The Contest for Rule in Eighteenth-Century Iran

This volume is dedicated to

Professor Bert Fragner (1941–2021)

Already available in *The Idea of Iran* series

Birth of the Persian Empire, Vol. 1
Edited by Vesta Sarkhosh Curtis (British Museum) and Sarah Stewart (SOAS, London).
ISBN: 978-1-84511-062-5

The Age of the Parthians, Vol. 2
Edited by Vesta Sarkhosh Curtis (British Museum) and Sarah Stewart (SOAS, London).
ISBN: 978-1-84511-406-0

The Sasanian Era, Vol. 3
Edited by Vesta Sarkhosh Curtis (British Museum) and Sarah Stewart (SOAS, London).
ISBN: 978-1-84511-690-3

The Rise of Islam, Vol. 4
Edited by Vesta Sarkhosh Curtis (British Museum) and Sarah Stewart (SOAS, London).
ISBN: 978-1-84511-691-0

Early Islamic Iran, Vol. 5
Edited by Edmund Herzig (University of Oxford) and Sarah Stewart (SOAS, London).
ISBN: 978-1-78076-061-2

The Age of the Seljuqs, Vol. 6
Edited by Edmund Herzig (University of Oxford) and Sarah Stewart (SOAS, London).
ISBN: 978-1-78076-947-9

The Coming of Mongols, Vol. 7
Edited by David O. Morgan (University Wisconsin-Madison) and Sarah Stewart (SOAS, London).
ISBN: 978 1 78831 285 1

Iran After the Mongols, Vol. 8
Edited by Sussan Babaie (The Courtauld Institute of Art, University of London).
ISBN: 978-1-7883-1528-9

The Timurid Century, Vol. 9
Edited by Charles Melville (University of Cambridge).
ISBN: 978-1-8386-0613-8

Safavid Persia in the Age of Empires, Vol. 10
Edited by Charles Melville (University of Cambridge).
ISBN: 978-0-7556-3377-7

The Contest for Rule in Eighteenth-Century Iran

The Idea of Iran

Volume XI

Edited By

Charles Melville

(University of Cambridge)

Supported by the Soudavar Memorial Foundation

SOUDAVAR
MEMORIAL FOUNDATION

I.B.TAURIS
LONDON • NEW YORK • OXFORD • NEW DELHI • SYDNEY

I.B.TAURIS
Bloomsbury Publishing Plc
50 Bedford Square, London, WC1B 3DP, UK
1385 Broadway, New York, NY 10018, USA

BLOOMSBURY, I.B. TAURIS and the I.B. TAURIS logo are trademarks of Bloomsbury Publishing Plc

First published in Great Britain 2022

Copyright © The Soudavar Memorial Trust, 2022

Charles Melville has asserted his right under the Copyright, Designs and Patents Act, 1988, to be identified as Editor of this work.

For legal purposes the Acknowledgements on p. xiii constitute an extension of this copyright page.

Cover image: Nader Shah of Persia, artist unknown, c. oil on canvas, 127 x 99 cm, F44. (© British Library)

All rights reserved. No part of this publication may be reproduced or transmitted in any form or by any means, electronic or mechanical, including photocopying, recording, or any information storage or retrieval system, without prior permission in writing from the publishers.

Bloomsbury Publishing Plc does not have any control over, or responsibility for, any third-party websites referred to or in this book. All internet addresses given in this book were correct at the time of going to press. The author and publisher regret any inconvenience caused if addresses have changed or sites have ceased to exist, but can accept no responsibility for any such changes.

A catalogue record for this book is available from the British Library.
A catalog record for this book is available from the Library of Congress.

ISBN: HB: 978-0-7556-4599-2
PB: 978-0-7556-4596-1
ePDF: 978-0-7556-4595-4
eBook: 978-0-7556-4597-8

Series: The Idea of Iran, volume 11

Typeset by P. Fozooni

Printed and bound in Great Britain

To find out more about our authors and books visit www.bloomsbury.com and sign up for our newsletters.

Contents

List of Illustrations	vii
Acknowledgements	xiii
Contributors	xv
Introduction *Charles Melville*	1
Nader Shah's Idea of Iran *Ernest Tucker*	9
Dismembering the Corporate: The Single Portraits of Nader Shah and the Changing Body Politic in Post-Safavid Iran *Janet O'Brien*	27
'The Persian State' and the Safavid Inheritance: Views from the Caspian, 1722–1781 *Kevin Gledhill*	57
Safavid Nostalgia in Early Qajar Chronicles *Assef Ashraf*	81
From the Chehel Sotun to the'Emarat-e Divani of Qom: The Evolution of Royal Wall Painting during the Reign of Fath-'Ali Shah *Kianoosh Motaghedi*	103
Diplomatic Gift Exchange between the Russian and the Persian Courts in the Early Nineteenth Century *Firuza Abdullaeva*	129
Proto-Nationalism in Early Modern Iran and Afghanistan *Sajjad Nejatie*	171
Fraying at the Edges: Iran and the Khanates of Central Asia *Fatema Soudavar Farmanfarmaian*	191
Sir William Jones and the Migration of the Idea of Iran to Indi *John R. Perry*	215
Index	227

Illustrations

Black and white figures (in text)

Full details of each image, which to save space in text are not all provided in the captions marked with an asterisk *.

Chapter 2

Shah 'Abbas II and the Mughal Ambassador, artist unknown, after 1647, fresco, approx. 3.3 × 5.7 m. Audience hall of the Chehel Sotun Palace, Esfahan. © Sussan Babaie.   33

Karim Khan Zand, attributed to Abu'l-Hasan Mostowfi Ghaffari Kashani, ca. 1750–75, Shiraz, opaque watercolour and gold on paper, image 25.2 × 20.2 cm. Musée du Louvre, Paris, MAO 800. (Author's own photo).   38

Karim Khan Zand on Horseback (Persian inscription misidentifies the subject as Nader Shah), attributed to Abu'l-Hasan Mostowfi Ghaffari Kashani, 18th century, Shiraz, opaque watercolour and gold on paper, 30 × 21.5 cm. Shalva Amiranashvili Museum of Fine Arts, Georgian National Museum, Tbilisi, 147. © Georgian National Museum, Shalva Amiranashvili Museum of Fine Arts.   39

Portrait of Karim Khan Zand, signed Mohammad Baqer, third quarter of the 18th century, Shiraz, tempera on varnished cardboard, 24.5 × 16 cm. Shalva Amiranashvili Museum of Fine Arts, Georgian National Museum, Tbilisi, 138. © Georgian National Museum, Shalva Amiranashvili Museum of Fine Arts.   40

Fath-'Ali Shah King of Persia, signed Mirza Baba, 1798–99 (1213 AH), Tehran, oil on canvas, 188 × 107 cm. British Library, London, Foster 116. © British Library.   41

Chapter 5

Painting in the *Naqqash khana* room in Golestan Palace, Tehran, ca. 1810, oil on canvas, in the European style (author's own photograph).   105

Karim Khan Zand amidst his close circle, Zand era, attributed to Ja'far, oil on canvas, in Pars Museum, Shiraz (author's own photograph).   107

Pre-Islamic stone reliefs: Achaemenid, Parthian and Sasanian, Fars province, Iran (author's own photograph).   111

(Left) Self-portrait by 'Abdollah Khan in the saff-e salam wall painting in   113
Negarestan Palace, Tehran. (Centre and right) saff-e salam wall painting
in Negarestan Palace. Photography ca. 1886. Source: Archive of
Ketabkhana-ye Majles, Tehran.

Comparison of 'Abdollah Khan's projects: (a) saff-e salam wall painting   117
in Negarestan Palace, Tehran, 1228 AH (1813) showing Fath-'Ali Shah
with 12 sons (formerly 118 figures); (b) saff-e salam wall painting in
Soleymaniya Palace, Karaj, 1228 AH (1813), showing Fath-'Ali Shah
with 14 sons; (c) saff-e salam wall painting from Qom royal residence,
1248 AH (1833), showing Fath-'Ali Shah with 99 sons (formerly 150
figures); (d) *Naqsh-e Khaqan* (Portrait of the King), relief in Shahr-e
Rayy, 1248 AH (1833), showing Fath-'Ali Shah with 16 sons (author's
own photographs).

Comparison between the style of saff-e salam wall painting from   119
Soleymaniya Palace, Karaj 1228 AH (1813), Qom royal residence 1248
AH (1833) and the relief in Shahr-e Rayy 1248 AH (1833). (First row)
left: Shahr-e Rayy; middle: Qom; right: Karaj; (second row) left: Karaj;
right: Shahr-e Rayy; (third row) left: Shahr-e Rayy; middle: Qom; right:
Karaj (author's own photographs).

Chapter 6

Mehr 'Ali, *Portrait of Fath-'Ali Shah, Standing*, 1809–10, VP-1107 ©   131
State Hermitage Museum. https://www.hermitagemuseum.org/wps/portal/
hermitage/digital-collec tion/01.+Paintings/78?lng=ru

Robert Lefèvre, *Portrait of Napoleon I in his Coronation Robes*, 1812,   131
26.789 © Museum of Fine Arts, Boston, William Sturgis Bigelow
Collection. https://collections.mfa.org/objects/32249

Solomon Enthroned, from a double frontispiece from a copy of Ferdowsi's   131
Shahnama, Iran, Shiraz, c. 1540–50, 83a/2006 © The David Collection,
Copenhagen. https://www.davidmus.dk/en/collections/islamic/materials/
miniatures/art/83b-2006-83a-2006

Marcin Zaleski (?), *Signing of the Turkmanchay Treaty by Count I.F.*   133
Paskevich and 'Abbas Mirza, 1840s © Gomel National Museum. This is
the imaginary interpretation of the Moshkov-Beggrov print, commissioned
by Paskevich for his palace in Gomel. In the painting he is moved into the
compositional centre. Griboedov and Khosrow Mirza are standing behind
the protagonists. Only a year later they were leading Russian and Persian
diplomatic missions to Persia and Russia.

Ball fan with Khosrow Mirza's autograph, № ЭРТ-6766 © State   141
Hermitage Museum.

Teacup with the portrait of Fath-'Ali Shah, 1825–30, Flight and Barr, soft-paste porcelain, hand-painted, № 1708 © Museum of Royal Worcester. https://www.museumofroyalworcester.org/collection/1708/   145

Robert Ker Porter, *Portrait of Fath-'Ali Shah Qajar*, Iran, ca. 1821–35, after a drawing made by the artist in 1819, Dreweatts, Chinese Ceramics and Works of Art (Part 2) and Japanese, Islamic and Indian Ceramics & Works of Art, London, 20 May 2021, lot 597. https://auctions.dreweatts.com/past-auctions/drewea1-10226/lot-details/271a29ee-65f4-4f95-8851-ad1100fcd329   146

Teacup with the portrait of 'Abbas Mirza, porcelain, gold, Royal Worcester, Flight Barr and Barr, early 1820s, height 6.8 cm © Golestan Palace Museum.   147

Royal order (farman) awarded by Fath-'Ali Shah to Sir Harford Jones-Brydges in Moharram 1224/March 1809, opaque watercolour, gold, ink, paper, 61.2 × 47.4 cm © Private collection.   148

Bowl with the portrait of Alexander I, porcelain, polychrome, gold, Imperial Porcelain Factory, St Petersburg 1815 (?) © Golestan Palace Museum.   150

Karl Gampeln, *Portrait of Khosrow Mirza*, St Petersburg, 1829, ЭРГ-19106 © Hermitage Museum.   153

Portrait of Khosrow Mirza, N 5682 © National Library of Iran, Tehran.   154

Sir Thomas Lawrence, *Portrait of Mirza Abu'l-Hasan Khan Ilchi*, London, 1810, 1964.100 © The Fogg Art Museum, Harvard University, Cambridge, Massachusetts. https://commons.wikimedia.org/wiki/Category:Mirza_Abolhassan_Khan_Ilchi#/media/File:Mirza_Abu'l_Hassan_Khan_by_Thomas_Lawrence,_1810_-_Fogg_Art_Museum_-_DSC02319.JPG   155

Thomas Baxter, *Cabinet cup with portrait of Mirza Abu'l-Hasan Khan*, Worcester, Flight Barr and Barr, ca. 1814–16 © Bonham's, London, 29 September 2021. https://www.bonhams.com/auctions/27326/lot/21/   155

Sir Godfrey Kneller, *Portrait of Peter I the Great, Tsar of Russia*, 1698, RCIN 405645 © Royal Collection. https://www.rct.uk/collection/search#/30/collection/405645/peter-the-great-tsar-of-russia-1672-1725   156

Colour Plates

Chapter 2

Plate Ia. *Madar-e vatan* (Motherland), signed Mirza Habib-Allah Khan, January/February 1924 (dated *Jomada al-thani* 1342 AH), painted in Shiraz and printed in Bombay, chromolithograph, 39.4 × 48.3 cm. Collection of Anil Relia, Ahmedabad. © Anil Relia.

Plate Ib. *Portrait of Nader Shah*, attributed to Mohammad Reza Hendi, ca. 1740, Esfahan, oil on canvas, 179 × 116.5 cm. V&A, London, IM.20-1919. © Victoria and Albert Museum.

Plate Ic. *Nader Shah of Persia*, artist unknown, ca. 1740, Iran, oil on canvas, 127 × 99 cm. British Library, London, F44. © British Library.

Plate Id. *Portrait of Nader Shah*, signed Bahram, 1743–44 (dated 1156 AH), Iran, gouache and gold on paper, image 22 × 14 cm. State Hermitage Museum, St Petersburg, VR-552. © The State Hermitage Museum, St Petersburg; photograph © The State Hermitage Museum, photo by Vladimir Terebenin.

Plate IIa. *Portrait of Nader Shah*, signed Mirza Jani, ca. 1740 (date illegible), Esfahan, ink on paper, 38.7 × 26.4 cm. Islamic Arts Museum Malaysia, Kuala Lumpur, 2003.6.26. © Islamic Arts Museum Malaysia.

Plate IIb. *Equestrian Portrait of Nader Shah*, attributed to Mohammad 'Ali ebn 'Abd al-Beg ebn 'Ali-Qoli Jebadar, ca. 1740–45, Esfahan, opaque watercolour and gold on paper, 22.7 × 16.7 cm. Museum of Fine Arts, Boston, 14.646. © Museum of Fine Arts, Boston.

Plate IIc. *Nader Shah*, in an album of paintings and calligraphy, signed Mohammad Sadeq, 1785–86 (dated 1200 AH), Esfahan, opaque watercolour and gold on paper, 43 × 28.5 cm. National Library of Russia, St Petersburg, PNS 383, fol. 5. © National Library of Russia.

Plate IId. *Portrait of Nader Shah*, frontispiece of a *Tarikh-e Naderi* manuscript, artist unknown, ca. 1870, Iran, opaque watercolour, gold and ink on paper, 28.8 × 17.5 cm. British Library, London, Or. 11947, fol. 1v. (author's own photograph).

Chapter 5

Plate III. (Left) *Fath-'Ali Shah on the Takht-e Naderi*, ca. 1805, by Mehr 'Ali, Golestan Palace, Tehran, oil on canvas (author's own photograph). (Right) King Darius on his throne, 500 BC, stone relief, Persepolis, Shiraz (author's own photograph). Studying these two images proves that the Qajar painters were inspired by ancestral themes.

Plate IV. Saff-e salam wall painting in Soleymaniya Palace, Karaj, ca. 1813, by 'Abdollah Khan.

Plate Va. Saff-e salam wall painting from Qom royal residence (before and after restoration), ca. 1833, attributed to 'Abdollah Khan (author's own photograph).

Plate Vb. Detail of the saff-e salam wall painting from Qom Royal Residence (after restoration), ca. 1833, attributed to 'Abdollah Khan (author's own photograph).

Chapter 6

Plate VIa. Vladimir Borovikovsky, *Portrait of Mortaza-Qoli Khan*, 1796, oil on canvas, 284 × 1895 cm, Ж-5010 © State Russian Museum. https://rusmuseumvrm.ru/data/collections/painting/18_19/borovikovskiy_vladimir_lukich_portret_murtazi_kuli_hana_1796/index.php

Plate VIb. Mohammad Ja'far, *Portrait of 'Abbas Mirza*, St Petersburg, 1824, opaque watercolour © Museum of the Russian Academy of Fine Arts.

Plate VIIa. Teacup with the portrait of Fath-'Ali Shah, porcelain, Royal Worcester, Flight Barr and Barr, early 1820s, height 6.8 cm, № V3-732; V3-741; Holders, Iran, 1820s, gold, polychrome enamel, height 7.4 cm © State Hermitage Museum. http://kronk.spb.ru/img/ivanov-lukonin-smesova-1984-121.jpg

Plate VIIb. Teacup with the emblem combining the Persian and the British national coat of arms porcelain, Spode and Copeland, early 1820s, height 6.6 cm © Golestan Palace Museum.

Plate VIIIa. Fedor Solntsev, Plate from the 'Shah' dinner service, Imperial Porcelain Factory, St Petersburg, 1838, hallmarked NI © Golestan Palace Museum.

Plate VIIIb. Fedor Solntsev, Plate from the Kremlin dinner service, 1837–38, МЗ-И-445 © State Hermitage Museum.

Plate VIIIc. Plate gifted to Tsarevich Alexey Petrovich by his grandmother Tsarina Natalya Kirillovna in 1694, Moscow, end of the 17th century, MP-3365 © Moscow Kremlin Museums. https://collectiononline.kreml.ru/entity/OBJECT/42294?query=тарелка%201694&index=0

Plate VIId. Gold tray in polychrome enamel mina'i, diameter 45.5 cm, V3-751 © State Hermitage Museum. https://kronk.St Petersburgru/img/ivanov-lukonin-smesova-1984-118.jpg

Acknowledgements

This eleventh volume in the 'Idea of Iran' series has, as in the case of previous proceedings, relied on the sustained support of many people, starting most notably with the Trustees of the Soudavar Memorial Foundation, particularly Mrs Fatema Soudavar Farmanfarmaian and Dr Layla Diba, both of whom are constantly ready with advice and encouragement, not least in the framing of the academic programme as we near modern times. For the first time, and in response to the problems and uncertainties caused by the Covid-19 pandemic, the symposium on which the present volume is based was held virtually, in November 2020, entitled 'Iran in transition to a new world order'. These arrangements required a different set of administrative and technical skills, ably provided by the Centre for Iranian Studies in the SOAS Middle East Institute.

Thanks go to my colleague, Dr Sarah Stewart, for her continuing support and assistance in overseeing the administration of the Soudavar Memorial symposium that is being published here, and Angelica Baschiera for handling the practicalities of the organization.

Parvis Fozooni has once more typeset and formatted the chapters and the colour plates as a labour of love, with great patience and attention to detail; there is now the additional work created by producing the Index. It is hard to see how the series could continue without him. Andy Platts has again been a pleasure to work with on the copy-editing, finding many ways to improve each chapter while maintaining that they reached her in such good condition that there was almost nothing left to be done.

Naturally, without the work of the authors to turn their presentations into publishable texts, the book could not exist at all and I thank them for fulfilling their obligations, and more, in this respect; they and I have all benefited additionally from the comments provided by two anonymous reviewers. Finally, thanks also go to Rory Gormley and Yasmin Garcha at I.B. Tauris/Bloomsbury for their care and patience over the production of this volume, which is dedicated to the memory of the late Professor Bert Fragner (27 November 1941–16 December 2021), who did so much to articulate the 'idea of Iran' and in numerous words and deeds explored its ramifications throughout the passages of history from the Mongols to the Qajars. For his scholarly career and tireless encouragement of the field we all, indeed, have much to acknowledge with gratitude.

Contributors

Firuza Abdullaeva graduated from Saint Petersburg University, where she completed her PhD and taught at the Iranian Department. As Associate Professor she left St Petersburg for Oxford to teach Persian literature and become a Fellow of Wadham College, where she was also Curator of the Ferdowsi Library. In 2010 she moved to Cambridge as the IHF Research Fellow at Pembroke College, where she is currently Director of Research of the Cambridge Shahnama Centre. Her research includes Persian literature and book art, Russian cultural Orientalism in Central Asia and the Caucasus, and Russo-Persian diplomacy of the early Qajar period.

Assef Ashraf is University Assistant Professor in the Eastern Islamic Lands and Persian-Speaking World at the University of Cambridge and a Fellow of Pembroke College. His research has been published in *Comparative Studies in Society and History*, the *Journal of the Economic and Social History of the Orient* and the *International Journal of Middle East Studies*. He has co-edited a volume entitled *The Persianate World: Rethinking a Shared Sphere* and is currently writing a book on the formation of Qajar Iran.

Kevin Gledhill is an Instructor in the Department of History at Sacred Heart University in Fairfield, Connecticut. He has previously taught at Yale University, Clark University and Quinnipiac University. He received his PhD from Yale in May 2020, his MA from the Center for Middle Eastern Studies at the University of Chicago (2011) and his BA in History and Spanish from La Salle University (2009). His work focuses on the history of Iran, southern Russia and the South Caucasus in the eighteenth and nineteenth centuries, arguing for the Caspian Sea as a unit of historical analysis.

Charles Melville is Emeritus Professor of Persian History at the University of Cambridge. He is currently President of the British Institute of Persian Studies (British Academy) and director of the Cambridge Shahnama Project. He is a Permanent Fellow at the Centre for the Study of Manuscript Cultures at Hamburg University, where he is working on 'Visualising Persian History' with an Emeritus Fellowship from the Leverhulme Trust.

Kianoosh Motaghedi is an artist and Islamic art historian. He has published a number of books and articles in the fields of Persian ceramics, calligraphy and Qajar arts. In both 2017 and 2018 he received fellowships from the French Ministry of Culture and Communication for his independent research. In 2019 he curated an exhibition and published a catalogue on *Calligraphic Paintings from the Qajar Era* for the Reza Abbasi Museum, Tehran. His latest publication is *From Golestan Garden to Golestan Palace* (2021). He has travelled extensively across the Middle East, Central Asia, India and Europe and has knowledge of Persian, Arabic and English.

Sajjad Nejatie is a Sessional Lecturer at the University of Toronto's Department of Near and Middle Eastern Civilizations. He specializes in the history, historiography and culture of early modern and modern Iran and Afghanistan. He is currently preparing for the publication of his first book manuscript, provisionally titled *The Pearl of Pearls: A History of the Abdali-Durrani Confederacy from its Origins to the Reign of Ahmad Shah Durr-i Durran, circa 1550–1772*.

Janet O'Brien is a final-year PhD candidate at The Courtauld Institute of Art and a recipient of the Soudavar Memorial Foundation Grant. She is also the Smithsonian Institution Predoctoral Fellow at the Freer Gallery of Art and Arthur M. Sackler Gallery in Washington DC. She previously served in curatorial and research positions at the Walters Art Museum in Baltimore, Museum of Fine Arts, Houston and Courtauld Gallery in London, and was an Associate Lecturer at The Courtauld. She is a contributing author of *Bestowing Beauty: Masterpieces from Persian Lands, Selections from the Hossein Afshar Collection* (2020).

John Perry is Professor of Persian Emeritus at the University of Chicago. His monographs include *Karim Khan Zand: A History of Iran, 1747–1779* (1979) and *Form and Meaning in Persian Vocabulary: The Arabic Feminine Ending* (1991). He is currently contributing editor of *Encyclopaedia Iranica*, and in 2019 received a Lifetime Achievement award from the American Association of Teachers of Persian. His current research is focused on the history of the Persian language, and in particular the mechanisms of the incorporation of Arabic vocabulary into Persian and its dissemination into other languages of the region.

Fatema Soudavar Farmanfarmaian, born in Tehran in 1940, is a trustee of the Soudavar Memorial Foundation and an independent historian who has written essays for academic journals and multi-authored books on a variety of subjects, primarily dealing with nineteenth-century Iran, and edited and partly authored two books in Persian. She has had privileged access to a trove of private and public archives, mainly in Iran but also in Russia, that shed light on little known episodes of this period's history.

Ernest Tucker has taught in the history department at the US Naval Academy since 1990, receiving the rank of full professor there in 2006. Tucker received his PhD in Middle Eastern history from the University of Chicago and spent time in the late 1980s and in 2005–6 living and doing research in Istanbul, Turkey as a Fulbright Scholar. He has published three books on Iran and the Ottoman Empire, his articles have appeared in a wide variety of scholarly journals, dictionaries and encyclopedias, and he has consulted for a variety of governmental and non-governmental organizations.

Introduction

Charles Melville
(University of Cambridge)

While most changes of dynasty involve periods of transition, of continuity and change, the era covered in this volume of 'The Idea of Iran' series is rather particular in witnessing a prolonged period of almost a century, between the collapse of the Safavids and the establishment of the Qajars, when Iran endured a succession of conflicting regimes, political instability and heightened violence. It can perhaps be compared with the shorter but equally turbulent period after the collapse of the central authority of the Ilkhanate in 1335, which permitted the emergence of several regional powers with different claims to sovereignty, the most successful and enduring of which – the Mozaffarids in Fars, Jalayerids in Iraq and the Karts in Herat – were absorbed into Timur's fiercely assembled conquests (at least for a while).[1] The long reign of the Safavids, from 1501 to 1722, with puppet shahs lingering for another 15 years, was followed by a correspondingly protracted void in power, with concomitant variations in government and different approaches to claiming legitimacy for rulership. The most substantial study of one of these regimes remains John Perry's fine book on the Zands in southern Iran,[2] not given any detailed treatment in the present volume, while Nader Shah has attracted the most attention, as here also.[3]

Late eighteenth-century Iran has been largely neglected as an unwholesome period of 'crisis and collapse' between two relatively stable regimes and although this perception has been somewhat rectified by the collection of studies edited recently by Michael Axworthy, which provide a reappraisal of existing scholarship and suggest some fruitful topics for further work,[4] these are not sufficient to disguise the basic breakdown of government and society and lack of security in large parts of the country. The perception of internal disorder and insecurity on the part of her neighbours was exemplified by the sharp decline in the number of travellers passing through Iran. Apart from the celebrated Jonas Hanway, very few spent any time in the country. Those who did make the journey either, like Hanway (1743–44), kept to the northern provinces, entering and leaving via Astrakhan,[5] were present in the region on the death of Nader Shah[6] or, like Edward Ives and several later employees of the East India Company, sailed up the Persian Gulf to Basra and by way of Baghdad and Mosul, returning from India to Europe via Aleppo.[7] In other words, skirting round Iran entirely. Later in the century, travellers such as

George Forster (in 1783–84) in north-east Iran and particularly the French diplomat Guillaume-Antoine Olivier (in 1796) in western Iran penetrated more deeply into the country and made interesting observations on commercial life and the state of the cities.[8] But this leaves us with very restricted views of Iran from outsiders and generally only from the peripheries: valuable, but under-exploited, while other interesting accounts from 'Central Europe' have recently been introduced by Giorgio Rota.[9]

The neglect of the period is thus partly due to a relative paucity of sources but, as John Perry's survey of the Zands[10] and Assef Ashraf's chapter on the historiography of the period show, there are a substantial number of chronicles covering the rise of the Qajars, which usefully reveal how the new rulers saw themselves. Dr Ashraf's chapter neatly opens up one of the underlying questions of the struggle for power in the post-Safavid vacuum: namely, what was the legacy of the Safavids and how was this expressed in the search for identity in the different regimes that replaced them? For a start, the Qajars were one of the Qezelbash tribes that underpinned the early Safavid cause and could look back to Safavid symbols to validate their coronation ceremonies and inform their models of administration and governance. Apart from the admiration expressed for Shah 'Abbas and an elaboration of the ideal attributes of kingship found in the first two Qajar monarchs, their claim to rule was based as much on their reunification of the heartlands of Iran that had constituted the Safavid Empire, and their restoration of just rule, as on any suggestion of deriving legitimacy from being the direct heirs of the Safavids. In fact, as the author notes, the Qajars did not look back nostalgically to the Safavids alone, but to earlier sources of identity in titulature such as *khaqan* and *saheb-qeran*, with Turkish and Timurid overtones that also referred to the pre-Islamic past and were not absent from the Safavids' own vision of Iran.

Some of the same multifaceted sources made up Nader Shah's idea of his rulership, but with the emphasis on the recreation of a Timurid world empire and emulation of Timur's conquests. Ernest Tucker discusses the different planks of this identity formation and sources of legitimacy, with its 'Persianate, Turko-Mongol and Islamicate aspects'. Arguably, the same elements are intermixed in all these ideas, differing only in emphasis in the regimes they underpinned. For Nader Shah, the new ingredient was the rejection of Iran's exclusively Shi'i identity and an attempt to embrace a more universal form of Islam. Starting as the champion of the Safavids, Nader also sought to reconstitute their empire by driving out the Ottomans and Afghans and regaining control of the Caucasus, going further in invading Transoxania and north India (and more successfully than the Safavids had been able to do), but based his immediate elevation to the throne on the endorsement of the Mongol-style *quriltay* that harked back to the Ilkhanate. At the same time, for domestic consumption at least, Nader did much to patronize the shrine of Emam Reza in Mashhad: mixed messaging, to say the least. If, as Tucker, suggests, Nader weakened the connection between royal and religious authority in Iran, once more in the manner of the Mongol regimes, this certainly marks a contrast between what went before and what came after. The early Qajars again patronized the religious establishment while embracing the pre-Islamic regal symbolism of monumental rock carvings. Interestingly, both Nader Shah and Fath-'Ali Shah had emulations of the *Shahnama* devoted to them, in the form of the *Shahnama-ye Naderi* of Mohammad 'Ali Tusi and the *Shahanshahnama* of Fath-'Ali Khan Saba,[11] offering an alternative to the Safavid model of sacred kingship.

Nader Shah's succession in the east[12] was partly acceptably 'legitimate' due to the fact that his grandson Shahrokh (r. 1748–96) was also the grandson of Shah Soltan-Hoseyn Safavi (d. 1726) and thus brought multiple points of reference to enhance his claims.[13] Far from reviving Safavid government and aspirations to maintain Nader's conquests, however, the Naderids found they were barely able to maintain themselves in the face of Afghan ambitions to make Nader's legacy their own. As Sajjad Nejatie's chapter shows, it was the Dorranis and the Qajars who actually contested for supremacy over Khorasan. The Qajars were depicted as hostile Qezelbash and the Dorranis looked back to a pre-Safavid, Sunni past as well as to the changes introduced by Nader Shah's career that had paved the way for Afghan hegemony in the region. This had been introduced already by the Safavids' arrangements for the government of Qandahar and the Abdalis' seizure of Herat. Competing claims to sovereignty over Herat could be traced back to a time well before the arrival of the Great Powers on the scene added a new dimension to the rivalry. For the Qajars, control of Khorasan would represent not only a restoration of the eastern territories of the Safavid Empire, but the more particularly personal recovery of their ancestral homeland. Fatema Soudavar's chapter explores this dynamic interaction between Iran and Central Asia in its historical context and argues for the long-term cultural connections between the two regions that persisted beyond the effective separation of Transoxania from Iran. Despite the ancient Turkification of 'greater Khorasan', it was still possible to view the territories of Balkh and Marv as part of the idea of Iran at least in linguistic terms and in the light of centuries of shared history.

However, although the idea of Iran at the end of the Safavid period, both culturally and territorially, might still have embraced the wider region that is currently sometimes called the 'Persianate world', and even been reinforced by Nader Shah's conquests in western Iran, Central Asia and Hindustan, within 50 years of his death the reality was rather different. Not only was Afghanistan about to be lost permanently, but also Georgia and important parts of the southern Caucasus, the scene of some of the most excessive brutalities of Nader Shah and Agha Mohammad Khan – leading directly, in the latter case, to his death and in both cases opening the door to the less unattractive inroads of the expanding power of Russia.

Kevin Gledhill's chapter addresses some of the earliest trading encounters between the Russians and the regional Iranian powers during the whole interval before the rise of the Qajars, as they affected the Caspian provinces and control of the Caspian Sea, but with a particular focus on how both parties viewed the Iranian state. Agha Mohammad Khan, in renewing early eighteenth-century Safavid-era treaties, saw himself explicitly as the heir to the Safavids and as having a mission to restore the empire (much as Nader Shah did also), including invoking an anti-Ottoman alliance. The latter feature of international affairs in this period created a triangular relationship between the Ottomans, Iran and expansionist Russia, which delayed the fulfilment of Russian ambitions in the south, witnessing instead their 'quiet encroachment' until the decisive advance under Catherine the Great in the last year of her reign (1796).[14] When Catherine became tsar in the 1760s, this notion of the unity of the Iranian kingdom was of course a fiction, especially with the Zands firmly entrenched in south-western Iran – and not particularly interested in the northern provinces – not to mention the effective loss of Khorasan, as noted above. By the reign of Mohammad Shah (r. 1834–48) the idea of Iran as a territorial concept required serious revision, even if culturally, or emotionally, the sense of identity remained largely intact.

One aspect of this splendid image can be seen in Firuza Abdullaeva's chapter on diplomatic gift exchanges between Iran and Russia in the wake of the disastrous second Perso–Russian war, culminating in the Treaty of Turkmanchay (1828) and the murder of the Russian envoy, Alexander Griboedov, in Tehran the following year. The selection of gifts on both sides, quite apart from underlining the importance of repairing relations in the aftermath of these events, also provided an opportunity to display 'typical' representations of their nations' cultural artefacts. On the Russian side, in addition to platinum coins, Griboedov brought the shah swords and armaments (always welcome), diamond decorations, crystal vases, sable furs and textiles, as well as a porcelain dinner service; more spectacular gifts accompanied the return of Khosrow Mirza to Iran following his successful 'redemption' mission to apologize for the murder, including more porcelain and crystal tableware. Interestingly, among the rather modest gifts brought to St Petersburg by the young Khosrow Mirza, was not only a selection of 18 precious Persian manuscripts, but a series of teacups for the tsarina. The author shows the hidden (but, nonetheless, decipherable) symbolism behind this set of beautiful pieces, combining English-made Worcester porcelain with traditional Persian cup holders. The point being that, in addition to the three-cornered relationship between the Ottomans, Russia and Iran already noted, the arrival of the English on the scene added an altogether new dimension to the range of interests and rival ambitions playing out in the Iranian space. The perception of Iran as a place to desire and also to exploit was beginning to take root in earnest.

English interest in Iran was largely due to British involvement in India and it was in India, during the early years of the East India Company's growing control of the country, that scholarly engagement with Persian literature and language blossomed, rather than in Iran itself. This is reflected, among other ways, in the enormous accumulation in private collections and ultimately in British (and other European) libraries of Persian manuscripts with an Indian provenance. The context of this growing interest is engagingly documented by John Perry, who refers to the migration of Iranian literati and bureaucrats to India after the collapse of the Safavids, continuing a trend that had indeed persisted throughout the heyday of the Mughal Empire in the previous century.[15] These émigrés provide at least a 'native' perception of Iran from within, as it were, with their motivations for leaving being a reflection on the situation there and the belief that they would find a more or less congenial and familiar refuge in India. The arrival of the English in India gave them their first encounter with Persian and in this the role of Sir William Jones is rightly emphasized – the first in a line of authors and bureaucrats to produce Persian grammars and to edit and translate Persian literary classics, which also helped to forge an idea of Iran in Britain.

One way to form an image of Iran is, of course, visually and, apart from the decorated teacups described above, the pictorial arts of the period ca. 1730–ca. 1830 also provide a window into the Iranian world of the time. Interestingly, whereas in earlier periods the arts of the book in precious manuscripts or single leaf drawings would be considered the chief representation of courtly or metropolitan social life, the chapters here focus on the growth of royal portraiture. Janet O'Brien's chapter discusses how the artists depicted Nader Shah as a powerful individual, reliant on his own strength, and as a 'personification of victory' in a remarkable series of portraits all dating from after the conquest of Delhi in 1739, which not only guaranteed his international fame but also testified to the success that justified his seizure of power and the riches with which he presented himself to the world. The few earlier depictions of the Safavid rulers placed them in a courtly setting, their authority underpinned by the entourage representing the ruling institutions of government. By contrast, Nader is depicted detached from any such power structure and, ironically, by the end of his reign he found himself alone indeed. While the depictions of Nader broke the mould of royal portrait painting, emulated under the Zands and indeed the early Qajar rulers – as on the Worcester porcelain teacups with their pictures of Fath-'Ali Shah and 'Abbas Mirza, for comparable reasons of promoting a particular message – Kianoosh Motaghedi's chapter discusses how, along with pictures of a dazzling, bejewelled, wasp-waisted shah (hardly a manly specimen, apart from his long beard), the Qajars revived the image of corporate, dynastic rule. The huge reception-hall mural paintings, heirs more recognizably to the murals in the Chehel Sotun in Esfahan than to the pictures of Karim Khan's small group of supporters, are distinct in their depiction of the enormous royal family of princes and cousins, with the enthroned shah in the centre an ethereal, almost abstract figure. In another telling contrast to Nader Shah's image and its development in the context of his spectacular victory in India, the paintings of Fath-'Ali Shah – and specifically the subject of this chapter, the recently restored mural from the 'Emarat-e divani in Qom – were commissioned after the humiliating defeat at the hands of Russia in the Russo-Persian war. An equally important moment to be affirming royal credentials, fabulous wealth and sustaining the majesty of the Safavid Empire to which the Qajars laid claim.

As before, this collection of chapters is based on the presentations at the Idea of Iran Symposium, held this time online on 28 November 2020 and organized through the continuing good offices of SOAS. I am grateful to the anonymous reviewers for their sometimes trenchant comments and generally helpful suggestions, not least in proposing that the focus of the volume was not so much on 'legitimacy' as on 'rulership', but also drawing attention to some omissions. Notably, there are no chapters devoted to the Zands, or that focus more closely on peripheral regions, such as Naderid rule in Khorasan or events in the Caucasus. It is, of course, difficult to fit all these topics into a one-day conference and it is not always the case that they will necessarily be treated in such a way as to explore the 'idea of Iran', or add new insights. John Perry's work on the Zands has left thin pickings for further discussion and Michael Axworthy's excellent conference volume on the eighteenth century, frequently referred to here, highlighted some areas that needed new research, such as the economy of the eighteenth century and, particularly, the intellectual life of the period.[16] The dust has not yet settled on these contributions, which are still fresh and do not need regurgitating. Readers of this volume may wish to read Axworthy's alongside it. Meanwhile, the next symposium, on the later nineteenth century, will provide another opportunity to consider religious developments in more detail, and particularly the evolution of relations between religion and the state, a topic opened up many years ago by Hamid Algar.[17]

I am particularly glad that it has been possible to include the work of younger scholars here, bringing their own fresh contributions to a neglected period of Iranian history and promising more for the future.

Notes:

1. Despite defeats at the hands of Timur, the Jalayerids eventually succumbed to pressure from the Black Sheep Turkomans only in 1411. The Sarbadars in Khorasan were eclipsed after 1386. For an overview of the whole period, see the convenient survey by H.R. Roemer in *The Cambridge History of Iran, vol. 6, The Timurid and Safavid Periods*, ed. Peter Jackson and Laurence Lockhart (Cambridge: Cambridge University Press, 1986), chapters 1–2, pp. 1–97.
2. John R. Perry, *Karim Khan Zand: A History of Iran, 1747–1779* (Chicago: University of Chicago Press, 1979).
3. The classic study is by Laurence Lockhart, *Nader Shah: A Critical Study based mainly upon Contemporary Sources* (London: Luzac & Co., 1938), essentially his PhD dissertation. More recent valuable work has been published by Michael Axworthy, *The Sword of Persia: Nader Shah, from Tribal Warrior to Conquering Tyrant* (London: I.B. Tauris, 2006) and Ernest S. Tucker, *Nadir Shah's Quest for Legitimacy in Post-Safavid Iran* (Gainesvillle: University Press of Florida, 2006), among others. For a fresh look, see Mohammad Parsa's recent dissertation, 'Iran's Last Empire: State Formation and Fragmentation in Nāderid Iran' (London: SOAS, 2021) and the chapter by Janet O'Brien in the present volume.
4. Michael Axworthy, ed., *Crisis, Collapse, Militarism and Civil War: The History and Historiography of 18th Century Iran* (New York: Oxford University Press, 2018).
5. For an appreciation of Hanway, see Lockhart, *Nader Shah*, pp. 308–10; his account includes the travels of G. Thompson, via Urgenj and Khiva to Mashhad; Th. Woodroofe, via Astrakhan and Enzeli (Anzali), and van Meirop, via Rasht, Qazvin and Mashhad; the latter found much of Khorasan, through which he passed, to be quite populous and flourishing. See also the account of Frère (Père) Louis Bazin, in *Lettres édifiantes et curieuses, écrites des missions étrangères* (Paris, 1780), vol. IV, pp. 322–64, for events on the death of Nader. The later Russian traveller, S.G. Gmélin (1770–72), *Histoire des découvertes faites par divers savans voyageurs dans plusieurs contrées de la Russie et de la Perse...*, vol. I (Berne: Société Typographique, 1779), made an interrupted botanical expedition that was again confined to the Caspian shores.
6. John Cook, *Voyages and Travels through the Russian Empire, Tartary, and Part of the Kingdom of Persia* (Edinburgh: printed for the author, 1770), vol. II, travelling from and returning to Astrakhan, as far as Anzali, where news came of Nader's death, p. 423. His account is full of observations on the state of Iran under Nader.
7. E. Ives, *A Voyage from England to India, in the Year MDCCLIV, including a Journey from Persia to England by an Unusual Route, in 1758–1759* (London: Edward and Charles Dilly, 1773). The 'unusual route' was up the Persian Gulf to Basra and on via Kirkuk and Diyarbekr to Aleppo, subsequently followed by many others; see Stephen Longrigg, *Four Centuries of Modern Iraq* (Oxford: Clarendon Press, 1925), pp. 333–35; Hugh Murray, *Historical Account of Discoveries and Travels in Asia: From the Earliest Ages to the Present Time*, 3 vols (Edinburgh: A. Constable and Co., 1820), vol. I, pp. 409–23.
8. George Forster, *A Journey from Bengal to England, through the Northern Part of India, Kashmire, Afghanistan, and Persia ...* vol. II (London: R. Faulder, 1798); G.-

A. Olivier, *Voyage dans l'Empire othoman, l'Égypte et la Perse...*, vol. III (Paris: H. Agasse, 1807).
9. Giorgio Rota, 'Persia 1700–1800: Some views from Central Europe', in Axworthy, ed., *Crisis, Collapse, Militarism*, pp. 183–213.
10. Perry, *Karim Khan Zand*, pp. 303–16.
11. Abbas Amanat, 'Shahnameh-ye Naderi and the revival of epic poetry in post-Safavid Iran', in *The Layered Heart. Essays on Persian Poetry. A Celebration in Honor of Dick Davis*, ed. A.A. Seyed-Ghorab (Washington DC: Mage, 2019), pp. 295–318; Layla S. Diba, 'Introducing Fath 'Ali Shah: Production and dispersal of the *Shahanshahnama* manuscripts', in *Shahnama Studies I*, ed. Charles Melville (Cambridge: Centre of Middle Eastern and Islamic Studies, 2006), pp. 239–58.
12. More aptly called the Naderids than the Afsharids, as argued by Axworthy, *Crisis, Collapse, Militarism*, introduction, p. 7.
13. See Tucker, *Nadir Shah's Quest*, pp. 37–38, recalling that Shahrokh was also the name of Timur's son.
14. Goodarz Rashtiani, 'Iranian–Russian relations in the eighteenth century', in Axworthy, ed., *Crisis, Collapse, Militarism*, pp. 163–82.
15. As documented by Masashi Haneda, 'Emigration of Iranian elites to India during the 16th–18th centuries', *Cahiers d'Asie Centrale* 3–4 (1997), pp. 129–43, and Benedek Péri, 'The ethnic composition of the "Iranian" nobility at Akbar's court (1574–1605)', in *Irano-Turkic Cultural Contacts in the 11th–17th Centuries*, ed. Éva M. Jeremiás (Piliscsaba: Avicenna Institute of Middle Eastern Studies, [2002] 2003), pp. 177–201; see also Sunil Sharma's chapter 'Local and transregional places in the works of Safavid men of letters', in *Safavid Persia in the Age of Empires: The Idea of Iran*, vol. 10, ed. Charles Melville (London: I.B. Tauris, 2021), pp. 309–29.
16. Willem Floor, 'The Persian economy in the eighteenth century: A dismal record', in Axworthy, *Crisis, Collapse, Militarism*, pp. 125–50; Sajjad Rizvi, 'Whatever happened to the School of Isfahan?: Philosophy in 18th-century Iran', in ibid., pp. 71–104.
17. Hamid Algar, *Religion and State in Iran 1785–1906: The Role of the Ulama in the Qajar Period* (Berkeley: University of California Press, 1969).

1

Nader Shah's Idea of Iran

Ernest Tucker
(US Naval Academy, Annapolis)

Nader Shah's reign, despite his relatively short time on the Iranian throne in the 1730s and 1740s, had a definite impact on ideas of Iran as they evolved from late Safavid times through the early Qajar era. He pursued his path to power in the unsettled milieu that arose after the collapse of Safavid state following the fall of Esfahan to Ghelzay Afghan invaders in October 1722. This prompted Nader to depart quite radically from concepts of Iran established under the Safavids. Visions of Iran developed during the Safavid heyday had fused traditions and tropes from a rediscovered pre-Islamic Persian past with the legacy of the Turkmen nomadic heritage, all against the backdrop of a rapidly evolving early modern Twelver Shi'i Iranian religious identity.

These diverse components of Safavid identity helped to frame an image of Safavid Iran often seen today as the precursor of more modern visions of the nation. By late Safavid times, any 'idea of Iran' had come to include powerful but distinct spheres of religious and secular identity. Both were supported by the dynasty's *farr* (royal reputation/charisma), which endured long after its material collapse.

Nader's meteoric rise from obscurity in the 1720s, his seizure of power and erasure of the formal vestiges of Safavid authority in the 1730s, defeat of the Mughals at Karnal (just north of Delhi) in early 1739, and continuing challenge to the Ottomans for control of Iraq and the Caucasus in the mid-1740s gave him the opportunity to reimagine Iran considerably. The evolution of his own idea of Iran appears through the evidence of contemporary chronicles and sources as his attempt to create an 'invented tradition', to borrow a term familiar from other historiographies of the early modern world.[1] His chroniclers ultimately portrayed his project as the creation of a Timurid-style 'world empire' in which Iran could shine as the jewel in the crown of a united *umma* (Muslim community) with distinctive Persianate, Turko-Mongol and Islamicate aspects.

In this system, other Islamic rulers, specifically those he conquered, such as the Mughals and Ozbeks, were to become subsidiary 'shahs' under Nader as the 'shahanshah' ('king of kings'): a concept harking back both to pre-Islamic Persian practice and to Turko-Mongol traditions of steppe governance.[2] Overlaid on this was the vision of a reunited Muslim umma with Twelver

Shi'ism brought back into the fold as a fifth *mazhab* (or rite) of Sunni Islam. Such an invention of tradition seems designed to have gone beyond the long period of sectarian discord with other Islamic polities that had sometimes accompanied Safavid rule.

The Ottomans played important roles in both these components of Nader's new idea of Iran. In the Turko-Mongol tribal context, presumed Ottoman lineage ties to Nader could be construed as familial, with Nader as a 'younger brother' to the Ottoman sultan 'older brother' of common Turkic or Turkmen ancestry. In the religious context, Nader offered to recognize the Ottoman ruler's status as guardian of Mecca and Medina, as well as his general role as leader of the Sunni world, in return for official Ottoman approval of Nader's reimagined version of Shi'ism as a more integral part of the Sunni world. The various parts of Nader's new idea of Iran sought thus to transcend the limitations of any Safavid ideas of Iran. Ultimately, Nader's project was quite short-lived, given his brief but tumultuous 11 years as monarch.

His reign has been depicted either as a time of brutal tyranny, the impact of which on Iran and the region was defined by what he destroyed and ruined, or as a moment when a powerful ruler, however flawed and cruel, took control in a way that definitively marked Iran's entrance into the early modern world. Nader's attempts to invent a new idea of Iran, had several enduring legacies. His time on the throne greatly widened a divide between royal and religious authority in Iran that began under the Safavids and continued into Qajar times. Nader's signing of the 1746 Kordan Treaty with the Ottomans also paradoxically created a space for Iran in an Islamic 'community of nations' that presaged Iran's place in the modern world. An examination of phases in the evolution of Nader's idea of Iran, may add depth to our overall understanding of the long-term historical impact of his rule.

Ideas of Iran immediately before Nader became Shah

Nader's story, in all its aspects, began in the period of Safavid demise, so it might be useful to begin by reviewing ideas of Iran current at that time. It is no secret that Safavid identity had been shaped from that dynasty's beginning through support for and connections to Twelver Shi'ism, seen early on in Shah Esma'il I's well-known allusions in mystical Turkish poetry to his descent from the Seventh Shi'i Imam, Musa al-Kazem.[3] As Safavid Shi'i identities matured throughout the sixteenth and seventeenth centuries, Iran grew into a great centre of Shi'i learning, with its scholars forging strong ties with Shi'i communities around the Muslim world, particularly in India, Lebanon and Iraq. The Safavid era's embrace of older Persianate forms of literary and poetic traditions, embodied in new versions of the *Shahnama* and other classic poems, completed and deepened this period's idea of Iran as well.[4] In turn, these literary excursions were paralleled by great creativity in other genres of Safavid intellectual achievement, epitomized by the works produced by the philosophers of the School of Esfahan.[5]

All of this fell into sudden turmoil with the arrival of the Ghelzay Afghans and the collapse of the Safavid dispensation in 1722. These staunchly Sunni Afghan horsemen must have been quite taken aback by their sudden capture of the Iranian heartland, a situation that ultimately only lasted a few years. Their conquest certainly did not allow the Afghans enough time to forge any meaningful concept of Iran to displace earlier versions kept alive by various Safavid pretenders and claimants who appeared during the 1720s and 1730s.

Uncertainty about any idea of Iran thus hovered over the country just as Nader first rose to prominence: a situation that gave him more room to develop his own innovative concepts as his importance as a military and political leader grew. One of Nader's earliest military achievements in his native Khorasan was to defeat Malek Mahmud Sistani, a leading warlord of the region, in 1726. Sistani, asserting his own right to rule, had begun to construct a novel idea of Iran with sovereignty being justified through claims of an eclectic ancestry from pre-Islamic Iranian royal families, like the Kayanids, as well as later Islamic dynasties, such as the Saffarids.[6]

Nader first made his name as a loyal commander in the struggle to restore the Safavid order. He became Safavid Shah Tahmasp II's main commander in campaigns against Afghan and Ottoman armies that had occupied large parts of the country. Gaining an initial reputation for military competence in Tahmasp's service, Nader's own continuous string of victories, together with a growing perception of Tahmasp's weakness and deficiencies as a ruler, soon persuaded him to oust Tahmasp as monarch. In 1732, not yet ready to take the throne himself, Nader installed Tahmasp's infant son as a figurehead with the regnal name 'Abbas III.

One of the major contemporary chronicles of Nader's career, the *Tarikh-e 'alam-ara-ye Naderi* of Mohammad Kazem Marvi, foreshadows the emergence of Nader's own idea of Iran in this work's account of how Nader replaced Tahmasp with 'Abbas. Overall, Marvi's work reveals him to have supported the Safavids as Iran's legitimate rulers: a sentiment that persisted among substantial groups of Iranians over many decades.[7] It shows how he saw Nader first as the Safavids' worthy champion, but then as a doomed usurper after he seized the throne, no matter how great his military prowess.

In Marvi's description of the installation of 'Abbas III, he has 'Abbas begin to cry when he received the crown. Marvi reports that Nader told his followers that, by crying, 'Abbas was indicating that he wanted to 'rule over the Afghans of Qandahar and the Ottoman sultan'.[8] Marvi then has Nader affirm: 'As ['Abbas] requested, I will throw reins around the necks of the Ottoman sultan, Hoseyn Shah Afghan, Mohammad Shah of India, and Abu'l-Feyz Khan ruler of Turan, and make them serve his magnificent court .... I will have prayers recited and strike coins in the name of this sovereign [Safavid] prince'.[9]

Although Marvi's work reveals a clear pro-Safavid slant here, his account also foreshadows aspects of the development of Nader's own ideas.

Marvi has Nader articulate the idea of an Iran that would dominate the Ottomans, Afghans, Mughals and Ozbeks as its vassals: figurative centre of a restored umma governed by domains linked through Turko-Mongol lineage ties and tradition. To tie this heritage even more closely to Nader's assertions of legitimacy as a ruler, Marvi and other contemporary chroniclers also recorded how Nader tried in various ways to make connections with the legacy of Timur: his epitome of Turko-Mongol rulership.[10]

Nader's Moghan Coronation: Beginnings of his new 'Idea of Iran'

Nader's striking coronation ceremony on the plain of Moghan in Azerbaijan in the spring of 1736 marks in many respects the real commencement of the evolution of Nader's idea of Iran. This coronation served to decouple Iranian concepts of royal legitimacy from ways in which they had evolved under Safavid rule. He ended royal support for the particularities of Shi'i belief and practice (such as *sabb*: the ritual cursing of the first three caliphs) that had generated a hostile division between Iran and its neighbours by the end of the Safavid era. At the same time, he continued to promote other aspects of Shi'ism, such as pilgrimages to the tombs of the Imams, that did not draw condemnation from other Muslims. The Moghan ceremony also marked the debut of Nader's clear attempt to 'invent tradition' in other ways by arranging a *quriltay* (assembly of delegations) of his subjects in imitation of the venerable Turko-Mongol tradition of gathering tribal elders on the steppe to choose and approve a new khan.

At this occasion, Nader called for Shi'ism to be integrated into Sunni Islam as a fifth mazhab, to enjoy the same status as the conventional four Sunni legal schools. He proposed that Twelver Shi'i Islam be redefined as the 'mazhab-e Ja'fari' in recognition of the importance of the Sixth Imam, Ja'far al-Sadeq, as its principal jurist. Shi'i departures from the various Sunni legal schools on interpretations of *shari'a* law would henceforth be treated just as another of the minor divergences between the conventional four Sunni legal schools that had been tolerated for centuries.

This new idea of Iran unveiled at Moghan departed from Safavid tradition in several ways. In religious terms, it made a basic appeal to the commonalities of the whole umma to argue for the equal status of all Muslims. Such a reimagining of Shi'ism would have nullified the classic Ottoman justification for war against the Safavids as heretics. It would also have provided Iran's ruler with a more legitimate status in connection with activities tied to pilgrimages to Mecca and Medina, specifically in the control of the annual hajj caravan with its tax and trade revenue potential. Perhaps to symbolize this unity, Nader introduced a new cap with four folds: the 'kolah-e Naderi'. It has variously been interpreted as alluding to the four 'rightly guided' caliphs, in place of the 12 red pleats of the headgear designed to honour the Twelve Imams so emblematic of the Qezelbash, or as a visual reminder of the domains of the four major contemporary Muslim dynasties and rulers: Nader in Iran along with the Ottomans, Ozbeks and Mughals.[11]

The convening of a quriltay also invoked the steppe tradition of approving a new tribal leader through a conclave of elders. This quriltay assembled not only representatives of the ruling nomadic warrior class (in this case, Turkmen tribal cavalry carried over from the Safavid Qezelbash forces who now supported Nader), but delegations from all communities under his rule, sedentary and nomadic, Muslim and non-Muslim. Such a gathering also offered, in addition to recalling Turko-Mongol tradition (not least a quriltay held 400 years earlier, in the late Ilkhanid period), a distant echo of the pre-Islamic Persian tradition of 'simultaneous rulership' over a vast panoply of subjects, reflected so famously in the ancient murals of Persepolis.[12]

Nader presented this new proposed juxtaposition of religious and cultural identities in an embassy dispatched to the Ottoman court a few months after the Moghan gathering. Seeking Ottoman sultan Mahmud I's acknowledgement of Nader's accession to the throne, the Iranian ambassador also described the religious component of Nader's new idea of Iran. He called on the Ottoman ruler, in his capacity as 'servitor of the Two Holy Places (Mecca and Medina) [*khadim al-harameyn al-sharifeyn*]', to erect a new pillar at the Ka'ba, commemorating the Ja'fari rite there and providing tangible proof of its equal status with other mazhabs at this principal meeting ground of the Islamic umma.[13]

Nader's emissary similarly invoked his revival of Turko-Mongol tradition. He argued for Nader's right to rule because he belonged to the 'noble Turkmen nation' ('*il-e jalil-e Torkman*').[14] Later official documents and contemporary court chronicles reused this phrase repeatedly as a reminder of his broad lineage ties to the Ottomans, Mughals and Central Asian rulers.[15] The official Ottoman account of the 1736 embassy, the *Tahkik ve Tevfik* by Koca Mehmet Rağıp Pasha (who later served as Ottoman Grand Vizier), mentions that Nader had begun to express such ideas in a letter to the Ottomans written even prior to the 1736 embassy.

Rağıp observed that this earlier letter was not written in Persian, the usual practice for any documents from the court chanceries of Iran, but in 'Iranian Turkish' (*İran türkisi*). Nader stated in it that,

> in the time of Chengiz Khan, the leaders of the Turkmen tribes, who left the land of Turan and migrated to Iran and Anatolia, were said to be all of one stock and one lineage. At that time, the exalted ancestor of the dynasty of the ever-increasing state [the Ottoman Empire] headed to Anatolia and our ancestor settled in the provinces of Iran. Since these lineages are interwoven and connected, it is hoped that when his royal

highness [the Ottoman sultan] learns of them, he will give royal consent to the establishment of peace between [us].[16]

In this phase of negotiations with the Ottomans, in fact, Nader's emissary held out the possibility that he might even allow himself to be considered a special Ottoman family associate, like the Crimean khan. Despite several days of talks, however, these initial negotiations failed to impress the Ottomans with Nader's new vision.[17]

It would be anachronistic and misleading to read such an invocation of Turkish blood ties now as some sort of early 'Pan-Turkism', however. These 1736 articulations of the components of Nader's idea of Iran were, rather, rough drafts of concepts that he would refine over the course of his 11 years in power with broad religious and political dimensions. A fuller articulation of his proposed religious innovations would be presented at the 1743 Council of Najaf, while his political reformulations would only take shape after his defeat of the Mughals and the rulers of Central Asia (see below).

Enduring Ottoman scepticism about Nader's concepts reflected how accustomed the Ottomans had become to the Safavids as Iran's rulers, despite their underlying and substantial religious enmity with these Shi'i neighbours, which occasionally erupted into major conflict. Aspects of Ottoman policy in Iran for decades after the fall of Esfahan paradoxically came to reflect a certain nostalgia for the parameters that had shaped this earlier relationship, notwithstanding the many times it broke down in hostility.

This can be perceived through the intermittent Ottoman promotion of Safavid pretenders of varying degrees of credibility to the Iranian throne after 1722. The Ottomans also continued to maintain as one of their primary diplomatic goals the restoration of as much as possible of the Safavid status quo ante in various phases of peace negotiations with Nader and other Iranian rulers.[18] Ottoman persistence in this regard testifies to some measure of real nostalgia for the largely peaceful interactions of the previous eight decades of the Ottoman–Safavid relationship that developed after the 1639 Treaty of Zohab. In the end, Nader too became compelled to accept the broad parameters of this Ottoman vision of the past upon his signing of the 1746 Treaty of Kordan, as shall be examined.

The Idea of Iran and Nader's Conquest of India

Soon after his initial attempt to persuade the Ottomans of the legitimacy of his idea of Iran immediately following his 1736 coronation, Nader shifted his attention eastward. His campaigns there, initially against the Afghans, culminated in his conquest of India, for which he became infamous in the subcontinent and beyond. His victory over the Mughals substantially affected how he viewed his relationships with other Muslim rulers.

The impact of his conquest of India on the development of Nader's idea of Iran became apparent in how contemporary official documents described him. After vanquishing the Mughals at the Battle of Karnal near Delhi in 1739, his official letters began to describe him as the 'shahanshah'.[19] This new title was to elevate his position vis-à-vis the Mughal emperor, Naser al-Din Mohammad, whose title Nader's documents now posited merely as 'Mohammad Shah': to show clearly his new status as Nader's subordinate. Nader treated the Ozbek Janid ruler Abu'l-Feyz Khan in a very similar fashion after his victory over him, renaming him 'Abu'l-Feyz Shah' to establish his equal status with the Mughal monarch.[20] An official letter from Nader to the Ottomans in the early 1740s, presenting new peace proposals following his conquests in India and Central Asia, now identified Nader as 'crown-giver of the kings of Turan and India'.[21] This turn of phrase, together with the image of a 'shahanshah' ruling over subsidiary 'shahs', both recalls descriptions of pre-Islamic hierarchies of monarchs and rulers and alludes to the familial, tribal relationships and connections of Turko-Mongol tradition and heritage.

Another aspect of these connections received more emphasis in documents composed after Nader's Indian campaign: Nader's attempt to associate himself with the farr of Timur and his descendants. The theme of connection with Timur, present in many of the contemporary chronicles of Nader and documents issued by his court, came into special focus upon his victory over the Mughals, depicted as paralleling Timur's own military triumphs in India.[22] Nader took pains to recognize Mughal rulers' status as legitimate based on their Timurid ancestry, but he took this a step further. The final peace treaty between Nader and Mohammad Shah also asserted their common ties of 'Turkmen' descent that Nader had introduced in exchanges with the Ottomans.[23] Following these new conquests in the east, Nader could now be seen as master of the fully developed version of his new idea of Iran at the centre of a reunified umma.

Nader's main court chronicler, Mirza Mahdi Khan Astarabadi, observes that although 'all of the provinces of India had come under the control of Nader's state' at the time of the conquest, Nader did not attempt to incorporate India *directly* into his own personal domains.[24] In fact, the final treaty carefully delineated the borders of the two empires and enumerated war reparations that the Mughals would be required to pay him.[25] After notoriously plundering the Mughal court's wealth and allowing his troops to wreck the city of Delhi in an unforgettable rampage, all Nader really did in political terms was to redefine Iran's relationship with India. Nader would now preside over the eastern part of a newly reunited Muslim umma, ruled by various families of Turko-Mongol descent linked by lineage, invented descent ties and actual marriage ties.

After glossing over the devastation caused by the infamous Delhi massacre, Astarabadi's chronicle immediately shifts to recounting 'an event to increase happiness': the marriage of a Mughal princess to Nader's son, Nasrollah Mirza.[26] The description of this marriage by Marvi, Nader's other major contemporary chronicler, also provided an occasion for him to mention Nader's 'Turkmen descent' concept again. He has Nader proclaim, 'Since the exalted lineage of the imperial deputy [Nader] is Turkmen, and the [Mughal] *padishah*, who is the wellspring of eloquence and politeness, is also Turkmen, there is no separation or discord observed between them'.[27] Although there was awareness of general ethnic ties between Timur and rulers of Turkmen lineage farther west, such as members of the Afshar tribe, such a bold assertion of kinship constituted an invention of tradition even more substantial than the links earlier adduced between Nader and the Ottomans.

Khorasan as Iran's new Centre: The Role of Kalat-e Naderi

It was also after his victories in India and Central Asia that Nader began to make tentative steps to re-centre his empire in the region of Khorasan. As his home territory, Khorasan had in many ways always served as his refuge, particularly the fortress plateau of Kalat-e Naderi located about 150 km north of Mashhad. Nader had structures built there beginning in the late 1730s, in particular the pavilion later known as the Qasr-e Khorshid ('Palace of the Sun'). This suggests that he was planning to make Kalat a secure repository for the vast treasures that he had taken from the Mughals and other conquered royal houses, as well as providing a convenient, secure location at which to convene his royal court on auspicious occasions.[28]

Kalat has been important in Khorasan since ancient times and was even mentioned in the *Shahnama*.[29] Nader came to treat it as a strategic refuge and retreat throughout his career. Most infamously, he seems to have brought there the extraordinary amounts of treasure he had seized and craftsmen he had captured from the Mughal court immediately after his conquest of India. The site became for him a fortified depot to guard his riches. Its location had numerous advantages. It was near Nader's birthplace and within the ancestral territory of his most loyal followers. Securing it and fortifying it would not require a great expenditure of resources. It was a unique *natural* fortress – a work of God available to Nader, and therefore more prestigious than any manmade structure. Nader could highlight the natural quality of his achievements of conquest in using Kalat to store conquered treasure.

Eighteenth-century Indian rulers celebrated finding or possessing treasures as important proofs of their legitimacy: a facet of kingship celebrated in the Indian tradition since the time of the *Arthashastra*, an ancient political manual.[30] Kalat seems to have been important for Nader in both respects. Early in his career, he discovered there a treasure left by Timur and, after his triumphs in India and elsewhere, he was able to make the fortress a secure location in which to guard and maintain his own conquered treasures. Marvi's chronicle presents an important premonition of Nader's future very early in his career, while describing one of his first significant military campaigns. He relates that, when camped near Kalat, Nader woke up in the middle of the night and noticed a faint glow from a distant mountainside. When he went to explore it, he discovered a rock inscription, near which was a hoard of buried treasure.

Marvi reveals the author of this inscription to be none other than Timur, who had placed it there to commemorate the resistance of Kalat to his armies:

> He who arrives here shall become the rarity of the age and lord of the conjunction ... they called me Timur-e Gurkan. ... I conquered ... [many] countries. ... Beware, lest you be carried away by the pomp and size of your army. In all situations, seek victory from God, since victory can only be granted by God. Even though 850,000 troops of ... [my] armies ... were assembled here, I still could not take the fortress of Kalat. When I turned my glance away from the army and instead relied upon divine grace, its conquest was made easy for me. ... Do not be proud when your army wins a victory but thank God.[31]

Marvi reports that Kalat was where Nader discovered Timur's treasure and saw the earlier conqueror's advice: omens presaging how Nader's career would parallel Timur's.

A rock inscription still visible near one of the entrances to Kalat-e Naderi testifies to Nader's enduring sense of connection to Timur. Not complete, but possibly dating from the end of Nader's reign, it is one of only a handful of Turkish-language inscriptions and documents from Nader's court that have come to light. The text is a paean to Nader that describes him as 'associated with the hearth of Timur'.[32] The clear invocation of the earlier conqueror, in this most intimate setting and in Nader's mother tongue, testifies to the strong association for Nader between the site and Timur's legacy.

Nader's chroniclers regularly make brief references to Kalat in the course of describing Nader's campaigns, with Marvi labelling it '*Kalat-e Dar al-Sebat*' ('Kalat, the Abode of Steadfastness'), recalling its quality as a refuge.[33] Descriptions of his 1736 Moghan coronation report that Nader asserted then that he would prefer to retire to Kalat and rest on his laurels as Iran's saviour than become its monarch, but relented when his subjects assembled there prevailed on him to take the throne.

As a key part of Nader's home territory, Kalat existed symbiotically with Mashhad, only a short distance to the south. Nader retained a strong attachment to the city of Mashhad itself, lavishing gifts on the shrine of Emam Reza there at important points during his career. During Nader's brief reign, Mashhad temporarily flourished as the hub of a revived trading network between India and Russia. It also continued to increase in importance as a pilgrimage centre with its shrine complex. Nader appears to have foreseen the possibilities of the development of Mashhad into a major commercial hub.

Jonas Hanway, an English trader who visited there in the early 1740s, characterized it as thriving at that time.[34] Nader also took steps to promote the city's prominence, such as the creation of an Armenian merchant community within Mashhad to be called 'New Nakhjavan'. This was reportedly modelled on Esfahan's 'New Jolfa', where Armenians from the traditional Armenian territories of the Caucasus had been resettled by the Safavids in a particular neighbourhood to promote that dynasty's participation in long-distance overland trade networks.[35] The re-centring of his domains in this new part of Iran, more advantageous for Nader than Esfahan, might also have helped to address one of the Safavids' continuing fiscal dilemmas: how to limit and control the constant flow of wealth out of Iran into India.

However, Mashhad's most important function during the Afsharid era continued to be its significance as a centre of religious veneration. Nader did much to encourage this, most notably erecting a marble fountain in one of the courtyards of the shrine of the Eighth Imam and gilding one of its principal gates in 1741.[36] He issued a *farman* to appoint a new custodian from among the ulema of Mashhad for that shrine in 1154/1742.[37] In these ways, Nader helped to preserve and bolster the spiritual glory of this pilgrimage destination that had already become very important in the Safavid period.

Despite such preliminary efforts to shift his seat of power to Khorasan though, the main focus of Nader's everyday activities, like those of his nomadic predecessors, always remained his mobile camp, which could resemble a small city in its expansiveness. Nader Shah's image as a ruler for whom 'the real capital of his empire was the seat of a saddle and the back of a horse' recalls the Ozbek ruler Shibani Khan's exclamation to Khonji, his court chronicler: 'Let our capital be our saddle'.[38] This ultimately became a problem because the demands of Nader's perpetually mobile army camp, constantly on campaigns unbroken by significant periods of rest, soon exceeded the financial carrying capacity of his domains. Occasional gestures to propitiate the shrines and improve the economic infrastructure of Mashhad at moments of victory, while hoarding treasures in Kalat, were insufficient to sustain a world empire whose leader could never devote enough attention to securing the basic prosperity of its newly located capital region.

Nader's Idea of Iran and the Ottomans again at Najaf

As the circumstances of his career of conquest dictated, Nader's attention shifted quickly back to his confrontation with the Ottomans on his western flank soon after his return from India and his visits to Kalat and Mashhad in Khorasan. An important part of this new campaign against the Ottomans, in contrast to his diplomatic exchanges with the Mughal ruler, was to put renewed pressure on the Ottomans to accept his innovative religious proposals, previously discussed as legitimate parts of Nader's new idea of Iran. This part of his new programme was a focal point in his negotiations with the Ottoman sultan, emphasizing the sultan's special status as guardian of Mecca and Medina.

The most detailed presentation of Nader's novel religious proposals took place in late 1743 at a council that Nader convened in the Iraqi shrine city of Najaf where he assembled Iranian, Ottoman and Central Asian ulema. This occurred soon after he had launched a new military offensive against the Ottomans in Iraq. One of its goals was to compel the Ottomans finally to agree to both the religious and the political aspects of Nader's new idea of Iran that they had continually put off accepting since Nader's investiture as Iran's sovereign.

An eyewitness account of this gathering by an Iraqi Sunni cleric, 'Abdollah al-Soweydi, presents his views on the religious aspects of Nader's new idea of Iran very clearly. At the beginning of his account, al-Soweydi mentions the political aspects of Nader's new concepts, previously discussed, observing how Nader emphasized his parallels with Timur and marriage alliances with several other Muslim dynasties to bolster his legitimacy.[39] Al-Soweydi describes how, at this meeting, when he himself tried to engage in real theological discussions with the Iranian religious authorities there, he soon got the impression that Nader did not intend to allow the assembled clerics to engage in debate on any details of theological controversies.

The Iranian spokesmen at Najaf used arguments to justify Nader's new religious concepts similar to those employed by the Iranian embassy to Istanbul in 1736. In both cases, Nader simply wanted the Ottomans to accept the idea that Iranian Muslims could legally and officially be considered Sunnis, without any discussion of theological intricacies. As a result, al-Soweydi and the other participants in the council signed an agreement at its conclusion that hardly mentioned the concept of Twelver Shi'ism as the Ja'fari mazhab of Sunni Islam, but focused on acknowledging mutually held principles of Islamic practice and belief. Al-Soweydi finishes his account by expressing his strong sentiment that the entire gathering felt like nothing more than an exercise in *taqiya* (ritual dissimulation: a long-established way for Shi'is to gloss over areas of theological dispute with other Muslims by dissimulation on controversial religious topics) by the Iranian delegation.[40]

Creative use of taqiya might have been one way for Iranian clerics to manage their presentation of Nader's proposal. Al-Soweydi's invocation of the concept of taqiya might help to explain how Nader's team avoided exploration of the more problematic aspects of his new religious ideas in either a domestic or a foreign context. This Ottoman account confirms the persistence and intensification, following his conquest of India, of Nader's campaign to get the Ottomans to accept in its entirety the new idea of Iran that he had been pushing since 1736 at his coronation in Moghan. Al-Soweydi also confirms how, by 1743, Nader had extended his concepts of political legitimation considerably from the simple assertions of Turkmen descent he had made at Moghan by now mentioning his marriage alliances forged and lineage ties recognized with other Muslim dynasties. Perhaps this simply shows that he felt more secure in promoting his ideas with the tangible achievements of his recent military victories in India and Central Asia.

Conclusion: The End of Conflict between Nader and the Ottomans

Despite the council of Najaf, Nader's last war with the Ottomans continued until he defeated them near Yerevan in August 1745. By this point in their conflict, both sides had become exhausted and depleted. Thus, Nader finally offered peace proposals in which he omitted his previous demand that the Ottomans withdraw from Iraq and no longer called on them to accept the specifics of his Ja'fari mazhab proposal. As his grip on Iran weakened during the winter of 1746 and spring of 1747 with a substantial round of domestic revolts erupting across his realm, Nader became more willing to accept Ottoman terms for a lasting peace settlement.

In September 1746, Nader met with an Ottoman emissary in the village of Kordan near Tehran, where he signed a treaty with the Ottomans to recognize their common 'Turkmen' origins and acknowledge Iran's respect for Sunni practices. This agreement was in many ways a restatement of the main provisions of the 1639 Ottoman–Safavid Treaty of Zohab. It restored the borders of that earlier time and guaranteed good treatment for Iranian pilgrims to the Shi'i shrine cities of Iraq or those performing the hajj. The Kordan Treaty signalled the end of a conflict between the Ottomans and the Iranians that had waxed and waned over the previous 25 years since the end of Safavid rule and cleared the way finally for the Ottomans to recognize Nader officially.

Although the treaty pledged Iran's allegiance to Sunni Islam, its language reveals that this was only at a superficial level.[41] One of the treaty's provisions secured the rights of Iranians making pilgrimages to the shrine cities of Iraq so revered by Shi'is and specifically admonished Ottoman officials from Baghdad not to demand oppressive taxes from Iranian pilgrims visiting those places.[42] It thus protected the safety and status of Iranians continuing to engage in distinctly Shi'i practices.

By signing the Treaty of Kordan, Nader formally abandoned attempts to get the Ottomans to affirm the Ja'fari mazhab idea while committing Iranians to respecting the outward manifestations of Sunni Islam. The treaty offered a way to protect essential rites of Shi'i piety, such as pilgrimages to the tombs of the Imams, while agreeing that Iranian Shi'is would not continue practices that offended the Sunnis but might, at least according to some interpretations, not be considered essential parts of Shi'ism. The Kordan agreement thus became the basis for the emergence of a modern Ottoman–Iranian relationship, presaging later ideas of Iran beyond the fleeting endurance of Nader's own projects. This new Iranian–Ottoman paradigm required the formal abandonment of the policy of using theological differences to justify war, in favour of establishing a relationship sanctioned according to Islamic principles respected by both empires. Despite Nader's assassination shortly after the signing of the treaty, it remained the basis for future relations long beyond his brief reign.

Unfortunately, the rapid disintegration of Nader's regime quickly followed the diplomatic achievement of the Treaty of Kordan. The tumult of Nader's era in the region became part of the general upheaval across the Muslim world in the eighteenth century with the ever greater involvement of European powers in all aspects of Muslim life in this part of the world. Nader's idea of Iran, though, despite its failure to take root, did set the stage for more modern ideas to take shape, beginning in Qajar times. The questions it raised about the nature of relationships across the sectarian divides of the Muslim umma, as well as its attempts through an invention of tradition to redefine relationships between Iran and the empires, polities and nations around it, are issues that continued to confront Iran throughout the next several centuries.

Notes:

1. The concept of 'invented traditions' can be traced back to the 1983 collection of essays edited by Eric Hobsbawm and Terence Ranger, *The Invention of Tradition*, but has since been adopted for many other historical settings and contexts.
2. For pre-Islamic Persian concepts of the 'king of kings', see R. Schmitt, 'Achaemenid dynasty'. For Central Asian steppe principles of political authority, see Thomas Allsen, 'Sharing out the empire', pp. 172–90.
3. Safavid-era uses of Imami Shi'i tradition in forging 'ideas of Iran' are discussed extensively in Sholeh A. Quinn, *Historical Writing during the Reign of Shah 'Abbas*; and H.R. Roemer, 'The Safavid period'.
4. See, for example, Sheila R. Canby, ed., *The Shahnama of Shah Tahmasp*.
5. See Seyyed Hossein Nasr, 'Philosophy in Islam', pp. 57–80.
6. Laurence Lockhart, *Nadir Shah*, p. 6.
7. For discussion of lingering nostalgia for the Safavids in the period after 1722, see John R. Perry, 'The last Safavids'.
8. Mohammad Kāzem Marvi and Mohammad Amin Reyāhi, *Tārikh-e 'ālam-ārā-ye Nāderi*, p. 234.
9. Ibid.
10. For discussion of Nader's attempts to model himself on Timur, see Ernest Tucker, 'Seeking a world empire', pp. 332–42.
11. See Layla S. Diba, 'Visual and written sources', pp. 84–96.
12. For discussion of 'simultaneous rulership' in this context, see Gene R. Garthwaite, '"What's in a name?"', pp. 9–19. It is worth noting that the quriltay summoned by Sheykh-'Ali son of 'Ali Qushchi in Khorasan in 1336 included several leading sheykhs as well as viziers, see Jean Aubin, 'Le *quriltai* de Sultân-Maydân'.
13. Koca Mehmet Rağıp Pasha, *Tahkik ve Tevfik*, p. 56.
14. Ibid., p. 42.
15. See Nader Shah's 1736 letter to the Ottoman Grand Vizier in 'Abd al-Hoseyn Navā'i, ed., *Nāder Shāh va bāzmāndagānash*, p. 284.
16. Rağıp Pasha, *Tahkik*, p. 25.
17. For a more detailed analysis of this embassy, see Ernest Tucker, 'Nadir Shah and the Ja'fari Madhhab reconsidered', pp. 163–79.
18. For discussion of one such episode, the Ottoman promotion of the Safavid pretender 'Safi Mirza' in 1744, see Ernest S. Tucker, *Nadir Shah's Quest for Legitimacy in Post-Safavid Iran*, pp. 95–97.
19. 'Abdollah al-Soweydi, *Ketāb al-hojjāj al-qat'iya*, p. 4.
20. Mirzā Mahdi Khān Astarābādi, *Tārikh-e jahāngoshā-ye Nāderi*, p. 352.
21. Ibid., p. 389.
22. For discussion of this, see Tucker, 'Seeking a world empire', pp. 332–42.
23. 'Fimābeyn-e hazrateyn nesbat-e torkmāni va ettehād va selsela-ye jensiyat tahaqqoq dārad' ('Between the two excellencies [Nader Shah and Mohammad Shah], the Turkmen relationship, unity and [common] lineage of [their] origin is confirmed'), Astarābādi, *Tārikh-e jahāngoshā*, p. 327. See also Riazul Islam, *A Calendar of Documents on Indo-Persian Relations*, vol. II, pp. 69, 81.
24. Astarābādi, *Tārikh-e jahāngoshā*, p. 328.

25. Not once in the treaty or in discussions with Mohammad Shah was the Ja'fari mazhab concept mentioned, a sign that this was important only in negotiations with the Ottomans as guardians of the Ka'ba.
26. Astarābādi, *Tārikh-e jahāngoshā*, p. 332.
27. Marvi and Reyāhi, *Tārikh-e 'ālam-ārā*, p. 751.
28. For discussion of Kalat, see Michael Axworthy, 'Basile Vatatzes and his History of Nāder Šāh', pp. 331–43; and Sussan Babaie, 'Nader Shah, the Delhi loot, and the 18th-century exotics of empire', pp. 215–34.
29. See Abu'l-Qāsem Ferdowsi, *The Epic of the Kings*, pp. 114–19.
30. D.H. Kolff, *Naukar, Rajput, and Sepoy*, p. 68.
31. Marvi and Reyāhi, *Tārikh-e 'ālam-ārā*, pp. 15–16.
32. Mohammad Rezā Khosravi, *Kalāt-e Nāderi*, pp. 66–67.
33. Marvi and Reyāhi, *Tārikh-e 'ālam-ārā*, p. 108.
34. Jonas Hanway, *An Historical Account of the British Trade over the Caspian Sea*, vol. I, pp. 23, 245.
35. Tanburi Arutin Efendi, an Ottoman-Armenian musician sent to Nader's court, visited Mashhad in 1740 and claims to have seen only the ruins of this 'New Nakhjavan' there, labelling it a failed experiment. See Tanburi Arutin Efendi, *Tahmas Kulu Han'ın Tevarihi*, p. 36.
36. Lockhart, *Nadir Shah*, p. 197.
37. Navā'i, ed., *Nāder Shāh*, pp. 480–81.
38. Lockhart, *Nadir Shah*, p. 197; and Fazlollāh b. Ruzbehān Khonji, *Mehmān-nāma-ye Bokhārā*, quoted in Monika Gronke, 'The Persian court between palace and tent', p. 20.
39. Al-Soweydi, *Ketāb al-hojjāj al-qat'iya*, p. 4.
40. Ibid., p. 28.
41. Astarābādi, *Tārikh-e jahāngoshā*, p. 418.
42. Ibid.

Bibliography:

Allsen, Thomas, 'Sharing out the empire: Apportioned lands under the Mongols', in *Nomads in the Sedentary World*, ed. Anatoly Khazanov and André Wink (Richmond, UK: Curzon, 2001), pp. 172–90.

Arutin Efendi, Tanburi, *Tahmas Kulu Han'ın Tevarihi*, ed. Esat Uras (Ankara: Türk Tarih Kurumu Basımevi, 1942).

Astarābādi, Mirzā Mahdi Khān, *Tārikh-e jahāngoshā-ye Nāderi*, ed. 'Abdollāh Anvār (Tehran: Kiyānush, 1377/1998).

Aubin, Jean, 'Le *quriltai* de Sultân-Maydân (1336)', *Journal Asiatique* 276 (1991), pp. 175–97.

Axworthy, Michael, 'Basile Vatatzes and his history of Nāder Šāh', *Oriente Moderno* 86, no. 2 (2006), pp. 331–43.

Babaie, Sussan, 'Nader Shah, the Delhi loot, and the 18th-century exotics of empire', in *Crisis, Collapse, Militarism and Civil War: The History and Historiography of 18th Century Iran*, ed. Michael Axworthy (New York: Oxford University Press, 2018), pp. 215–34.

Canby, Sheila R., ed., *The Shahnama of Shah Tahmasp: The Persian Book of Kings* (New Haven: Yale University Press, 2014).

Diba, Layla S., 'Visual and written sources: Dating eighteenth-century silks', in *Woven from the Soul, Spun from the Heart: Textile Arts of Safavid and Qajar Iran 16th – 19th Centuries*, ed. Carol Bier (Washington: Textile Museum, 1987), pp. 84–96.

Ferdowsi, Abu'l-Qāsem, *The Epic of the Kings*, trans. Reuben Levy (Chicago: University of Chicago Press, 1967).

Garthwaite, Gene R., '"What's in a name?": Periodization and "18th-century Iran"', in *Crisis, Collapse, Militarism and Civil War: The History and Historiography of 18th Century Iran*, ed. Michael Axworthy (New York: Oxford University Press, 2018), pp. 9–19.

Gronke, Monika, 'The Persian court between palace and tent: From Timur to 'Abbas I', in *Timurid Art and Culture: Iran and Central Asia in the Fifteenth Century*, ed. Lisa Golombek and Maria Subtelny (Leiden: Brill, 1992), pp. 18–22.

Hanway, Jonas, *An Historical Account of the British Trade over the Caspian Sea*, 2 vols (London: Osborne, Brown et al., 1761).

Hobsbawm, Eric and Terence Ranger, eds, *The Invention of Tradition* (Cambridge: Cambridge University Press, 1983).

Khosravi, Mohammad Rezā, *Kalāt-e Nāderi* (Mashhad: Entešārāt-e Āstān-e Qods-e Razavi, 1367/1988).

Kolff, D.H., *Naukar, Rajput, and Sepoy: The Evolution of the Military Labour Market in Hindustan, 1450–1850* (Cambridge: Cambridge University Press, 1990).

Lockhart, Laurence, *Nadir Shah. A Critical Study based mainly upon Contemporary Sources* (London: Luzac & Co., 1938).
Marvi, Mohammad Kāzem and Mohammad Amin Reyāhi, *Tārikh-e 'ālam-ārā-ye Nāderi* (Tehran: Zavvār, 1364/1985).
Nasr, Seyyed Hossein, 'Philosophy in Islam', *Studia Islamica* 37 (1972), pp. 57–80.
Navā'i, 'Abd al-Hoseyn, ed., *Nāder Shāh va bāzmāndagānash: hamrāh bā nāma-hā-ye saltanati va asnād-e seyāsi va edāri* (Tehran: Entesharāt-e Zarrin, 1368/1989).
Perry, John R., 'The last Safavids, 1722–1773', *Iran* 9 (1971), pp. 59–69.
Quinn, Sholeh A., *Historical Writing during the Reign of Shah 'Abbas Ideology, Imitation and Legitimacy in Safavid Chronicles* (Salt Lake City: University of Utah Press, 2000).
Rağıp Pasha, Koca Mehmet, *Tahkik ve Tevfik*, ed. Ahmet Zeki İzgöer (Istanbul: Kitabevi, 2003).
Riazul Islam, *A Calendar of Documents on Indo-Persian Relations*, 2 vols (Karachi: Mirza Muhammad Sadiq, 1982).
Roemer, H.R., 'The Safavid period', in *The Cambridge History of Iran, vol. 6, The Timurid and Safavid Periods*, ed. Peter Jackson and Laurence Lockhart (Cambridge: Cambridge University Press, 1986) pp. 189–350.
Schmitt, R., 'Achaemenid dynasty', *Encyclopaedia Iranica, vol. I (1983)*, pp. 414–26, online at http://www.iranicaonline.org/articles/achaemenid-dynasty [accessed 25 March 2021].
al-Soweydi, 'Abdollāh, *Ketāb al-hojjāj al-qat'iya li-ettifāq al-ferāq al-Eslāmiya* (Cairo: al-Maktaba al-Ḥalabiya, 1323 AH/1905).
Tucker, Ernest, 'Nadir Shah and the Ja'fari Madhhab reconsidered', *Iranian Studies* 27, no. 1–4 (1994), pp. 163–79.
— *Nadir Shah's Quest for Legitimacy in Post-Safavid Iran* (Gainesville: University Press of Florida, 2006).
— 'Seeking a world empire: Nadir Shah in Timur's path', in *History and Historiography of post-Mongol Central Asia and the Middle East: Studies in Honor of John E. Woods*, ed. Judith Pfeiffer and Sholeh Quinn (Wiesbaden: Harrassowitz, 2006), pp. 332–42.

2

Dismembering the Corporate: The Single Portraits of Nader Shah and the Changing Body Politic in Post-Safavid Iran

Janet O'Brien
(The Courtauld Institute of Art, University of London)

In 1924, a poster depicting Reza Khan as the protector of Iran was circulated in the Parsi community in India (Plate Ia)*. Painted in Shiraz and printed in Bombay, it shows *Madar-e vatan* (Motherland) – a female personification of Iran whose verdant robe drapes over her territory – leaning on the soon-to-be shah (r. 1925–41) of the new Pahlavi dynasty and holding his freshly commissioned crown. It was distributed at a time when Reza Khan was canvassing the support of Bombay Parsis for his nationalist project and encouraging their repatriation.[1] Loaded with rhetoric and evocation, this image deserves a deeper unpacking and I hope to publish a fuller study in the near future. What first intrigued me was the presence of Nader Shah (r. 1736–47) in the top right corner, next to Shapur (r. 239–70) and Darius (r. 522–486 BC), who are joined by Cyrus (r. 559–530 BC) in the form of a four-winged rock figure standing guard at the feet of *Madar-e vatan*. Parsis derive their Zoroastrian identity from ancient Iran, and images of Sasanian and Achaemenid kings are part of that identity.[2] But why is Nader, the only ruler present from the Islamic period, ranked among them?

Like the ancient greats, Nader was celebrated for his vast empire, and his conquest of India would have been a source of pride for the Parsis. Furthermore, he was a hero of Reza Khan,[3] and his self-styling as Iran's saviour played into the Pahlavi brand of nationalism,[4] which explains his instruction to Reza Khan to protect the distressed motherland and to raise his sword against the enemies of Iran.[5] What this composition also demonstrates, and what is pertinent to this chapter, is the powerful and enduring resonance of Nader's image. Thanks to his many portraits, the extent of which had never been seen before him, Nader became a personification of victory and an emblem of Iran's last mighty empire and, in this case, a constituent of the 'idea of Iran' constructed by Reza Khan for the Parsis.

The bust image of Nader in this poster is modelled after a widely reproduced engraving, which was first published in John Malcolm's *The*

History of Persia in 1815.[6] The engraving itself was copied 'From an Original Persian Painting', most likely the oil painting of *Nader Shah Crowning Reza-Qoli Mirza* by Abu'l-Hasan Mostowfi Ghaffari Kashani dated 1189/1775–76, now at the Sa'adabad Palace.[7] This fascinating journey from an eighteenth-century oil canvas in Tehran to a twentieth-century chromolithograph in British Bombay via an engraving printed in London is proof of the vast space and time, and diverse media, that Nader's image had traversed. Numerous cross-media iterations have continued to the present day. Nader is recreated in the flesh in theatres, heroized in a bronze sculpture, animated in children's books and cartoons, and he battles on in the virtual world of video games.[8] The resemblance of all these representations to his first depictions is a testament to a three-century-long visual lineage. Yet, with the exception of Layla Diba, Abolala Soudavar and Adel Adamova,[9] authors of Persian painting texts have paid little attention to Nader and have dismissed his turbulent period as an era of artistic darkness. Significantly, his portraits constitute the earliest extant corpus of recognizable single-figure representations of an Iranian ruler, but they have never been studied collectively as a phenomenon that heralded the emergence of royal portraiture in Iran.

The visual legacy of Nader can be traced back to a number of portraits created during his reign and shortly after his death in 1747 (Plates Ib–IIb)*.[10] Crucially, all of them were made after his Delhi conquest of 1739, the event that made him, in the words of the contemporary English writer Jonas Hanway, 'the most powerful of all the monarchs of the East'.[11] I shall discuss them in turn in a moment, but viewing them as a group allows us to observe that, despite the different settings, styles and media, a distinct iconography of Nader has emerged. They share a remarkable consistency, not only in terms of his four-pointed hat and jewels looted from Delhi, but also his proud-chested, arms-akimbo swagger, his unflinching gaze and resolute look, his face turned towards his left to show off the feather *jeqqa* worn on the right side of his hat to signal his sovereign status, and his head slightly tilted back to give an air of pride that befits a conqueror. It is this depiction from his early portraits that has come to be recognized as the image of Nader.

The legend of Nader began with his meteoric ascent from tribal soldier from Khorasan to commander-in-chief of Tahmasp II. He ended the Afghan occupation of Iran (1722–29) and restored the Safavid ruler to the throne (r. 1729–32). He eventually deposed the Safavids to found the Afsharid dynasty in 1736. His conquests formed an empire stretching from the Caucasus to India and earned him admirers among other great conquerors, including Napoleon and the Duke of Wellington.[12] Nader's invasion and sack of Delhi in 1739 generated a frenzy of reports from St Petersburg to Istanbul in the London newspapers, and news of his plans for an offensive against the Ottoman Empire was widely circulated on the heels of his Indian victory.[13] Armed with a war chest overflowing with the riches of the Mughal Empire, and following his campaigns in Central Asia and Dagestan, Nader turned his attention to the Ottomans in 1743.[14] It was speculated that he planned to expand as far west as Europe and as far east as China.[15] Mohammad 'Ali Tusi, a poet commissioned by Nader to versify his heroic deeds, predicted that his royal patron would 'do the same to the rulers of Rum, as Genghis did to the world' and, like Eskandar (Alexander), Nader too 'will move from Zang [Africa] ... to Farang [Europe]'.[16]

Such a radical change in the political landscape of Iran was accompanied by a makeover of the royal image. This chapter introduces the core findings abstracted from a larger investigation into why Nader's portraits were novel; specifically, how they decoupled the shah from the collective ruling body and how that visual break-up was linked to contrasting notions of rule between Nader's self-referential authority and the dynastic institution of the Safavids.[17] Theories of the body politic, never before applied in Persian painting, provide a methodological tool to contrast their divergent displays of power and ideologies of kingship. The theory most often cited is 'the King's Two Bodies' – the dual concept of the immortal 'body politic' and the mortal 'body natural' of the king. Despite the attention this medieval doctrine has garnered among scholars, the body politic is, in fact, an ancient concept rooted in Hinduism, with parallels in Zoroastrianism. It was further developed in Iranian and Indian political discourse in the Islamic period. To summarize my analysis of the different but often convergent interpretations, the body politic may refer to a corporate power structure with the king as its soul, head, or heart. Alternatively, it may embody the dignity and sanctity of the royal office, which, I argue, may be derived from certain attributes that reside in the individual capacity of the shah, including *farr* (divine glory), *javanmardi* (chivalric manliness) and his qualities as *ensan-e kamel* (the Perfect Man). This constellation of ideas, as will be further referenced in this chapter, provides a theoretical means to trace the transformation of the political image of the shah from being the head of a corporation to the sole embodiment of the sovereign office.

It is not feasible to introduce the full corpus of Nader's representations in this short chapter,[18] or to consider their transcultural identities more globally in the context of his empire-building aspirations. Instead, I shall focus on his single portraits created in Iran and how they embody his personality-driven rule. I begin with an oil painting from Iran, ca. 1740, in the Victoria and Albert (V&A) collection (Plate Ib)*. It is the earliest surviving life-size Persian portrait of an Iranian ruler. It depicts Nader seated back on his heels, arms akimbo, with one hand resting on his belt and the other on his lap. As an upstart, he needed to carry his soldier body with regal bearing, and this traditional pose of a Safavid shah lends dignity to his nascent kingship. But, unlike representations of Safavid or earlier rulers in Iran, Nader is draped in looted jewels from Delhi, seated on a Mughal carpet in a Mughal tent.[19] Bearing the fruits of his victories, his body functions as a most resplendent triumphal monument of his conquest of the Mughal Empire. Layla Diba has attributed the painting to Mohammad Reza Hendi,[20] who was active in Iran and India in the mid-eighteenth century and whose works comprise royal portraits from the Afsharid and Mughal courts. While there is no direct evidence of it being ordered by Nader himself, the meticulous rendering of the royal accoutrements – including the birds on the enamelled hilts of the dagger and the sword, the *kundan* designs of the jewelled objects, the gold and silver threads in the carpet, and the double twists of the prayer beads that rest on the floor – suggests that it was probably a royal commission, and that Nader might have even sat for it. We also know from textual records that Nader ordered multiple paintings of himself after the Delhi conquest.[21] As for its intended function, again, there is no information. But, according to travellers' accounts, Nader's palaces in Esfahan, Mashhad, Qazvin and Behshahr were decorated with figurative paintings,[22] and traces remain in the Qasr-e Khorshid in Kalat.[23] One could picture this portrait adorning one of his palaces, and its triumphal message would have made it a fitting choice for an audience hall.[24]

In Persian painting, the deployment of the king's body as an exclusive sight and site of power was a trend that emerged under Nader.[25] In this composition, his body dominates the tight space and commands our full attention. His stocky torso, wide girth, and bulky thighs exude physical robustness. His masculinity is further amplified by his strong and well-defined face, and a full, perfectly groomed beard.[26] This representation closely resembles eyewitness descriptions of his imposing presence and manly appearance,[27] and would have been readily recognized by those who had met him. More significant is the focus on his body and what it means. In Islamic thought, bodily perfection of the king is indexical of the health of the body politic,[28] and there are ample contemporary references to Nader's physical vigour, self-discipline and ability to endure hardship alongside his soldiers.[29] In the V&A portrait, and in others, Nader, who was in his fifties, is depicted in the fullness of health and, metaphorically, in command of his empire. His vitality, strength and manliness are core attributes of *javanmardi*, a Persian concept associated with invincible heroes such as Rostam, Iran's national defender in the *Shahnama*.[30] His perfect, omnipotent body may also be a visual evocation of the Islamic notion of *ensan-e kamel*, the Perfect Man who is the manifestation of God.[31]

The primacy of the victor's body over other kingly qualities is emphasized by al-Ghazali in his celebrated work *Nasihat al-moluk* (*Book of Counsel for Kings*): 'If a king is going to be victorious, he will (carry) certain marks of victory: he will be strong of body'.[32] This emphasis on bodily strength is visualized through the solidity of Nader's painted body, which contrasts markedly with the more flatly rendered bodies of Safavid shahs.[33] The slender frames of Safavid rulers may be associated with the articulation of their legitimacy, which was dependent more on their role as the head of the royal household and ruling corporation and less on their battle-tested prowess, and this is borne out by the dominance of audience scenes over battle scenes in Safavid royal representation. This contrast in body types was noted by contemporary observers in Iran and Europe. Nader was described as 'manly' with a large and robust body, in contrast to the 'effeminacy' of Tahmasp II who was deposed by Nader.[34] Shah Soltan Hoseyn (r. 1694–1722) was dismissed as pallid, meek and timid,[35] and his father, Soleyman (r. 1666–94), was disparaged for being 'a little too effeminate for a monarch who should be a warrior'.[36] One might argue that these were exaggerated topoi linking the Safavid decline to a weak body,[37] but such corporeal metaphors would only serve to illustrate why it was imperative for Nader, who relied on his image as God's chosen one who 'restored order to Iran',[38] to project a visually powerful body.

Nader's heavily built figure bears more resemblance to the ideal male body type in India – his conquered land – where a firm-waisted (*kamar-band*) body was a marker of battle-readiness and manliness.[39] Also, in India, unlike Iran, portraiture had long been a primary mode of representing kingship, and it was undergoing a revival under the reigning emperor, Mohammad Shah (r. 1719–48).[40] As mentioned earlier, Mohammad Reza Hendi, painter of the present work, was a portraitist active in India as well as Iran. Some of Nader's portraits were painted in the Mughal style by Indian artists, and the portrait albums he brought back from Delhi might also have inspired his painters in Iran to create single portraits of him in their own visual language.

However much raw power a body exudes, unless it is cloaked in royal attributes, it remains the body of a mortal. In this painting, Nader's body functions as the ultimate showcase for the exotic Indian jewels,[41] similar to the public exhibition of his war trophies, including the Peacock Throne, which he put on in Herat[42] and the gift-laden embassies he sent to the Russian and Ottoman courts to announce his victory.[43] The sparkling display can also be viewed, literally and symbolically, as the luminosity of Nader's divine glory or farr.[44] As Abolala Soudavar writes, victories over non-Iranians (*an-Iran*) generated 'the most potent of all *farr*s',[45] and it could hardly be more potent than the farr earned from defeating one of the richest empires in the world. Contemporary viewers would have been awestruck by this unprecedented display of jewels on the shah's body. Persian painting up until now rarely showed kings bedecked with jewellery, and this depiction prefigures the gem-encrusted body of Fath-'Ali Shah (r. 1797–1834) in the Qajar period.

I also argue that Nader was desirous of body markers that would project the image of himself as a universal sovereign for peoples of different creeds and cultures in his expanding empire. The most prominent sign, as we see in his portraits, is the substitution of the turban by his hat. Some believe the four tips of his hat represent the four 'rightly guided' caliphs in Sunni Islam, though turbans were a 'mark of Islam' and the 'crowns of the Arabs' according to the *Hadith*,[46] and replacing the turban by his hat would seem to run counter to its presumed Sunni connection. It has also been suggested that his hat symbolizes the four corners of his empire, as foretold by a dream of a white fish with four horns.[47] In his eyewitness account of Nader's coronation, Catholicos Abraham of Crete describes the hat as 'cross-like'.[48] What is important is not to decide which interpretation is 'correct' (and there are no records of Nader's true intentions), but rather to recognize that the ambiguity might have been part of a strategy to offer different meanings to an audience comprising different faiths. This is consistent with the religious ambivalence of Nader and his convoluted attempts to appease both Shi'is in Iran and Sunnis in the Mughal and Ottoman Empires by concocting a new sect, *Ja'fari*, and calling for unity of all Muslims.[49] Nader also took steps to present himself as the deliverer of Christians from Ottoman rule; he issued decrees to protect Christians in the Caucasus, cultivated relations with church leaders and attended church services.[50] He ordered the translation of the Bible, Talmud and Qur'an into Persian, in a further signal of his aspirations to unite a multifaith empire.[51]

In addition to his crown-like hat, the diadem and jeqqa are transcultural symbols of kingship. Rulers in the Mughal, Safavid and Ottoman Empires all wore jeqqas on their turbans. The diadem was a symbol of kingship associated with ancient rulers in both the East and the West, from Neo-Assyrian, Achaemenid, and Sasanian kings to Eskandar, but it disappeared in the Islamic period. Its reintroduction by Nader could be read as an attempt to invoke Eskandar, who adopted the diadem when he was proclaimed 'king of Asia'.[52] Nader was likened to Eskandar by both his biographer and poet,[53] and he too assumed the mantle of king of Asia after his victories in India and Central Asia. Donning this 'triple crown' in his portraits, Nader is now *shahanshah* (king of kings),[54] a title that is inscribed on objects associated with his Indian victory, including two representations by Mughal court painter Mohammad Panah,[55] coins,[56] a ceremonial axe[57] and several priceless gemstones from the Mughal treasury.[58]

Another symbol that carries a shared meaning across divides is the prayer beads (*tasbih*) clutched in Nader's hand (Plates Ib, Ic and IIc)*. In Persian poetry, prayer beads are usually associated with pious ascetics.[59] There are Sufis holding tasbih in Safavid painting, but not kings.[60] In Nader's case, the prayer beads were used in the main religions in his heterogenous empire, including Sunni and Shi'i Islam, Hinduism, Buddhism and Sikhism in India, and Christianity in the Caucasus.[61] As a universal mark of piety, the prayer beads offer a pictorial means to present Nader as the *shah-e din* (king of faith), as he is titled on one of his coronation coins.[62] This non-sectarian sentiment is evidenced on other coins and seals that he adopted after he became shah; they refer to him simply as God's chosen one, without the Shi'i or Sunni invocations found on coins issued during the Safavid period and Afghan occupation respectively.[63]

In a second oil painting, now hung in the British Library, Nader assumes a standing pose more typical of a European monarch (Plate Ic)*. This is the first

Persian portrait depicting a shah in a European three-quarter stance. His thrusting elbows, 'the Renaissance elbow', are a sign of masculinity that calls to mind the portrait of Henry VIII by Hans Holbein the Younger,[64] but this arm gesture is also an established kingly pose in Persian painting (Figure 1).

Fig. 1. Shah 'Abbas II and the Mughal Ambassador, *artist unknown, after 1647, fresco, approx. 3.3 × 5.7 m. Audience hall of the Chehel Sotun Palace, Esfahan.* © Sussan Babaie.

This blending of Persian and European royal postures is fitted inside a painted oval, which was in vogue in Europe as a framing device for portrait series of great men. Little is known about its actual audience, except that it was brought back from India by Henry Vansittart, who entered the service of the East India Company in Madras in 1746 and succeeded Robert Clive as Governor of Bengal.[65] We know from contemporary correspondence that a portrait of Nader was presented to the British President of Madras in 1740 soon after the Delhi conquest,[66] and it is likely that the British Library painting was a similar gesture. We might consider this consciously anglicized portrayal an invitation to its British audience to view him in the same light as the greatest monarchs represented in portrait galleries in Britain and Europe. The V&A oil painting was also brought back to Britain from India, and it too might have been a diplomatic gift (as an alternative to my earlier suggestion of it being displayed in one of Nader's palaces). Such gifts, as John McAleer, a historian of the British Empire, has suggested, might have served to keep the Iranian conqueror at the forefront of the British authorities' calculations and reminded them of his presence in India.[67]

For someone whose legitimacy rested critically on his achievements on the battlefield, equestrian imagery was essential to Nader's identity (Plates Id–IIb)*. Representations of rulers on horseback are deeply rooted in the visual culture of Iran, from the Sasanian rock relief of Shapur I at Naqsh-e Rostam to the Safavid mural of Shah Esma'il at the Battle of Marv in the Chehel Sotun Palace in Esfahan,[68] not to mention the battle scenes of ancient kings and mythical heroes in the *Shahnama*. But the painters also looked westwards for inspiration. Mohammad 'Ali probably modelled his depiction of Nader, now at the Museum of Fine Arts, Boston (MFA), on a European prototype that was popular in the late seventeenth and early eighteenth centuries (Plate IIb)*. Some of the most portrayed monarchs, like Louis XIV and Peter the Great, were represented in a similar manner, seated on a rearing horse in the foreground, gazing directly at the viewer while a battle rages in the distance.[69] One such painting of Louis XIV was presented to Shah Soleyman, for whom Mohammad 'Ali's grandfather, 'Ali-Qoli Jebadar, worked.[70] The drawing by Mirza Jani at the Islamic Arts Museum Malaysia is similarly formulated but without the battle in the background (Plate IIa)*. The intended audiences of these portraits are not known, but by evoking both Persian and European archetypes of the triumphant warrior and their shared ideals of chivalry and heroism,[71] the painters have created an image of the Iranian conqueror through the lens of global empires. What these three works also have in common is a landscape setting, a feature mostly absent from Safavid equestrian portraits.[72] The visual connection between the body of Nader and the land of Iran (whether restored or conquered) underscores his image as the protector of *Iran-zamin*. In the *Shahnama-ye Naderi* by Mohammad 'Ali Tusi, Iran-zamin is depicted as a *Shahnama*-like land liberated by his royal patron.[73] Tusi compares Nader to Fereydun, the patriarchal hero who drove the evil Arab king Zahhak out of Iran-zamin.[74] According to Abbas Amanat, Tusi uses the term Iran-zamin to denote not only a geographic territory, but also a politically conceived entity whose prosperity and order are dependent on Nader coming to the rescue.[75] The term fell into disuse after the Ilkhanid period (1260–1335) and only reappeared under Nader, as he himself proclaims on a coin commemorating his coronation: 'Nader of *Iran-zamin* and the conqueror of the world'.[76]

Whether he is portrayed as a national saviour or world conqueror, the self-centric nature of Nader's image mirrors his highly personalized polity. With no hereditary or religious lineage to boast, he cultivated a brand of authority based on his own military genius and charisma. His self-reliance was widely noted, as his obituary in a London paper reads, 'not being dependent on anyone but himself for the crown, he was resolved to manage it by his own will without any external helps'.[77] The notion of the royal self as the sole source and symbol of power is figuratively expressed by his own historian, Mirza Mahdi Khan Astarabadi: 'the trenchant blade owes its excellence to its temper, not to the iron mine … after divine grace, his prevailment is by his own sword'.[78] This self-referentiality is asserted across a wide range of biographical material, including chronicles, poetry, coins, seals and other objects, which is set out more fully in my thesis. I argue, in particular, that the unusually large corpus of biographies of Nader, in contrast to the dominance of dynastic histories during the Safavid era, provides further evidence of his success in constructing a personalised identity, and, in that light, there is a compelling case for regarding his single portraits as part of that endeavour and as the visual counterpart of Naderi history.

The exclusive focus on the shah's body would have been a novelty to the contemporary viewer as royal portraits were virtually absent in Safavid Iran. From the two-century rule of the Safavids, we really only have the amorous portrait of 'Abbas I and his page by Mohammad Qasem, dated 1036/1627, in which 'Abbas's body is treated as a private object of his beloved's intoxicated gaze rather than a public spectacle of kingship.[79] There is also an Indianized painting of Shah Soleyman attributed to Sheykh 'Abbasi, ca. 1670.[80] But I have found no other individual portraits of Safavid shahs painted in Iran during their lifetime. This is all the more perplexing considering the fact that single-figure painting was experiencing phenomenal popularity in the seventeenth century, and the most powerful members of the ruling elite are among those portrayed, including several grand viziers.[81] The persistent dearth of royal portraits amid such a flourishing period in portrait-making stands as an art historical quandary, and the explanation lies not in where the shah is absent but rather where he is present.

Safavids shahs are embedded in courtly gatherings and scenes of historical events. The most well-known are the three audience scenes in the Chehel Sotun Palace in Esfahan, painted after 1647 (Figure 1).[82] Despite an evident change in court ceremonials from the relative informality under 'Abbas I (r. 1587–1629) to the strict hierarchy under 'Abbas II (r. 1642–66), all three banquet scenes adhere to an almost identical triangular configuration.[83] This is curious indeed when one observes that the successive Safavid courts are represented in the dress and headgear of the day but not the ceremonial protocol of the day. I argue that by featuring the shah at the apex of a repeated triangular structure buttressed by an anonymous support cast of courtiers, this series forms a pictorial *selsela* (chain) of dynastic continuity as kingship 'migrates' from Tahmasp I (r. 1524–76) to 'Abbas I and to 'Abbas II. In his analysis of the doctrine of 'the King's Two Bodies', Ernst Kantorowicz explains that the body corporate may be eternalized horizontally as 'a plurality of persons collected in one body' and vertically as 'a plurality in succession'.[84] The Chehel Sotun group scenes combine both dimensions into an emphatic image of the Safavid dynastic body.

These paintings also promote the *gholam* (elite slave) hegemony as the face of the Safavid power structure – front-row grandees, beardless eunuchs and young Georgians wearing fur-brimmed caps.[85] They dominated the upper echelons of the administration and military under 'Abbas II.[86] Their critical role in physically supporting the ruling hierarchy was underscored by titles such as 'pillars of the mighty state' (*arkan-e dowlat*) for principal officers and 'prop of the state' (*e'temad al-dowla*) for the grand vizier.[87] The court scenes were formulated by members of the gholam elite in the court of 'Abbas II,[88] who commissioned the palace as the architectural centrepiece of his reign. Gholam power had reached its peak by this time as 'Abbas II began his efforts to curb their influence, though they would continue to occupy high offices for some time.[89] The fact that their dominance was under threat would have been all the more reason to stake out their place in these most prominent representations of Safavid power. Taken as a whole, the Chehel Sotun pictorial cycle traces the ascent of the gholams, beginning with their substitution of the Qezelbash revolutionaries who helped Esma'il I (r. 1501–24) to found the Safavid dynasty and through the reigns of Tahmasp I, 'Abbas I, and 'Abbas II.[90] Seated in the highest and nearest place to the shah, their physical closeness binds the elite slaves to their royal master in one corporate body. Such inseparability also reflects the body politic discourse of Nasir al-Din Tusi, a towering figure in Twelver Shi'i thought, in which he equates household slaves with the hands, feet and eyes of the body.[91] The shah, acting as the head and soul of the body politic,[92] must balance the different functionaries in order to maintain its well-being,[93] and the triangular composition may serve as a metaphor for the power equilibrium between the shah and his court. The physical proximity may be further read as a pictorial articulation of the Shi'i ethos of sociability and accessibility of the shah, which was a mark of the Safavid charisma derived from the Twelfth Imam.[94]

The Chehel Sotun scenes are the most monumental expressions of the Safavid body corporate, but they are by no means an isolated experiment. Group painting served as the predominant, if not exclusive, mode of royal representation in the second half of the seventeenth century. Among them are several court gatherings painted by 'Ali-Qoli Jebadar in the St Petersburg Album.[95] In my thesis, I argue that the courtiers represent members of the *andarun* or inner household (*khassa*), whose close proximity to the shah signals their positions as his 'intimates' (*moqarraban*).[96] I query if these group portraits might have been intended as a counterpoint to the grand vision of the *birun* or outer court (*divan*) in the Chehel Sotun paintings.[97]

The Safavid court assemblies represent kingship as a shared office. This collective body has all but disappeared from Nader's images. The figure of the shah has been transplanted from the horizontal frame of the historicizing painting to the vertical format of a single portrait. What was once a constituent part of a pluralized entity is now singular, monumental and whole. The Safavid body politic has thus been visually decapitated and dismembered, liberating the shah's body to stage his one-man show.

The breaking away of the king from the courtly bodies echoes Nader's purges of the bureaucratic establishment. As Amanat has observed, 'his disgust for the machinery of government was evident in his consistent crushing of the old Safavid bureaucracy and haphazard replacement of it with a military elite'.[98] The Qezelbash roots of his Afshar clan might have added to his contempt for the Safavid model of centralized administration dominated by the gholam class. The isolation of Nader's body also signals a divergence from the Shi'i ethos of sociability practised by Safavid shahs. Unlike the Safavids, Nader's charisma was not dependent on staging a show of hospitality. In fact, he is rarely depicted in a feasting scene. Rather, his portraits emphasize his farr earned from victories on the battlefield, as well as other warrior attributes, such as javanmardi. These immortal qualities reside in his individual capacity as shah and grant dignity and sanctity to his office.[99]

The early representations of Nader served as prototypes for a long line of later iterations extending into the nineteenth century. They are beyond the scope of this chapter, but I shall briefly mention two examples that illustrate how Qajar rulers might have played a part in perpetuating Nader's victorious image for their own agendas, similar to Reza Khan's borrowing of Nader's portrait in the *Madar-e vatan* poster. The first is an album composition by Mohammad Sadeq dated 1200/1785–86 in the National Library of Russia (Plate IIc)*. It retains the iconography established in the V&A oil painting but has two additional reminders of Nader's Indian victory. He is attended by a Mughal youth holding a Mughal-style fan. On his diadem are three huge diamonds; judging by their shapes and sizes, they probably represent the *Darya-ye nur*, *Kuh-e nur* and *Taj-e mah* from his Delhi loot. Mohammad Sadeq recreated this mace-wielding, blue-clad Nader a decade later in a wall painting of his defeat of the Mughals at the Battle of Karnal, located in the Chehel Sotun audience hall.[100] This mural was created for the Qajar founder, Agha Mohammad Khan, in 1796, the year he was crowned on the Moghan steppe in emulation of Nader, who held his coronation there six decades earlier.[101] As Nader's image continued into the nineteenth century, its interpretation took on contemporary accents and idiosyncrasies, like the frontispiece portrait in a *Tarikh-e Jahāngoshā* manuscript in the British Library (Plate IId)*. It features a 'Qajarized' Nader dressed in a Qajar-style overcoat and his four-pointed hat is morphed into a black astrakhan cap. It was probably not a royal commission, but the manuscript was copied in ca. 1870 during the reign of Naser al-Din Shah, who considered himself a second Nader Shah after his recapture of Herat from the Afghans, who had seized the city in the aftermath of Nader's death.[102] The two highly unusual scenes in the manuscript, both concerning the Afghans, have prompted me to query if the manuscript might have been made to commemorate the Qajar shah's victory.

The primary aim of this chapter was to give a sense of the novelty and longevity of Nader's imagery and how it was reinvented from the Safavid mode of royal representation. But the visual legacy of Nader went far beyond his own images. His portraits valorized the shah's body, and this new impulse of self-display led to the establishment of portraiture as a principal mode of royal image-making in the Zand (1751–94) and Qajar (1789–1925) periods. Ghaffari, painter of *Nader Shah Crowning Reza-Qoli Mirza* mentioned near the beginning of this chapter, also painted a number of portraits of Karim Khan Zand (r. 1751–79).[103] In two of them, the Zand founder shares the same body and pose as Nader in the works of Bahram and Mirza Jani (Figures 2 and 3, cf. Plates Id and IIa)*, while another equestrian painting bears a striking resemblance to Mohammad 'Ali's depiction of Nader,[104] though all three lack a background.

Fig. 2. Karim Khan Zand, *attributed to Abu'l-Hasan Mostowfi Ghaffari Kashani, ca. 1750–75, Shiraz, opaque watercolour and gold on paper, image 25.2 × 20.2 cm. Musée du Louvre, Paris, MAO 800 (Author's own photograph).*

Fig. 3. Karim Khan Zand on Horseback *(Persian inscription misidentifies the subject as Nader Shah), attributed to Abu'l-Hasan Mostowfi Ghaffari Kashani, 18th century, Shiraz, opaque watercolour and gold on paper, 30 × 21.5 cm. Shalva Amiranashvili Museum of Fine Arts, Georgian National Museum, Tbilisi, 147. © Georgian National Museum, Shalva Amiranashvili Museum of Fine Arts.*

A seated representation of Karim Khan by Mohammad Baqer mirrors Nader's posture and masculine, monumental body type in the V&A oil painting, despite its more modest scale (Figure 4).

Fig. 4. Portrait of Karim Khan Zand, *signed Mohammad Baqer, third quarter of the 18th century, Shiraz, tempera on varnished cardboard, 24.5 × 16 cm. Shalva Amiranashvili Museum of Fine Arts, Georgian National Museum, Tbilisi, 138. © Georgian National Museum, Shalva Amiranashvili Museum of Fine Arts.*

Two early oil paintings of Fath-'Ali Shah by Mirza Baba, a student of Mohammad Sadeq, in 1213/1798–99 carry the unmistakable DNA of Nader's V&A portrait: the Europeanized style and modelling technique; the monumental figure in a tight pictorial space decorated with drapery and carpet; and the bejewelled body in a nearly identical pose complete with similar accoutrements. One is at the British Library (Figure 5) and the other in a private collection. X-ray imaging of the latter revealed that it was originally painted

Fig. 5. Fath-'Ali Shah King of Persia, *signed Mirza Baba, 1798–99 (1213 AH), Tehran, oil on canvas, 188 × 107 cm. British Library, London, Foster 116. © British Library.*

with a tasbih in Fath-'Ali Shah's left hand,[105] which suggests that Mirza Baba was looking back at Nader's portraits, either the one by Mohammad Reza Hendi at the V&A or a later interpretation, like the album painting by his teacher, Mohammad Sadeq (Plate IIc)*. Another portrait of Fath-'Ali Shah by Mirza Baba in a copy of the *Divan-e Khaqan* written by the Qajar ruler, dated 1216/1802, is also reminiscent of Mohammad Sadeq's depiction of Nader.[106] Mehr 'Ali, another prominent artist at the Qajar court, painted two works, both dated ca. 1231/1815–16, that show Nader and Fath-'Ali Shah in identical compositions, making the same gestures.[107] They closely resemble the established iconography of Nader and provide further proof of the direct lineage between the representations of the two rulers.

In her paper 'Persian painting in the eighteenth century: Tradition and transmission', Layla Diba presents her pioneering investigation into the familial and student–teacher relationships of eighteenth-century artists.[108] Building on her work, I argue that the painters of Nader's portraits hailed from a lineage stretching back to the late Safavid court and extending forward to the Zand and Qajar periods. Ghaffari's family was in the service of Nader and, as a young man, he was encouraged by Nader to paint.[109] He became the historiographer of Karim Khan and painted his portraits. Mohammad Baqer's father was Mohammad 'Ali,[110] Nader's chief painter to whom the MFA equestrian composition is attributed, and Mohammad Baqer's grandfather, 'Abd al-Beg, and great-grandfather, 'Ali-Qoli Jebadar, were both leading painters of the Safavid court. Both Mohammad Baqer and Mohammad Sadeq were commissioned by Nader's historiographer, Astarabadi, to reassemble the St Petersburg Album, one of the painting albums looted from Delhi, and they would presumably have worked with Mohammad Reza Hendi, who also painted the bust portrait of Nader in the St Petersburg Album.[111] They continued their practice at the Zand and Qajar courts, and Mohammad Sadeq's student, Mirza Baba, became an eminent painter in the early Qajar period. These court portraitists served as a crucial inter-epochal link that carried their innovations in royal portraiture into the Zand and Qajar future.

By tracing this web of artistic lineages, I aim to situate royal portraiture in Iran properly, not as a genre that suddenly burst onto the scene during the Qajar period, or as mere imitations of portraits of European monarchs, but as a negotiated phenomenon set in motion by Nader and his image-makers. These painters drew inspiration from sources as diverse as Iranian, Indian and European royal imagery to devise a representational mode befitting Nader's world-conquering rhetoric. The variety in scale – from album page to life-size – and in medium – from oil on canvas to watercolour on paper and ink drawing – also speaks to an enthusiasm to search for the new. Ultimately, they created more than just portraits of Nader; they ushered in a paradigm shift in the representation of kingship that placed the royal body at the centre of a new political order.

For all the heroization and immortalization of Nader's body in the pictorial realm, his actual body met an early and brutal demise. On 20 June 1747, after a mere 11 years on the throne, he was ambushed in his tent and assassinated by his own courtiers at the instigation of his nephew, who seized the throne as 'Adel Shah (r. 1747–48). A London newspaper reports the gruesome mutilation: 'They cut off his head, took out his heart and burnt it, and cut his body in pieces'.[112] Nader's own poet, Tusi, gives a more ruminative lament in the *Shahnama-ye Naderi*: 'When the night was young, his mind was set on killing and plunder, By dawn his frame had no head and his head no crown. A single turn of the wheel of fate, Spared neither Nader nor the Naderi [empire]'.[113] The body natural perished, and his body politic did not survive. But Nader and the Naderi live on in his portraits, offering not just a visual register for the era but a long-lasting legacy in royal portraiture in Iran.[114]

Notes:

* For additional information; please see the List of Illustrations on page vii.
1. Dinyar Patel, 'Caught between two nationalisms', pp. 1–37.
2. For Reza Khan's invocation of ancient Iran to legitimize his own rule, see Abbas Amanat, *Iran*, p. 439.
3. Michael P. Zirinsky, 'Imperial power and dictatorship', p. 656. Reza Khan was also hailed as a second Nader Shah; Amanat, *Iran*, pp. 423 and 438.
4. Nader's self-constructed image as the national saviour is pronounced on his coronation seal: 'God restored order to Iran in the name of Nader' (بنام نادر ایران قرار داد خدا); Hyacinth Louis Rabino di Borgomale, *Coins, Medals, and Seals of the Shâhs of Irân*, p. 52.
5. The inscription to the right of Nader's head reads (my translation): 'Now that she is leaning on you, this mother, without refuge and distressed, out of kindness you must embrace her like your own life, against the enemy of the water and earth of Iran, like the lightning of your fire sword'.
6. British Museum, 1873,0712.621, https://www.britishmuseum.org/collection/object/P 1873-0712-621.
7. On the museum website, the figure being crowned is misidentified as Mohammad Shah; http://sadmu.ir/detail/7433. For the correct identity, see Mohammad 'Ali Karimzāda Tabrizi, *Ahvāl va āsār-e naqqāshān-e qadim-e Irān*, vol. I, p. 37, and the discussion in my thesis.
8. For plays, see *Du ru-ye revāyat-e Nāderi*, https://mehrnews.com/news/2917126. For sculpture, see the equestrian bronze at the Mausoleum of Nader Shah, https://commons.wikimedia.org/wiki/File:Tomb_of_Nader_Shah.JPG.
   For children's books, see *Nadir Shah* by Pavitra Kumar Sharma, https://www.amazon.in/Nadir-Shah-Pavitra-Kumar-Sharma/dp/8184912226.
   The Curse of Nader Shah by Sutapa Basu, https://www.amazon.com/Curse-Nader-Shah-Sutapa-Basu-ebook/dp/B07XT8QRQD.
   For video games, see *Quest of Persia: Nader's Blade*, http://www.questofpersia.com/nader/, and *The Afsharids*, https://steamcommunity.com/sharedfiles/filedetails/?id=407643560.
9. Layla S. Diba and Maryam Ekhtiar, *Royal Persian Paintings*, pp. 137–45; Abolala Soudavar, *Art of the Persian Courts*, pp. 381–85; and A.T. Adamova, *Persian Painting and Drawing of the 15th–19th Centuries*, pp. 83–84.
10. See two further portraits of Nader at the Art Institute of Chicago, 1919.952, http://www.artic.edu/aic/collections/artwork/76888?search_no=1&index=72, and Golestan Palace Library, Tehran, published in Badri Ātābāy, *Fehrest-e moraqqa'āt-e ketābkhāna-ye saltanati*, cat. 137.
11. Jonas Hanway, *An Historical Account of the British Trade*, vol. IV, p. 227.
12. Rudi Matthee, 'Nader Shah in Iranian historiography'.
13. The news reports are too numerous to list in a note. They were obtained from my searches of the Burney Collection at the British Library.
14. Nader's dream of defeating the Ottoman Empire was ultimately unfulfilled; the Ottoman–Persian war was protracted for three years (1743–46) and ended with the status quo unaltered; Laurence Lockhart, *Nadir Shah*, pp. 223–37 and 246–56.

15. Aniruddha Ray, 'Invasion of Nadir Shah and the origins of French imperialist thought', p. 371.
16. Abbas Amanat, 'Shahnameh-ye Naderi and the revival of epic poetry', pp. 309–11.
17. The necessary brevity of this chapter has meant that I am only able to present the conclusions of these findings. The reader is urged to refer to my thesis for the full analysis; Janet O'Brien, 'Nādir Shāh: The Emergence of Royal Portraiture'.
18. They include single, double and group portraits, as well as battle and court scenes, made in a variety of styles and media in both Iran and India.
19. It was Layla Diba who first pointed out the resemblance to a Mughal tent; Diba and Ekhtiar, *Royal Persian Paintings*, p. 138.
20. Ibid.
21. Nader commissioned a half-English, half-Prussian painter named Cassels to 'paint eight pictures, and make them as like as possible'; John Cook, *Voyages and Travels Through the Russian Empire*, vol. II, pp. 515–17. A picture of Nader, 'one of several made "at Industan"', was gifted to Richard Benyon, President of Madras, a year after the Delhi invasion; Henry Dodwell, *A Calendar of the Madras Records, 1740–44*, p. 30.
22. Hanway, *Historical Account*, vol. I, p. 231; Xavier Hommaire de Hell, *Voyage en Turquie et en Perse*, vol. II, p. 270; and Adamova, *Persian Painting*, p. 83.
23. For Qasr-e Khorshid, see Sussan Babaie, 'Nader Shah, the Delhi loot, and the 18th-century exotics of empire', pp. 215–34.
24. Persian wall paintings tend to be made to fit an arch-shaped niche or a dedicated rectangular space. I have not found anything among the V&A archives to confirm that the canvas has been trimmed to fit the modern frame.
25. Michel Foucault developed the theory of treating the body as a site of power. While he deals with the condemned man, an 'inverted figure of the king', his theory flows from the idea that the king's body serves as the site of 'surplus power'; idem, *Discipline and Punish*, pp. 25–29.
26. For masculine signifiers for Persian kings, see Lloyd Llewellyn-Jones, *King and Court in Ancient Persia*, pp. 56–57.
27. James Fraser, *The History of Nadir Shah*, p. 227; 'Abd al-Karim al-Kashmiri, *The Memoirs of Khojeh Abdulkurreem*, p. 47; and Père Louis Bazin, 'Mémoires sur dernières années du règne de Thamas Kouli-Kan', pp. 315–16.
28. Nasir al-Din Tusi, *The Nasirean Ethics*, pp. 193–94 and 228; Abu'l-Fażl Allāmī, *Aīn-i Akbarī*, vol. I, p. iv; Rosalind O'Hanlon, 'Kingdom, household and body history', pp. 894–97 and 908–9; and Monica Juneja, 'Translating the body into image', pp. 235–60.
29. Fraser, *Nadir Shah*, pp. 227–30; and Hanway, *Historical Account*, vol. IV, p. 268.
30. The concept of javanmardi encompasses both physical and character traits of an idealized warrior: youthfulness, vitality, strength, bravery, self-command, fortitude, resilience against pain and hardship, self-sacrifice, comradeship, generosity, and so forth; Lloyd Ridgeon, 'The felon, the faithful and the fighter', pp. 1–27; Rosalind O'Hanlon, 'Manliness and imperial service in Mughal north India', pp. 56–67; and Ali Anooshahr, 'The king who would be man', pp. 329–32. As this discussion concerns the visual representation of Nader, it necessarily focuses on the more tangible qualities. Javanmardi, as a code of conduct, was also

professed by warriors on the frontiers of Khorasan, from where Nader hailed; Mohsen Zakeri, 'Javānmardi'.
31. Gerhard Böwering, 'Ensān-e kāmel'; Allāmī, *Aīn-i Akbarī*, p. 181; and O'Hanlon, 'Kingdom', pp. 890–97. An additional link to this idea is an inscription on Nader's seal: 'Nader is the manifestation of divine grace' (مظهر لطف الهی نادر است); British Library, Or. 4935, fol. 16.
32. Abu Hāmid Mohammad al-Ghazāli, *Ghazālī's Book of Counsel for Kings*, p. 91.
33. Scholars have observed the prioritization of the 'real face' over the 'flat body' in Safavid portraits; Sussan Babaie, 'The penchant for "portraits"' (forthcoming); and Massumeh Farhad, 'Artists, paintings and their publics'. This 'face-focused' preference extends to the depiction of Safavid shahs. Royal bodies in the late Safavid period, such as those of 'Abbas II and Soltan-Hoseyn, are more volumetric but they are not afforded the muscularity and monumentality of Nader's warrior body.
34. 'Extract of a letter from Venice, dated June 16', *London Evening Post*, issue 1342, 22–24 June 1736.
35. Rudi Matthee, 'Solṭān Ḥosayn'.
36. Idem, 'Solaymān I'.
37. Idem, *Persia in Crisis*, p. xxv.
38. See note 4 above.
39. Sajida Sultana Alvi, *Advice on the Art of Governance*, pp. 88 and 194; O'Hanlon, 'Manliness' pp. 64–65; and Juneja, 'Translating the body', pp. 246–47.
40. Malini Roy, 'The revival of the Mughal painting tradition', pp. 17–23.
41. The fact that he dressed plainly in real life and shunned the luxurious trappings of royalty only adds to the intentionality of the visual rhetoric. According to Hanway, 'His dress was not remarkable; his mind seemed to be superior to external pomp or luxurious softness'; idem, *Historical Account*, vol. IV, p. 268.
42. Al-Kashmiri, *Memoirs*, pp. 26–27.
43. Lockhart, *Nadir Shah*, p. 157; Mirzā Mahdi Khān Astarābādi, *Tārikh-e jahāngoshā-ye Nāderi*, p. 337.
44. For discussions on regalia and precious gems as symbols of farr, see Anna Malecka, 'Daryā-ye nur', pp. 72–78; and Llewellyn-Jones, *King and Court*, pp. 43 and 61–66.
45. Abolala Soudavar, 'Looking through *The Two Eyes of the Earth*', pp. 29 and 31.
46. Robert Dankoff, 'Turban and crown'.
47. Michael Axworthy, *The Sword of Persia*, p. 76; also see Astarābādi, *Tārikh-e Jahāngoshā*, pp. 67 and 809.
48. Abraham of Crete, *The Chronicle of Abraham of Crete*, p. 84.
49. Ernest Tucker, 'Nadir Shah and the Ja'fari Madhhab reconsidered', pp. 163–79; and Astarābādi, *Tārikh-e Jahāngoshā*, pp. 268–69.
50. Abraham, *Chronicle*, pp. 32–34, 47–48 and 66.
51. Lockhart, *Nadir Shah*, p. 280.
52. E.A. Fredricksmeyer, 'The origin of Alexander's royal insignia', pp. 97–109.
53. Astarābādi, *Tārikh-e Jahāngoshā*, p. 210; Amanat, 'Shahnameh-ye Naderi', pp. 295–318; and Abraham, *Chronicle*, p. 145.

54. The title dates back to the Achaemenid and Sasanian Empires. It was revived by the Shi'i Buyids (934–1062) as a defiant gesture against the caliphal rule of the 'Abbasids and Arab Islam, and they too swapped the turban for a crown; Tilman Nagel, 'Buyids'. The title fell into disuse, then reappeared when Shah Esma'il, the Safavid founder, proclaimed himself the *shahanshah-e Iran*; Amanat, *Iran*, pp. 9 and 33.
55. V&A, IM.237-1921, http://collections.vam.ac.uk/item/O120816/nadir-shah-painting-muhammad-panah/; and Bodleian Library, MS. Ouseley Add. 173, fol. 29v, https://digital.bodleian.ox.ac.uk/inquire/p/5d1ebd55-34d1-4dc3-8284-b85ad7fc0a14.
56. David Collection, C334, https://www.davidmus.dk/en/collections/islamic/dynasties/safavids/coins/c334.
57. National Museum, New Delhi, 58.47/3, http://www.nationalmuseumindia.gov.in/en/collections/index/9.
58. Susan Stronge, Joanna Whalley and Anna Ferrari, *Bejewelled Treasures*, pp. 38–39; and Victor B. Meen and A. Douglas Tushingham, *Crown Jewels of Iran*, pp. 46–47 and 64–67.
59. Annemarie Schimmel, *A Two-Colored Brocade*, p. 91.
60. I am aware of two exceptions: prayer beads lying on the ground before an 'Abbas I-lookalike *Gushtasp* in a *Shahnama* manuscript, 1014/1605, Iran, Staatsbibliothek zu Berlin, MS of. fol. 4251, fol. 460r; and prayer beads tucked into the waist sash of 'Abbas II in *Shah 'Abbas II Receiving a Mughal Ambassador*, Abu'l-Hasan Mostowfi Ghaffari Kashani, ca. 1780–94, Shiraz, Aga Khan Museum, AKM00110.
61. The Islamic tasbih consists of 100 beads. Around 70 beads are visible in the V&A painting, not including the section clutched in his hand. Prayer beads used by Buddhists, Hindus and Sikhs have 108 beads and an Orthodox Christian rosary has 100 knots or beads.
62. Abraham, سکه بر زر کرد نام سلطنت را در جهان / شاه دین نادر قلی اسکندر صاحبقران; *Chronicle*, p. 145.
63. Tucker, 'Nadir Shah', p. 170; and Rabino di Borgomale, *Coins*, pp. 51–53.
64. Tatiana C. String, *Art and Communication in the Reign of Henry VIII*, p. 71.
65. Lucy S. Sutherland, 'Vansittart, Henry (1732–?70), of Foxley, Berks'.
66. Dodwell, *A Calendar of the Madras Records*, p. 30.
67. John McAleer, *Picturing India*, p. 136.
68. See https://www.livius.org/pictures/iran/naqs-e-rustam/naqs-e-rustam-relief-of-shapur-i/naqs-e-rustam-relief-of-shapur-i/; and Sussan Babaie, 'Shah 'Abbas II, the conquest of Qandahar', fig. 4.
69. Mikhailovsky Palace, Ж-4901, https://rusmuseumvrm.ru/data/collections/painting/17_19/tannauer_i_g_petr_i_v_poltavskoy_bitve_1724_zh_4901/index.php?lang=en; and Château de Versailles, MV 2156, http://ressources.chateauversailles.fr/ressources-pedagogiques/Louis-XIV-vetu-a-la-romaine-et-couronne-par-la-Victoire-devant-Maestricht-en.
70. Layla S. Diba, 'Lacquerwork of Safavid Persia', p. 260 and illustration 57.
71. For javanmardi, see note 30 above. For chivalric qualities in eighteenth-century Europe, see Philip Carter, 'An "effeminate" or "efficient" nation?', pp. 436–38.

72. See, for example, *Equestrian Portrait of Mirza Mohammad Taqi*, signed Mo'in Mosavver, 1096/1685, Khalili Collections, MSS 1003, https://www.khalilicollections.org/collections/islamic-art/khalili-collection-islamic-art-album-page-with-an-equestrian-portrait-of-mirza-muhammad-taqi-tabrizi-mss-1003/.
73. Amanat, 'Shahnameh-ye Naderi', pp. 302, 309 and 318. In Ferdowsi's *Shahnama*, *Iran-zamin* refers to the pre-Islamic Iranian empire stretching from Mesopotamia and the Caucasus to Central and South Asia, as distinct from its rival *Turan-zamin*, a historical region in Central Asia.
74. Ibid. The mace that Nader is holding in all three equestrian portraits is also associated with Fereydun, who used it to defeat Zahhak. Nader's chronicler too makes the connection between the two heroes when he writes, 'with the *farr* of Fereydun ... [Nader] stepped onto the world throne' (با فر فریدونی ... قدم بر فراز تخت جهانبانی گذاشته); Astarābādi, *Tārikh-e Jahāngoshā*, p. 272.
75. Amanat, 'Shahnameh-ye Naderi', p. 302.
76. Rabino di Borgomale, *Coins*, p. 51. سکه بر زر کرد نام سلطنت را در جهان / نادر ایران زمین و خسرو گیتی ستان ;
77. 'The character of Nadir Shah, Thamas Kuli Kan', *Whitehall Evening Post of London Intelligencer*, issue 255, 29 September–1 October 1747.
78. تیغ برنده را فخر بجوهر خداداد خویش است نه بکان آهن ... که بعد از لطف الهی استظهارش بشمشیر خویش است ; Astarābādi, *Tārikh-e Jahāngoshā*, p. 26.
79. Musée du Louvre, MAO 494, https://collections.louvre.fr/ark:/53355/cl010321123. There is a small bust portrait of 'Abbas I but it appears to have been copied from a group scene, signed by Reza 'Abbasi, that shows the shah receiving the Mughal ambassador, Khan 'Alam. Both are in an album at the National Library of Russia, Dorn 489, fols. 77v and 74r.
80. Chester Beatty Library, Per 298.7, https://twitter.com/iamkristinesr/status/1300764098305626113.
81. For portraits of grand viziers Khalifa Soltan and Shah-Qoli Khan, see Soudavar, *Art of the Persian Courts*, cats 118 and 153. Also see the portraits of Mirza Mohammad Taqi in note 72 above and at Stanford University, 2005.97, https://arts.stanford.edu/phd-candidate-explores-persias-safavid-empire-in-her-exhibition-at-the-cantor/.
82. For the other two scenes featuring Tahmasp I and 'Abbas I, see Babaie, 'Shah 'Abbas II', figs. 5 and 6.
83. For the seating orders under 'Abbas I and 'Abbas II, see Jean Chardin, *Les Voyages du chevalier Chardin en Perse et autres lieux de l'Orient*, vol. V, pp. 470–73; and Babaie, 'Shah 'Abbas II', pp. 137–39.
84. Ernst Hartwig Kantorowicz, *The King's Two Bodies*, pp. 310–13. While the medieval Christian theology origin of this doctrine does not translate into Iranian ideologies of kingship, as Ali Anooshahr has pointed out in idem, 'The body politic and rise of the Safavids', pp. 22–23, the more general notion of the immortal body politic does seem to have more universal application and is rooted in India with parallels in Iran; see note 94 below and Kantorowicz, *Two Bodies*, pp. 496–506. The theories relating to the body politic are addressed in detail in my thesis.

85. For the rise of gholam power in the Safavid ruling hierarchy, see Sussan Babaie *et al.*, *Slaves of the Shah*.
86. Ibid., p. 139; and Vladimir Minorsky, *Tadhkirat al-Mulūk*, pp. 47 and 118.
87. Minorsky, *Tadhkirat*, pp. 44–55; and Roger M. Savory, 'The Safavid state and polity', p. 180.
88. Babaie *et al.*, *Slaves*, p. 135.
89. Ibid., pp. 45 and 139.
90. A representation of Esma'il's Battle of Marv forms part of this four-part cycle; Babaie, 'Shah 'Abbas II', fig. 4.
91. Tusi, *Ethics*, p. 181.
92. Ibid., pp. 193–94 and 228; Aziz al-Azmeh, *Muslim Kingship*, p. 120; and Anooshahr, 'The body politic', p. 23.
93. See note 28 above.
94. Tusi counsels on the need for a synthesis (*ta'lif*) of all individuals cooperating together like the organs of the body (*ālāt-e badan*), and his notion of synthesis encompasses sociability, close association and affection; Tusi, *Ethics*, pp. 195, 228, 234 and 318. For the physical proximity to the shah as a measure of power in the Safavid hierarchy, see Babaie *et al.*, *Slaves*, p. 16; and Matthee, *Persia in Crisis*, pp. 32–33.
95. Institute of Oriental Manuscripts of the Russian Academy of Sciences, Album E-14, fol. 98r. They also share the horizontal orientation with the Chehel Sotun murals, and one wonders if they were designs for wall paintings in the harem.
96. Minorsky, *Tadhkirat*, pp. 55–69 and 126–39.
97. For the dynamics between the birun and andarun of the Safavid court, see Babaie *et al.*, *Slaves*, p. 11.
98. Amanat, *Iran*, pp. 151–52.
99. The eternal body politic may refer to the dignity and sanctity of the royal office itself, as an alternative interpretation to it being a collective body with the king as its head; Kantorowicz, *Two Bodies*, pp. 383–450.
100. See https://archnet.org/collections/1283/media_contents/121287.
101. Abbas Amanat, 'Qajar Iran', p. 17.
102. Abbas Amanat, *Pivot of the Universe*, p. 280.
103. Ghaffari's portraits of Karim Khan were the subject of my master's dissertation; Janet O'Brien, 'Historian as Painter, Portrait as Memory: Re-Presenting Karīm Khān Zand and the Portrait of the King in Eighteenth-Century Iran'.
104. Sotheby's, London, 6 October 2010, lot 91, https://www.sothebys.com/en/auctions/ecatalogue/2010/arts-of-the-islamic-world-l10223/lot.91.html, cf. Plate IIb.
105. Diba and Ekhtiar, *Royal Persian Paintings*, pp. 180–81 and 180n18.
106. Royal Collection Trust, RCIN 1005020, fol. 12v, https://www.royalcollection.org.uk/collection/1005020/divan-i-khaqan-dywn-kh-q-n.
107. Layla S. Diba, *Naqqāshi-hā-ye Zand va Qājār*, figs. 17 and 19.
108. Layla S. Diba, 'Persian painting in the eighteenth century', pp. 147–60.
109. Karimzāda Tabrizi, *Naqqāshān*, vol. I, p. 34.
110. Yaghoub Azhand, 'Kārestān-e honari-ye Mohammad Bāqer'.
111. See note 10 above.

112. 'London', *London Evening Post*, issue 3105, 26–29 September 1747.
113. سر شب سر قتل و تاراج داشت، نه تن سر نه سر تاج داشت. به یک گردش چرخ نیلوفری، نه نادر بجا ماند و نه نادری ; Amanat, 'Shahnameh-ye Naderi', p. 298.
114. I would like to thank the Soudavar Memorial Foundation for the opportunity to participate in the *Idea of Iran* symposium and publication and for the generous grant for my PhD research. This paper is written as part of my Smithsonian Institution Predoctoral Fellowship at the Freer Gallery of Art and Arthur M. Sackler Gallery, and I am grateful for their support and the guidance of my fellowship adviser, Dr Massumeh Farhad.

Bibliography:

Press reports

'Extract of a letter from Venice, dated June 16', *London Evening Post*, issue 1342, 22–24 June 1736.
'London', *London Evening Post*, issue 3105, 26–29 September 1747.
'The character of Nadir Shah, Thamas Kuli Kan', *Whitehall Evening Post of London Intelligencer*, issue 255, 29 September–1 October 1747.

Other sources and studies

Abraham of Crete, *The Chronicle of Abraham of Crete*, trans. George A. Bournoutian (Costa Mesa, CA: Mazda, 1999).
Adamova, A.T., *Persian Painting and Drawing of the 15th–19th Centuries from the Hermitage Museum* (St Petersburg: Slaviia, 1996).
'Allāmī, Abu'l-Fażl, *Aīn-i Akbarī*, trans. H. Blochmann, 3 vols (Kolkata: Asiatic Society of Bengal, 1873, originally written c. 1590).
Alvi, Sajida Sultana, ed. and trans., *Advice on the Art of Governance: An Indo-Islamic Mirror for Princes: Mau'iẓah-i Jahāngīrī of Muḥammad Bāqir Najm-i S̱ānī* (Albany: State University of New York Press, 1989, originally written 1612).
Amanat, Abbas, 'Qajar Iran', in *Royal Persian Paintings: The Qajar Epoch, 1785–1925*, ed. Layla S. Diba and Maryam Ekhtiar (London: I.B. Tauris and Brooklyn: Brooklyn Museum of Art, 1998), pp. 14–29.
— *Pivot of the Universe: Nasir al-Din Shah Qajar and the Iranian Monarchy* (London: I.B. Tauris, 2008).
— *Iran: A Modern History* (New Haven: Yale University Press, 2017).
— 'Shahnameh-ye Naderi and the revival of epic poetry in post-Safavid Iran', in *The Layered Heart: Essays on Persian Poetry: A Celebration in Honor of Dick Davis*, ed. Ali A. Seyed-Gohrab (Washington, DC: Mage Publishers, 2018), pp. 295–318.
Anooshahr, Ali, 'The king who would be man: The gender roles of the warrior king in early modern history', *Journal of the Royal Asiatic Society* 18, no. 3 (2008), pp. 327–40.
— 'The body politic and rise of the Safavids', in *Safavid Persia in the Age of Empires: The Idea of Iran*, vol. 10, ed. Charles Melville (London: I.B. Tauris, 2021), pp. 13–28.
Astarābādi, Mīrzā Mahdi Khān, *Tārikh-e jahāngoshā-ye Nāderi*, ed. 'Abdollāh Anvār (Tehran: Donyā-ye ketāb, 1390/2011).
Ātābāy, Badri, *Fehrest-e moraqqa'āt-e ketābkhāna-ye saltanati* (Tehran: Chāp-e zibā, 1353/1974).
Axworthy, Michael, *The Sword of Persia: Nader Shah, from Tribal Warrior to Conquering Tyrant* (London: I.B. Tauris, 2006).

Azhand, Yaghoub, 'Kārestān-e honari-ye Mohammad Bāqer', *Honar-hā-ye-zibā: Honar-hā-ye-tajassomi* 20, no. 4 (2016), pp. 27–37.

Al-Azmeh, Aziz, *Muslim Kingship: Power and the Sacred in Muslim, Christian and Pagan Polities* (London: I.B. Tauris, 2001).

Babaie, Sussan, 'Shah 'Abbas II, the conquest of Qandahar, the Chihil Sutun, and its wall paintings', *Muqarnas* 11 (1994), pp. 125–42.

— 'Nader Shah, the Delhi loot, and the 18th-century exotics of empire', in *Crisis, Collapse, Militarism and Civil War: The History and Historiography of 18th Century Iran*, ed. Michael Axworthy (New York: Oxford University Press, 2018), pp. 215–34.

— 'The penchant for "portraits": Representing bodies in early modern Persian painting' (forthcoming).

Babaie, Sussan, Kathryn Babayan, Ina Baghdiantz-McCabe and Massumeh Farhad, *Slaves of the Shah: New Elites of Safavid Iran* (London: I.B. Tauris, 2004).

Bazin, Père Louis, 'Mémoires sur dernières années du règne de Thamas Kouli-Kan et sa mort tragique', in *Lettres édifiantes et curieuses écrites des missions étrangères* (Paris: J.G. Merigot, 1780, letter originally written Bandar Abbas, 1751), vol. IV, pp. 277–321.

Böwering, Gerhard, 'Ensān-e kāmel', *Encyclopaedia Iranica*, vol. VIII (1998), pp. 457–61, online at http://www.iranicaonline.org/articles/ensan-e-kamel [accessed 23 April 2021].

Carter, Philip, 'An "effeminate" or "efficient" nation? Masculinity and eighteenth-century social documentary', *Luxurious Sexualities: Textual Practice* 11, no. 3 (1997), pp. 429–44.

Chardin, Jean, *Voyages du Chevalier Chardin en Perse, et autres lieux de l'Orient*, 10 vols, ed. Louis Mathieu Langlès (Paris: Le Normant, 1811).

Cook, John, *Voyages and Travels Through the Russian Empire, Tartary, and Part of the Kingdom of Persia*, 2 vols (Edinburgh: printed for the author, 1770).

Dankoff, Robert, 'Turban and crown: An essay in Islamic civilization', 2015, online at https://www.academia.edu/13435409/Turban_and_Crown_An_Essay_in_Islamic_Civilization [accessed 23 April 2021].

Diba, Layla S., *Naqqāshi-hā-ye Zand va Qājār az majmu'a-hā-ye khosusi: 9 Khordād-29 Khordād* (Tehran: Anjoman-e Irān va Emrikā Kānun-e Farhangi, 1974).

— 'Persian painting in the eighteenth century: Tradition and transmission', *Muqarnas* 6 (1989), pp. 147–60.

— 'Lacquerwork of Safavid Persia and its Relationship to Persian Painting', doctoral dissertation (New York University, 1994).

Diba, Layla S. and Maryam Ekhtiar, *Royal Persian Paintings: The Qajar Epoch, 1785–1925* (London: I.B. Tauris and Brooklyn: Brooklyn Museum of Art, 1998).

Dodwell, Henry, *A Calendar of the Madras Records, 1740–44* (Madras: Madras Government Press, 1917).

Farhad, Massumeh, 'Artists, paintings and their publics: Safavid albums in the seventeenth century', *The Yarshater Lectures in Persian Art*, SOAS, University of London, 16, 17, 20 and 21 May 2019.

Foucault, Michel, *Discipline and Punish: The Birth of the Prison*, trans. Alan Sheridan (New York: Vintage Books, 1995).

Fraser, James, *The History of Nadir Shah* (London: A. Millar, 1742).

Fredricksmeyer, E.A., 'The origin of Alexander's royal insignia', *Transactions of the American Philological Association* 127 (1997), pp. 97–109.

al-Ghazāli, Abu Hāmid Mohammad, *Ghazālī's Book of Counsel for Kings (Nasīhat al-Mulūk)*, trans. F.R.C. Bagley (London: Oxford University Press, 1964, originally written Tus, ca. 1109–11).

Hanway, Jonas, *An Historical Account of the British Trade over the Caspian Sea*, 4 vols (London: Dodsley *et al.*, 1753).

Hommaire de Hell, Xavier, *Voyage en Turquie et en Perse*, 4 vols (Paris: P. Bertrand, 1854).

Juneja, Monica, 'Translating the body into image: The body politic and visual practice at the Mughal court during the sixteenth and seventeenth centuries', in *Images of the Body in India*, ed. Axel Michaels and Christoph Wulf (New Delhi: Routledge, 2011), pp. 235–60.

Kantorowicz, Ernst Hartwig, *The King's Two Bodies: A Study in Mediaeval Political Theology* (Princeton: Princeton University Press, 1957).

Karimzāda Tabrizi, Mohammad 'Ali, *Ahvāl va āsār-e naqqāshān-e qadim-e Irān*, 3 vols (London: M.'A. Karīm'zādah Tabrīzī, 1985–1991).

al-Kashmiri, 'Abd al-Karim, *The Memoirs of Khojeh Abdulkurreem: A cashmerian of distinction, who accompanied Nadir Shah on his return from Hindostan to Persia ...* , trans. Francis Gladwin (Kolkata: Mackay, 1768).

Llewellyn-Jones, Lloyd, *King and Court in Ancient Persia 559 to 331 BCE* (Edinburgh: Edinburgh University Press, 2013).

Lockhart, Laurence, *Nadir Shah: A Critical Study based mainly upon Contemporary Sources* (London: Luzac & Co., 1938).

McAleer, John, *Picturing India: People, Places and the World of the East India Company* (London: British Library, 2017).

Malcolm, Sir John, *The History of Persia. From the Most Early Period to the Present Time*, 2 vols (London: John Murray, 1815).

Malecka, Anna, 'Daryā-ye nur: History and myth of a crown jewel of Iran', *Iranian Studies* 51, no. 1 (2018), pp. 69–96.

Matthee, Rudi, *Persia in Crisis: Safavid Decline and the Fall of Isfahan* (London: I.B. Tauris, 2012).

— 'Solaymān I', *Encyclopaedia Iranica*, online edition (2015), at http://www.iranicaonline.org/articles/solayman-1 [accessed 23 April 2021].

— 'Solṭān Ḥosayn', *Encyclopaedia Iranica*, online edition (2015), at http://www.iranicaonline.org/articles/soltan-hosayn [accessed 23 April 2021].
— '*Nader Shah in Iranian historiography: Warlord or national hero?*' (Institute for Advanced Study, 2018), online at https://www.ias.edu/ideas/2018/matthee-nader-shah [accessed 23 April 2021].
Meen, Victor B. and A. Douglas Tushingham, *Crown Jewels of Iran* (Toronto: University of Toronto Press, 1968).
Minorsky, Vladimir, ed. and trans., *Tadhkirat al-Mulūk: A Manual of Ṣafavid Administration (circa 1137/1725). Persian Text in Facsimile (B.M. Or. 9496)* (Cambridge: E.J.W. Gibb Memorial Trust, 1980).
Nagel, Tilman, 'Buyids', *Encyclopaedia Iranica*, vol. IV (1990), pp. 578–86, online at http://www.iranicaonline.org/articles/buyids [accessed 23 April 2021].
O'Brien, Janet, 'Historian as Painter, Portrait as Memory: Re-Presenting Karīm Khān Zand and the Portrait of the King in Eighteenth-Century Iran', master's dissertation (The Courtauld Institute of Art, 2015).
— 'Nādir Shāh: The Emergence of Royal Portraiture and a New Body Politic in Eighteen-Century Iran', doctoral dissertation (The Courtauld Institute of Art, forthcoming, 2022).
O'Hanlon, Rosalind, 'Manliness and imperial service in Mughal north India', *Journal of the Economic and Social History of the Orient* 42, no. 1 (1999), pp. 47–93.
— 'Kingdom, household and body history, gender and imperial service under Akbar', *Modern Asian Studies* 41, no. 5 (2007), pp. 889–923.
Patel, Dinyar, 'Caught between two nationalisms: The Iran League of Bombay and the political anxieties of an Indian minority', *Modern Asian Studies* (2020), pp. 1–37.
Rabino di Borgomale, Hyacinth Louis, *Coins, Medals, and Seals of the Shâhs of Irân, 1500–1941* (Hertford, Hertfordshire: S. Austin and Sons, Oriental and General Printers, 1945).
Ray, Aniruddha, 'Invasion of Nadir Shah and the origins of French imperialist thought', *Proceedings of the Indian History Congress* 33 (1971), pp. 362–88.
Ridgeon, Lloyd, 'The felon, the faithful and the fighter: The protean face of the chivalric man (*javanmard*) in the medieval Persianate and modern Iranian worlds', in *Javanmardi: The Ethics and Practice of Persianate Perfection*, ed. idem (London: Gingko, 2018), pp. 1–27.
Roy, Malini, 'The revival of the Mughal painting tradition during the reign of Muhammad Shah', in *Princes and Painters in Mughal Delhi, 1707–1857*, ed. William Dalrymple and Yuthika Sharma (New York: Asia Society Museum, 2012), pp. 17–23.

Savory, Roger M., 'The Safavid state and polity', *Iranian Studies* 7, no. 1–2 (1974), pp. 179–212.

Schimmel, Annemarie, *A Two-Colored Brocade: The Imagery of Persian Poetry* (Chapel Hill: University of North Carolina Press, 1992).

Soudavar, Abolala, *Art of the Persian Courts: Selections from the Art and History Trust Collection* (New York: Rizzoli, 1992).

— 'Looking through *The Two Eyes of the Earth*: A reassessment of Sasanian rock reliefs', *Iranian Studies* 45, no. 1 (2012), pp. 29–58.

String, Tatiana C., *Art and Communication in the Reign of Henry VIII* (London: Routledge: 2017).

Stronge, Susan, Joanna Whalley and Anna Ferrari, *Bejewelled Treasures: The Al-Thani Collection* (London: V&A Publishing, 2015).

Sutherland, Lucy S., 'Vansittart, Henry (1732-?70), of Foxley, Berks', *The History of Parliament*, online at https://www.historyofparliamentonline.org/volume/1754-1790/member/ vansittart-henry-1732-70 [accessed 23 April 2021].

Tucker, Ernest, 'Nadir Shah and the Ja'fari Madhhab reconsidered', *Iranian Studies* 27, no. 1–4 (1994), pp. 163–79.

Tusi, Nasir al-Din, *The Nasirean Ethics by Nasir ad-Din Tusi*, trans. George M. Wickens (London: Allen and Unwin, 1964).

Zakeri, Mohsen, 'Javānmardi', *Encyclopaedia Iranica*, vol. XIV (2008), pp. 594–601, online at https://iranicaonline.org/articles/javanmardi [accessed 23 April 2021].

Zirinsky, Michael P., 'Imperial power and dictatorship: Britain and the rise of Reza Shah, 1921–1926', *International Journal of Middle East Studies* 24, no. 4 (1992), pp. 639–63.

3

'The Persian State' and the Safavid Inheritance: Views from the Caspian, 1722–1781

Kevin Gledhill[1]
(Sacred Heart University)

Introduction: A Safavid Inheritance on the Caspian Coast

On 12/23 September 1781,[2] Count Marko Voĭnovich, the commander of Russia's naval squadron in the Caspian Sea, composed a message from Mazandaran to Grigoriĭ Potemkin in St Petersburg. Voĭnovich, a Montenegrin naval commander who entered Russian service during the most recent Russo-Ottoman War (1768–1774), had been sent by Potemkin to establish a settlement for trade in the south-eastern corner of the Caspian Sea. Officials of the central Russian state had long seen Mazandaran and Astarabad as potentially advantageous sites for a such an outpost. Since the early 1770s, they had accelerated efforts to survey the region and open commerce via Iran to Central Asia and India.[3] Attracted by invitations from Yomut Turkmen emissaries and by the prospects of expanded fishing, seal hunting and oil revenues, they began planning an expedition in the mid-1770s. Potemkin, who coordinated Russia's diplomacy with Iran in his capacity as viceregent of the territories between Astrakhan and the northern shores of the Black Sea, oversaw the project and assigned General A.V. Suvarov, and later Voĭnovich, to command.[4] Seeing an opportunity to divert trade from India to the Caspian–Volga–Baltic route while Russia's imperial rivals were preoccupied with the American War of Independence, Potemkin dispatched Voĭnovich to Iran and the Turkmen coast to lay the foundations for trade.[5]

The 12/23 September 1781 dispatch from Voĭnovich detailed his negotiations with Agha Mohammad Khan Qajar, the eldest son of Mohammad Hasan Khan Qovanlu (d. 1759). A eunuch since his childhood and long-time prisoner of Karim Khan Zand, Agha Mohammad would consolidate his control of Iran by expanding outwards from the Caspian coast by 1792. He established Qajar dynastic rule officially with his enthronement as shah in 1796. Agha Mohammad Khan had only returned to the north from captivity in Shiraz in 1779 and had recently taken control of Astarabad at the time of Voĭnovich's arrival. He assumed a pre-eminent position in the south-eastern corner of the Caspian Sea through competition with half-brothers Mortaza-Qoli Khan and Reza-Qoli Khan.[6]

While Agha Mohammad came to distrust the Russian officers (he arrested Voĭnovich in December of 1781), he initially welcomed them. Contemporary Qajar sources claim that the ten-year-old Fath-'Ali Khan (the future Fath-'Ali Shah) received the Russians' petition for a small plot of land for their settlement, which he granted.[7] In reality, Agha Mohammad Khan offered the land to Voĭnovich himself in a letter carried by the Greek merchant (and later Astrakhan-based caviar magnate) Ioannis Varvakis.

Agha Mohammad's letter to Voĭnovich and the subsequent 12/23 September message from Voĭnovich to Potemkin offer unique insights into the Qajar dynastic founder's idea of Iranian identity and the Safavid inheritance, as well as the meanings of Iranian statehood in the Caspian diplomatic and commercial environment.

The documents first reveal a mutual commitment among both the Qajars and Russian officers and diplomats to uphold a fiction of a unified Iranian state that inherited Safavid dynastic legitimacy. For the Russians, this fiction developed over the course of the eighteenth century and was connected to a series of commercial treaties that granted tariff-free trading privileges to subjects of Peter I and Anna Ivanovna, whose representatives negotiated these agreements between 1717 and 1735. For Agha Mohammad Khan, Safavid authority passed to the Qajars as the last faithful servitors of the old dynastic order. The Qajars drew on historical narratives of continuity between them and their Safavid predecessors, framing the campaigns of Agha Mohammad Khan as a project of Safavid restoration. Like the Russian notion of Iranian statehood, this idea also developed over decades, beginning with the career of Agha Mohammad's father, Mohammad Hasan Khan. This rhetoric of the Qovanlu Qajars' right to rule a single Iranian state passed to them from the court of Esfahan is apparent in Agha Mohammad's correspondence (which survives in translation in Potemkin's papers) with Voĭnovich. Agha Mohammad drew on the phrasing and terminology employed by the Russian consuls in Gilan and in the Rasht Treaty of 1732, asserting that 'there is an unbreakable friendship between the Russian and Iranian states'.[8] Russian officials often applied this language, borrowed directly from the treaties, in their correspondence with the autonomous rulers of the southern Caspian coastal regions. Agha Mohammad then added that just as Voĭnovich received instructions from Catherine II, he similarly commanded 'officers and notables in Astarabad and Mazandaran, who are entirely at my disposal'. He authorized his appointed governors, Rahim Khan Qajar (Davolu) and Reza Khan Qajar (Qovanlu) to negotiate the specifics and assist Voĭnovich in building a commercial outpost in the Bay of Astarabad.[9]

Thus, Agha Mohammad framed the negotiations around his claim to equivalent status with Catherine II, speaking as a sovereign ruler responsible for the maintenance of the 'eternal friendship' between the two states.[10] In doing so, he found some common ground with Russian diplomats, who frequently expressed a desire to find a single, stable authority to offer protection to Russian subjects beyond the northern ports and into the interior of Iran. For example, Consul Ivan Tumanovskiĭ wrote from Anzali (Enzeli) in 1782 about the obstacles to trade presented by the political divisions within Iran and of the instability created by the absence of a unified state.[11] Russian economic interests made the language of Safavid continuity and simple state-to-state relations a central part of Caspian diplomacy in the eighteenth century. It offered a framework for officials in Astarabad, Rasht, Baku, Quba and Derbent to recognize Russian commercial privileges, hoping to attract merchants from Astrakhan and generate revenues through trade. Agha Mohammad Khan, at least at the beginning of his negotiations with Voĭnovich, embraced this framework. Economic relations with Russia, therefore, forged a specific idea of Iranian statehood, incentivizing northern khans to adhere to narratives of continuity and Safavid succession.

Russian appeals to past treaties with the Safavids and Afshars, as well as their desire for a centralized polity with which to negotiate, had limits. The idea of continuity with the Safavids provided a legal basis for trade. It legitimized consular establishments and provided a language in which to advocate for the interests of merchants who operated between Gilan and Astrakhan. However, officers and consuls on the ground adapted to conditions in the southern Caspian, negotiating directly with local rulers and even establishing protectorates (as in Kartli-Kakheti in 1783) that violated the principle of a territorially restored Iran. St Petersburg offered only a partial commitment to Safavid restoration and Iranian unification. Furthermore, officials serving under Catherine II did not recognize Agha Mohammad as the 'sovereign' of that unified Iran and they continued to cultivate other Iranian allies, including 'Ali Morad Khan Zand in Shiraz and Mortaza-Qoli Khan Qajar in Mazandaran.

The question of where to build the Russian trading post revealed the depth of Qajar commitment to a Safavid restorationist ideology through which Agha Mohammad Khan legitimized his authority. Voĭnovich asked for the right to control the fortress at Ashraf, once the site of a residence of 'Abbas I Safavi (r. 996–1038/1588–1629). On 10/21 September, Voĭnovich wrote to Potemkin praising the town as a location for a settlement by pointing to its supply of water, access to a secure harbour (a rare feature in the Caspian) in the Bay of Astarabad, easily defended fortress, fertile agricultural lands and its location at the junction of long-distance trading routes.[12] He wrote to Agha Mohammad for permission to build there, hoping to rename the town Melisopol (Greek for 'City of Honey').[13]

For Agha Mohammad Khan, this cession was impossible because it conflicted with his own project of Safavid restoration and sense of a Qajar inheritance from the Safavids. Voĭnovich makes this clear in the 12/23 September dispatch. In his description of Agha Mohammad's refusal, he notes that the Qajar ruler offered him 'any other suitable location' along the coast, but that he would not negotiate over the rights to Ashraf. Voĭnovich informed Potemkin that Agha Mohammad agreed to the construction of a settlement, 'only, he cannot give us Ashraf, because this is a place of [belonging to] the sovereign and he greatly hopes sometime to restore respect for the Shah throughout Persia'; this effort would be imperiled by turning Ashraf over to Russian rule.[14] The phrase used in the document is 'this is a place of [i.e. belonging to] the sovereign' (*mesto onoe gosudarskoe*). This term may refer to the designation of Mazandaran as *khassa*, or land with revenues assigned to the shah's treasury, in the time of 'Abbas I.[15] It seems that Agha Mohammad either narrowed the area designated as khassa to include only the specific location of the residence of 'Abbas I, or merely sought to protect a place of ideological significance irrespective of its legal status in the Safavid era.

Agha Mohammad's Safavid revivalism was not the same as the Russian idea of a unified state that inherited the obligations to Russia of its predecessors. The two sides developed a partially shared vocabulary to use in commercial negotiations. Though they arrived at their ideas of unified Iranian statehood for different reasons, these notions gave Agha Mohammad Khan and Voĭnovich, as well as Nikita Baskakov, who rebuilt the Russian settlement in Mazandaran in 1782, a shared language in which to negotiate in matters of trade. However, the differences between their senses of the meaning of that language opened possibilities for misunderstanding and conflict, as occurred by the end of 1781.

These documents reveal significant features of the early Qajar relationship to the Safavid past and a sense of continuity from it, while also demonstrating a separate economic and diplomatic commitment to the idea of a unified Iranian counterpart to Russia in the former Safavid lands. Ideological justifications for Qajar rule that emerged independently in the borderlands of Astarabad, Khorasan and the Turkmen Steppe combined with commercial considerations to manufacture the notions of Iranian statehood that formed the basis of relations with the Russian Empire. As a result, both Agha Mohammad Khan and Voĭnovich recognized the binding nature of Safavid-era treaties and the existence of a legitimate and cohesive Safavid inheritance. Their encounter reflects an eighteenth-century Caspian world connected, in part, by a fiction of an 'Iranian state' unbroken by the multi-sided wars that followed the assassination of Nader Shah. This chapter will examine the development of this idea of Iran between the fall of Esfahan in 1722 and the Voĭnovich expedition in 1781 and its distinct meanings to ruling elites on both the southern and northern sides of the Caspian Sea.

Russia's Caspian Diplomacy and the 'Persian State'

From the point of view of the Russian imperial court and the Presidents and boards of the Colleges of Commerce and Foreign Affairs (forerunners of the ministries, first established under Peter I), relations with Iran and trade in the Caspian Sea were rooted in bilateral agreements with the Safavid shahs. As Russia's victory over Sweden in the Great Northern War (1701–21) appeared certain, Peter I undertook efforts to link his new holdings in the Baltic to the Volga–Caspian commercial route and to redirect transit trades between Asia and Western Europe to run through Russian territory. Diplomatic outreach was embedded within a larger project of gathering intelligence and mapping the Caspian Sea and adjoining lands, beginning in 1715.[16] Between 1715 and 1718, Artemiĭ Volynskiĭ travelled in Iran, negotiating the first permanent Russo-Iranian commercial treaty at the court of Shah Soltan-Hoseyn.

Following the Safavid collapse in 1722, Russian forces occupied the Caspian shores between Daghestan and Gilan. Tahmasp II, a Safavid prince who had escaped from the Ghelzay Afghan siege of Esfahan and launched an attempt to regain power from the north, recognized Russian territorial claims as far east as Astarabad in the south-eastern corner of the Caspian. He committed to mutual defence against the Ottomans and agreed to supply Russian armies in the north with meat, salt and horses.[17] After nearly a decade of costly occupation, General Vasiliĭ Levashov negotiated the first of two treaties that returned these lands to Tahmasp in 1732.

The Treaty of Rasht (1732) set the terms of state-to-state relations across the Caspian Sea, establishing a legal regime of trade, diplomacy and travel that lasted until the outbreak of the Russo-Iranian Wars in 1804. Its text begins by reaffirming the historical friendship between the two states, maintaining that Empress Anna continued the Petrine-era policy of supporting the legitimate claims of the Safavid shah to his ancestral throne.[18] Under the terms of the agreement, Russian troops were to abandon the area west of the Sefidrud in Gilan within one month of ratification and all territories south of the Kura River within five months. The return of this territory to the shah is framed in the treaty as an act of goodwill.[19] Most of the pact consisted of commercial and diplomatic terms, assuring tariff-free trade throughout Iran for Russian subjects, who also received guarantees from the Iranian court that it would ensure recovery of their property lost to theft or shipwrecks.[20] These terms were affirmed and extended in the Treaty of Ganja in 1735, in which all lands to the Sulak River in Daghestan were ceded to Iran and each side pledged itself to an anti-Ottoman alliance.[21] As Oleg Nikonov has noted, the Russian Empire benefited by legitimizing its diplomatic and military presence in the Caspian, and gained assurances that Iranian officials would protect its economic interests in the silk trade and transit routes to India. Through the Colleges of Commerce and Foreign Affairs, the Russian Empire also began to institutionalize its diplomatic services in Iran with the establishment of a consulate at Rasht, which the Treaty of Ganja permitted.[22]

The economic terms of the Treaty of Rasht were highly advantageous to Russian merchants. It granted them the right to travel freely throughout all of Iran and prohibited officials within Iran from collecting 'any customs or other taxes from Russian subjects'. It further prohibited bureaucrats from compensating for these lost revenues by other means, such as gift exchanges. Tax exemptions extended not only to goods produced in Russia and Iran, but to Indian and Western European commodities as well. Finally, the treaty offered a means for petition against abuses with the founding of consulates and a residency at the shah's court, but it also called for the construction of storehouses and caravanserais and required officials to account for and send back inheritances to heirs in Russia if a subject of the Russian Empire died in Iran.[23]

Despite the shifts in Russian policy and ambitions from the reign of Peter I (1682/89–1725) to that of his niece, Anna (r. 1730–1741), St Petersburg's representatives consistently framed their actions in the region in terms of the continuation of a historic friendship with a single Iranian state. While Peter's 1722 war manifesto cited Lezgi uprisings and plunder from Russian traders in Shamakhi as the immediate cause for war, it added that the emperor intended to punish insurgents and ensure respect for the shah's authority.[24] This claim is repeated in the 1723 agreement signed at St Petersburg by the representatives of Tahmasp II, in which the shah acknowledged the *Nizovoï Korpus*, the Russian military command in the southern Caspian, as invited guests who had come into Iran for the purpose of Safavid restoration.[25] The Treaty of Ganja further elaborated on the idiom of state–state relations and long-standing alliance. It included an appeal that 'both exalted monarchies' interests demand that favourably established trade be upheld, and that there be no disturbances to subjects of both sides setting out for trade, on which depends common benefit'.[26] To this end, both the Russian Empire and 'Persian State' (*Persidskoe gosudarstvo*) granted the other's subjects access to piers and storehouses without interference, and Russia was allowed to establish a consulate in Rasht to protect its merchants.[27]

This language of friendship and alliance between two states, along with the specific commercial clauses of the treaties, offered Russian diplomats and traders in the lands of the former Safavid Empire a powerful rhetorical tool to advocate for their interests to Afsharid, Zand, Qajar and local officials throughout the rest of the eighteenth century. The protection of trading privileges became the leading priority of Russian consuls, who appealed to the treaties as clearly elaborated legal bases for their interventions in matters of commerce. In the instructions sent to Consul Semën Arapov in 1737 from the College of Foreign Affairs, he was reminded of the state's interest in expanding Iranian trade, with an emphasis on his responsibility to ensure the recognition of the treaty clauses concerning tariffs. The college's board also highlighted the right of Russian subjects to carry Indian goods via Iran to Russia with the same exemptions.[28] The former commander of Russian troops in Iran, Vasiliĭ Levashov, sent Arapov the full text of Articles Three to Eight of the Rasht Treaty, and reminded him of his right to press Iranian governors to provide caravanserais, shops and storehouses, as well as to recover goods from shipwrecks and to enforce security of roads.[29] Many of these points are repeated verbatim, though with additional elaboration, in the College of Foreign Affairs' instructions to Consul Grigoriĭ Merk in 1776.[30]

Consuls invoked the treaties frequently in their relations with Iranian elites. In 1768, Gavrilo Bogolīubov composed a set of reforms for consular administration and the conduct of trade, favouring Astrakhan's Russian traders over more recently arrived Armenian subjects of the Russian Empire. In his proposal, Bogolīubov cited violation of the 'Ganja Treaty of 1732' (conflating the two agreements of the 1730s) by Hedayatollah Khan of Rasht. Bogolīubov used this evidence of abuses of legally established privileges to advance his proposal to move the consulate to Talesh, though opposition of the College of Foreign Affairs and some merchants invested in Gilan led to the abandonment of this plan.[31] But Bogolīubov applied references to the treaties in other portions of his reform proposal. In Article Six of the Rasht Treaty, the residencies established at both courts were assigned the task of 'maintaining frequent exchange [of goods] ... and to ensure full satisfaction and justice for their subjects'.[32] This clause had already become the basis for extraterritorial authority, allowing the consuls to mediate disputes between Russian subjects and to submit criminal cases to the magistrate in Astrakhan.[33] Bogolīubov suggested new ways to structure this judicial authority, calling for the ruler of Gilan and the consul to appoint panels of two or three merchants each to hear complaints and to render judgements to be finalized by joint review of khan and consul. Appeals to the treaties continued. As relations between Hedayatollah Khan and this Russian outpost deteriorated in the 1780s, then-Consul Ivan Tumanovskiĭ denounced alleged treaty violations by the ruler of Gilan and by Malek Mohammad Khan of Baku. He accused them of collecting *rahdari* dues (road tolls) from Russian subjects carrying cargoes into the interior from the ports.[34] The Rasht and Ganja Treaties thus became the legal basis through which Russian diplomats understood their responsibilities in Iran and they raised their disputes with and appeals to local rulers and the Zand court within the framework of these treaties. The position of the Russian central state, that Karim Khan Zand held the legitimate authority that assured their trading rights in Iran, did not prevent its representatives from negotiating with local elites separately as though they were sovereigns, too. Relations with these rulers required flexibility that framed them as 'Persian' (the term used in Russian documents of the period) when such a framing suited Russian interests, and as independent in other cases. In doing so, Russian agents had to navigate the ideological claims of local rulers with their own relationship to the Safavid past.

While Russian traders and diplomats in the South Caucasus, Gilan and the Caspian Sea maintained a fiction of a single Iranian state in a direct line of succession from the last Safavids for commercial reasons, the autonomous rulers with whom they interacted did so according to their own motives. For elites in Astarabad, Quba, Rasht and Baku, the treaties offered a framework within which to conduct relations with Russia, bringing needed revenues into their territories and denying them to rivals. However, the presence of Safavid pretenders, appeals to rank and office-holding in the Safavid era and historical narratives of service to the former shahs all provided ideological tools to justify the rule and expansion of post-Safavid rulers along the southern and western shores of the Caspian Sea. This trend is especially pronounced in the case of the Qajars, Mohammad Hasan Khan (d. 1759) and his son Agha Mohammad Khan (d. 1797), the first Qajar shah. Appeals to the Safavid past and dynastic continuity were used in a more limited and selective way by Fath-'Ali Khan of Quba in Shirvan and Daghestan.

Fath-'Ali Khan of Quba engaged extensively with the Caspian economic and diplomatic environment through Derbent, Salyan and later through the subordination of the ruling house of Baku. After a three-year absence from 'Persia', the Russian court sought to re-engage diplomatically and commercially with Iran after the accession of Catherine II in 1762. This policy brought new opportunities for expansion and consolidation of power to rulers in the South Caucasus. On 20/31 July 1762, the empress issued an edict (*ukaz*) requiring the establishment of two consulates and trading centres in Iran. With this order, Catherine limited merchant activity elsewhere due to political instability. At the two designated sites of Anzali and Baku, the consuls relied on merchant intermediaries to enforce the regulation of trade. Catherine authorized the consuls to employ six merchants to implement imperial policy and inspect cargoes. Their task was to ensure that trading agents of larger merchant houses exchanged goods at the prices set by state officials and by their employers in Moscow, St Petersburg and Astrakhan.[35] This edict marked the beginning of a sustained effort by the Russian court to promote trade in the Caspian. When tariff collections in Astrakhan had not risen as expected by 1767, the empress and the College of Commerce authorized an investigation of the causes. Since 1764, tariff collections at Astrakhan had fallen from 40,658 rubles to only 13,588.[36] Mikhaïl Suliakov, the Consul in Baku, claimed that he was unable to contribute to the investigation, blaming the merchants for keeping fraudulent records in order to avoid taxation.[37]

By launching this investigation, St Petersburg officials neglected to consider events on the ground in Shirvan, where a war, fought at least in part for control of silk trading centres and routes to the Caspian, broke out in 1766. One side in this conflict was led by Fath-'Ali Khan, the ruler of Quba, a town located between the coastal strip of the Caspian and the Caucasus, approximately 95 kilometers south of Derbent. He emerged during this period as the leading figure in the military and political affairs of the eastern Caucasus. Between his coming to power in 1758 and his death in 1789, Fath-'Ali Khan was one of the most powerful figures in the region, ruling Quba, Derbent and Salyan at the mouth of the Kura River, as well as subjugating the ruling houses of Baku, Lankaran and other khanates and competing for influence with the rulers of Karabagh and Kartli-Kakheti.

The conflict between Quba and Shamakhi in the mid-1760s reveals the close relationship that Fath-'Ali Khan maintained with the Russian consuls and merchants during this period. Chronicle sources from the region say little about the war. 'Abbas-Qoli Bakikhanov, writing in the mid-nineteenth century, states only that Fath-'Ali Khan marched against Shamakhi in 1181/May 1767–April 1768 in alliance with Hoseyn Khan of Sheki. They divided the region between themselves (*mamlekat ra taqsim kard*) after their victory and Fath-'Ali Khan took possession of Shirvan and rebuilt the city of Shamakhi.[38] In fact, the war began earlier than this and Fath-'Ali Khan's correspondence with Suliakov reveals an economic dimension. In a letter received at the consulate in Baku on 4/15 April 1766, the Quban ruler noted the robbery and captivity of Russian merchants on the road to the Shamakhi and positioned himself as a guarantor of their safety, securing the route by ordering his *eshik-aqasi-bashi*, Musa Bek, to ensure their passage to markets there. This title of *eshik-aqasi-bashi* originally signified the task of gatekeeper of the inner household of the shah, though in practice it typically required the management of officials and close proximity to and influence over the shah as one of the leading figures at the Safavid court. In exchange for Musa Bek's protection, Fath-'Ali Khan asked Russians and Armenians not to travel in caravans jointly with the merchants of Baku or Shamakhi, which would expose them to raids when mistaken for these rivals.[39] Musa Bek also wrote to the consul and reassured him of his protection, repeating the request to exclude the traders of Shamakhi from their caravans.[40] In offering this protection, Fath-'Ali Khan ensured a closer relationship with Russian officials, seeking increased access to this commercial hub and centre of silk production.

Given the official Russian commitment to the idea of a single Iranian state that provided legal sanction for its consulate under the treaties of the 1730s, it seems likely that Fath-'Ali Khan would stress his place within that Iranian state in correspondence with Baku. Often, however, he rejected Zand authority over his holdings in Shirvan and Daghestan while promising to uphold the terms of the treaties independently. Historians of eighteenth-century Iran acknowledge the effective reach of Karim Khan Zand's authority, which was limited north of the Aras River and the Alborz Mountains.[41] Despite this, the Zands nominally recognized Fath-'Ali Khan's authority in the South Caucasus as part of a larger Iranian polity with its capital in Shiraz; court chronicler Abu'l-Hasan Ghaffari refers to Fath-'Ali Khan as the *beglerbegi* of all of Shirvan.[42] In 1775, Fath-'Ali Khan sent a letter to the Russian court that sought to define his relationship with the Zands and Romanovs in different terms. He explained that he had rejected the overtures of Karim Khan's deputies, sent from Shiraz with gifts to persuade him to serve and recognize the *vakil*'s authority. He explained his refusal in terms of his sincere wish for Russian protection over his territory. Like other rulers of this period, Fath-'Ali Khan held out the possibility of a subordinate status to the Russian throne, though it is difficult to assess how literally this offer was intended.[43] In making this appeal, he almost certainly hoped to offset pressure from Shiraz, using Russian protection as a counterweight.

These exchanges reveal the nuances and adaptability of relations between northern Iranian rulers and the Russian Empire under the Rasht and Ganja Treaties. Russian officials sought assurances that local elites would protect the property of subjects of St Petersburg and their rights to trade without tariff obligations. Figures such as Fath-'Ali Khan were able to cultivate friendly relations with Russia by upholding these privileges. However, Fath-'Ali Khan maintained distance from the nominal authority of the Zand rulers of the south, even if Russia recognized the Zands as the ultimate guarantors of the treaties' terms across Iran. Rather than insist on the legality of Zand power, Russian state agents came, over the course of the eighteenth century, to construct separate relationships with the khans of the north, disregarding the language of a unified 'Persian' state as needed, even as they applied it consistently in defence of their own merchants in Iran.

Furthermore, the khans' occasional offers to enter into a protectorate relationship or their use of language indicating a complete break with the south were not consistent. In the 1780s, Fath-'Ali Khan utilized a Safavid pretender to advance and justify expansionist projects. John Perry has argued that Safavid pretenders played a significant role in organizing resistance to Afghan and Ottoman occupations in the 1720s. They served as symbols of legitimate authority at that time, before their use declined sharply in the post-Nader era. The paradigm of rule had shifted and, while Safavid pretenders remained in some cases, the idea of restoration was mainly only taken up by the Qajars in the latter half of the century.[44]

Following the death of Karim Khan Zand in 1779, a new round of fighting began in the South Caucasus and Gilan. As Fath-'Ali Khan campaigned to the south, the Russian consul in Anzali reported that the Quban Khan retained a supposed Safavid claimant, who called himself 'Abbas III. Merchant informants of the consulate reported in April of 1783 that 'Abbas had emerged around Salyan and intended to march on Ardabil to announce a Safavid restoration.[45] 'Abbas lacked an independent base of support and funding; consequently, Fath-'Ali Khan prevented his march and held him in reserve under the protection of his vassal, Malek Mohammad Khan, at Baku.[46]

Post-Safavid rulers positioned themselves as guarantors of the treaty privileges of Russian merchants with the intention of attracting trade and monopolizing control of revenues in the north. Mutual interests enabled Russo-Iranian trade and provided incentives to enforce the terms of past agreements across the southern Caspian. However, Russian officials negotiated with the khans independently of any central authority, despite the fiction of a unified Iran. While maintaining political autonomy through his relationship with the Russian consulate, Fath-'Ali Khan also drew on the language of a legitimate Safavid imperial order when advantageous. With the possibility of direct Zand rule increasingly remote after Karim Khan's death in 1779, Fath-'Ali Khan briefly chose to compete with rivals through an idiom of Safavid restoration as he campaigned in Talesh and Gilan. This type of appeal could still be a potent ideological tool, though it received its most complete expression when wielded by Agha Mohammad Khan Qajar.

Safavid Restoration and Continuity among the Qajars

The Qovanlu Qajars of Astarabad demonstrated a stronger commitment to Safavid restoration and continuity than the rulers of the South Caucasus. By the 1790s, Agha Mohammad Khan, the Qajar dynastic founder, claimed a right to rule as the legitimate heir to the Safavids, with the Qajars as their last faithful servants. He territorialized this claim in his assertion of the natural right of the shah to recognition by the *vali*s of Kartli and Kakheti, by then a unified east Georgian kingdom ruled by Erekle II. Since the Treaty of Georgievsk in 1783, this kingdom had enjoyed the status of a Russian protectorate. According to court chronicler Mohammad Fathollah b. Mohammad Taqi Saru'i, Agha Mohammad demanded the subjugation of Erekle's kingdom and justified his claims there as an expression of Safavid restoration. In a letter to Erekle, he wrote of a historical reality in which:

> 'Gorjestan [Georgia] was [a possession] of the kings of Iran, such that [it was so] since the time of Shah Esma'il Safavi until the beginning of our imperial dispensation [*dowlat-e homayun-e ma*]; for this reason, the path of wisdom and course of wise advice is this, that that *velayat* be placed under the shelter of the foot of the throne'.[47]

In addressing this letter to the east Georgian king, Agha Mohammad Khan placed himself in a direct line of succession from the Safavid dynastic founder, ruling over an Iranian state with a clearly defined territory, of which Tiflis was a part. In doing so, he drew on an ideological project of Safavid succession that developed under his father Mohammad Hasan Khan and grandfather Fath-'Ali Khan.

In 1726, Fath-'Ali Khan Qajar Qovanlu was executed on the order of the future Nader Shah, who replaced him as the leading military commander in the service of Tahmasp II. Fath-'Ali Khan Qajar's son, Mohammad Hasan Khan, found refuge among the Yomut Turkmens after his father's death. The Afsharid chronicler Mohammad Kazem Marvi mentions the protection Mohammad Hasan Khan received from a maternal uncle, Bekanj 'Ali Beg Yomut, during his time on the Turkmen Steppe.[48] Mohammad Hasan made several bids to return to power in Astarabad and to resist Afshar control in the borderlands. In the course of his attempts to suppress these Qajar revolts, 'Adel Shah Afshar captured the young Agha Mohammad and had him castrated.[49] Mohammad Hasan regained his position in Astarabad and from 1749 to 1759, he was among the most powerful rulers in the former Safavid lands, engaged in conflicts with Karim Khan Zand and Azad Khan Afghan between Azerbaijan, Astarabad and Fars.

While Qajar chronicles make no mention of Mohammad Hasan Khan's role in Afsharid succession disputes in Mashhad, this activity enabled him to build a military coalition. It also may reveal the early origins of an ideological programme of Safavid restorationism present in his later career. During the winter of 1749–1750, Mohammad Hasan Khan participated in the elevation of Mir Sayyed Mohammad Mar'ashi to the throne as shah in Mashhad.[50] Mir Sayyed Mohammad was a maternal descendant of Shah Soleyman Safavi (r. 1077–1105/1666–1694) and administrator (*motavali*) of the shrine of Emam Reza in Mashhad. Mohammad Hasan Khan's involvement in the removal of Shahrokh Shah Afshar and the brief reign of Mir Sayyed Mohammad (with the regnal name of Soleyman II) is attested in the writings of Mir Sayyed Mohammad's grandson, Soltan Hashem Mirza Mar'ashi.

Soltan Hashem Mirza places Mohammad Hasan among a group of 16 amirs who came to Mashhad in 1749. They stated that they had no desire to rule and made clear that the support they had previously given to Shahrokh had been due to his maternal ancestry from the 'Exalted Safavid line [*eradat va ata'at keh ba u dashtim ... beh sabab-e selsela-ye 'aliya bud*]'.[51] They praised the 'aptitude [*qabeliyat*] and personality [*tashakhkhos*] and mentality [*zehn*] and judiciousness [*zaka*]' of the early Safavids, which had made them uniquely suited to rule Iran, but lamented misrule by the heirs of the dynasty. Shahrokh attempted to flee from this assembly, only to be captured, deposed and blinded.[52] The subsequent enthronement of Soleyman II is framed as a restoration, attended by the 'khans and commanders' of the peoples who had served the Safavids from the beginning, who had been left disappointed and deprived by a long period of misrule.[53] They offered their allegiance to Soleyman II and received offices and recognition of their authority. Mohammad Hasan Khan was named *eshik-aqasi-bashi*.[54]

The rule of Soleyman II was short-lived and Shahrokh returned to power quickly in Mashhad. Despite this, Mohammad Hasan Khan incorporated Safavid restoration into his ruling ideology and made it central to his claims to authority. He passed a narrative of Safavid restoration to Agha Mohammad Khan; it is clearly present in the chronicle by Saru'i, completed just after Agha Mohammad's assassination in 1797.

The history of the Qajars of Astarabad in Saru'i's text is defined by service to the Safavids. Their settlement in Astarabad began, according to his account, with an order from Shah 'Abbas I to relocate to the north-eastern frontier in order to protect it against raids by the Sa'in Khani Turkmens. The shah singled out the Qajars for their bravery and service, dividing them into two settlements at Marv and Mobarakabad, outside Astarabad, to prevent raids from Central Asia.[55] This story was probably already informing the identity of the Qajars in this region in the time of Mohammad Hasan Khan and certainly did before the rise of Agha Mohammad to power. Members of the ruling elite around Astarabad told the story of their relocation from the South Caucasus by Shah 'Abbas to the traveller and botanist Samuel Gottlieb Gmelin in 1773. In this account, a force of 1,000 Qajars had distinguished themselves by defeating a much larger Ottoman army in Shirvan, which inspired the gratitude and trust of the shah. When the need arose to defend the borderlands from the Turkmens, 'Abbas recalled this service and relocated the Qajars to the north-eastern frontier.[56]

In both the late eighteenth-century history by Saru'i and in the earlier actions of Mohammad Hasan, it is possible to find evidence of a Safavid revivalist project. Saru'i advances the narrative of faithful service to the Safavids by the Qajars in his account of the fall of the Safavid capital in 1722. According to this fictionalized account, Fath-'Ali Khan Qajar rallied Qajar forces to relieve the capital, then under siege. Despite his march to the relief of Shah Soltan-Hoseyn and his 'manly battle' with the Afghans, his efforts were thwarted by the selfishness and cowardice of the shah's courtiers, leading to the fall of Esfahan.[57] Three decades later and after the downfall of Soleyman II, Mohammad Hasan captured the Safavid pretender Esma'il III, in whose name he had coins struck; he also seems to have resided at Ashraf, using it as his capital to emphasize his ties to the Safavid past.[58]

Saru'i further highlighted his Qajar patrons' Safavid-loyalist credentials through the use of the term 'Qezelbash'. As Mana Kia has demonstrated, this term had a shifting meaning over time and should not be assumed to refer only to the *oymaq*s that had initially provided the spiritual followers and military class of the sixteenth-century Safavids. By the post-Safavid period, it had come to signify an association with the lands of the former dynasty, service to it and Shi'i religious identity. This meaning of Qezelbash would have been clear in Iran and South Asia as part of a shared Persianate vocabulary of identity.[59] In the borderlands between the Turkmen regions and Astarabad and Khorasan, the term retained some of its earlier polemical usage. This meaning is evident in an account of the Afsharid campaign against Qarshi in 1737, as related by Bukharan chronicler Mohammad Qazi Vafa Karminagi. In this text, the author describes the invasion by Reza-Qoli Mirza Afshar as a '*fitna* [revolt] of the insurgent Qezelbash'. Prominent figures in the Bukharan administration rallied their forces in response to the approaching 'contingent of [Shi'i] heretics [*ravafez*]'.[60] These terms, 'Qezelbash' and 'heretic', are used interchangeably in the text and contrasted with the Bukharan 'army of Islam' whose counterattacks inspired fear among the 'ravafez'.[61]

Saru'i's use of the 'Qezelbash' label for the Qajars occurs specifically in the context of battles with Sunni enemies, allowing the Qajars to retain their seventeenth-century status as defenders of the Shi'i dynasty and believers. Given the wider Persianate use of the word 'Qezelbash' in this period, this term allowed a further association between the emerging power of the Qajars and the Safavid past. When Dorrani Afghan armies invaded Khorasan in 1754, Mohammad Hasan Khan led a coalition of amirs who had fled to his protection at Damghan. This force now advanced to resist the Dorrani army. Qajar forces battled the Afghans at Moghisa, outside Sabzavar. There, the 'advance guard of the appointed armies of the Qezelbash (*qaravolan-e jonud-e mo'ayyena-ye Qezelbashiya*)' did battle with the Afghan advance guard. Ultimately, the Qajar forces 'put them to flight in terror, [with the Afghans] turning on their commanders and hurriedly fleeing through Sabzavar and Holy Mashhad without turning back'.[62]

Saru'i employs similar language in his description of Mohammad Hasan's battles with Azad Khan Afghan, who controlled much of Azerbaijan in the 1750s. Saru'i casts Azad Khan's rule in Orumia and Tabriz as a time of oppression of the faithful. He writes, 'free men of Azerbaijan were brought under Afghan bondage ... the servants of God ... prayed for relief' for which 'the slaves of the Soltan [Mohammad Hasan Khan] went to Azerbaijan to remove them by force'.[63] The battle is depicted in decidedly religious terms, as well as linguistic-cultural ones. The 'Sunni left flank and the Shi'i right flank and the left and right flanks of the reverse and the Afghan centre and the centre of the army of Turk and Tajik' clashed.[64] In defence of their camp, the Afghans are described as attacking the 'Qezelbash army' (*sepah-e Qezelbash*). But the Qezelbash were not deterred, 'responding fearlessly to the call of the khedive of that time to take up arms, the Qezelbash, from dread of the khan and fear for their lives put their shields behind them and bore their chests as shields'. Finally, they forced Azad to flee to Tiflis and looted his camp.[65]

For the eighteenth-century Qajar rulers, the Safavid legacy was inseparable from their own aspirations and claims to authority within Iran. Having failed to oust Afsharid forces from Astarabad with attacks launched from the Turkmen Steppe, Mohammad Hasan Khan aligned himself with a project of Safavid restoration in Mashhad in 1749. While Soleyman II ruled only briefly, Mohammad Hasan emerged as one of the leading contenders for power in the post-Nader Shah era, laying siege to Shiraz before his final defeat at the hands of Karim Khan Zand and rivals within the Qajar ruling families. There is significant evidence that he legitimized his claims to power in the language of Safavid loyalty and revival, given his use of pretenders and residence in Ashraf. Furthermore, a historical narrative emerged in which the Qajars came into the south-eastern Caspian borderlands as servitors of the shah and had remained faithful, even beyond the collapse of the dynasty. This story was written into the official histories of the Qajars during the reigns of Agha Mohammad Shah (d. 1797) and Fath-'Ali Shah (r. 1797–1834).

Conclusions: The Question of Ashraf

These ideological claims help to explain the negotiations over the site of the Russian outpost in 1781. When Agha Mohammad Khan protested that he could not relinquish control over land that belonged to the sovereign, he defended an idea of Iran as a political unit inherited from the Safavids. Given the close association of Ashraf with Shah 'Abbas I, the most celebrated ruler of the Safavid period and the one with whom Qajar historians emphasized their own association through the story of their forced migration, the refusal to cede Ashraf is laden with symbolic political meaning. Voïnovich perceived some of the significance of this claim when he informed Potemkin that Agha Mohammad had refused his request to build on the site 'because it belongs to the sovereign and he greatly hopes to restore respect for the shah throughout Persia', and that he feared the loss of this respect if he ceded Shah 'Abbas' settlement in Mazandaran.[66] Qajar legitimacy depended on the ideology of Safavid revival.

Throughout the eighteenth century, a new set of military elites emerged within the former Safavid lands, resulting in a series of wars that only ended with the establishment of a decentralized Qajar monarchy in most of the territory of the former Safavid Empire. In this environment, Qajar claims to Safavid restoration offered a unique claim to authority, distinct from the imperial vision of Nader Shah, which drew on military power and appeals to the Timurid past, Turkmen ancestry and the experiment of rebranding Shi'i jurisprudence as the Ja'fari *mazhab* in negotiations with the Ottomans.[67] The Qajar use of the past was equally distinct from the ideology of Karim Khan Zand, who sidestepped questions of Safavid legitimacy and never officially took the title of shah. Agha Mohammad did take the throne, though only after the sack of Tiflis and completion of Safavid territorial restoration in the South Caucasus. According to John Malcolm, he then travelled to the Safavid dynastic shrine at Ardabil and bound on the sword of Esma'il I.[68] Though it had significant applications in the competitive environment of post-Safavid Iran, Qajar self-identification as Qezelbash guardians against Afghan Sunni incursions also drew on the particular resonances of the 'Qezelbash' label in the borderlands with Central Asia.

It would be easy, therefore, for Agha Mohammad Khan to assimilate this label and ideological framing into a new diplomatic context of encounter with imperial Russia. In doing so, he aligned two different motivations: a legitimizing strategy based on Safavid revivalism in which authority transferred to the loyal Qajar lineage and an economic incentive to recognize Safavid continuity as a means to attract Russian traders by honouring the privileges they received in treaties with Tahmasp II. Despite appeals to the treaties of the 1730s, Russian merchants and diplomats continued to acknowledge Zand claims at this time and simultaneously cultivated local partnerships with the khans of other regions of the Caspian littoral.[69]

When Agha Mohammad Khan and Marko Voïnovich began their correspondence in September 1781, the Safavid past permeated the negotiations. For Voïnovich, Agha Mohammad's support of a settlement offered the possibility of finally realizing Russian ambitions for expanded trade in Central and South Asia. Like other rulers of northern Iran, Agha Mohammad's independent power was an inescapable reality, but trade brought the promise of new revenues and required that the khan accept the terms of the Rasht and Ganja Treaties. Both the Russians in their appeal to the treaties and Agha Mohammad in his claims to Safavid restoration embraced the legitimacy of these agreements and the idea of a unified Iranian state. The Russian commitment to this concept was conditional and it was easily de-emphasized in dealings with Rasht, Quba or Astarabad. Agha Mohammad Khan could not compromise on the Safavid idea and consequently refused to allow settlement at Ashraf. When the fortification of Voïnovich's settlement appeared to threaten his sense of his own sovereign power, he ordered the arrest of the Russian officers and the destruction of their buildings. The Safavid dynastic appeal was inescapable in the southern and western Caspian; it resurfaced in times of conflict within the former Safavid lands and it imposed an idea of Iranian statehood that defined relations between the rulers of the northern coastal khanates and the Russian Empire. By the end of the century, it contributed to the Qajars' conflict with Russia over competing claims in Georgia.

Notes:

1. Research for this chapter was supported in part by the Title VIII Combined Research and Language Training Program, which is funded by the US State Department, Title VIII Program for Research and Training on Eastern Europe and Eurasia (Independent States of the Former Soviet Union) and administered by American Councils for International Education: ACTR/ACCELS. The opinions expressed herein are the author's own and do not necessarily represent the views of either the US Department of State or American Councils.
2. Throughout the eighteenth century (and until after the Bolshevik Revolution), the Russian state used the Julian calendar, which differed from the Gregorian, standard in Russia since the Bolshevik Revolution, by 11 days at the time of the Voĭnovich expedition.
3. Travelling for the Russian Academy of Sciences between 1770 and 1774, Königsburg-born botanist Samuel Gottlieb Gmelin called for the creation of a Russian monopolistic company to operate in Mazandaran, connecting routes into Iran, Central Asia and India. He favoured Mazandaran both as a location for these routes and for the area's potential to support a settlement with rice cultivation. While this region was suited to expanding trade and offered lower prices than neighbouring Gilan, Gmelin cautioned that the governor at the time, Mohammad Khan Savadkuhi, discouraged trade through monopolistic purchasing of goods; Samuel Gottlieb Gmelin, *Travels through Northern Persia*, pp. 240, 245.
4. Kh.A. Ataev, *Torgovo-èkonomicheskie svîazi Irana s Rossieĭ v XVIII – XIX vv.*, p. 369.
5. Capt. Karl von Gablits, *Istoricheskiĭ zhurnal"*, p. v.
6. For more detail on these early campaigns, see Gavin Hambly, 'Āghā Muḥammad Khān', pp. 114–20.
7. Mohammad Fathollāh b. Mohammad-Taqi Sāru'i, *Tārikh-e Mohammadi*, f. 72v.
8. RGVIA, f. 52, o. 1/194, d. 244, l. 46.
9. Ibid.
10. In this regard, the letter confirms the view, expressed by Muriel Atkin, *Russia and Iran*, p. 35, that Agha Mohammad negotiated with Russian officials as an equal, rather than a provincial governor with a subordinate status, from the beginning of his rule.
11. RGADA, f. 276, o. 1, d. 651, l. 3ob.
12. RGVIA, f. 52, o. 1/194, d. 244, ll. 28–30.
13. Ibid., l. 31; Lt. Rading, 'O proisshestviakh sluchivshikhsîa pri osnovaniĭ Russkago seleniîa', p. 40.
14. RGVIA, f. 52, o. 1/194, d. 244, l. 33.
15. Ibid.; for the status of all of Mazandaran as *khassa*, inherited from Shah 'Abbas' mother in the 1590s, see V. Minorksy, 'Commentary', in *Tadhkirat al-Mulūk*, p. 169.
16. For the impact of Russian victories in the Baltic on strategic thinking regarding Iran, see Oleg Nikonov, *Iran vo vneshnepoliticheskoĭ strategii Rossiĭskoĭ Imperii*, pp. 11–14, 37. For efforts to map Iranian and Central Asian geography and the strategic and military recommendations of Russian officials there, see P.P.

Bushev, *Posol'stvo Artemiîa Volynskogo v Iran*, pp. 9–11; I.V. Kurukin, *Persidskiĭ pokhod Petra Velikogo*, pp. 23–39.
17. *Dogovory Rossii s vostokom"*, ed. T. Îuzefovich, pp. 187–88.
18. Ibid., pp. 194–95.
19. Ibid., p. 196.
20. Ibid., pp. 197–200.
21. Ibid., pp. 202–7.
22. Nikonov, *Iran vo vneshnepoliticheskoĭ strategii*, p. 171.
23. *Dogovory*, pp. 197–99.
24. Fëdor Ivanovich Soĭmonov, *Opisanie Kaspiĭskago Morîa*, p. 50.
25. *Dogovory*, pp. 194–95.
26. Ibid., p. 206.
27. Ibid., pp. 206–7.
28. V.A. Ulîanitskiĭ, *Russkiîa konsul'stva za granitseîu*, vol. II, pp. CCCVI–CCCXII.
29. Ibid., p. CCCXXIII.
30. RGVIA, f. 52, o. 1/194, d. 135, ch. 2, ll. 35–45ob.
31. RGADA, f. 276, o. 1, d. 644, ll. 76–76ob.
32. *Dogovory*, pp. 201–2.
33. E.V. Safronova, *Stanovlenie i razvitie konsulskoĭ sluzhby*, pp. 177–78. V.O. Kulakov has shown the close coordination between the consuls in Gilan and the Governorate in Astrakhan on judicial matters, including the transfer of prisoners from the consulate to Astrakhan and referrals of civil cases to the city's authorities. See V.O. Kulakov, *Astrakhan' v persidskoĭ politike Rossii*, pp. 40–43.
34. RGADA, f. 276, o. 1, d. 652, l. 2ob.
35. PSZ, vol. 16, no. 11,630, pp. 35–36.
36. RGADA, f. 276, o. 1, d. 642, l. 1ob.
37. Ibid., l. 4ob.
38. 'Abbās-Qoli Āqā Bakikhanuf, *Golestān-e Eram*, pp. 186–87.
39. RGADA f. 276, o. 1, d. 641, ll. 6–6ob; for the responsibilities of the *eshik-aqasi-bashi*, see Roger M. Savory, 'Ešīk-āqāsī-bāšī', pp. 600–601.
40. Ibid., l. 8.
41. John R. Perry, *Karim Khan Zand*, pp. 212–13; Gholām Rezā Varahrām, *Tārikh-e siyāsi va ejtemā'i-ye Irān*, p. 92. Perry notes the failure of Zand efforts to establish bonds with the khans of the South Caucasus by marriage. By contrast, historians in the Soviet Union and independent Azerbaijan have regarded this period as one of fragmented, self-consciously Azerbaijani khanates. V.N. Leviatov, *Ocherki iz istorii Azerbaĭdzhana v XVIII veke*, viewed these khanates as divided by their feudal structures. This economic-political structure left them unable to defend themselves against expansionism from Iran and the Ottomans and led to unification with Russia, which could provide security. More recently, Huseyn Rahimli has argued that these khanates drew Russian, Iranian and Ottoman competition for resources and trade routes, but sought to maintain their status as independent Azerbaijani states, which Fath-'Ali Khan strove to unify. See Guseĭn Ragimli, *Azerbaĭdzhanskie khanstva v diplomaticheskikh otnosheniîakh*. These latter interpretations presume a national framework in a region that the Russian and Persian-language sources consistently call 'Shirvan' or 'Daghestan' (in the north), and part of Iran. The policies of Fath-'Ali Khan do offer significant

contrasts with the Zands and Qajars, but the evidence of a specifically 'national' concept is not evident in the sources.

42. Abu'l-Hasan Ghaffāri Kāshāni, *Golshan-e morād*, p. 610. This reference comes in the context of Fath-'Ali Khan organizing the restoration of Hedayatollah Khan to power in Gilan after his escape from the Qajars by sea with Russian assistance at Anzali.
43. Doc. No. 13, in G. B. Abdullaev, *Iz istorii severo-vostochnogo Azerbaĭdzhana*, p. 169.
44. John R. Perry, 'The last Safavids', p. 68.
45. RGADA, f. 23, o. 1, d. 13, ch. 3, l. 157ob.
46. Ibid., l. 342ob.
47. Sāru'i, *Tārikh-e Mohammadi*, fols. 211v–212r.
48. Mohammad Kāzem Marvi, *Nāma-ye 'ālam-ārā-ye Nāderi*, vol. II, l. 67.
49. Hambly, 'Āghā Muḥammad', pp. 110–11.
50. His role in service to Mir Sayyed Mohammad has been noted elsewhere. See Gholām Hoseyn Zargarinezhād, *Tārikh-e Irān dar dowra-ye Qājāriya*, p. 180. Zargarinezhad states that Mohammad Hasan Khan supported Ebrahim Shah Afshar in his war against 'Adel Shah and that he then joined the supporters of Mir Sayyed Mohammad. Some sources, such as Golestana's history, place Mohammad Hasan on the steppe among the Yomut at that time: Abu'l-Hasan b. Mohammad Amin Golestāna, *Mojmal al-tavārikh pas az Nāder*, pp. 349–50. However, the Mar'ashi sources themselves place him in Mashhad, alongside many figures who later appear as allies of Mohammad Hasan in Qajar chronicles.
51. Soltān Hāshem Mirzā Mar'ashi, *Zabur-e Āl-e Dāvud*, p. 104.
52. Ibid., pp. 104–6.
53. Ibid., p. 107.
54. Ibid., p. 108.
55. Sāru'i, *Tārikh-e Mohammadi*, f. 9v.
56. Gmelin, *Travels through Northern Persia*, p. 249.
57. Sāru'i, *Tārikh-e Mohammadi*, f. 11v.
58. For the striking of coins in the name of the Safavid claimant, see Priscilla Soucek, 'Coinage of the Qajars', p. 56; for Mohammad Hasan's residence at Ashraf, see Gmelin, *Travels through Northern Persia*, p. 249.
59. Mana Kia, *Persianate Selves*, pp. 147–52.
60. Muḥammad Qāżī Vafā' Karmīnagī, *Tuhfat al-Khānī*, p. 75.
61. Ibid., pp. 75–76.
62. Sāru'i, *Tārikh-e Mohammadi*, fols. 16r–16v.
63. Ibid., fols. 17r–17v.
64. Ibid., f. 17v.
65. Ibid., fols. 17v–18r.
66. RGVIA, f. 52, o. 1/194, d. 244, l. 33.
67. Ernest S. Tucker, *Nadir Shah's Quest for Legitimacy in Post-Safavid Iran*.
68. Sir John Malcolm, *The History of Persia*, vol. II, p. 194.

69. For example, Anzali and Rasht in Gilan, ruled by Hedayatollah Khan, had been the key nodes in Russo-Iranian trade over the Caspian for decades. I address the Russian relationship with Hedayatollah Khan in Gilan during this period, including his abandonment by consular officials during a Qajar invasion in 1786 and a subsequent investigation of his death in St Petersburg, in a forthcoming article in *Iranian Studies* (Kevin Gledhill, 'Betrayed into the hands of the enemy'). At the time of Voĭnovich's arrival, Agha Mohammad was still away from Astarabad on a campaign to the west in which he drove Hedayatollah Khan out of Rasht and to the protection of Fath-'Ali Khan of Quba. Agha Mohammad's army looted the palace at Rasht and Hedayatollah Khan returned by January 1782 after they had departed. The Qajar ruler moved to eliminate Anzali as an alternative to Mazandaran as a potential port. When Russian ships returned to rebuild the Mazandaran settlement in 1782 (despite the previous arrest of Voĭnovich and his officers), Agha Mohammad invested money in the project and demanded in return that Russian merchants cut off operations in other ports of the southern Caspian. He named Anzali, Baku, and Salyan specifically in his note to Captain Nikita Baskakov and called for the piers there to be destroyed. See: RGVIA, f. 52, o. 1/194, d. 288, l. 7.

Bibliography:

Abdullaev, G.B., *Iz istorii severo-vostochnogo Azerbaĭdzhana v 60 – 80-kh gg. XVIII v.* (Baku: Izdatel'stvo Akademii Nauk Azerbaĭdzhanskoĭ SSR, 1958).
Ataev, Kh.A., *Torgovo-èkonomicheskie svîazi Irana s Rossieĭ v XVIII – XIX vv.* (Moscow: Nauka, 1991).
Atkin Muriel, *Russia and Iran, 1780–1828* (Minneapolis: University of Minnesota Press, 1980).
Bakikhanuf, 'Abbās-Qoli Āqā, *Golestān-e Eram: tārikh-e Shirvān va Dāghestān az āghāz tā janghā-ye Irān va Rus*, ed. 'Abd al-Karim 'Alizadeh (Tehran: Qaqnus, 1383/2004).
Bushev, P.P., *Posol'stvo Artemiîa Volynskogo v Iran v 1715–1718 gg. (po russkim arkhivam)* (Moscow: Izdatel'stvo Nauka, Glavnaîa Redaktsiîa Vostochnoĭ Literatury, 1978).
Dogovory Rossii s vostokom", politicheskie i torgovye, ed. T. Îuzefovich (St Petersburg: Tipografiîa O.M. Bakhsta, 1869).
Ghaffāri Kāshāni, Abu'l-Hasan, *Golshan-e morād*, ed. Gholāmrezā Tabātabā'i Majd (Tehran: Enteshārāt-e zarrin, 1369/1990).
Gledhill, Kevin, "Betrayed into the hands of the enemy:' The 1795–96 Russian investigation of the death of Hedayat-Allah Khan of Gilan', *Iranian Studies*.
Gmelin, Samuel Gottlieb, *Travels through Northern Persia, 1770–1774*, trans. Willem Floor (Washington: Mage, 2007).
Golestāna, Abu'l-Hasan b. Mohammad Amin, *Mojmal al-tavārikh pas az Nāder*, ed. Mohammad-Taqi Modarres Razavi (Tehran: Chāpkhāna-ye sherkat-e tab'-e ketāb, 1320/1941).
Hambly, Gavin, 'Āghā Muḥammad Khān and the establishment of the Qājār dynasty', in *The Cambridge History of Iran, vol. 7, From Nadir Shah to the Islamic Republic*, ed. Peter Avery, Gavin Hambly and Charles Melville (Cambridge: Cambridge University Press, 1991), pp. 104–43.
Karmīnagī, Muḥammad Qāżī Vafā', *Tuḥfat al-Khānī yā tārīkh-i Muqīm Khānī*, ed. Mansur Sefatgol with the collaboration of Nobuaki Kondo (Fuchu, Tokyo: Research Institute for Languages and Cultures of Asia and Africa, 2015).
Kia, Mana, *Persianate Selves: Memories of Place and Origins before Nationalism* (Stanford: Stanford University Press, 2020).
Kulakov, V.O., *Astrakhan' v persidskoĭ politike Rossii v pervoĭ polovine XVIII v.* (Astrakhan: Astrakhanskiĭ Universitet, 2012).
Kurukin, I.V., *Persidskiĭ pokhod Petra Velikogo: Nizovoĭ Korpus na beregakh Kaspiîa (1722–1735)* (Moscow: Kvadriga, 2010).
Leviatov, V.N., *Ocherki iz istorii Azerbaĭdzhana v XVIII veke* (Baku: Izd. Akademii Nauk Azerbaĭdzhanskoĭ SSR, 1947).
Malcolm, Sir John, *The History of Persia*, vol. II (London: John Murray, 1829).

[Mar'ashi], Soltān Hāshem Mirzā, *Zabur-e Āl-e Dāvud: sharh-e ertebāt-e sādāt-e Mar'ashi bā salātin-e Safaviya*, ed. 'Abd al-Hoseyn Navā'i (Tehran: Mirās-e Maktub, 1379/2000).

Marvi, Mohammad Kāzem, *Nāma-ye 'ālam-ārā-ye Nāderi* (facsimile), vol. II (Moscow: Dānesh, 1960).

Minorsky, V., 'Commentary,' in *Tadhkirat al-Mulūk: A Manual of Ṣafavid Administration (circa 1725)*, ed. and trans. V. Minorsky (repr. Cambridge: Cambridge University Press, 1980).

Nikonov, Oleg A., *Iran vo vneshnepoliticheskoĭ strategii Rossiĭskoĭ Imperii v XVIII v.* (Vladimir: Izd. Vladimirskogo Universiteta, 2009).

Perry, John R., 'The last Safavids, 1722–1773', *Iran* 9 (1971), pp. 59–69.

— *Karim Khan Zand: A History of Iran, 1747–1779* (Chicago: University of Chicago Press, 1979).

Polnoe sobranie zakonov Rossiĭskoĭ Imperii (PSZ), vol. 16 (St Petersburg, 1830).

Rading, Lt., 'O proisshestviakh sluchivshikhsia pri osnovanii Russkago seleniia na beregu Astrabadskago zaliva v 1781 godu', in *Zhurnal" Ministerstva Vnutrennikh Del"*, ed. P.B. Butkov (St Petersburg, 1839).

Ragimli, Guseĭn, *Azerbaĭdzhanskie khanstva v diplomaticheskikh otnosheniĭakh Turtsii, Rossii i Irana (vtoraia polovina XVIII – nachalo XIX vekov* (Baku: IPO Turkhan, 2018).

Rossiĭskiĭ Gosudarstennyĭ Arkhiv Drevnikh Aktov (RGADA), f. 23, o. 1, d. 13, ch. 3.

— f. 276, o. 1, dd. 641, 642, 644, 651, 652.

Rossiĭskiĭ Gosudarstennyĭ Voenno-Istoricheskiĭ Arkhiv (RGVIA), f. 52, o. 1/194, d. 135, ch. 2; dd. 244, 288.

Safronova, E.V., *Stanovlenie i razvitie konsulskoĭ sluzhby Rossiĭskoĭ Imperii v XVIII – nachale XIX v.* (St Petersburg: Yuridicheskiĭ Tsentr Press, 2002).

Sāru'i, Mohammad Fathollāh b. Mohammad-Taqi, *Tārikh-e Mohammadi*, Add Ms. 27243, dated 1222/1807, British Library, London.

Savory, Roger M., 'Ešīk-āqāsī-bāšī', *Encyclopaedia Iranica*, vol. VIII, fasc. 6 (1998), pp. 600–601, online at https://iranicaonline.org/articles/esik-aqasi-basi [accessed 30 April 2021].

Soĭmonov, Fëdor Ivanovich, *Opisanie Kaspiĭskago Moria i chinenykh na onom rossiĭkikh zavoevanii* (St Petersburg: Imperatorskaya Akademiya Nauk, 1763).

Soucek, Priscilla, 'Coinage of the Qajars: A system in continual transition', *Iranian Studies* 34, no. 1–4, 'Qajar Art and Society' (2001), pp. 51–87.

Tucker, Ernest S., *Nadir Shah's Quest for Legitimacy in Post-Safavid Iran* (Gainesville: University Press of Florida, 2006).

Ulianitskiĭ, V.A., *Russkiia konsul'stva za granitseiu v XVIII veke*, vol. II (Moscow: Tip. G. Lissnera i A. Geshelia, 1899).

Varahrām, Gholām Rezā, *Tārikh-e siyāsi va 'ejtemā'i-ye Irān dar 'asr-e Zand* (Tehran: Mo'ayyin, 1385/2006).

[von Gablits, Capt. Karl], *Istoricheskiĭ zhurnal" byvshikh v 1781 i 1782 godakh na Kaspiĭskom more Rossiiskoĭ èskadry pod komandoîu flota kapitana vtorago ranga Grafa Voĭnovicha* (Moscow: Tipografiîa S. Selivanovskogo, 1809).

Zargarinezhād, Gholām Hoseyn, *Tārikh-e Irān dar dowra-ye Qājāriya, 'asr-e Āqā Mohammad Khān* (Tehran: Sazmān-e motāla'a va tadvin-e kotob 'olum-e ensāni-ye Dāneshgāh [Samt], Markaz-e tahqiq va tuse'a-e 'olum-e ensāni, 1395/2016).

4

Safavid Nostalgia in Early Qajar Chronicles

Assef Ashraf
(University of Cambridge)

The eighteenth century has long been viewed as a disruptive period in Iranian history. The collapse of the Safavid Empire in 1722; the Afghan occupation of Esfahan; the brief reigns of Nader Shah (r. 1736–47) and Karim Khan Zand (r. 1751–79); the rise of Agha Mohammad Khan in the 1780s – together, these episodes seem to present a picture of disintegration, discontinuity and disruption in the eighteenth century. Although both Nader Shah and Karim Khan attempted to establish dynasties that would outlast their own lifetimes, neither of them was successful. Upon their deaths, various claimants to the throne competed and fought with one another for political control. Meanwhile, war, famine and natural disasters took their toll on society, upending lives, creating economic hardship and leading some cities to be depopulated.[1] Any cursory reading of the sources from the period – whether in the form of chronicles, memoirs, travel accounts or literature – would provide plenty of support for the view that the eighteenth century was a turbulent time. It is no surprise, therefore, that the century has been characterized by scholars as a 'period of political contraction and economic decline', an 'interregnum' between the Safavid and Qajar eras, and a time of 'crisis' and 'collapse'.[2] The periods of rule by Nader Shah and Karim Khan – both the subject of some scholarship – have been described as 'islands' of stability amidst a 'morass of anarchy'.[3] Most recently, it has been argued that the eighteenth century marked the end of a long period in Iranian history, stretching back to the Mongol invasions of the thirteenth century, which may serve as a point of departure from which to mark the beginning of the 'modern' era of Iranian history.[4] The rise to power of the Qajars in the late eighteenth century, meanwhile, is perceived to have stabilized the situation, and drawn Iran's time of troubles to a close.[5]

But all was not lost in the eighteenth century. A closer reading of the sources reveals continuities running throughout the course of Iran's eighteenth century. The Safavid pretenders who made claims to the throne long after the fall of Esfahan in 1722, the survival of Safavid concepts and institutions and even the fact that Karim Khan preferred to take the title *vakil* (deputy or regent) rather than 'shah' all suggest that the memory of the Safavids persisted long after the collapse of the empire.[6] Much of early Qajar history is also difficult to understand without a basic familiarity with Safavid-era terminology, discourse and institutions.[7] Qajar-era administrative and governance practices, such as land assignment, gift giving and petitioning, had their roots in the Safavid era – and further back – and early nineteenth-century chronicles situated the Qajars within a long history and tradition of kingship in the Iranian and Islamic world. These facts, however, beg their own questions: how, exactly, did the memory of the Safavids survive? How did Persian-language historiography of the later eighteenth century and early nineteenth century depict the Safavids? Why did early Qajar chronicles depict the Qajars' relationship to the Safavids in the ways that they did?

One place to begin the story is with Agha Mohammad Khan's coronation. In March 1796, Agha Mohammad Khan, the founder of the Qajar dynasty, crowned himself shah. But his coronation had been a long time coming. Since 1779, when he fled Shiraz after the death of Karim Khan Zand, who had been holding him captive, Agha Mohammad Khan had carefully and painstakingly consolidated political power. Beginning first with his homeland of Mazandaran in northern Iran, he began a series of military campaigns aimed at conquering the various corners of what the sources called 'the Guarded Domains of Iran' (*mamalek-e mahrusa-ye Iran*), wresting control of provinces from the Zands and building alliances with tribal khans. By 1794, Agha Mohammad Khan had conquered the provinces of Fars and Kerman in central Iran and defeated his remaining Zand rival, Lotf-'Ali Khan. And yet, he did not declare himself shah at that point. He waited until he had also conquered Georgia and made headway in Khorasan, two provinces that had been part of the erstwhile Safavid Empire. Only when he had achieved those goals, did he crown himself with the so-called Kayanid crown in an elaborate coronation ceremony.[8]

That Agha Mohammad Khan only felt fit to take the title of shah in 1796, after he had conquered most of the former Safavid territories, suggests not only that the Safavid Empire remained vivid in the cultural memory, even seven decades after the empire's collapse, but also that associating himself with the Safavid rulers and the empire over which they ruled was a critical part of Agha Mohammad Khan's – and by extension, the Qajars' – political legitimacy. A number of scholars have illustrated the various ways that the institution of kingship to which the Qajars were heir had been shaped by centuries of Iranian, Islamic and Turko-Mongolian terms, concepts and ideas stretching back centuries.[9] Meanwhile, historians such as Ernest Tucker and Abbas Amanat have written on eighteenth- and nineteenth-century trends in Persian historiography, highlighting stylistic aspects, like an increase in decorative and ornamental writing in the immediate aftermath of the Safavid collapse, and Persian historiography's contribution to a 'proto-nationalist' discourse in Iran.[10] In recent years, attention has been turned to sources like travelogues and other commemorative texts, such as *tazkera*s, to try to determine how the collapse of the Safavid Empire may have shaped people's sense of identity, belonging and kinship with one another.[11] But the questions of how early Qajar chronicles and historiography remembered and depicted the Safavids, and what role the memory of the Safavids played in Qajar political culture and the construction of Qajar political authority have yet to receive any sustained attention.

The fundamental claim of this chapter is that the memory of the Safavids can be detected in early Qajar sources and was especially strong in early Qajar chronicles. Indeed, one could go even further and argue that early Qajar chronicles exhibited a sense of nostalgia for Safavid rule, a yearning for an imagined past during which justice and good governance prevailed and rightful kings reigned. The authors of these chronicles drew comparisons and made connections between Safavid and Qajar rule – sometimes in an explicit manner, other times more implicitly – in order to highlight the ways in which early Qajar monarchs, especially Fath-'Ali Shah (r. 1797–1834), differed from their Zand and Afsharid predecessors, and were heirs to a style of rule embodied by the Safavid monarchs. Shah 'Abbas (r. 1587–1629) was most often singled out as a particular paragon of ideal kingship. Of course, early Qajar chronicles compared Qajar shahs with rulers of earlier periods as well and, as far as the terminology and discourse of kingship under the Qajars was concerned, there was a rich and very long tradition beyond the Safavids on which the early Qajar chronicles drew. But the construction of Qajar legitimacy and political authority during the early nineteenth century relied, in part, on a claim articulated in the chronicles of the period that the Qajars had restored justice, balance, order and other characteristics associated with kingship and the rule of the Safavids – if not resurrected the Safavid Empire itself.

Early Qajar Chronicles

The sources referred to here as 'early Qajar chronicles' are those that were written during the reigns of Agha Mohammad Khan and Fath-'Ali Shah – that is between the years 1785 and 1834 – and focus primarily on the events related to the rise of the Qajars and the first few decades of their rule. Several histories, of varying length, focus and state of completion, were written under Agha Mohammad Khan and Fath-'Ali Shah, but six of the more important and comprehensive chronicles are, in order of completion date, *Tarikh-e Mohammadi* (also known as *Ahsan al-tavarikh*), *Mofarreh al-qolub, Ma'aser-e soltaniyya, Tarikh-e jahan-ara, Tarikh-e Saheb-Qerani* and *Tarikh-e Zu'l-Qarneyn*. Of these six, *Tarikh-e Mohammadi* was finished in the final year of Agha Mohammad Khan's reign, with a continuation related to events in 1212/1797–98 after his death; the other five were completed during the reign of Fath-'Ali Shah. *Mofarreh al-qolub* and *Tarikh-e jahan-ara* have not been published and are available solely in manuscript form, while the other four have been published.[12]

In their length, their level of detail, which events and individuals they focus on, and even their style of writing, the six chronicles exhibit a fair degree of variety. Saru'i's *Tarikh-e Mohammadi*, for instance, is relatively short and concise as far as historical detail is concerned but, on the other hand, is written in a difficult and abstruse style that bears some resemblance to the chronicles of the late Safavid and Afsharid periods. The chronicle's writing style may be explained by the fact that Saru'i had been a student of Mirza Mahdi Astarabadi, the court chronicler under Nader Shah, and therefore may have been influenced by a style of writing best exemplified by Astarabadi's *Dorra-ye Naderi* – a verse history, itself modelled on the highly ornamental fourteenth-century chronicle by Vassaf.[13] At the other end of the stylistic spectrum is *Tarikh-e Saheb-Qerani*, which is written in comparatively direct and straightforward language that is shorn of the ornate writing found in much eighteenth-century historiography. The other chronicles fall in the middle of the spectrum and help to illustrate the gradual evolution towards a simpler Persian prose style over the course of the nineteenth century.

In terms of their content also, the chronicles exhibit some variety. Mirza Fazlollah 'Khavari' Shirazi's *Tarikh-e Zu'l-Qarneyn* is the most comprehensive in its range and its detail. Khavari, who was the court chronicler (*vaqaye'-negar*) under Fath-'Ali Shah, wrote his history in an annalistic form that proceeds in a year-by-year format. Unlike the histories written by the other court chroniclers under Fath-'Ali Shah – Mirza Mohammad Reza Tabrizi's *Zinat al-tavarikh* and Mirza Mohammad Sadeq Marvazi's *Tarikh-e jahan-ara* – Khavari's history covers the totality of the early Qajar period. The published edition of the text is two volumes and over one thousand pages long. Although some have argued that 'Abd al-Razzaq 'Maftun' Donboli's *Ma'aser-e soltaniyya* is foremost among the chronicles of the Fath-'Ali Shah period – for its details on 'Abbas Mirza's modernizing efforts and for being among the earliest Persian books to be published by the printing press established in Tabriz in 1817 – in its scope and detail, *Tarikh-e Zu'l-Qarneyn* is arguably more important.[14]

Nevertheless, what unites these chronicles is their authors' positions, their relationship to the Qajars and the focus of the chronicles themselves. They were all written by court chroniclers, ministers or, in the case of *Tarikh-e Saheb-Qerani*, by a Qajar prince – Mahmud Mirza was the fifteenth son of Fath-'Ali Shah.[15] The chronicles therefore should be read as texts that articulated a vision and projected an image of the Qajar dynasty which the Qajars would have wanted to broadcast. They are, for the most part, sympathetic to, and indeed have a bias towards, the Qajars.

However, by selecting the early Qajar chronicles whose authors were patronized by the first two Qajar shahs, a substantial number of contemporaneous sources that offer different historical perspectives on the period, and even on the memory of the Safavids have been excluded. There are, for instance, histories and memoirs, like *Ruznama-ye Mirza Mohammad Kalantar-e Fars* and *Rostam al-tavarikh*, which have distinct authorial voices and often advance a particular interpretation of history, but which were written outside the context of the royal court. There are even late eighteenth-/early nineteenth-century histories, like *Majma' al-tavarikh*, *Fava'ed-e Safaviyya* and *Tazkera-ye Al-e Davud*, whose authors were descendants of the Safavid dynasty and which were openly pro-Safavid works that in some cases called for a Safavid restoration, but were written in South Asia, outside the context of Qajar Iran.[16] Conversely, there are anthologies of poetry and commemorative texts (*tazkera*), many of which were written in the court by the same authors of chronicles and which, by their very nature, were intended to 'remember' the past, but which primarily served literary and cultural, rather than political, purposes. Good examples of these sorts of sources from the early Qajar period are *Tazkera-ye Anjoman-e Khaqan*, *Tazkera-ye Khavari*, *Tazkera-ye Negarestan-e Dara* and *Safinat al-Mahmud*. All of these texts, while of immeasurable importance to both historians and literary scholars, should be distinguished from the kinds of sources represented by the court chronicles selected here, in that they do not, it would be safe to say, explicitly present an official 'Qajar' interpretation of history. Finally, there are a number of local and provincial histories that offer accounts of particular regions during the early nineteenth century, which have not been included because of their more narrow scope.[17]

One other point about the sources should be mentioned before proceeding. Chronicles obviously often tell us very little about knowledge, perceptions or attitudes beyond the royal court. The texts were written primarily for the shah, governors, princes or princesses, or other patrons in the court, and even those chronicles that were widely copied – as some of the early Qajar chronicles were – or those that were printed – such as, for example, *Ma'aser-e soltaniyya* – were not intended for a mass audience. Thus, the questions of how widespread the memory of the Safavids remained in the early nineteenth century or to what extent a nostalgia for the Safavids prevailed in society cannot be answered using chronicles. What the sources can tell us, however, is how and why the memory of the Safavids figured in the Qajars' vision of themselves.

Links to the Safavids

The effort by early Qajar chronicles to establish a link between the Qajars and the Safavids is evident in aspects of their structure and content. Most of the chronicles begin by recounting the exploits of Fath-'Ali Khan Qajar and Mohammad Hasan Khan Qajar, the grandfather and father, respectively, of Agha Mohammad Khan. Fath-'Ali Khan Qajar had served as a military commander during the final years of the Safavid Empire, and came to the aid of Shah Soltan-Hoseyn during the Afghan siege of Esfahan in 1722.[18] After the fall of Esfahan, he became one of the closest advisers to the young Safavid prince Tahmasp II, even earning for himself the title of Vakil al-Dowla.[19] He was eventually killed in 1726 as a result of increasing tension with his main rival, Tahmasp-Qoli, who would later become Nader Shah.[20] *Tarikh-e Mohammadi*, *Tarikh-e jahan-ara*, *Tarikh-e Zu'l-Qarneyn* and *Tarikh-e Saheb-Qerani* all narrate these events very early in their accounts. In fact, early Qajar chronicles provide little by way of a history of the Safavids themselves, or of the Safavid period, and instead place the history of the empire's collapse in the context of the rise of the Qajars. By beginning their accounts with the career of Fath-'Ali Khan, authors of early Qajar chronicles literally framed the late eighteenth-century rise of the Qajars as a story that had begun in the late Safavid period.

Alongside, and at times preceding, their accounts of Fath-'Ali Khan and Mohammad Hasan Khan's careers, early Qajar chronicles also explain the genealogy of the Qajars (*zekr-e nasab-e il-e jalil-e Qajar*) – complementing, in a sense, the distinction (*hasab*) of the Qajars in their service to the Safavids.[21] Saru'i's *Tarikh-e Mohammadi* only mentions in passing that the Qajars are descendants of the Turks, claiming that they are from Syria (*sham*), but other chronicles go into more, albeit conflicting, detail. All of the chronicles claim Turkic ancestry for the Qajars, although there is discrepancy between the accounts of what exactly that ancestry was, and who the Qajars were actually descended from. Some claimed that the Qajars were descended from a Turk by the name of Qajar Khan, who settled in Iran with Oghuz Khan. They later, it is said, joined the Aq Qoyunlu before eventually joining the Qezelbash confederacy under the Safavids.[22] During the reign of Shah 'Abbas, the Qajars' role expanded further, as they were appointed to important offices, including commanders-in-chief (*qurchibashi*) of the royal guards and governorships of Karabakh and Ganja.[23] Other sources elaborate on the early history of the Qajars and claim that Qajar Khan was a son of Sertaq b. Saba from the Jalayerid tribe.[24] Yet others wrote that the Qajars were descended from Japheth son of Noah, or from Oghuz Khan himself.[25]

The lack of consistency among the chronicles raises the question of just how important it was for both the chroniclers and their patrons to provide a historically accurate presentation of the Qajars' genealogy. At the very least, it reminds us that almost all genealogical claims in pre-modern chronicles served a political rather than a factual purpose. In the case of the Qajars, it may be, as Kondo has recently argued, that the Qajars simply did not rely on genealogy as a way of legitimizing their rule and saw 'no benefit in forging a legendary genealogy' – unlike earlier Central Asian rulers, or indeed even the Safavids.[26] On the other hand, however, there is a common theme in the genealogies of the Qajars: they almost always highlight the Qajars' service to the late Safavid rulers, and sometimes even in earlier periods of Safavid rule. In the words of Marvazi, the author of *Tarikh-e jahan-ara*:

> in the age of Shah 'Abbas – may God illumine his proof! – due to the necessities of good administration and by his powerful order (*beh eqteza'-ye tadbir va emza'-ye ahkam-e taqdir*) each of the branches of

this glorious tribe came to be appointed to political positions in one of the regions of Iran' (*soghur-e mamlekat-e Iran*).[27]

The high esteem in which early Qajar chronicles had held Shah 'Abbas – a theme to which this chapter will return – is also evident in Marvazi's use of the phrase of veneration and salutation following 'Abbas's name. He does not add a similar phrase when writing about other pre-Qajar shahs elsewhere in his chronicle.

But it is really in the chronicles' portrayal of the rise of Agha Mohammad Khan, his accession to the throne in 1796 and the beginning of Qajar rule in Iran that one can detect just how important the memory of the Safavids was to Qajar claims of legitimacy. The extended passage in *Tarikh-e Mohammadi* about the coronation ceremony of Agha Mohammad Khan, which was mentioned above, goes on for several pages in the published edition, and Saru'i describes in detail the Kayanid crown and the jewels worn by Agha Mohammad Khan, the gifts that were offered to him, the ulema and sayyeds who came to pay their respects to him, the prayer leaders who gave sermons in his honour, the drummers and musicians who played in celebration of him and the wine-bearers who held feasts for him, among other tributes. Agha Mohammad Khan himself went on pilgrimage to the shrine of Emam Reza in Mashhad, and then went out on a hunting expedition.[28] The tone and tenor of the passage is one of celebration – in honour of someone who was held to be a rightful ruler, and who was, therefore, deservedly fêted by his subjects.

The chronicles make a point of contrasting the Qajars with the Zands, Afsharids and Afghans who preceded them. The Afghans who besieged Esfahan are almost universally described as having brought about oppression and tyranny (*zolm*) and having caused the desolation of Iran (*virani-ye Iran*).[29] But even the successors of Nader Shah and Karim Khan Zand are the object of scorn in Qajar chronicles. Consider, for instance, how Mahmud Mirza, the author of *Tarikh-e Saheb-Qerani*, describes the circumstances in which Agha Mohammad Khan became shah:

> When the Jamshid-like shah [i.e. Agha Mohammad Khan], as a result of heavenly affirmations, divine prosperity, favoured fortune, came to be king (*malek*) over the kingdom (*molk*) of Iran – which was the realm of his forefathers – and had purified it [Iran] of the stains of the impure existence of the scions of Nader Shah Afshar and Karim Khan Zand, the country's leaders and governors, and its khans and army chiefs – near and far, obedient and rebellious – one and all, from Tbilisi to Khorasan, from Gorgan to the coasts of Oman, tied the band of obedience and placed their heads upon the neck of royal order.[30]

Agha Mohammad Khan's rise to power, aside from being presented as divinely ordained, is cast as a restorative event. He did not simply defeat his main Afshar and Zand rivals and conquer territory, he 'purified' (*pak kard*) Iran of the 'stains' (*lows*) that the Afshars and Zands represented and crowned himself shah over a dominion which was part of his heritage and, in a sense, belonged to him (*mowrus-e ajdad-e niyakan*). Agha Mohammad Khan – at least according to the chronicles themselves – restored Iran's political state of affairs to its proper and rightful order.

The idea that the Qajars not only defeated their rivals but righted the course of Iran's political destiny is a point to which the final portion of this passage – in which the geographic extent and reach of Qajar rule is briefly mentioned – alludes. The chronicle claims that Agha Mohammad Khan won the loyalty of provincial notables and tribal khans from west to east, from north to south, across the wide expanse of Iran. Whether all of the notables across such a vast region had *in reality* pledged their allegiance to Agha Mohammad Khan is not especially relevant; the point is that the chronicle *claims* that they did. Mahmud Mirza seems to be suggesting that Agha Mohammad Khan had finally reunited the far-flung regions of Iran under his command after a period of time during which rulers had been unable to do so.

Every Inch a King

A theme that emerges from the chronicles is of the contrast between Qajar rule and the Zands and Afsharids before them and, more specifically, a sense that the Qajars had restored justice, balance and order to Iran. This is a theme that chroniclers often did not make explicit, but which appears as a subtext in their chronicles. The praise that Marvazi offered Shah 'Abbas in the passage above is a clue. The Safavid ruler was admired and held in high esteem by the Qajars, and even served as a model to emulate. Chroniclers presented the Qajars as worthy inheritors of the mantle of kingship, and Fath-'Ali Shah was specifically singled out as a just, generous and merciful king in a succession of rightful monarchs – as the latest example of a ruler who was 'every inch a king'.

A critical element in depicting the Qajars as fitting holders of the throne was the sometimes lengthy sections in chronicles devoted to describing the virtues and attributes of Fath-'Ali Shah, emphasizing his kingly attributes.[31] 'Homa' Marvazi's *Tarikh-e jahan-ara*, for instance, has a long section that praises Fath-'Ali Shah and which has as its heading 'the commencement of the story is of the transfer of kingship to his honorable caliphate and a brief description of his outwardly and inner virtues (*mahsanat-e suri va ma'navi*) along with the kingly character (*akhlaq-e malekana*) of the world-conquering emperor'.[32] The section begins with Marvazi writing in praise of the shah's physical appearance including, in his words, his handsome face and figure (*hosn-e surat va khubi-ye shamayel*), before moving on to list and describe his attributes: his bravery, largesse, justice and fairness.[33]

Khavari's *Khatema-ye Ruznamcha-ye homayun*, however, which was written as an appendix to the chronicle *Tarikh-e Zu'l-Qarneyn* and which provides details on the shah's personal character and his household, devotes even more space to praising the shah's attributes. Khavari wrote the *Khatema* at the request of the shah but completed it after Fath-'Ali Shah's death.[34] It can therefore be read as a memorial for the shah, in which his portrayal as a fitting and rightful king was one of its central goals. In the edition published in 2001, Khavari's descriptions of the shah's virtues span 20 pages. In introducing the section, Khavari writes that the attributes he will describe are 'the necessities for the essence of kingship' (*az lavazem-e zat-e saltanat*).[35]

The *Khatema* itself is divided into three parts (*bab*) with the first part divided into two sections (*fasl*) and parts two and three into three sections each. The first bab is devoted to describing Fath-'Ali Shah's qualities, while the other two introduce the children, wives and grandchildren of the shah. It is unusual to find personal details about a shah, and at the level of detail found in Khavari's *Khatema*, in a court chronicle – certainly during the early Qajar period. The only other narrative source that compares to the *Khatema* in terms of the level of detail about the shah's personal life, his children and his grandchildren is the *Tarikh-e 'Azodi*, a memoir of life in the royal court written by Soltan-Ahmad Mirza 'Azod al-Dowla, the forty-ninth son of Fath-'Ali Shah.[36] Both Khavari's *Khatema* and 'Azod al-Dowla's memoir are themselves unusual in the Persian historiographical tradition for the amount of information they provide about the shah's children, which may be due to the simple fact that the shah had such a large number of offspring (over one hundred of whom survived infancy) but which may also reflect the importance that marriages, and the children who were born of them, had in early Qajar political life.

Like *Tarikh-e jahan-ara*, Khavari begins his *Khatema* by praising the shah's physical appearance. He gives thanks that the shah had been blessed with both inner attributes (*mahasen-e bateni*) and outer qualities (*hosn-e zaheri*). The shah's face radiated kindliness (*tal'atash mehri-ye foruzan*) and his figure was as graceful as a cypress tree (*qamatash sarvi kheraman*). Fath-'Ali Shah, Khavari says, looked the part of a king, such that even foreign dignitaries understood in whose presence they stood and would thus present him with gifts and tributes (*hadaya va tohaf*) on behalf of the world's kings.[37] Textual sources like the *Khatema* and *Tarikh-e jahan-ara*, that praise Fath-'Ali Shah's physique and describe it as one that is befitting a shah, offer an interesting complement to the visual sources we have, in the form of large portraits, of the shah's stature and physical appearance. Many of these portraits were themselves gifted to foreign kings and dignitaries.[38]

The bulk of the first bab in the *Khatema*, however, is devoted to describing the virtues that are essential, according to Khavari, for kingship and which Fath-'Ali Shah is said to have possessed. Eight 'pillars of kingship' are selected and presented at length: justice (*'edalat*); bravery (*shoja'at*); generosity (*sakhavat*); manliness (*moruvvat*); piety (*diyanat*); modesty (*'esmat*); mildness, diffidence and humility (*helm, haya'* and *tavazo'*); and loftiness, authority and governance (*jalalat, satvat* and *siyasat*).[39] For each of these kingly virtues,

Khavari briefly explains the meaning of the terms before providing anecdotes or episodes from Fath-'Ali Shah's reign that illustrate each quality. In the entry on bravery, for instance, he describes the shah's courage and leadership in battle.[40] In the section on generosity, Khavari explains that Fath-'Ali Shah was known to give salaries to soldiers from the royal treasury (*khazane-ye 'amera*) and, in those instances when service went beyond expectations (*khedmat-e taza*), he would bestow land grants in the form of perpetual *toyul*, in addition to their salaries. During the Russo-Persian wars, the shah sent 200,000 *toman*s each year, according to Khavari, in the form of gold coins to offset the costs of the soldiers in Azerbaijan.[41] These kinds of descriptions can be read as a court historian extolling his patron in the ways one would expect, and certainly should not be read as evidence for Fath-'Ali Shah's true character or even as reflecting reality. Nevertheless, the fact that Khavari devoted so much space to praising the shah, and that he did it as an appendix to his chronicle, long after the shah had died, tells us something about the chronicle's effort to present Fath-'Ali Shah as a worthy – and legitimate – king.

A clue to why Khavari wrote the *Khatema* in the way that he did, and what its intended purpose was, may be provided by comparing it with a similar text from the Safavid era: Eskandar Beg Monshi's *Tarikh-e 'alam-ara-ye 'Abbasi*. Like Khavari's chronicle, Eskandar Beg's history of Shah 'Abbas's reign is one of the few chronicles to include separate and extended sections in praise of the shah's attributes. In the case of *Tarikh-e 'alam-ara*, Eskandar Beg divides the first volume of his chronicle into 12 discourses (*maqala*), the first of which focuses on the genealogy and rise to power of the Safavids – by far the longest of the 12 discourses and comprising nearly the entire first volume. The remaining 11 discourses then describe – like Khavari's text – the qualities and virtues of the shah. Eskandar Beg chooses to highlight Shah 'Abbas's piety, judgement, good fortune, justice, authority and autocratic behaviour (*nafad-e amr-e qahhari*), policy-making and administration, the simplicity of his lifestyle, his concerns for the rights of his servants, knowledge of world affairs, public works and battles and victories.[42]

Khavari's and Eskandar Beg's texts do differ in their respective depictions of Fath-'Ali Shah and Shah 'Abbas. The qualities chosen by Khavari generally overlap with those that Eskandar Beg chose, but there are fewer in Khavari's list, there are some slight differences in the qualities, and the order they are placed in also differs. Eskandar Beg, for example, begins his discourses with Shah 'Abbas's piety (*esteghraq beh dargah-e elahi*, a different terminology from Khavari), unlike Khavari who begins with justice (which is the subject of the fifth discourse in Eskandar Beg's text). The discourse on piety begins by emphasizing Shah 'Abbas's ancestors as having been sayyeds – making the shah related to the house of the Prophet Mohammad – and other men of spiritual authority. The most excellent gifts (*mavaheb-e 'ozma*) of the shah's spiritual forefathers, including their ability to perform miracles (*khavareq-e* '*adat*) were, according to Eskandar Beg, passed down to the shah himself. Khavari makes no such assertion about Fath-'Ali Shah, a reflection of the fact that the Qajars did not claim – as did the Safavids – to be descended from the Prophet, but also perhaps an indication that the idea of a 'sacred king' who was blessed with supernatural powers – so prevalent in the narratives of political authority in the sixteenth and seventeenth centuries – had waned by the early nineteenth century.[43]

Although the descriptions written by Khavari and Eskandar Beg are not identical, their overall similarities are striking. While some of the terms differ, both Fath-'Ali Shah and Shah 'Abbas are praised for their justice, their piety, their policies and administration and their authority. Some of the apparent differences in terminology in fact mask commonalities. Khavari, for instance, does not include the construction of public works (*asar-e kheyr va ensha' va ehdas-e 'emarat*) as a separate 'pillar of kingship' to define Fath-'Ali Shah – as Eskandar Beg does – but he does devote space to describing this facet of Fath-'Ali Shah's character. In the section on justice, Khavari writes:

> To demonstrate this commendable attribute [i.e. justice] there are a number of convincing proofs at hand ... Among these irrefutable proofs is the building and cultivation (*abadi va ma'muri*) of Iran's boundaries (*marz-e Iran*). A just king develops [his kingdom] and a tyrant destroys it. Iran was in disrepair (*virani*) from the days of Afghan rebellion until the end of Zand rule – like an owl's nest. During the few years of his reign, Agha Mohammad Shah – may God illumine his proofs! – did not exhibit much interest in repairing Iran ... but then [during Fath-'Ali Shah's reign] destroyed villages were built into small towns (*qasabat*) and ruined small towns (*qasabat-e virana*) also developed beyond well-known cities. Iran's population returned to such a state that people moved out of the confines of cities and built homes in the mountains and plains. Foreign tradesmen, craftsmen and merchants (*ghoraba'-ye ahl-e herfat va san'at va tejarat*) from surrounding countries came and settled in Iran.[44]

Even if one accepts that Khavari may have been painting a rosier picture than reality, the point still stands that Fath-'Ali Shah was being portrayed as a king who, like Shah 'Abbas, built and repaired his kingdom.[45] Although no explicit comparison is made between Fath-'Ali Shah and Shah 'Abbas, by writing that Iran fell into a state of disrepair from the time of the Afghan invasion onwards, Khavari is implicitly tying Qajar rule back to the Safavid period. In addition, by comparing Fath-'Ali Shah to Agha Mohammad Khan, Khavari is also carefully distinguishing the former as standing out even among the Qajars.

The contrast that Khavari makes between Fath-'Ali Shah's reign, on the one hand, and the Afghans, Afsharids, Zands – and even Agha Mohammad Khan – on the other, brings to the fore a recurring theme in these sources: that the

Qajars restored a balance to Iran's political order that had last been seen under the Safavids. It is worth mentioning that none of the Zand chronicles have sections that are analogous to the *Khatema* or to the discourses in *Tarikh-e 'alam-ara-ye 'Abbasi*, and even those Afsharid chronicles that portray Nader Shah as Iran's saviour after the collapse of the Safavid Empire tend to emphasize his conquests and military campaigns rather than his kingly virtues.[46]

In the Persian tradition of advice literature and political ethics, the idea that balance and order are brought about in the world as a result of a rightful and just ruler is most famously presented in the form of the so-called 'circle of justice'. The origins of the idea can be traced back to ancient Mesopotamia, but its most well-known formulation is attributed to the Sasanian ruler Ardashir, who is reported to have said that 'There is no kingdom without an army, no army without wealth, no wealth without prosperity, and no prosperity without justice'.[47] Various iterations of the maxim appear in political ethical literature over the centuries, but it was used in the early Qajar period specifically to portray the Qajars as having restored balance to Iran's political affairs. A notable example is found in Mohammad 'Nadim' Barforushi's *Mofarreh al-qolub*, which is a moral work – rather than a traditional chronicle – that describes the moral virtues that everyone, but especially kings, should cultivate. The treatise is divided into five parts (*bab*), each divided into two sections (*fasl*), and a lengthy appendix (*khatema*). The appendix, which takes up more than half the text, is an account of the reigns of Agha Mohammad Khan and the first few years of Fath-'Ali Shah to 1220/1805–6.[48]

The virtues that Barforushi chooses to focus on include employing correct etiquette in speaking (*adad-e sokhan*), modesty (*haya'*), mildness (*helm*), intelligence (*zaka'*), bravery (*shoja'at*) and humility (*forutani*) – similar to the qualities found in Khavari's *Khatema*. Finally, in a noteworthy passage, Barforushi writes that the order of the world and of the kingdom (*nezam-e 'alam va entezam-e mamlekat*) are contingent on justice (*'edalat*), and that injustice (*zolm*) leads to the destruction of the realm (*enhedam-e mamlekat*).[49] He goes on to describe Fath-'Ali Shah as having restored order, before finally writing that, as he appointed his sons to provincial governorships, he urged them to uphold justice in the respective provinces over which they would rule. The shah then quoted for his sons, according to Barforushi, a variation of the adage attributed to Ardashir, who is himself held up as a role model of the ideal king in the *Shahnama*: 'there is no kingdom without men, and no men without wealth, and no wealth without prosperity, and no prosperity without justice and punishment'.[50] Fath-'Ali Shah is presented as a latter-day Ardashir, offering wise counsel to his sons as they take their posts.

An Empire restored

This sense of a return to order pervades the sources, especially those from the reign of Fath-'Ali Shah, who is often depicted as a just and fitting king. One might wonder: what does that have to do with the Safavids? How was this idea of order being restored linked to the Safavids specifically? Although there were plenty of ways in which the Qajars were implicitly linked back to the Safavids, as the above discussion has demonstrated, Khavari's *Tarikh-e Zu'l-Qarneyn* offers one of the more explicit connections. Towards the beginning of the chronicle, Khavari describes all of the various provinces and regions – from the Caucasus, to Khorasan, to Fars – that comprise the 'Guarded Domains' of Iran. He describes their geographical features, their agricultural production and their economies. The point here is subtle but still clear: these are all regions that make up Iranian lands, and any ruler who claims to rule Iran should rule over all of these regions. Then, in case the subtext proved too subtle to make the point, Khavari proceeds a short while later to compare and contrast the Safavids, Afsharids, Zands and Qajars. He writes that Shah Tahmasp (r. 1524–76) and Shah 'Abbas used force (*zarb-e shamshir*) and governance (*tadbir*) to expand the Safavid Empire's borders, and then continues:

> But then during the time of the Afghan conquests, it was all lost. Nader Shah accomplished courageous acts but he did not have the acumen to ensure his longevity (*az ru-ye ferasat nabud keh davami dashta bashad*), while the Zands lost due to their ineptitude (*bi 'orzegi*). When it became this glorious dynasty's turn to rule (*nowbat-e dara'i keh beh in selsela-ye jalila resid*) – despite the conquests made by the Ottomans, Russians, Afghans and Ozbeks – kingly deeds, which shall be recorded in this book, were restored within Iran's boundaries (*baz kar-ha-ye molukana dar hodud-e Iran shod*).[51]

This praise for the Qajars, and the harsh words for Nader Shah and especially the Zands, can be explained by the fact that a Qajar shah was Khavari's patron, and should be read with some scepticism. But Khavari's passage provides a few crucial clues to how the Qajars articulated their legitimacy. First, the Qajars are legitimate because they reunited all of the territories and kingdoms of the 'Guarded Domains' of Iran. Second, like the Safavids, they did 'kingly deeds' (*kar-ha-ye molukana*). And, finally, those king-like or regal accomplishments included 'conquest' but, perhaps more importantly, they also included 'governance', political acumen and political skill.

The link that Khavari draws between the Qajars and the Safavids is one of the clearest and most explicit examples of an early Qajar chronicle articulating the claim that the Qajars were not only heirs to the style of rule embodied by the Safavids, but in fact had restored what had been lost with the Safavids' collapse. If one were to look beyond the claims put forward in the chronicles, however, one would find additional ways in which the Qajars sought to present themselves as heirs to the Safavids. The administrative offices created by Agha Mohammad Khan and Fath-'Ali Shah resembled those that existed under the late Safavids. Offices such as prime minister (*sadr-e a'zam*), imperial treasurer (*mostowfi al-mamalek*) and imperial secretary (*monshi al-mamalek*) were re-established under the Qajars, and although these offices also existed under their Zand and Afsharid predecessors, by the end of Fath-'Ali Shah's reign the administrative chancery (*divan*) was the largest it had been since the Safavid era.[52] In some cases, the individuals who held those offices could even trace their family's service back to the Safavid period. A noteworthy example was the Farahani family, whose prominence in the early Qajar court rivalled even that of the prime minister, who were close advisers to Fath-'Ali Shah and the crown prince 'Abbas Mirza, and who were given the title of Qa'em-Maqam. Ancestors of Mirza 'Isa, the first Qa'em-Maqam under the Qajars, had served successive shahs and, by the late Safavid period, were the 'keepers of the seal' of the Safavids. There were, of course, other families who served in political and administrative positions under the Qajars whose ancestors had not served the Safavids, but being able to claim a long heritage of administrative service added to the prestige of individuals. As 'Maftun' Donboli put it when writing about the Farahani family: 'the majority of his [Mirza Abu'l-Hasan 'Isa] ancestors, ancestor after ancestor, grandee after grandee, served in the ministries of illustrious sultans'.[53]

In their patronage of the arts and architecture, the early Qajars, and especially Fath-'Ali Shah, also took up the Safavid mantle. The level and extent of construction and renovation projects during the early Qajar period arguably matched the Safavids' achievements. Fath-'Ali Shah constructed, renovated or reconstructed more buildings than any ruler since Shah 'Abbas, including extensions to the Golestan Palace in Tehran, major works to city walls, to religious shrines in Mashhad and Qom, and other projects in cities across Iran.[54] The enormous wall paintings that lined the Negarestan palace walls, depicting Fath-'Ali Shah seated on the throne in the centre, surrounded by princes, tribal khans and foreign dignitaries; the massive rock reliefs that were constructed in Firuzkuh, Rayy and Shiraz – the first such reliefs since the Sasanian period; and lavish court ceremonies and rituals, like the annual Nowruz processions that were revived under Fath-'Ali Shah, together give one an idea of the scope and imperial pretensions of the early Qajar court.[55] Many of these practices and ceremonies were not unique to the Qajars or to the Safavids, and indeed in the realm of public ceremonial spaces there were significant differences between the Qajars and the Safavids. As Sussan Babaie has shown, the principal spaces for public performances of kingship under the Qajars compare poorly with those of the Safavids, and it is really in the sphere of private and leisure palaces that a fruitful comparison between the Qajars and Safavids can be made.[56] Nevertheless, the royal and courtly ceremonies under the Qajars do seem to suggest a conscious effort to present themselves as worthy of the throne and as imperial rulers comparable with other dynasties in Iran's past – including the Safavids. John Malcolm, the first European emissary to travel to Iran after the collapse of the Safavid Empire, remarked upon visiting the court of Fath-'Ali Shah that 'on extraordinary occasions nothing can exceed the splendour of the Persian court. It presents a scene of the greatest magnificence, regulated by the most disciplined order'.[57]

It would be a mistake to think that early Qajar chronicles placed the Qajars in a tradition of royal authority and rule that was exclusively associated with the Safavids, or even that it was *only* the memory of the Safavids which was retained in the chronicles. There are numerous examples of how the chronicles placed the Qajars within a much longer historical tradition, stretching back beyond the Safavids to the Ilkhanate and even to pre-Islamic Iranian dynasties. The Kayanid crown with which Agha Mohammad Khan crowned himself shah in 1796, in both the textual and the visual sources, and some of the titles that Qajar shahs used for themselves – such as *khaqan* and *saheb-qeran* – are potent reminders of the ways in which much older and deeper traditions were used for the purposes of legitimizing Qajar rule. The authors of chronicles themselves wrote about how they were continuing in the tradition of Persian historical writing exemplified by earlier historians like Vassaf, Yazdi, Idris Bedlisi and Astarabadi. An over-emphasis on the memory of Safavid rule in the Qajar period might lead one to overlook other historical connections. It is not *only* in early Qajar chronicles that one can detect a sense of nostalgia for the Safavids. Nevertheless, the memory of the Safavids does pervade the early Qajar chronicles. And while it might be expected to find that theme running through Qajar historiography, it is worth considering *how* that theme appears in the chronicles. Given the context in which the Qajars rose to power in the late eighteenth century, and both the basis of and the limits to their claims to royal authority, greater attention to this theme would surely serve to shed further light on how the Qajars consolidated their power and political authority.

Notes:

1. For one eyewitness account, see Mirzā Mohammad Kalāntar-e Fārs, *Ruznāma-ye Mirzā Mohammad Kalāntar-e Fārs*.
2. Ann K.S. Lambton, 'The tribal resurgence and the decline of the bureaucracy', p. 108; see also Michael Axworthy, *Crisis, Collapse, Militarism and Civil War*.
3. John R. Perry, 'The last Safavids', p. 59. Studies of Nader Shah and Karim Khan include, in addition to a number of journal articles and the essays in *The Cambridge History of Iran*, vol. 7 and *Encyclopaedia Iranica*, amongst others, a few monographs: Laurence Lockhart, *Nadir Shah*; Michael Axworthy, *Sword of Persia*; Ernest S. Tucker, *Nadir Shah's Quest for Legitimacy*; John R. Perry, *Karim Khan Zand*.
4. Gene R. Garthwaite, '"What's in a name?"'.
5. On the rise of the Qajars being a 'watershed' moment, see Ann K.S. Lambton, 'Persian trade under the early Qajars', p. 110.
6. On Karim Khan and the title of *vakil*, see John R. Perry, 'The Vakil Al-Raʻaya'.
7. On the survival of Safavid concepts, see Perry, 'The last Safavids', p. 59.
8. Abbas Amanat, 'The Kayanid crown and Qajar reclaiming of royal authority'.
9. Ann K.S. Lambton, 'The Qājār dynasty'; Gavin Hambly, 'Āghā Muḥammad Khān and the establishment of the Qājār dynasty'; idem, 'Iran during the reigns of Fatḥ ʻAlī Shāh and Muḥammad Shāh'; S.A. Arjomand, *The Shadow of God and the Hidden Imam*; Abbas Amanat, *Pivot of the Universe*; Nobuaki Kondo, 'How to found a new dynasty'.
10. Ernest Tucker, 'Persian historiography in the eighteenth and early nineteenth centuries', pp. 258–91; Abbas Amanat, 'Legend, legitimacy and making a national narrative', pp. 292–366.
11. Mana Kia, *Persianate selves*.
12. I have used the British Library's copy of Barforushi's *Mofarreh al-qolub* in this essay. For more on this source, completed in or around 1220/1805–6, see Ann K.S. Lambton, 'Some new trends in Islamic political thought', pp. 95–128; Charles Rieu, *Supplement to the Catalogue of the Persian Manuscripts*, pp. 251–52. Manuscript copies of *Tārikh-e jahān-ārā*, completed in or around 1233/1817–18, exist in the Majles Library (Tehran), the Khuda Bakhsh Oriental Public Library (Patna), the British Library (London), the Library of the Royal Asiatic Society (London) and the National Library of Russia (Saint Petersburg). I have used the Majles Library's copy, which is complete, in this chapter. References for the chronicles used are listed in the bibliography. I have omitted from this chapter Sāruʼi's *Tārikh-e Fath-ʻAli Shāh-e Qājār*, which was left unfinished and has large gaps in its account; Cholavi Māzandarāni's *Tārikh-e Molk-ārā*, the only manuscript of which is defective and only goes up to 1794–95; and al-Sabalāni's *Tārikh-e Āl-e Qājār*, which stops at 1805. For more on these and other early Qajar chronicles, see C.A. Storey, *Persian Literature*, vol. I, pp. 332–38. I have also omitted Mohammad Reza 'Banda' Tabrizi's *Zinat al-tavārikh*, a universal history which, in its final part, covers the Qajar era up to 1221/1806–7. On this source, see Storey, *Persian Literature*, vol. I, p. 147.

13. On Saru'i's relationship with Astarabadi, see *Tārikh-e Mohammadi*, p. 13. For more on Vassaf, Astarabadi and Saru'i, and their stylistic similarities, see Charles Melville, 'The historian at work'; idem, 'The Mongol and Timurid periods'; Tucker, 'Persian historiography'.
14. On *Ma'āser-e soltāniyya* being the foremost early Qajar chronicle, see Amanat, 'Legend, legitimacy and making a national narrative', p. 298.
15. For more on Mahmud Mirza, see Dominic P. Brookshaw, 'Maḥmud Mīrzā''.
16. These sources are briefly discussed in Tucker, 'Persian historiography', pp. 269–70. All three of these texts have now been published. There is also an unpublished and untitled history of Iran from the death of Shah Soltan-Hoseyn to the death of Karim Khan Zand, written by a Razi al-Din Tafreshi, held in the British Library. On this source, see Charles Rieu, *Catalogue of the Persian Manuscripts in the British Museum*, vol. II, pp. 798–99.
17. Examples include Mohammad Taqi Nuri, *Ashraf al-tavārikh* (Tehran, 2008); Nāder Mirzā, *Tārikh va joghrāfi-ye Dār al-Saltana-ye Tabriz* (Tabriz, 1994); and Hasan Fasā'i, *Fārsnāma-ye Nāseri* (Tehran, 1988).
18. Mohammad Sadeq Marvazi, *Tārikh-e jahān-ārā*, fol. 11v.
19. Hambly, 'Āghā Muḥammad Khān', pp. 107–8.
20. For more on Fath-'Ali Khan Qajar, see 'Abd al-Hoseyn Navā'i, 'Fatḥ-'Alī Khān Qājār'.
21. See, for instance, Marvazi, *Tārikh-e jahān-ārā*, fol. 10r. On *hasab* and *nasab* defining a man's worth, see Roy Mottahedeh, *Loyalty and Leadership in an Early Islamic Society*, pp. 98–104.
22. Mahmud Mirzā Qājār, *Tārikh-e Sāheb-Qerāni*, pp. 3–4; Marvazi, *Tārikh-e jahān-ārā*, fol. 10r–v.
23. Marvazi, *Tārikh-e jahān-ārā*, fol. 11r–v.
24. Lambton, 'The Qājār dynasty', p. 1. Lambton is quoting *Tārikh-e rowzat al-safā-ye Nāseri*, the chronicle written under Naser al-Din Shah (r. 1848–96) as an addendum to Mirkhvānd's chronicle *Tārikh-e rowzat al-safā* – another, albeit later, example of the Qajars' efforts to establish a historical link with the Safavids. On Mirkhvānd's chronicle, see Sholeh Quinn, *Historical Writing During the Reign of Shah 'Abbas*, pp. 39–42.
25. Kondo, 'How to found a new dynasty', p. 278.
26. Ibid., p. 280.
27. Marvazi, *Tārikh-e jahān-ārā*, fol. 11v.
28. Sāru'i, *Tārikh-e Mohammadi*, pp. 283–86.
29. See, for example, ibid., pp. 29–30.
30. Mahmud Mirzā, *Tārikh-e Sāheb-Qerāni*, p. 82.
31. On 'kingly virtues' in Persian chronicles, see Sholeh Quinn, *Persian Historiography across Empires*, pp. 155–201.
32. Marvazi, *Tārikh-e jahān-ārā*, fol. 222r.
33. Ibid., fols. 223r–225v.
34. Storey, *Persian Literature*, vol. I, p. 337.
35. Mirzā Fazlollāh Khāvari, *Tārikh-e Zu'l-Qarneyn*, vol. II, p. 951.
36. Soltān-Ahmad Mirzā, *Tārikh-e 'Azodi*; trans. Manoutchehr M. Eskandari as *Life at the Court of the Early Qajar Shahs*.
37. Khāvari, *Tārikh-e Zu'l-Qarneyn*, vol. II, pp. 949–50.

38. See Julian Raby, *Qajar Portraits*; Layla Diba and Maryam Ekhtiar, eds, *Royal Persian Paintings*.
39. Khāvari, *Tārikh-e Zu'l-Qarneyn*, vol. II, pp. 951–68.
40. Ibid., vol. II, pp. 952–53.
41. Ibid., vol. II, pp. 953–54.
42. Eskandar Beg Monshi, *Tārikh-e 'ālam-ārā-ye 'Abbāsi*, vol. II, pp. 1099–1116. The translation of these terms is from Roger Savory, *The History of Shah 'Abbas the Great*, vol. I, pp. 515–44.
43. On 'sacred kingship' in the sixteenth and seventeenth centuries, see A. Azfar Moin, *The Millennial Sovereign*.
44. Khāvari, *Tārikh-e Zu'l-Qarneyn*, vol. II, p. 951.
45. On economic recuperation under the early Qajars, see Charles Issawi, *The Economic History of Iran*; Lambton, 'Persian trade under the early Qajars'.
46. On Nader Shah being portrayed as Iran's saviour, see Peter Avery, 'Nādir Shāh and the Afsharid legacy', p. 11.
47. See Ann K.S. Lambton, 'Justice in the medieval Persian theory of kingship', p. 100; Linda Darling, *A History of Social Justice and Political Power in the Middle East*.
48. See Lambton, 'Some new trends'; Rieu, *Supplement*, pp. 251–52.
49. Mohammad Barforushi, *Mofarreh al-qolub*, fol. 199a.
50. Barforushi, *Mofarreh al-qolub*, fol. 208a. On Ardashir, see Nasrin Askari, *The Medieval Reception of the* Shāhnāma.
51. Khāvari, *Tārikh-e Zu'l-Qarneyn*, vol. I, p. 18.
52. For a comparison with the Zand chancery, see Perry, *Karīm Khān Zand*, pp. 217–18. On the development of the early Qajar administrative structure, see Colin Meredith, 'Early Qajar administration'; Vanessa Martin, 'An evaluation of reform'.
53. 'Abd al-Razzāq Donboli, *Tazkera-ye Negārestān-e Dārā*, p. 145.
54. Jennifer Scarce, 'The arts of the eighteenth to twentieth centuries'; eadem, 'The architecture and decoration of the Gulistan Palace'; Yahyā Zokā', *Tārikhcha-ye sākhtemān-hā-ye Arg-e Saltanati-ye Tehrān*.
55. On early Qajar painting, see Layla Diba, 'Images of power and the power of images'; on Qajar rock reliefs, see Paul J.P. Luft, 'The Qajar rock reliefs'.
56. Sussan Babaie, 'In the eye of the storm'.
57. Sir John Malcolm, *History of Persia*, vol. II, p. 555.

Bibliography:

Primary Sources

'Azod al-Dowla, Soltān-Ahmad Mirzā Qājār, *Tārikh-e 'Azodi*, ed. 'Abd al-Hoseyn Navā'i (Tehran: 'Elm, 1376/1997); trans. Manoutchehr M. Eskandari as *Life at the Court of the Early Qajar Shahs* (Washington, DC: Mage Publishers, 2014).

Barforushi, Mohammad 'Nadim', *Mofarreh al-qolub*, ca. 1220/1805, Ms. Or. 3499, British Library, London.

Donboli, 'Abd al-Razzāq Beg 'Maftun', *Ma'āser-e soltāniyya*, ed. Mohammad Bāqer Tabrizi (Tabriz: Dar al-Entebā'-e Dār al-Saltana, 1241/1826).

— *Tazkera-ye Negārestān-e Dārā*, ed. 'Abd al-Rasul Khayyāmpur (Tabriz: Ketābforushi-ye Tehrān, 1342/1963).

Eskandar Beg Monshi Torkamān, *Tārikh-e 'ālam-ārā-ye 'Abbāsi*, ed. Iraj Afshār, 2 vols (Tehran: Amir Kabir, 1350/1971); trans. Roger M. Savory as *The History of Shah 'Abbas the Great*, 2 vols (Boulder, CO: Westview Press, 1978).

Kalāntar-e Fārs, Mirzā Mohammad, *Ruznāma-ye Mirzā Mohammad Kalāntar-e Fārs*, ed. 'Abbās Eqbāl (Tehran: Sherkat-e sehāmi, 1325/1946).

'Khāvari' Shirāzi, Mirzā Fazlollāh, *Tārikh-e Zu'l-Qarneyn*, ed. Nasir Afshārfar, 2 vols (Tehran: Ketābkhāna, muza va markaz-e asnād-e majles-e shurā-ye eslāmi, 1380/2001).

Mahmud Mirzā Qājār, *Tārikh-e Sāheb-Qerāni: Havādes-e tārikh-e selsela-ye Qājār (1190– 1248 A.H.)*, ed. Nādera Jalāli (Tehran: Majles, 1389/2010).

Malcolm, Sir John, *The History of Persia from the Most Early Period to the Present Time*, 2 vols (London: John Murray, 1815).

Marvazi, Mohammad Sādeq 'Homā', *Tārikh-e jāhān-ārā*, n.d. Ms. 8623, Majles Library, Tehran.

Sāru'i, Mohammad, *Tārikh-e Mohammadi: Ahsan al-tavārikh*, ed. Gholāmrezā Tabātabā'i Majd (Tehran: Mo'assasa-ye enteshārāt-e Amir Kabir, 1371/1992).

Secondary Sources

Amanat, Abbas, *Pivot of the Universe: Nasir al-Din Shah Qajar and the Iranian Monarchy, 1831–1896* (Berkeley and Los Angeles: University of California Press, 1997).

— 'The Kayanid crown and Qajar reclaiming of royal authority', *Iranian Studies* 34, no. 1–4 (2001), pp. 17–30.

— 'Legend, legitimacy and making a national narrative in the historiography of Qajar Iran (1785–1925)', in *A History of Persian Literature, volume X, Persian Historiography*, ed. Charles Melville (London: I.B. Tauris, 2012), pp. 292–366.

Arjomand, S.A., *The Shadow of God and the Hidden Imam* (Chicago: Chicago University Press, 1984).

Askari, Nasrin, *The Medieval Reception of the* Shāhnāma *as a Mirror for Princes* (Leiden: Brill, 2016).

Avery, Peter, 'Nādir Shāh and the Afsharid Legacy', in *The Cambridge History of Iran, vol. 7, From Nadir Shah to the Islamic Republic*, ed. Peter Avery, Gavin Hambly and Charles Melville (Cambridge: Cambridge University Press, 1991), pp. 3–62.

Axworthy, Michael, *Sword of Persia: Nader Shah, from Tribal Warrior to Conquering Tyrant* (London: I.B. Tauris, 2006).

— ed., *Crisis, Collapse, Militarism and Civil War: The History and Historiography of 18th Century Iran* (New York: Oxford University Press, 2018).

Babaie, Sussan, 'In the eye of the storm: Visualizing the Qajar axis of kingship', *Artibus Asiae* 66, no. 2 (2006), pp. 35–54.

Brookshaw, Dominic Parviz, 'Maḥmud Mīrzā', *Encyclopaedia Iranica*, online edition (2006) at https://iranicaonline.org/articles/mahmud-mirza [accessed 13 April 2021].

Darling, Linda T., *A History of Social Justice and Political Power in the Middle East: The Circle of Justice from Mesopotamia to Globalization* (New York: Routledge, 2013).

Diba, Layla S., 'Images of power and the power of images: Intention and response in early Qajar painting (1785–1834)', in *Royal Persian Paintings: The Qajar Epoch, 1785–1925*, ed. Layla S. Diba and Maryam Ekhtiar (London: I.B. Tauris and Brooklyn: Brooklyn Museum of Art, 1998), pp. 30–49.

Diba, Layla S. and Maryam Ekhtiar, eds, *Royal Persian Paintings: The Qajar Epoch, 1785–1925* (London: I.B. Tauris and Brooklyn: Brooklyn Museum of Art, 1998).

Garthwaite, Gene R., '"What's in a name?" Periodization and "18th-century Iran"', in *Crisis, Collapse, Militarism and Civil War: The History and Historiography of 18th Century Iran*, ed. Michael Axworthy (New York: Oxford University Press, 2018), pp. 9–19.

Hambly, Gavin, 'Āghā Muḥammad Khān and the establishment of the Qājār dynasty', in *The Cambridge History of Iran, vol. 7, From Nadir Shah to the Islamic Republic*, ed. Peter Avery, Gavin Hambly and Charles Melville (Cambridge: Cambridge University Press, 1991), pp. 104–43.

— 'Iran during the reigns of Fatḥ 'Alī Shāh and Muḥammad Shāh', in *The Cambridge History of Iran, vol. 7, From Nadir Shah to the Islamic Republic*, ed. Peter Avery, Gavin Hambly and Charles Melville (Cambridge: Cambridge University Press, 1991), pp. 144–73.

Issawi, Charles P., *The Economic History of Iran, 1800–1914* (Chicago: University of Chicago Press, 1971).

Kia, Mana, *Persianate Selves: Memories of Place and Origin before Nationalism* (Stanford, CA: Stanford University Press, 2020).

Kondo, Nobuaki, 'How to found a new dynasty: The early Qajars' quest for legitimacy', *Journal of Persianate Studies* 12, no. 2 (2019), pp. 261–87.

Lambton, Ann K.S., 'Justice in the medieval Persian theory of kingship', *Studia Islamica* 17 (1962), pp. 91–119.

— 'Some new trends in Islamic political thought in late 18th and early 19th century Persia', *Studia Islamica* 39 (1974), pp. 95–128.

— 'The tribal resurgence and the decline of the bureaucracy in the eighteenth century', in *Studies in Eighteenth Century Islamic History*, ed. Thomas Naff and Roger Owen (Carbondale: Southern Illinois University Press, 1977), pp. 108–29.

— 'Persian trade under the early Qajars', in *Qājār Persia: Eleven Studies* (Austin: University of Texas Press, 1987), pp. 108–39.

— 'The Qājār dynasty', in *Qājār Persia: Eleven Studies* (Austin: University of Texas Press, 1987), pp. 1–32.

Lockhart, Laurence, *Nadir Shah: A Critical Study based mainly upon Contemporary Sources* (London: Luzac & Co., 1938).

Luft, J.P., 'The Qajar rock reliefs', *Iranian Studies* 34, no. 1–4 (2001), pp. 31–49.

Martin, Vanessa, 'An evaluation of reform and development of the state in the early Qājār period', *Die Welt des Islams* 36, no. 1 (March 1996), pp. 1–24.

Melville, Charles, 'The historian at work', in *A History of Persian Literature, vol. X, Persian Historiography*, ed. Charles Melville (London: I.B. Tauris, 2012), pp. 56–100.

— 'The Mongol and Timurid periods, 1250–1500', in *A History of Persian Literature, vol. X, Persian Historiography*, ed. Charles Melville (London: I.B. Tauris, 2012), pp. 155–208.

Meredith, Colin, 'Early Qajar administration: An analysis of its development and functions', *Iranian Studies* 4, no. 2–3 (Spring–Summer 1971), pp. 59–84.

Moin, A. Azfar, *The Millennial Sovereign: Sacred Kingship and Sainthood in Islam* (New York: Columbia University Press, 2012).

Mottahedeh, Roy, *Loyalty and Leadership in an Early Islamic Society* (Princeton: Princeton University Press, 1980).

Navā'i, 'Abd al-Hoseyn, 'Fath-'Alī Khān Qājār', *Encyclopaedia Iranica*, vol. IX, fasc. 4 (1999), pp. 406–7, online at https://www.iranicaonline.org/articles/fath-ali-khan-qajar [accessed 13 April 2021].

Perry, John R., 'The last Safavids, 1722–1773', *Iran* 9 (1971), pp. 59–69.

— *Karim Khāan Zand: A History of Iran, 1747–1779* (Chicago: University of Chicago Press, 1979).

— 'The Vakil Al-Ra'aya: A pre-modern Iranian Ombudsman', in *Iran Und Iranisch geprägte Kulturen: Studien zum 65. Geburtstag von Bert G. Fragner* [Iran and Iraniate cultures: Studies for Bert G. Fragner on his 65th birthday], ed. M. Ritter, R. Kauz and B. Hoffmann (Wiesbaden: Dr Ludwig Reichert Verlag, 2008), pp. 41–50.

Quinn, Sholeh A., *Historical Writing during the Reign of Shah 'Abbas: Ideology, Imitation and Legitimacy in Safavid Chronicles* (Salt Lake City: University of Utah Press, 2000).

— *Persian Historiography across Empires* (Cambridge: Cambridge University Press, 2020).

Raby, Julian, *Qajar Portraits* (New York: I.B. Tauris, 1999).

Rieu, Charles, *Catalogue of the Persian Manuscripts in the British Museum*, 3 vols (London: British Museum, 1876).

— *Supplement to the Catalogue of the Persian Manuscripts in the British Museum* (London: British Museum, 1895).

Scarce, Jennifer M., 'The arts of the eighteenth to twentieth centuries', in *The Cambridge History of Iran, vol. 7, From Nadir Shah to the Islamic Republic*, ed. Peter Avery, Gavin Hambly and Charles Melville (Cambridge: Cambridge University Press, 1991), pp. 890–958.

— 'The architecture and decoration of the Gulistan Palace: The aims and achievements of Fath 'Ali Shah (1797–1834) and Nasir al-Din Shah (1848–1896)', *Iranian Studies* 34, no. 1–4 (2001), pp. 103–16.

Storey, C.A., *Persian Literature: A Bio-bibliographical Survey*, 2 vols (London: Luzac & Co., 1927).

Tucker, Ernest S., *Nadir Shah's Quest for Legitimacy in Post-Safavid Iran* (Gainesville: University Press of Florida, 2006).

— 'Persian historiography in the eighteenth and early nineteenth centuries', in *A History of Persian Literature, vol. X, Persian Historiography*, ed. Charles Melville (London: I.B. Tauris, 2012), pp. 258–91.

Zokā, Yahyā, *Tārikhcha-ye sākhteman-hā-ye Arg-e Saltanati-ye Tehrān* (Tehran: Anjoman-e āsār-e melli, 1349/1970).

5

From the Chehel Sotun to the 'Emarat-e Divani of Qom: The Evolution of Royal Wall Painting during the Reign of Fath-'Ali Shah

Kianoosh Motaghedi
(Independent Researcher in Islamic Art, Tehran)

The eighteenth century in Iran was a period of strife and confusion; from a historical perspective, Iran underwent drastic changes in its cultural and socio-political environment leading into the nineteenth century.[1] Nevertheless, the power of artistic patronage under the Qajar dynasty (1785–1925) in directing artists and thus in shaping the history of art in this era cannot be overlooked, making it one of Iran's most remarkable periods of artistic history in the field of painting.

The most prominent feature of eighteenth-century Persian painting is the decline of book illustration. In its place, artists devoted their talents to large-scale oil paintings and, increasingly, to the decoration of small objects of lacquered papier mâché or wood.[2] Wall painting formed an important means for displaying royal themes and monumental works in the eighteenth century. There were many murals adorning palaces and buildings of that period, the majority of which have been destroyed; however, some descriptions, pictures and even a few restored buildings are available for observation and study. Subsequent Qajar wall painting could be regarded also as the transmission of an even earlier Safavid era tradition, which manifested itself in scenes of hunting, feasts and battle, most notably at the Chehel Sotun Palace in Esfahan.

As an artistic medium, the seventeenth-century deployment of murals in Esfahan marks a turning point. There, the murals were enjoyed by a royal elite in the seclusion of their palaces and pavilions inside the walled boundaries of the imperial domain. However, the evidence also suggests an unprecedented preponderance of mural decoration in urban and vernacular spaces that is also notably figural and narrative instead of floral and calligraphic, which is often the preferred mode of public representational displays in cities in the lands of Islam.[3]

Such a time-honoured tradition was carried over into subsequent eras, i.e. under the Afsharid and Zand dynasties, taking on a more narrative function for the impressive display of the ruler's authority shortly thereafter. While Zand art may be seen as a local school in Shiraz, Qajar art, due to the many regional palaces of the Qajar princelings decorated with paintings, had a national reach. This achievement was a consequence of the Qajars' political inclinations. In the early Qajar period, the active patronage of Fath-'Ali Shah was central to the establishment of new artistic styles and methods.[4] Aware of the need to legitimize Qajar rule in Iran and impress on the populace the magnificence and authority of the monarchy, Fath-'Ali Shah developed a sophisticated system of court etiquette and ceremonial protocols.[5]

Historical Perspective of Wall Painting in Iran

Before delving into the main subject of this chapter, I would like to mention some aspects of the history of wall painting and its evolution up to the eighteenth century. This topic has a long history, dating back to the pre-Islamic period in Iran.

Wall paintings in Kuh-e Khvaja, Sistan (dating from the third–fourth centuries AD) and Panjikent, modern Tajikistan (from the seventh century), are among the special cases that survive in eastern Iran from the pre-Islamic era. Furthermore, a similar artistic procedure was adopted to decorate palaces and monuments in Mesopotamia (Samarra and Baghdad), which was under the influence of the Byzantine and Hellenistic traditions.

The tradition of wall painting underwent a revival during the Islamic period from the Seljuq era onwards. Examples of this could be seen in the murals of Sultan Mahmud Ghaznavi's palace in Lashkari Bazar. Thereafter, the decoration of Timurid and Safavid palaces and buildings provided an opportunity for the formation of a new artistic genre through the beautification of the interiors of royal buildings and the houses of the elite.[6]

Safavid wall painting consisted of images of groups in feasts, battles and hunts, as well as European scenes and royal portraits. The adoption of Esfahan as the capital of the Safavids undoubtedly created the opportunity for the development of a wall painting tradition that had already been established in Qazvin. In this context, and as a result of the style of palace building developed by Shah 'Abbas and his successors in Esfahan, as well as their patronage of the arts, the tradition of wall painting evolved dramatically.

The reign of 'Abbas I (r. 1587–1629) marks the beginning of a sustained interaction between pre-modern Iran and seventeenth-century Europe. The artistic outcome of this moment of encounter, when the two parts of the globe still met as equals, can be seen in some paintings. That exchange on an equal footing, however, was temporary. The conflicts that Iran experienced following the fall of the Safavids until the arrival of the Qajars tipped the scales in favour of the West.[7]

According to Sussan Babaie, the location and themes of the wall paintings at the Chehel Sotun Palace were governed by a deliberate scheme, whereby the events documented included the relations between the Safavid court and its eastern neighbours, royal feasts and literary themes of romance. Wall paintings constitute the most important part of the palace's decorative programme. Thematically, the narrative paintings at the Chehel Sotun Palace can be divided into four broad categories. Prominent among these are historical scenes and the portraits of kings. The Safavid painter chose a specific ceremonial format as a more effective visual means to deliver a political message.[8]

The wall painting tradition in Esfahan was not restricted to royal palaces, but rather propagated in the public sphere in the houses of Esfahan's residents, especially those of the aristocrats and the Armenians. An example of this expansion into a wider arena could be seen in the wall paintings of the portal of the new imperial market, the Qeysariya bazaar, which was built off the north end of the Meydan-e Shah and connected to the existing bazaars behind the square. In these murals, we can see battle and hunting scenes of the shah as well as feasts, banquets and drinking in the European style.[9] The packed gathering of European revellers in the large panel on the east flank of the portal fits into a kind of conceptual space, where the image distils aspects of Persian views on European ways of being and doing.[10] The same theme reappears about 200 years later during the reign of Fath-'Ali Shah Qajar in the wall paintings decorating the *Naqqash khana* room at Golestan Palace, Tehran (Figure 1).[11]

Fig. 1. Painting in the Naqqash khana *room in Golestan Palace, Tehran, ca. 1810, oil on canvas, in the European style (author's own photograph).*

After the fall of the Safavids in 1722, Shah 'Abbas's legendary status was enhanced by virtue of comparison with what followed. For most of the rest of the eighteenth century, the lives of many Iranians were blighted by insecurity, economic depression and violence, with the possible exception of the reign of Karim Khan Zand in Shiraz (r. 1750–79).[12] Initially, the dominant figure was Nader Shah (r. 1736–47), who chose for his base and construction of monuments the mountain stronghold of Kalat-e Naderi, located in a fertile region in northern Khorasan. Despite extensive field research and study of the historical sources of that period, I could find evidence of few figurative murals from the time of Nader Shah and, unfortunately, our knowledge of the art of his time is limited. Today, a record of Kalat and its buildings remains from the Naser al-Din Shah period (late nineteenth century), from which we can obtain detailed information about the buildings and gates at that time.[13]

According to historical records, most of the time Nader lived in camps (*ordu*), of which no traces remain. Leaving aside Kalat-e Naderi, we should note that Nader was not a great builder of palaces. Those structures he had built in Kalat-e Naderi that were made of wood have been entirely lost; hence, we cannot know how they were decorated. One famous building of Nader Shah's time of which a record survives,[14] however, is the so-called Qurchi Palace, part of a large complex that has been demolished with no trace remaining in situ. The main monument still in existence there is the Khorshid Palace, generally considered to be Nader's tomb, or possibly his treasury, partly built and decorated by Indian workers, where today there are a few traces of figurative wall paintings.[15]

One outstanding example here is the seated portrait of a person, probably Nader Shah, painted in natural colours on plaster in a niche in the main hall.[16] Apart from this, the only ornaments dating from that period are some vegetal motifs, besides the *gol-o-morq* (bird and flower) designs in the Indian style that are painted on the walls of this palace. It should also be noted that some of these ornaments were added to the monument after Nader Shah's death.

Otherwise, Nader Shah's victory over the Mughals at Karnal in India in 1739 was made the subject of a huge fresco in the Chehel Sotun pavilion at Esfahan, and when Charles Texier, the French archaeologist and traveller (1802–71) was in Iran, in around 1840, he was informed that it was the work of the painter Aqa Sadeq.[17]

In contrast to Nader Shah, Karim Khan, who preferred the title *vakil* (regent) to that of shah, did not demand that his painters beautify his appearance, even in monumental canvases.[18] He was happy to be shown at an informal and unpretentious gathering, in a modest architectural setting. According to historical evidence, during this period Shiraz was the birthplace of a style that would flourish some 50 years later under the reign of Fath-'Ali Shah. The best examples of this style in its early stages are probably the murals in the Pars Museum and the Haft-Tanan Mansion. Most of the Zand buildings during the reign of Karim Khan were decorated with murals. In the Pars Museum we can see an oil painting of Karim Khan's audience hall (Figure 2).

Fig. 2. Karim Khan Zand amidst his close circle, Zand era, attributed to Ja'far, oil on canvas, in the Pars Museum, Shiraz (author's own photograph).

This monumental portrait of Karim Khan Zand and his kinsmen is an official image of the ruler.[19] It looks decidedly less formal than the large single figure portraits of Fath-'Ali Shah from the early Qajar period and does not follow the principle of showing king or ruler in the splendour of his court. The informal and modest tone of most of the paintings that depict Karim Khan thus contrasts sharply with the later vainglorious images of Fath-'Ali Shah and his court.[20] Layla Diba notes that the figures in this painting are melancholy and the tone sombre, suggesting that it might have been a posthumous portrait of the ruler, who died in 1779, painted for his kinsmen.[21]

We can infer from the study of murals in the Zand era that the tradition of royal wall painting on plaster, in which the king was portrayed in the centre of the composition, reappeared in a new form and function on the wall paintings of Zand buildings in Shiraz.

Wall Painting in the Reign of Agha Mohammad Khan (1785–97)

Interestingly, when the Qajars came to power, they deliberately sought to portray themselves as revivers of the Safavid state and pre-Islamic dynasties, because they knew how much this idea resonated with the Iranian people.[22] Consequently, Agha Mohammad Khan appropriated both the monuments and the visual language of Safavid power. With the rise of the Qajar dynasty, Tehran was chosen as the new capital of Iran (in 1786) and fundamental changes were made to its urban structure, involving the construction of a number of buildings and monuments.

A close examination of Qajar royal paintings demonstrates that they were political both in essence and in their themes. Although Tehran was chosen as the capital by Agha Mohammad Khan, he returned to his birthplace, Astarabad, to build his ceremonial palace and audience hall. According to historical documents, the murals in the palace at Sari consisted of a collection of paintings which took as their subject the battles and victories of Iran's most important warriors of the last 300 years, i.e., Shah Esma'il Safavi and Nader Shah.[23] The buildings at Sari and Astarabad also contain traces of two other subjects, feasting and fighting, which were influential in the formation of early Qajar wall painting during Agha Mohammad's reign. His commissioning of such paintings was simply the continuation of the wall painting tradition and homage to traditional ornamentation in the Safavid palaces, such as the Chehel Sotun. To date, we still cannot identify any murals with Agha Mohammad Khan's portrait on the walls of the Astarabad buildings. However, only two decades later, under the patronage of the second Qajar monarch Fath-'Ali Shah, this practice took a different turn.[24]

The first manifestation of this new focus was a wall painting by 'Abdollah Khan[25] in the Soleymaniya Palace,[26] Karaj, portraying Agha Mohammad Khan beside his brothers and kinsmen in an idealized manner. Interestingly, in the painting of Agha Mohammad we can see the Peacock throne (*Takht-e tavus*), on which the king is seated in the usual pose holding a sword and covered in jewellery. But we know that this throne was built after Agha Mohammad's time, during the reign of Fath-'Ali Shah. Incorporating such an element could be considered an interesting innovation on the part of the court painter, 'Abdollah Khan, intended to heighten, retrospectively, the majesty of Fath-'Ali Shah's predecessor and the founder of the dynasty.

Development of Wall Painting in the Reign of Fath-'Ali Shah (1797–1834)

Fath-'Ali Shah, Agha Mohammad Khan's nephew and the governor of Fars, came to power on his uncle's death. He was born in Damghan in 1771. In 1798, the coronation of Fath-'Ali Shah took place in Tehran, the recently established capital of the Qajars. He constructed an imperial image to rival that of the most illustrious rulers of Iran. This period could be regarded as the heyday of royal portraiture in the art history of Iran.

At that time, Fath-'Ali Shah was confronting both domestic and foreign threats. Locally, he felt the need to legitimize and consolidate his power, gain the support of the ulema (religious authorities) and enhance the grandeur of his monarchy. On the international front, the shah's aim was to bolster foreign alliances and counter border attacks. The Russians had been gaining much territory, annexing Armenia and northern Azerbaijan as well as the territories north of the Aras River.

During the early decades of the nineteenth century, Iran was involved in the inconclusive first Perso-Russian War (1805–13) and the ultimately disastrous second Perso-Russian war (1826–28). Nevertheless, occasions for elaborate ceremonials were devised, from New Year *salam*s to public levees, diplomatic receptions and poetic gatherings. The court was the perfect setting for displays of pageantry and loyalty. It was also a period of consolidation of royal power characterized by a massive building programme and the creation of a powerful dynastic image. Lavish decorative cycles of the ruler and his sons played a critical role in the construction of this image, and were displayed in the numerous palaces, pavilions and gardens of the ruler and his many sons and prince-governors.[27]

From an historical perspective, during this period Persian art, and in particular court painting, underwent a significant evolution, as did the tradition of creating rock reliefs and architecture under the shah's supervision. As a great patron of Shi'i religious officials, Fath-'Ali Shah began a programme of construction of new religious buildings (mosques and schools) and the restoration of other similar places in imitation of the Safavids. At the same time, he made himself into a patriotic personality cult figure by displaying an inclination towards the pre-Islamic history of Iran and other ancestral themes.

It seems that Fath-'Ali Shah's personal taste and his understanding of the arts led to the realization of the significance of image production. In this period, images of the shah were manifested in different art media, from coins and miniatures to rock reliefs. When he began his rule, Fath-'Ali Shah viewed himself as the rightful heir to the tradition of Persian kingship rooted in the past.[28] In contrast to Karim Khan, who modestly called himself *vakil al-ro'aya* (Regent for the subjects), Fath-'Ali Shah styled himself *shahanshah* (the King of kings). He was known for his lavish court, his strict etiquette and bejewelled kingly appearance. In Tehran, Fath-'Ali Shah enlarged the Golestan Palace and decorated it with paintings and figurative tiled wall revetments reflecting court life.

Evidence of both construction and iconography inspired by Iran's pre-Islamic heritage can be traced in the architecture and decoration of the period of his reign and gradually became a strong socio-cultural and artistic movement, which lasted until the end of the Pahlavi period.[29]

The three prominent painters of this period, Mirza Baba, Mehr 'Ali and 'Abdollah Khan, were actually discovered by Fath-'Ali Shah and through his patronage a new trend was established in Persian art. These three artists were the pillars of this new artistic movement. Mirza Baba is considered to be the first artist to paint a portrait of Fath 'Ali Shah, and he may have been the designer of the 'Allah-o-Akbar' Mountain rock relief outside Shiraz as well.

Mirza Baba's works evince the modelling and soft facial effects of his Zand school origins and, after him, Mehr 'Ali specialized in iconic portrayals of the ruler, distinguished by their elongated proportions and stylized – almost delicate – facial features, with eyebrows that appear to be delineated with kohl, and masterfully rendered jewels. Layla Diba comments that through the constant ordering and displaying of his portrait, his court and accoutrements in paintings, particularly in murals, Fath-'Ali Shah Qajar sought to consolidate his power and monarchy.[30]

Such a royal figure demanded an appropriate setting, and apart from an extensive programme of palace building, Fath-'Ali Shah commissioned several new or refashioned thrones, notably the *Takht-e tavus* (Peacock throne, originally known as the *Takht-e khorshid*, Sun throne),[31] *Takht-e Naderi* and *Takht-e marmar* (Marble throne).[32] He also commissioned not only a new crown but an array of regalia.[33]

His aim to promote his royal status is clearly manifested in various murals, records of which can be traced from different sources, in buildings such as the Negarestan Palace, Khorshid Mansion, 'Eshrat-ayin, Behesht-ayin and Soleymaniya Palace.

His most impressive achievement in the early years of his rule was arguably the striking of a balance between two ideas: ancestral themes (or primitivism) and the support of Shi'i ideology. Achieving this equilibrium allowed him to gain the approval of the religious authorities by restoring and constructing religious buildings, while continuing his ambitious projects to construct glorious royal palaces in the form of terrestrial paradises. His commitment to his vision of royal grandeur resulted in the significant advancement of both wall painting and rock reliefs.[34] Under Fath-'Ali Shah a series of rock reliefs was carved around the capital Tehran and in the provinces, in clear imitation of those of the pre-Islamic Parthian and Sasanian Empires.[35]

As we know, the idea of portraying royal receptions and enthronements with courtiers and distinguished guests standing humbly in rows dates back to ancient times. Such a theme can be seen in the Achaemenid and Sasanian reliefs,[36] in which the king is located at the centre of the work looking at the viewer, flanked by courtiers and servants (Figure 3).

Fath-'Ali Shah was a remarkable figure, who well understood the importance of an impressive appearance. Among the overwhelmed European visitors to his court at Tehran was the traveller and artist, Sir Robert Ker Porter (1777–1842),[37] whose description in 1818 corresponds to a portrait of the shah by Mehr 'Ali, one of his principal painters. He is shown as a slim, elegant figure dressed in a gold silk brocade robe and wearing a gem-encrusted crown, belt, sword, arm and wrist bands, all from the collections of the crown jewels.[38]

In a seated portrait of Fath-'Ali Shah painted by Mehr 'Ali in 1804,[39] the Achaemenid aesthetic, especially that of the reliefs in Persepolis, is evident. Here the shah is depicted with a long beard on a bejeweled throne, wearing the

Fig.3. Pre-Islamic stone reliefs: Achaemenid, Parthian and Sasanian, Fars province, Iran (author's own photograph).

imperial crown on his head.[40] He has the *Taj-e mah* (Crown of the Moon) and *Darya-ye nur* (Sea of light) jewels on his arms and a golden mace in his right hand, symbolizing kingly authority (Plate III)*. In its form and composition, this painting resembles the Darius relief on the eastern staircase of the Apadana Palace in Persepolis.[41] In this relief, the Achaemenid king Darius is depicted sitting in profile on the royal throne, holding his royal mace in one hand and a lotus flower in the other. He is also wearing a crown and has a long beard, all of which seems to have been adopted by the Qajar painter, Mehr 'Ali, in his work. This tradition of kingly portrayal continued right into the Islamic period in other artistic media, such as illustrated manuscripts and stucco carvings. An example of the latter can be seen in a stuccowork relief of the Seljuq ruler, Toghrel Beg, discovered in Rayy, which is now preserved in the Museum of Philadelphia.[42]

The creation of royal portraits by Mehr 'Ali and Mirza Baba in the first decade of Fath-'Ali Shah's reign developed into a new genre of Persian painting. The styles, poses and scenic elements remained relatively unchanged for about three decades. Such paintings on canvas were mainly promotional in nature and were presented to other rulers as a means of conveying the glory and authority of the Persian monarchs.

While Mehr 'Ali's standing portrait of Fath-'Ali Shah conforms to the new standards of nineteenth-century painting, it is 'Abdollah Khan who should be regarded as the pioneer of this aesthetic in royal portraiture. 'Abdollah had risen through the ranks of the court workshop system, sharing the honours with Mirza Baba and Mehr 'Ali, all of whom were celebrated for their portraits of the ruler that were sent abroad as diplomatic gifts. Although all three artists worked in both small format and monumental paintings, only one single signed work by 'Abdollah still exists, dated 1807, comparable in quality and sensitivity with the magnificent portrayals of Fath-'Ali Shah by the other two artists.[43]

Besides these works, a series of wall paintings were also commissioned for palace interiors. There is considerable evidence that images of the ruler, in myriad forms, sizes and media, played an integral role in the nineteenth-century exercise of power, both at home and abroad.[44] It was during this period that the need to create a larger and more impressive image of the king was felt, hence the evolution of wall painting into a new and different art medium.

'Abdollah Khan was looking for new media into which he could extend his artistic patterns and standards. Besides being chief painter, he was also regarded as the chief carver and architect. This provided him with new opportunities to experiment on a large scale with new expressions in his paintings and reliefs of the shah. His work was actually to harmonize different visual elements with the architectural space. In royal residences, paintings functioned as units of a rich array of decorative programmes. Battle and hunting scenes rank among the common themes in the wall paintings of such places. Despite having been destroyed, today we still have some information about the murals in the Golestan Palace, Tehran. Many buildings of this palace were ruined during the era of Naser al-Din Shah,[45] and later in the Pahlavi period. Fortunately, some of the paintings have survived on linen canvases dating back to Fath-'Ali Shah's period, such as an equestrian portrait of the young shah at the conquest of Ganja, Azerbaijan, depicted as a victorious king. This painting was once located on the wall of the Tanabi Palace.[46]

If we are to present a categorization of the royal portraits during the reign of Fath-'Ali Shah, we can list them under three groups: the first is the seated ruler on the throne with royal accoutrements;[47] the second shows the ruler in hunting or battle scenes;[48] and the third group would be dedicated to a special, innovative theme, i.e. the salam ceremony or royal reception (*saff-e salam*). The formation of such a new theme in the art of that period, and in particular on palace murals, was mostly for the purpose of representing the power, legitimacy and alliances of the Qajars. This last genre was pioneered by the chief painter, 'Abdollah Khan, whose artistic contribution over the six decades of his life led to the stabilization and development of royal wall painting in the nineteenth century and was regarded as a prototype for other painters of the time and manifested itself in other art media as well. 'Abdollah Khan's most celebrated work, acclaimed by virtually every foreign traveller from Ouseley to Curzon, was the enormous life-size fresco of the ruler and his court covering three sides of the audience hall of the now vanished Negarestan Palace in Tehran (Figure 4).[49] It was commissioned by the shah and executed by 'Abdollah Khan and his team in 1812–13 on the walls of the Delgosha audience hall.[50]

Fig. 4. (Left) Self-portrait by 'Abdollah Khan in the saff-e salam wall painting in Negarestan Palace, Tehran. (Centre and right) saff-e salam wall painting in Negarestan Palace. Photography ca. 1886. Source: Archive of the Ketabkhana-ye Majles, Tehran.

Some experts, however, have suggested that this work is of an imaginary New Year reception rather than a real event. Here we should also add that this was the first instance of a painter being allowed by the shah, as the commissioner of the work, to paint his portrait in a courtly, ceremonial mural.[51] Large-scale portraits of Fath-'Ali Shah were given to visiting ambassadors and envoys as gifts. John Malcolm (in 1800), Pierre Amedée Jaubert (1806), Sir Gore Ouseley (1812) and Alexander Ermolov (1817) were among the earliest recipients of such portraits.[52]

The innovation of his style appeared once more in the Soleymaniya palace in Karaj, also dated 1228 AH (1812–13). In this palace, 'Abdollah Khan executed two large wall paintings, including Fath-'Ali Shah and his sons as well as Agha Mohammad Khan and his blood relatives (Plate IV)*.

Generally, most of the 'royal reception' murals from Fath-'Ali Shah's reign were executed on plaster, and surviving examples are now located at Tehran, Karaj and Qom. A further series of panels from a single salam ceremony painting, the original location of which remains unknown, is preserved today in different collections inside and outside Iran. It bears no signature of the artist; however, one of its panels, recently presented at Christie's auction house in 2021, has been attributed to 'Abdollah Khan's school by Layla Diba.[53] She has also introduced another new-found case, which is thought to have been located at the Hasht Behesht Palace, Esfahan, dated 1243 AH (1827).[54]

'Emarat-e Divani, Qom and the last Mural from Fath-'Ali Shah's Reign

Another aspect of Fath-'Ali Shah's patronage was the repair and embellishment of shrines and the construction of new mosques, which enhanced his reputation among the ulema. He directed much attention towards the shrine city of Qom where, towards the end of his life, he prepared his own tomb. The shrine was embellished with a golden gate and, in 1833, the *ivan* was covered with marble and tile work.[55] Fath-'Ali Shah had very firm beliefs about religious issues, undertaking several pilgrimages to the holy shrines of the Shi'i imams. The religious status of Qom, as the location of the tomb of Hazrat-e Ma'suma, Emam Reza's sister, was so immense at that time that Fath-'Ali Shah would go there whenever he was travelling to the other cities of central Iran. The shah restored this holy place in the early years of his reign (in 1800) and he also had a school and hospital constructed next to the shrine. In 1807, he ordered the construction of a residential building and a great palace called *'Emarat-e divani* (the Government mansion)[56] near the shrine, where he would reside during his visits to Qom (Plate Va)*.

In the last years of his reign, Fath-'Ali Shah appointed his 28th son, Kay Kavus Mirza, to the governorship of Qom (1832–35). Kay Kavus Mirza constructed a royal audience hall (*Talar-e salam*)[57] and ordered for it a large wall painting with the theme of a royal reception, in recognition of his father. The painting was completed during the last two years of the shah's life. Unfortunately, this palace was abandoned after Fath-'Ali Shah's death and was on the verge of destruction during the reign of the subsequent ruler, Mohammad Shah.

The oldest historical account of this Divani mansion has been provided by Naser al-Din Shah, Fath-'Ali Shah's great grandson, during his trip to Qom on 8 February 1868: 'We went from *darbcheh* (small door) to the mansion and then on the pilgrimage ... We went to visit the grave of the late king [Fath-'Ali Shah] and we found ourselves in *Talar-e salam* [site of the royal reception painting], and then took a nap. We ordered restoration and other things'.[58] A few days after shah's return to Tehran, Sani' al-Molk,[59] the chief architect, was sent to Qom to undertake the intended restoration work.

Later in the reign of Naser al-Din Shah, the building underwent partial restoration twice more, in 1873 and in 1879.[60] According to some documents, the restoration began in 1879 and continued until 1884.[61] In his diary, Naser al-Din Shah recorded some interesting accounts of this building and its wall painting, the last of which dates back to 1887–88. On 6 April 1888, Naser al-Din Shah visited the site once more and stated that the restoration process had been carried out in a modest way.

Furthermore, other Qajar dignitaries have offered some accounts of this mansion. E'temad al-Saltana, for instance, has written about the restoration of the building and its grand painting in 1301 AH (1884).[62] On 12 Rajab 1313/29

December 1896, Mohammad-Qasem Khan also provided a detailed description of the place in his travel account: 'In the middle of the hall in five sections there is the portrait of the late king with all his sons and grandsons, totalling 110 in number. In the middle of another hall with three sections there is again the portrait of the king with two other personalities'.[63] Farid al-Molk Hamadani was another person to have visited the mansion during Mohammad-'Ali Shah's reign (r. 1907–11). He has pointed out that the building was on the verge of destruction at that time.[64]

As almost no foreign travellers or diplomats were allowed inside the precincts of Muslim holy shrines, where the mansion is situated, there is little information available from foreign sources. We can only read some details in the accounts by Lord Curzon, Comte de Sercey and Henry-René D'Allemagne,[65] mostly based on what they had heard rather than seen. Curzon described it as a mansion connected to the shrine.[66] De Sercey also had an opportunity to visit the place and refers to the impending destruction of a grandiose palace. He mentions a pool full of water as well as the nice mural in the building painted in gold and warm colours.[67]

Finally, the building and its halls were destroyed in 1954 to allow for renovation and expansion and were replaced by a mosque (1954–59). Fortunately, before the demolition, some experts gave themselves the task of detaching the paintings from the wall and transferring them to another location. The detached painting was carried to Tehran in 54 plaster blocks. The pieces were preserved for some time in the treasury of the Parliament of Iran, and in 2005 they were transferred to the treasury of the Golestan Palace.[68] Then, in 2015, the mural was brought out after 60 years in storage and the pieces were installed on the walls of the Negarestan Palace Museum and Garden in 2017, following two years of restoration.[69]

The wall painting of the royal mansion in Qom may arguably be considered a masterpiece and could be regarded as the quintessence of all former achievements in painting during Fath-'Ali Shah's reign. But who could the painter of such a masterpiece be? Exactly like the works of other chief painters, such as Mehr 'Ali, Mirza Baba and 'Abdollah Khan, the mural once again depicts Fath-'Ali Shah in a central position, seated on the Peacock throne, flanked by his elder sons in hierarchical order. The first figure on the left is the crown prince, 'Abbas Mirza, who passed away a couple of months after the completion of this work.

By analogy with the known Negarestan palace model, the mural from Qom originally consisted of a central image of Fath-'Ali Shah seated on the Peacock throne with his eldest sons (now missing from the two ends of the Qom mural). The Qom mural panels present two straight rows of figures, organized according to age and rank and divided by balustrades. Their features are idealized. The princes are dressed in elaborate court ceremonial attire and either crowned or turbaned according to their rank. The clothing is richly detailed and exquisitely rendered with the precision of 'Abdollah Khan's style. Unlike in other examples, here the ranks of personages are observed and the figures depicted in different sizes with distinguishable characteristics (Plate Vb)*.

When observing the centre of the composition, we can see the glorious throne of the shah there. The brilliantly coloured golden throne (*Takht-e tavus*), the rich detailing in gold paint of the brocades, shawl fabrics, fur collars and most of all armlets, epaulettes, crowns, daggers and swords worn by the princes, all impart an air of luxury and wealth to Fath-'Ali Shah and his sons, skilfully evoking the splendours of the imperial court.[70] In this painting there are no foreign officials or governmental authorities, only the shah's own sons and grandsons. The actual size of this painting was far greater than what we can observe today. In the original work there were 150 figures, but today we can only see 99.

Here it should be noted that in the original painting before restoration there were some names inscribed beside the figures, now effaced. Some of them were even rewritten in the past, however incorrectly. We may suppose that the artist's signature was written, as was common practice, under the throne near a leg, in the centre of the whole painting, but today there is no trace of it.

Mina Ramezan-Jama'at has attributed this mural to Mirza Mohammad-'Ali.[71] She has come to this conclusion by relying on a small copy of a royal reception painting dated 1250 AH (1834) in the Hermitage Museum, which is close in time and composition to this mural. Although some of this artist's lacquer works survive and his name is documented as a painter of fine artworks,[72] there is no account of him creating wall paintings.

According to Mohammad Hoseyn Naser al-Shari'at, who wrote the history of Qom (*Tarikh-e Qom*), this mural should be attributed to Mehr 'Ali. He also mentioned that there were three different portraits of Fath-'Ali Shah on the wall but, unfortunately, no trace of these remains.[73]

In my view, the Qom painting may be attributed to 'Abdollah Khan and his large team of workshop painters. The royal workshops were crucial for the execution of major projects such as this. The execution of giant decorative cycles would have required the very special talents of 'Abdollah Khan as designer and chief of the royal workshops and the service of a vast army of painters. The royal reception theme in Qajar wall painting was a symbol of royal authority that became a prototype in that period and was manifested in other art media. The perfect example for this theme was the mural first accomplished by 'Abdollah Khan in the Negarestan Palace, as noted above, and reproduced in other places within the capital later.

The three wall paintings already discussed and one rock relief presented in (Figure 5),[74] clearly demonstrate that 'Abdollah Khan's composition remained unchanged for about two decades and it could have been adopted once more in the mural located in the 'Emarat-e divani in Qom.

Fig. 5. Comparison of 'Abdollah Khan's projects: (a) saff-e salam wall painting in Negarestan Palace, Tehran, 1228 AH (1813) showing Fath-'Ali Shah with 12 sons (formerly 118 figures); (b) saff-e salam wall painting in Soleymaniya Palace, Karaj, 1228 AH (1813), showing Fath-'Ali Shah with 14 sons; (c) saff-e salam wall painting from Qom royal residence, 1248 AH (1833), showing Fath-'Ali Shah with 99 sons (formerly 150 figures); (d) Naqsh-e Khaqan *(Portrait of the King), relief in Shahr-e Rayy, 1248 AH (1833), showing Fath-'Ali Shah with 16 sons (author's own photographs).*

An important point to mention here concerns the two projects that were conducted simultaneously by 'Abdollah Khan in 1812–13, i.e. the two wall paintings in the Negarestan and Soleymaniya palaces. It seems that such paintings were functioning, as mentioned earlier, as symbols of power and legitimacy, and they were painted immediately after the drafting the Golestan Treaty between Iran and Russia in the aftermath of the first Russo-Persian war. Such an approach seemed absolutely necessary again, some 20 years later, when 'Abbas Mirza passed away, in order to regain the image of power and recall a forgotten glory. That is why the other two works were once again undertaken in the same year, 1248 AH (1832), one in Rayy and the other in Qom, by the same artist (Figure 6).

In my opinion, the Qom royal residence painting, in terms of style and composition, is exactly similar to the other two murals in the Negarestan and Soleymaniya palaces. The painting also shares close affinities, in its composition, the figures' poses and other elements in the scene, with the *Naqsh-e Khaqan* rock relief in Shahr-e Rayy,[75] which, according to available accounts and documents,[66] was designed and supervised by 'Abdollah Khan in 1831, and completed in 1832.[77]

Consequently, we can also attribute the wall painting from Qom to 'Abdollah Khan, because at the same time in 1832 he was working on two parallel projects in which he used the same methods and style to compose a royal scene. Moreover, in the same year, 1248 AH (1832–33), 'Abdollah Khan was commissioned by Fath-'Ali Shah to design his tombstone (for the Qom shrine), which can be viewed as further proof that he may have stayed in that region for a while. According to Lesan al-Molk Sepehr, 'the shah would visit the tombstone daily and pressure the masons into completing the job…'.[78]

Considering the stylistic features of 'Abdollah Khan's artworks over the three decades of his artistic career during Fath-'Ali Shah's reign, it appears entirely logical to associate him with the royal reception mural in Qom. Shared painterly ornaments and elements in such scenes, like the personages' poses and arrangement, garments, crowns, daggers and, most importantly, the fact that the shah's figure and his throne are all the same in size and structure, offer convincing proofs of 'Abdollah Khan's supervision over all these projects.

The last years of Fath-'Ali Shah's reign brought about a period of hardship and conflicts for the Qajar government. This crisis was due to the difficult situation provoked by internal and external tensions. 'Abbas Mirza's heavy defeat by the Russians, in addition to other factors, resulted in the country experiencing diminished prestige, especially the adverse conditions in its central and eastern regions after the campaigns against Herat. Given such unfavourable circumstances, the act of creating a great work of art was nothing but an attempt to show and strengthen family ties as well as to maintain the legitimacy of the Qajars. Now, with the reappearance of the monumental painting from the royal residence at Qom, we have enough evidence in hand to

Fig. 6. Comparison between the style of saff-e salam wall painting from Soleymaniya Palace, Karaj 1228 AH (1813), Qom royal residence 1248 AH (1833) and the relief in Shahr-e Rayy 1248 AH (1833). (First row) left: Shahr-e Rayy; middle: Qom; right: Karaj; (second row) left: Karaj; right: Shahr-e Rayy; (third row) left: Shahr-e Rayy; middle: Qom; right: Karaj (author's own photographs).

truly understand the scope and ambition of dynastic wall paintings of the Fath-'Ali Shah era. If we take a look at the calm face of the shah and the glory of his court, we can recognize the image of power embodied here.

Notes:

I should like to take this opportunity to express my gratitude to Dr Layla S. Diba for her comments and valuable guidance. I also wish to thank Dr Negar Habibi for sharing her knowledge of Safavid painting with me.

* For additional information; please see the List of Illustrations on page vii.
1. Abbas Amanat, 'Qajar Iran: A historical overview', pp. 15–16. For a recent reappraisal of the eighteenth century, particularly in the spheres of theological and philosophical inquiry, see Michael Axworthy, *Crisis, Collapse, Militarism and Civil War*.
2. Basil W. Robinson, 'A survey of Persian painting', p. 60.
3. Sussan Babaie, 'Frontiers of visual taboo', p. 137.
4. Layla S. Diba and Maryam Ekhtiar, *Royal Persian Paintings*, p. 52.
5. Stephen Vernoit, *Occidentalism*, p. 95.
6. Layla S. Diba, 'Invested with life', p. 7.
7. Negar Habibi, *'Ali Qoli Jebādār*, p. 226.
8. Sussan Babaie, 'Shah Abbas II', p. 139.
9. See Markus Ritter, 'Painting in Safavid Iran (1501–1722) and European pictures', pp. 270–75 for a discussion of European influences and idem, 'Battle painting and trophies at the Bazaar portal in Safavid Isfahan', p. 185 for the dating of the paintings and later restorations.
10. Babaie, 'Frontiers of visual taboo', p. 142.
11. Kianoosh Motaghedi, *From Golestan Garden*, pp. 76–77.
12. Amanat, 'Qajar Iran: A historical overview', p. 16.
13. See Mohammad Hasan Khan, E'temād al-Saltana, *Matla' al-shams*, p. 166.
14. Mohammad Kāzem Marvi, *'Ālam-ārā-ye Nāderi*, pp. 825–28.
15. See the doctoral dissertation of Melisande Bizoirre, 'La hache et le rossignol', and the discussion in Sussan Babaie, 'Nader Shah, the Delhi loot and the 18th-century exotics of empire', esp. pp. 227–30. See also Ernest Tucker, 'Nader Shah's Idea of Iran', in this volume, pp. 16–18 [ed.].
16. See also Janet O'Brien, 'Dismembering the corporate', in this volume, p. 30 and n. 23 [ed.].
17. Robinson, 'Survey of Persian painting', p. 60; and idem, 'Persian painting under the Zand and Qājār dynasties', p. 873. For more information and a bibliography of Āqā Sādeq, see Yaq'ub Ažand, 'Mohammad Sādeq', pp. 5–12.
18. O'Brien, 'Dismembering the corporate', pp. 38–40 also suggests that portraits of Karim Khan often follow Naderid prototypes.
19. Sotheby's auction house, London, 12 October 2000, lot 5; and Diba and Ekhtiar, *Royal Persian Paintings*, pp. 152–53. A similar example of this painting in the treasury of Niavaran Palace, Tehran, has recently been studied by this author: it is a mid-Qajar copy from the original, not previously identified. The painting is signed by 'Ali-Akbar Hajjarbāshi, an apprentice of Esma'il Jalayer.
20. Julian Raby, *Qajar Portraits*, p. 36.
21. Diba and Ekhtiar, *Royal Persian Paintings*, p. 153.
22. See Sussan Babaie, 'In the eye of the storm', pp. 35 –36 and 54; see also Assef Ashraf's chapter 'Safavid nostalgia in early Qajar chronicles', in this volume [ed.].
23. Diba and Ekhtiar, *Royal Persian Paintings*, p. 34.

24. Fath-'Ali Shah was interested in the arts from his youth and learned painting and calligraphy from the masters of his time (Mirza Baba Naqqash and Mirza 'Abbas Nuri). Some of his calligraphic practices are preserved in museums, inside Iran and abroad.
25. 'Abdollah Khan was not only *naqqashbashi*, or painter laureate, to Fath-'Ali Shah, but also court architect, as well as a skilled enamel painter, Diba and Ekhtiar, *Royal Persian Paintings*, p. 52. According to Murdoch Smith, 'he died at a great age at the beginning of the present Shah's reign' (sc. Naser al-Din Shah) (Basil W. Robinson, 'The court painters of Fath 'Ali Shah', p. 190). See 'Ali Asghar Mirzāei-Mehr, "Abdollāh Khān', p. 23. Mohammad 'Ali Karimzāda Tabrizi, *Ahvāl va āsār-e naqqāshān-e qadim-e Iran*, p. 301.
26. The Soleymaniya Palace was built in 1810 by the order of Fath-'Ali Shah in a vast garden and hunting ground, near Tehran. After its completion, 'Abdollah Khan painted two royal murals, which are still in their original place. See Wolfram Kleiss and Hubertus von Gall, 'Der Qajaren-Pavilion Sulaymanieh in Karaj', pp. 325–39. Also see Fereydoun Barjasteh van Waalwijk and Kamran Najafzadeh, 'Behin miva-ye khosravāni', pp. 22–43.
27. See the similar painting in Layla S. Diba, 'When history was writ large'.
28. Diba and Ekhtiar, *Royal Persian Paintings*, p. 35.
29. Tallinn Grigor, 'Kingship hybridized', pp. 219–33.
30. Diba and Ekhtiar, *Royal Persian Paintings*, p. 31.
31. *Takht-e tavus* was commissioned by Fath-'Ali Shah in 1215 AH (1801) and made in Esfahan. It was completed a year later. This royal throne is made of wood and covered with gold, jewels and precious stones. It was originally named *Takht-e khorshid* (the Sun throne) but was later called *Tavus* following Fath-'Ali Shah's marriage with Lady Tavus. The throne was restored during the reign of Naser al-Din Shah (in 1858) and some inscriptions in *nasta'liq* were added.
32. The *Marmar* and *Naderi* thrones were both made five years after the *Tavus* throne by the order of Fath-'Ali Shah in 1221 AH (1806).
33. Raby, *Qajar Portraits*, p. 10.
34. Under the rulers of the Qajar dynasty in the nineteenth century, rock reliefs were created that tie in with pre-Islamic traditions. These important monuments of the Qajar period have recently been systematically studied for the first time, see Hubertus Von Gall and Paul Luft, *Die Qajarischen Felsreliefs*, who also reproduce the Persian inscriptions and provide their translation as well as an identification of the persons depicted.
35. Some of Qajar reliefs are comparable with *Khong Aždar* and *Kul-Farokh* in Izeh (from the Parthian era) and also with *Tang-e Chugan* in Shiraz (from the Sasanian era).
36. Most of these reliefs have been located on the main routes, near water. Choosing such locations seems to have been an imitation of the pre-Islamic Sasanian practice.
37. See Robert Ker Porter, *Travels in Georgia, Persia, Armenia, Ancient Babylonia*, p. 325.
38. Currently about 25 portraits in oils of Fath-'Ali Shah produced over a period of 20 years have been identified, of which more than 15 were sent to contemporary rulers. See Robinson, 'The court painters', pp. 191–92 for Mehr 'Ali and Mirza Baba, and

pl. XXXIII–XXXVI; also idem, 'Persian painting', pp. 874–77 and pl. 9, 12, 14; and Diba and Ekhtiar, *Royal Persian Paintings*, pp. 180–88.
39. This oil painting by Mehr 'Ali is one of the oldest and most important portraits of Fath-'Ali Shah (1804) and was – with another painting – intended for the decoration of the audience hall of the Golestan Palace. It was installed in the upper right niche of the hall until the end of the Qajar era, but was moved to the Almas Hall, Golestan complex, after the Islamic Revolution.
40. A new royal crown was designed for Fath-'Ali Shah. This royal headgear was named the Kayanid crown, which, according to the tradition of the *Shahnama*, was worn by the ancient kings of Iran.
41. Michael Roaf, 'Sculptures and sculptors at Persepolis', p. 128. See also Jebrael Nokandeh, *A Survey of the History of Iran*, pp. 72–73.
42. Plaster panel with enthroned ruler (Toghrel) and courtiers, from the vicinity of Rayy, second half of the twelfth century. See Sheila R. Canby *et al.*, *Court and Cosmos*, pp. 76–77.
43. See Moya Carey, *Persian Art: Collecting the Arts of Iran for the V&A*, p.103. It is the only standing portrait of Fath-'Ali Shah signed by 'Abdollah Khan, kept in the Victoria and Albert Museum (V&A:707-1876). See also Mirzāei-Mehr, ''Abdollāh Khān', p. 22.
44. Diba and Ekhtiar, *Royal Persian Paintings*, p. 31.
45. For some information on the wall painting tradition and its continuation in the Naseri period, as well as a comparative study of this art medium between the Fath-'Ali Shah and Naser al-Din Shah periods, see also Alireza Baharlou and Marziyeh Qasemi, 'Barrasi-ye tatbiqi-ye divārnegāra-ye Saff-e Salām-e Kākh-e Negārestān'.
46. See Layla Diba, 'Making History', pp. 97–101. This work is now preserved at the National Museum of Iran, Islamic Department.
47. This style of painting was pioneered by Mehr 'Ali and Mirza Baba. Some paintings in this style were presented as diplomatic gifts to the kings and rulers of other countries. Some examples can be seen in Iran, in the *Naqqash khana* or *Gushvara* room, at the Audience Hall of Golestan Palace: an under-glass painting signed by Mehr 'Ali (1802); and two oil paintings by Mehr 'Ali (1804) in the Almas Hall, Golestan Palace.
48. A unique example with this theme is a large oil painting, probably kept at the Tanabi Palace, Golestan Complex, today preserved at the *Bonyad-e Mostaz'afan* Museum (Motaghedi, *From Golestan Garden*, p. 85); also, in the Ashoka Hall of the Rashrapati Bhavan, Former Viceroy's Residence, New Delhi (Diba and Ekhtiar, *Royal Persian Paintings*, p. 51).
49. Robinson, 'A survey of Persian painting', pp. 63, 66.
50. Mirzāei-Mehr was the first to mention the name of Delgosha audience hall, see Mirzāei-Mehr, ''Abdollāh Khān', p. 16. The saff-e salam mural from Negarestan was copied by Samsam ebn Zu'l-faqar (Mosavvar al-mamalek) in 1904, before the palace was demolished in the Mozaffarid era, but the copy was not exhibited until 1917. See Gwenaëlle Fellinger, *L'Empire des roses*, pp. 294–97. The date and signature were seen sometime in 1887–88 by E.G. Browne and recorded in his work, *A Year Amongst the Persians*, p. 96.
51. See Baharlou and Qasemi, 'Barrasi-ye tatbiqi-ye divārnegāra-ye Saff-e Salām-e', p. 53.

52. Vernoit, *Occidentalism*, p. 102.
53. Two panels of this large painting with a royal reception theme are kept at the treasury of the Saheb-Qeraniya Palace, Niavaran Complex, Tehran and one piece was formerly kept at Bonnet House Museum in Florida. See Diba, 'When history was writ large'.
54. See Layla S. Diba, 'From the miniature to the monumental'. Lord Curzon also saw this painting at Esfahan; see George Nathaniel Curzon, *Curzon's Persia*, p. 46.
55. Vernoit, *Occidentalism*, p. 100.
56. For more information about *'Emārat-e divāni Qom*, see Mohammad Hoseyn Nāser al-Shari'at, *Tārikh-e Qom*, pp. 190–91.
57. Similar to the Negarestan Palace in Tehran.
58. Majid 'Abd-e Amin, *Ruznāma-ye khāterāt-e Nāser al-Din Shāh*, p. 48.
59. At that time Sani' al-Molk was the title of Haj Mirza Hoseyn-'Ali Esfahani. See Mohammad Hasan Khan, E'temād al-Saltana, *Ruznāma-ye khāterāt*, p. 315.
60. In 1873 and 1879, E'tezad al-Dowla (governor of Qom) and Kamran Mirza (the Regent) engaged in correspondence while allocating funds to the restoration of the Divani Mansion, see Minā Ramezān-Jamā'at, *The Saff-e Salam Wall Painting*, p. 33.
61. E'temād al-Saltana, *Ruznāma-ye khāterāt*, p. 112.
62. E'temad al-Saltana referred to the mansion and its painting in his daily accounts on 25 Rajab 1301/8 April 1888, *Ruznāma-ye khāterāt*, p. 947.
63. 'Alirezā Abazari, *Safarnāma-ye Mohammad Qāsem Khān*, p. 674.
64. Mas'ud Farid, *Khāterāt-e Farid*, p. 253.
65. See the illustration of 'Fath-Ali-Shah entouré de ses fils et vizirs' by Henry-René D'Allemagne, *Du Khorassan au pays des Backtiaris*, p. 86.
66. Curzon, *Curzon's Persia*, vol. II, p. 12.
67. Comte Laurent de Sercey, *Une ambassade extraordinaire*, p. 167.
68. Ramezān-Jamā'at, *The Saff-e Salam Wall Painting*, p. 32, and also 'Abbās Feyz, *Ganjina-ye āsār-e Qom*, pp. 620–76.
69. Registered in the inventory of the national works of Iran, 2 August 2017 (Inv. No.: 765).
70. Diba, 'When history was writ large'.
71. Ramezān-Jamā'at, *The Saff-e Salam Wall Painting*, p. 44.
72. Karimzāda Tabrizi, *Ahvāl va āsār-e naqqāshān-e qadim-e Irān*, p. 912.
73. Nāser al-Shari'at, *Tārikh-e Qom*, p. 191.
74. See Von Gall and Luft, *Die Qajarischen Felsreliefs*, p. 73. The 12 sons of Fath-'Ali Shah in this painting may have been a reference to the 12 imams in Shi'i ideology.
75. Mirzā Afzal Shirāzi Khāvari, *Tārikh-e Zu'l-Qarneyn*, pp. 877–78.
76. E'temād al-Saltana, *Ruznāma-ye khāterāt*, p. 241.
77. In *Mer'āt ol-boldān* by E'temād al-Saltana, vol. IV, p. 2216, there is a record of this relief. The writer refers to 'Abdollah Khan Esfahani, the chief painter and architect of the Qajar court, as the artist who started this project in 1831 and completed the work a year later. We should note that there was formerly one more rock relief of Fath-'Ali Shah in Shahr-e Rayy, located at the Tabarak Mountain, depicting the king in a hunting scene in battle with a lion. This work was also designed by 'Abdollah Khan in 1831.
78. Lesān al-Molk Sepehr, *Nāsekh al-tavārikh*, vol. I, p. 135.

Bibliography:

'Abazari, 'Alirezā, 'Safarnāma-ye Mohammad Qāsem Khān Sāheb Jām be Qom', *Payām-e Bahārestān* 15 (2012), pp. 639–79.

'Abd-e Amin, Majid, *Ruznāma-ye khāterāt-e Nāser al-Din Shāh Qājār: Rajab 1284 AH – Safar 1287 AH* (Tehran: Afshar Foundation and Publication, 1397/2018).

Amanat, Abbas, 'Qajar Iran: A historical overview', in *Royal Persian Paintings: The Qajar Epoch 1785–1925* (London: I.B. Tauris, 1999), pp. 14–29.

Ashraf, Assef, 'Safavid nostalgia in early Qajar chronicles', in *The Contest for Rule in Eighteenth-Century Iran: The Idea of Iran*, vol. 11, ed. Charles Melville (London: I.B. Tauris, 2022), pp. 81–102.

Axworthy, Michael, ed., *Crisis, Collapse, Militarism and Civil War: The History and Historiography of 18th Century Iran* (New York: Oxford University Press, 2018).

Ažand, Yaq'ub, 'Mohammad Sādeq', *Golestān-e honar* 12 (1394/2015), pp. 5–12.

Babaie, Sussan, 'Shah Abbas II, the conquest of Qandahar, the Chihil Sutun, and its wall paintings', *Muqarnas* 11 (1994), pp. 125–42.

— 'In the eye of the storm: Visualizing the Qajar axis of kingship', *Artibus Asiae* 66, no. 2 (2006), pp. 35–54.

— 'Frontiers of visual taboo: Painted indecencies in Isfahan', in *Eros and Sexuality in Islamic Art*, ed. Francesca Leoni and Mika Natif (Aldershot, Hampshire: Ashgate, 2013), pp. 131–55.

— 'Nader Shah, the Delhi loot, and the 18th-century exotics of empire', in *Crisis, Collapse, Militarism and Civil War: The History and Historiography of 18th Century Iran*, ed. Michael Axworthy (New York: Oxford University Press, 2018), pp. 215–34.

Baharlou, Alireza and Marziyeh Qasemi, 'Barrasi-ye tatbiqi-ye divārnegāra-ye Saff-e Salām-e Kākh-e Negārestān va 'Emārat-e Nezāmiya (A Comparative Study on the Murals of Royal Reception in Negarestan Palace and Nezamiya Mansion)', *Motāle'āt-e tatbiqi-ye honar* 10, no. 19 (1399/2020), pp. 49–67.

Barjasteh van Waalwijk, Fereydoun and Kamran Najafzadeh, 'Behin miva-ye khosravāni derakht, the Soleimanieh murals – some thoughts and pictures', in *The International Qajar Studies Association*, vol. XIV–XV (Gronsveld, Santa Barbara, Tehran, 2015), pp. 22–43.

Bizoirre, Melisande, 'La hache et le rossignol. Productions artistiques en Iran après la chute d'Esfahān (1135/1722–1163/1750)', doctoral dissertation (Aix-Marseille University, 12 November 2020).

Browne, E.G., *A Year Amongst the Persians: 1887–1888* (Cambridge: Cambridge University Press, 1927).

Canby, Sheila R., Deniz Beyazit, Martina Rugiadi and A.C.S. Peacock, eds., *Court and Cosmos: The Great Age of the Seljuqs* (New York: Metropolitan Museum, 2016).

Carey, Moya, *Persian Art: Collecting the Arts of Iran for the V&A* (London: V&A publishing, 2017).

Curzon, George Nathaniel, *Curzon's Persia*, ed. Peter King (London: Pan Macmillan, 1986).

D'Allemagne, Henry-René, *Du Khorassan au pays des Bakhtiaris: trois mois de voyage en Perse* (Paris: Hachette, 1911).

Diba, Layla S., 'Invested with life: Wall painting and imagery before the Qajars', *Iranian Studies* 34, no. 1–4 (2001), pp. 5–16.

— 'Making history: A monumental battle painting of the Perso-Russian wars', *Artibus Asiae* 66, no. 2 (2006), pp. 97–110.

— 'When history was writ large: The Bartlett monumental painting of the court of Fath-'Ali Shah', lot essay, Christie's auction catalogue, 1 April 2021, Lot 30, online at https://www.christies.com/en/lot/lot-6308183 [accessed 1 March 2021].

— 'From the miniature to the monumental: The Negarestan Museum painting of the sons of Fath-'Ali Shah', online conference in Khamseen 2020, at https://www.google.com/url?sa=t&rct=j&q=&esrc=s&source=web&cd=&c ad=rja&uact=8&ved=2ahUKEwikvo2XubDwAhVbRhUIHbl9DkcQFjABe gQIAhAD&url=https%3A%2F%2Fsites.lsa.umich.edu%2Fkhamseen%2F2 020%2F10%2F&usg=AOvVaw0nYlRsnzmI-MdP6HtQCrBi [accessed 6 April 2021].

Diba, Layla S. and Maryam Ekhtiar, eds, *Royal Persian Paintings: The Qajar Epoch 1785–1925* (London: I.B. Tauris and Brooklyn: Brooklyn Museum of Art, 1998).

E'temād al-Saltana, Mohammad Hasan Khan, *Matla' al-shams, dar joghrāfi va tārikh-e ba'zi az belād va amāken-e Khorāsān*, vol. I (lith. Tehran, 1301/1884).

— *Mer'āt al-boldān*, ed. 'Abd al-Hoseyn Navā'i and Mir Hāshem Mohaddes, 4 vols (Tehran: Tehran University Press, 1367/1988).

— *Ruznāma-ye khāterāt-e E'temād al-Saltana*, ed. Iraj Afshār (Tehran: Amir Kabir, 1368/1989).

Farid, Mas'ud, *Khāterāt-e Farid (Mirzā Mohammad 'Ali Khān Farid al-Molk Hamadāni 1291–1334 AH)* (Tehran: Zāvar, 1354/1975).

Fellinger, Gwenaëlle, with Carol Guillaume, *L'Empire des roses: chefs-d'oeuvre de l'art persan du XIXe siècle* (Lens: Musée Louvre-Lens and Gand: Snoeck, 2018).

Feyz, 'Abbās, *Ganjina-ye āsār-e Qom* (Qom: Mehr Ostovar, 1350/1971).

Grigor, Talinn, 'Kingship hybridized, kingship homogenized: Revivalism under the Qajar and the Pahlavi dynasties', in *Persian Kingship and Architecture: Strategies of Power in Iran from the Achaemenids to the Pahlavis*, ed.

Sussan Babaie and Talinn Grigor (London: I.B. Tauris, 2015), pp. 218–54.
Habibi, Negar, *'Ali Qoli Jebādār et l'occidentalisme safavide: une étude sur les peintures dites* farangi sāzi, *leurs milieux et commanditaires* (Leiden: Brill, 2018).
Karimzāda Tabrizi, Mohammad 'Ali, *Ahvāl va āsār-e naqqāshān-e qadim-e Iran: The Lives and Arts of Old Painters of Iran & a Selection of Masters from The Ottoman & Indian Regions*, vol. II (London: Mostowfi, 1369/1990), p. 912.
Ker Porter, Robert, *Travels in Georgia, Persia, Armenia, Ancient Babylonia*, vol. I (London: Longman and Hurst, 1822).
Khāvari, Mirzā Afzal Shirāzi, *Tārikh-e Zu'l-Qarneyn*, vol. II, ed. Nāser Afshārfar (Tehran: Majles, 1380/2001).
Kleiss, Wolfram and Hubertus Von Gall, 'Der Qajaren-Pavilion Sulaymanieh in Karaj', *Archaeologische Mitteilungen aus Iran* 10 (Berlin: Dietrich Reimer Verlag, 1977), pp. 325–39.
Marvi, Mohammad Kāzem, *'Ālam-ārā-ye Nāderi*, ed. Mohammad Amin Riyāhi (Tehran: Zavvār, 1364/1985).
Mirzāei-Mehr, 'Ali Asghar, '"Abdollāh Khān', *Golestān-e honar* 16 (1395/2016), pp. 16–23.
Motaghedi, Kianoosh, *From Golestan Garden to Golestan Palace* (Tehran: Danyar, 1400/2021).
Nāser al-Shari'at, Mohammad Hoseyn, *Tārikh-e Qom*, ed. 'Ali Davāni (Tehran: Rahnamon, 1383/2004).
Nokandeh, Jebrael, ed., *A Survey of the History of Iran on the Basis of Iran National Museum Collections* (Tehran: Iran National Museum; Baloot Noghrei Institute, 2018).
O'Brien, Janet, 'Dismembering the corporate: The single portraits of Nader Shah and the changing body politic in post-Safavid Iran', in *The Contest for Rule in Eighteenth-Century Iran: The Idea of Iran*, vol. 11, ed. Charles Melville, (London: I.B. Tauris, 2022), pp. 27–55.
Raby, Julian, *Qajar Portraits* (New York: I.B. Tauris, 1999).
Ramezān-Jamā'at, Minā, *Divār negāra Saff-e Salām-e Fath-'Ali Shāh (The Saff-e Salam Wall Painting of Fath-'Ali Shah: Tracing the History of the Work, from the Divani Building in Qum to the Negarestan Palace-Museum of Tehran University)* (Tehran: Pooneh, 1398/2019), pp. 21–35.
Ritter, Markus, 'Painting in Safavid Iran (1501–1722) and European pictures Malerei im safawidischen Iran (1501–1722) und europäische Bilder', *Global Lab: Art as Message, Asia and Europe: Kunst als Botschaft, Asien und Europa* (Ostfildern: Hatje, 2009), pp. 270–75.
— 'Battle painting and trophies at the Bazaar portal in Safavid Isfahan Schlachtenbild und Trophäen des Basarportals im safawidischen Isfahan, Iran 17. Jahrhundert', *Inszenierung des Sieges – Sieg der Inszenierung:*

Interdisziplinäre Perspektiven, (Innsbruck: StudienVerlag, 2011), pp. 181–98.

Roaf, Michael, 'Sculptures and sculptors at Persepolis', *Iran* 21 (1983), pp. 1–164.

Robinson, Basil W., 'Persian painting under the Zand and Qājār dynasties', in *The Cambridge History of Iran, vol. 7, From Nadir Shah to the Islamic Republic*, ed. Peter Avery, Gavin Hambly and Charles Melville (Cambridge: Cambridge University Press, 1991), pp. 870–89.

— 'A survey of Persian painting', in idem, *Studies in Persian Art* (London: Pindar Press, 1993), vol. I, pp. 1–70.

— 'The court painters of Fath 'Ali Shah', in idem, *Studies in Persian Art* (London: Pindar Press, 1993), vol I., pp. 182–200.

Sepehr, Lesān al-Molk, *Nāsekh al-tavārikh*, ed. Jamshid Kiānfar, vol. I (Tehran: Enteshārāt-e asātir, 1377/1998).

De Sercey, Comte Laurent, *Une ambassade extraordinaire: la Perse en 1839–1840* (Paris: L'Artisan du Livre (Paris, 1928).

Tucker, Ernest, 'Nader Shah's Idea of Iran', in *The Contest for Rule in Eighteenth-Century Iran: The Idea of Iran*, vol. 11, ed. Charles Melville, (London: I.B. Tauris, 2022), pp. 9–26.

Vernoit, Stephen, *Occidentalism*, The Nasser D. Khalili Collection of Islamic Art, vol. XXIII (London: The Noor Foundation, 1997).

Von Gall, Hubertus and Paul Luft, *Die Qajarischen Felsreliefs* (Berlin: Dietrich Reimer, 2020).

6

Diplomatic Gift Exchange between the Russian and the Persian Courts in the Early Nineteenth Century

Firuza Abdullaeva
(University of Cambridge)

This chapter explores how diplomatic gift exchange between the Persian and the Russian courts during the early Qajar period reflects the relationship between the two countries at the outset of the Great Game and how the diplomatic gifts, especially of Persian royal portraiture, reflect the national idea. The choice of gifts and their subtle meanings also allude to the wider international scene, drawing Britain and Russia into existing rivalries between Iran and the Ottomans in the Caucasus, and even reflect domestic contests for the throne within the Qajar family. I shall focus on two special missions: the Russian one led by Alexander Griboedov, diplomat, playwright, composer, poet as well as statesman and businessman,[1] and the 'reciprocal' so-called Redemption embassy under the 16-year-old Qajar Prince Khosrow, also a diplomat and a poet, sent to St Petersburg to apologize for the murder of Griboedov and the members of his mission in Tehran in February 1829.

The art of diplomatic gift exchange has been known since ancient times. The purpose was not only to entertain a spoilt ruler with yet another precious gift of high monetary value but also to represent the highlights of the cultural, military and economic achievements of the whole country, expressing the crème de la crème of its national identity in the most sublime way, aiming to impress with its power and amuse with its uniqueness. That is why such gifts included not only masterpieces of arts and crafts but also live exotic animals, like giraffes. Often they would serve both purposes: practical, such as snakes for pharmaceutical needs or falcons for hunting, as well as propagandistic, to demonstrate majestic power, like elephants or lions.[2] Simple or sophisticated, expensive or modest they were intended to show the links and friendship between the two monarchs and the nations they represented.[3]

The amusement component of a diplomatic gift sometimes contained a special message, often hidden in an object, which was expected to be understood by the recipient.[4] One of the most famous examples of such a puzzle exchange was the dialogue between Alexander the Great and the

Achaemenid king Darius: Darius sent Alexander a ball and a polo stick to convey the message that Alexander was still a child and was not ready for a serious battle with him. Alexander interpreted the ball as the Earth, and thanked Darius for giving him a sign that he would rule the world. This old legend, known in several versions, demonstrates how important it is to be understood correctly; in diplomatic communication it is of paramount importance to be able to avoid any dangerous ambiguity while sending a sophisticated gift full of elegant symbolism. Both the missions that are the focus of this chapter had indeed a very special status.

Royal portraiture, boosted by the Napoleonic propaganda machine, had become by this time particularly popular in diplomatic gift exchange between Persia and the European courts: in the Golestan Palace there is a whole collection of such portraits sent to the shahs by their European counterparts. Of course, such depictions were known since antiquity, being used not only for displaying power but for practical purposes; for example, arranging royal marriages or exchanging news of the latest fashions. By the early Qajar period, Persian painting started actively to adopt the European style of royal representations in both imagery and technique, as has been revealed by the major exhibitions specifically dedicated to Qajar art.[5]

The 2019 film *Of Kings and Paintings*[6] is one of the best among the most recent examples of how the Qajars mastered the use of Western visual art for promoting the image of the great imperial ruler by merging it with much more ancient native paradigms and motifs. The first Qajar rulers were particularly effective at appropriating the visual propaganda borrowed from the Western courts to project their image through both worlds – East and West, Christian and Islamic, ancient and contemporary.[7]

When the now iconic image of Fath-'Ali Shah in the State Hermitage Museum (see Figure 1), or the David Collection, was distributed among the main European courts, the Western recipients could not fail to recognize the famous prototype of the greatest emperor of their time, the conqueror of the universe, modern-day Alexander the Great (see Figure 2), while those more enlightened about Persian culture were expected to see the Qur'anic epitome of ancient kingship – Solomon with the hoopoe of wisdom as his attribute instead of Napoleon's eagle of war (see Figure 3).

The Russian Mission to the Persian Court

In January 1829, the newly appointed minister plenipotentiary Alexander Griboedov and his entourage arrived in Tehran for a supposedly very short visit: only to present his credentials to the Qajar ruler Fath-'Ali Shah as the new envoy of the Russian Empire. However, on the eve of their departure, the mission was attacked by the bazaar mob and all members except one, Ivan Maltsev, were massacred; all possessions, all royal gifts from both sides and top secret documents were looted.

Fig. 1. Mehr 'Ali, Portrait of Fath-'Ali Shah, Standing, *1809–10, VP-1107 © State Hermitage Museum.**

Fig. 2. Robert Lefèvre, Portrait of Napoleon I in his Coronation Robes, *1812, 26.789 © Museum of Fine Arts, Boston, William Sturgis Bigelow Collection.**

Fig. 3. Solomon Enthroned, *from a double frontispiece from a copy of Ferdowsi's* Shahnama, *Iran, Shiraz, c. 1540–50, 83a/2006 © The David Collection, Copenhagen.**

The attitude towards the mission, and particularly its head, has been so controversial for almost two hundred years that his name is surrounded by myths and legends of exceptional variety: opinions range from admiration for his ability as a diplomat with stately vision, to hatred of his role as an ardent colonialist, to doubts concerning his ability to play the Great Game, and ignorance in deliberately eliminating his name from the annals of history.[8]

D.P. Costello, in his *Murder of Griboedov*, explains this tragic event (apart from several other contributing circumstances) by advancing the idea that the Persians, the Qajars and, particularly, Fath-'Ali Shah 'had no very exalted notion of the sacrosanctity of diplomatic premises or persons'. To illustrate this he mentions a story about Henry Willock, British chargé d'affaires, who fled Persia after receiving a letter from the shah, on 1 April 1822, threatening that Prince 'Ali Khan 'was ordered to come and strike his head off' unless a card debt was paid by Willock from the money promised by the British, within five days.[9] Such extraordinary behaviour by the shah towards the foreign diplomats in Persia had long roots and strong causes.

The period in question is known as the gambit stage of the so-called Great Game when, after the fall of Napoleon, there were only two foreign countries represented in Persia: Russia and Britain, the superpowers of the day. Both were equal in their influence on the government of Persia, both had equally keen geopolitical interests in the region. Britain, alarmed by the southward advances of Russia, especially after her overwhelming military successes in Europe against France, as well as in Turkey and Persia, was trying to protect the main source of her colonial wealth, India. Thus, Persia became a natural buffer zone between the Russian contingents in the Caucasus, managed from St Petersburg and Tiflis, and their British counterparts under the direction of the Foreign Office in London and the East India Company (EIC) in Calcutta, respectively. The Anglo-Russian rivalry was also complicated by the internal conflicts that made this tournament of rather colourful shadows more exciting, as the agents, mostly soldiers of fortune of various national and social backgrounds from Europe, dispersed between the Caucasus and India, were often of dubious loyalties.[10]

There are many theories about the reasons for the tragedy of the Russian mission in Tehran, but usually it is linked with the Turkmanchay Peace Treaty, which was drafted by Griboedov when he was still the secretary of the embassy. The treaty caused a great national humiliation of Persia, as a result of which she lost her very important territories in the Caucasus. It was signed in February 1828, exactly a year before the attack on the Russian mission, at the end of the second Perso-Russian war, which was initiated by the crown prince 'Abbas Mirza in an attempt to regain the territories lost during the previous war. The borders drawn by the treaty exist to this day. It is impossible to overestimate the importance of the Turkmanchay Treaty in determining the whole course of the relationship between the three countries, as thereafter

Russia not only acquired extensive commercial rights and political influence in Persia but established herself dangerously close to British India (see Figure 4). The treaty set the stage for a long duel between Russia and Britain, which spread from Persia and the Caucasus to Central Asia, the Crimea and the whole Middle East.[11]

Fig. 4. Marcin Zaleski (?), Signing of the Turkmanchay Treaty by Count I.F. Paskevich and 'Abbas Mirza, *1840s © Gomel National Museum.*

This is the imaginary interpretation of the Moshkov-Beggrov print, commissioned by Paskevich for his palace in Gomel. In the painting he is moved into the compositional centre. Griboedov and Khosrow Mirza are standing behind the protagonists. Only a year later they were leading Russian and Persian diplomatic missions to Persia and Russia.

Griboedov had his own very ambitious plans related to the newly acquired Caucasian territories, which he hoped to turn into an independent province flourishing economically on the fertile lands of Georgia, with the clear intention of expanding even further, opening up to the Black Sea and turning Batumi into the porto franco as the main logistical hub of his Russian Trans-Caucasian Company (RTCC). He submitted his proposal about the RTCC to the tsar via General Ivan Paskevich, newly appointed governor of the Caucasus and his brother-in-law, only four months before his murder in Tehran. It seems that his original plan followed the colonial patterns of not only the existing Russian companies in California and Alaska but, above all, the EIC, which was famous for its very special independent status, allowing it to have its own army, mint its own money, make serious political decisions and even send diplomatic missions on behalf of the king without consulting the London Foreign Office.

The original text of Griboedov's proposal has not survived. However, a very thorough study of the related sources allowed Nadezhda Tarkhova to reconstruct its main ideas.[12] The RTCC aimed to develop agricultural, industrial and trading infrastructure in Georgia and turn it into the key point on the Russian overland trade route between Asia and Europe. The final text was produced with the assistance of Petr Zaveleysky, who was the treasurer of the Russian Georgian government and civil governor of Tiflis since 1829. However, both Zaveleysky and Griboedov's father-in-law Alexander Chavchavadze, who was the governor of Erivan province, were later accused of being part of the revolt of the Georgian Princes of 1832 and both were dismissed, although not for long. Chavchavadze, after his short exile in Tambov, was allowed to return to Georgia and Zaveleysky was promoted and sent to Siberia in charge of the governmental plan to cultivate the region, bringing state serfs from central Russia.

The plan to establish such a company had come into Griboedov's mind much earlier. Among those who influenced his thinking were prominent statesmen and first-hand practitioners of colonial policy who acquired their experience during their extensive travels. Kondraty Ryleev (1795–1826), was the treasurer of the Russian American Company (1799–1881), which by that time was the most profitable semi-governmental trading business managed by the Russian navy. Griboedov and Ryleev had a lot in common: they were both members of the same Freemason Lodge, 'Flaming Star' and its branch 'Free Society of the Lovers of Russian Literature'. Both had extremely pragmatic, sharp and stately minds, believing that they were destined to direct their country to a much more progressive future. It is quite paradoxical that Ryleev, being among the main managers and shareholders of the Company, had very pro-American views.[13] As one of the five main organizers of the anti-monarchist plot of December 1825, Ryleev was executed after a long trial. His incriminating archive was rescued by Faddey Bulgarin (Jan Tadeusz Krzysztof Bułharyn), a very close friend of Griboedov, who, thanks to this invaluable help, managed to avoid not only execution but even a Siberian exile.

Another person whose ideas resonated well with those of Griboedov was Dmitry Zavalishin (1804–92), a young naval officer who, in 1822–24, participated in Admiral Mikhail Lazarev's circumnavigation, aiming to inspect the state of the Russian American Company. Zavalishin's personal role in expanding the Californian part of Russian America is impossible to overestimate. However, after such a brilliant success he was called back and advised by the Russian Foreign Office to restrain his zeal in order to avoid confrontation with his British counterparts. Disillusioned in the competence of the government, Zavalishin developed the most extreme anti-monarchist ideas. After the failure of the Decembrist uprising, Zavalishin and Griboedov were arrested and imprisoned together while awaiting trial in the Peter and Paul Fortress, which was the main political prison of the Russian Empire. Zavalishin left the Fortress for Siberia but Griboedov was not only totally rehabilitated but highly promoted, appointed minister plenipotentiary and sent back to Persia. The reason for this was partly because the High Investigation Committee did not find enough evidence against him, but mainly thanks to his brother-in-law General Ivan Paskevich, who was a member of the Committee and keen to have Griboedov's assistance on his new appointment in the Caucasus to replace General Alexey Ermolov, Griboedov's first superior. By this time Griboedov not only had a rich diplomatic and intelligence experience in Persia and the Caucasus but was the most educated civil servant among all his colleagues, including both contingents of the Russian and British Legations in Persia: he had two degrees in history, law and European languages from Moscow University, and had also learnt Persian and Turkish.

Griboedov's RTCC project was rejected for various reasons, one of which could be that it had striking and alarming similarities with the structure of the Russian American Company (free farmers' labour versus the use of serfs) and the British EIC (with its own military and monetary system), which caused him to be suspected of the separatist ambitions that had been exercised by General Ermolov, who had unlimited power and authority among the army in the Caucasus.

Crucially, it was Griboedov who was appointed to deliver the signed Turkmanchay Treaty to the tsar, a ceremony signalled by a 201-gun salute. For this exceptional military and diplomatic service Griboedov was promoted to the rank of State Councillor, awarded the order of St Anne with diamonds and given 4,000 gold roubles. He was hoping to stay in St Petersburg and go with his fellow literati (Pushkin, Krylov and Vyazemsky) to London and Paris and write their collective literary travelogue. However, against his will,[14] Griboedov had to go back to Persia – the price of his salvation by Paskevich and his spectacular promotion – but, in return for his freedom and ultimately his life, he had to sacrifice everything that he saw to be the purpose of his existence: music, theatre, high society in glittering St Petersburg and his literary fame.

Griboedov tried to delay his departure for Persia as long as he could for various reasons, one being his belief that the longer he was expected the warmer his reception would be.[15] More importantly, he was waiting for the gifts for the shah and his family to be selected, even specially produced and dispatched. He had many problems to solve: the outstanding indemnity, the territorial dispute and the return of the Russian subjects, including the deserters who were already a part of the Persian regular army. The gifts were essential for the negotiations.

Apart from revolutionary-minded Ryleev and Zavalishin, Griboedov's ideas had been influenced by his travels to Persia, the Caucasus and the Crimea and by people such as Alexander Vsevolozhsky (1793–1864), an archivist in the Foreign Office originating from a wealthy family in Astrakhan, and Jean-Pierre-Theodor Hettier (1795–1846), a French officer in charge of 'Abbas

Mirza's regular army, whom he met in Tabriz in 1820 and with whom he had discussed his plans ever since. Griboedov's intimate acquaintance with the structure of the British EIC was due to his closeness to John Kinneir MacDonald (1782–1830), the Company's envoy to Persia since 1824.[16] Their professional collaboration started with their work together on the preparation of the Turkmanchay Treaty and continued until his death. The level of trust that Griboedov had in MacDonald can be proved by the fact that he left his heavily pregnant 16-year-old wife Princess Nina Chavchavadze in Tabriz with him, not with the Russian consul Andrey Amburger (1794–1830).

Griboedov and MacDonald had quite a lot in common: both found themselves in Persia on the recommendation and under the protection of their powerful brothers-in-law in charge of colonial policies: General Count Ivan Paskevich (1782–1856), governor of the Caucasus, and Major-General Sir John Malcolm (1769–1833),[17] governor of Bombay, respectively. Both were talented and keen litterateurs,[18] interested in a wide range of subjects from history and literature to politics and economics and both were extremely ambitious due to their illegitimate birth. The most decisive factor that brought them together was their internal rivalries: Griboedov's lack of support from his superiors in the Russian Foreign Office, and personally from Minister Count Karl Nesselrode, who introduced the young secretary Ivan Maltsev as his agent in Griboedov's mission. MacDonald, sent to Persia on behalf of the EIC, even had to deal with a rival embassy, sent by the London Foreign Office: Henry Willock and his secretary and the mission's doctor John McNeill (1795–1883),[19] who was originally sent to Persia from India in 1820 and, thanks to his profession, became a confidant of the shah and his wives. This allowed Willock and McNeill to be close to the court while MacDonald was waiting in Tabriz for two years for his chance to present his credentials to the shah. The rivalry was not only vicious but complicated.

Willock had already been in Persia for 18 years by the time of MacDonald's appointment and was expecting to be appointed envoy himself; however, even though at times he was running the whole British Legation almost singlehandedly, his rank was never higher than chargé d'affaires. When MacDonald's credentials were eventually accepted, Willock left for London but soon, knighted, returned via St Petersburg, where he introduced himself to Count Nesselrode as the new British ambassador to Persia. Griboedov received an official note from Nesselrode recommending him to welcome Willock as his counterpart only three weeks before the tragedy. However, instead of greeting Willock in his new capacity, Griboedov immediately warned MacDonald about the 'Willock's affair'.[20] It seems that relations between the two envoys Griboedov and MacDonald, were as good as those between their superiors. This could be one of the main reasons for the attack on the Russian Legation, during which not only many valuables disappeared but also the mission's entire top secret documentation, which could have been hoped to compromise both Griboedov and MacDonald.

This multi-board chess game thus ended tragically for Griboedov, torn to pieces by the mob in February 1829; MacDonald died a year later in less dramatic but no less tragic circumstances with the duplicitous Dr McNeill by his bedside. Willock was called back to England. The absolute winner on the British side was McNeill, who in 1836 was appointed the minister plenipotentiary and the only envoy in Persia representing the British crown.

Even more illustriously successful was the career of Ivan Maltsev (1807–80), Griboedov's secretary and the only survivor of the Russian mission. It was he who was allowed to establish and promote the Russian Transcaucasian 'Society' (not 'Company' – to avoid unnecessary associations) which gained unlimited rights of tax-free trade in and with Persia. He finished his career with the highest rank in the Foreign Office, sometimes even replacing Minister Nesselrode, who served in this post for 40 years. Maltsev was orphaned at a very young age. His mother Princess Anna Mescherskaya was from one of the noblest families in Russia, his father Sergey Maltsev was one of the richest men in the Empire, owning various properties, including mansions and estates in both capitals, St Petersburg and Moscow, the Crimea and the Urals. Among his businesses were steel factories in the Urals, glass and crystal manufactures in Gus' Khrustalnyi and vineries in Simeiz on the Black Sea. Being qualified for a junior diplomatic rank, he joined the Persian mission as a secretary and as an informal sponsor of Griboedov's Trans-Caucasian Company, bringing a significant sum for investment. However, his task was more to inform St Petersburg about the situation in Persia, and particularly within the Russian mission.

Already in Georgia, during his short stop in Tiflis Griboedov used his time to marry the daughter of Prince Alexander Chavchavadze, the newly appointed Governor of Erivan, who was not present at the official ceremony in the main Tiflis Cathedral. This was chiefly because Griboedov, as an ambassador, had to secure permission for his marriage from the Foreign Office, which he feared would not be granted.

There are two versions of the events preceding the tragedy. The first, which was based on the original reports of Griboedov, testified that his meetings with the shah and other courtiers were a great success. The shah received him with unprecedented pomp, not accorded to any other foreign ambassador. Fully satisfied with the results of his mission, Griboedov and his staff were packing their luggage ready to depart when the attack happened, triggered by the arrival of the Armenian eunuch, who for 15 years had been the treasurer of the shah's harem, Mirza Ya'qub (Markaryants) with his most valuable possessions, asking for refuge.[21] Due to the Turkmanchay Treaty, he obtained the right to return to Armenia as a newly proclaimed Russian subject.

During the aftermath of the attack, other records of rather a legendary nature started to appear, refocusing on two formerly Christian women who also arrived at the mission for the same reason and who were already the wives of one of the shah's courtiers. Those rather imaginary records were summed up in the famous *Blackwood* 'Narrative', published 'anonymously' in Scotland under the name of Griboedov's Persian *mehmandar* (host), which aimed to show how Griboedov's numerous mistakes made him responsible for his own death.[22] The main message of the British 'Narrative' coincided with the official line which was formulated by 15 March 1829 by the Russian court:[23] Griboedov was too zealous in the performance of his duties, providing shelter to the Armenian eunuch, insulting the shah and allowing his new Georgian entourage to abuse the local population by constantly drinking alcohol, breaking bottles and fighting in the bazaar, apart from harassing the populace and confiscating enormous amounts of provisions for their personal consumption en route. Another fatal mistake ascribed to Griboedov was his overly long conversation (50 minutes) with the shah. While the Russian envoy was trying to discuss the situation of the indemnities and the war captives, dozens of the shah's sons were suffering due to their uncomfortable court uniform, as was the shah with his elaborate and immensely heavy Kayani crown and jewels richly decorating his head and body, with an enormous detachable diamond aigrette and black heron feathers.

It is remarkable that this 'Narrative' was immediately printed in a French periodical,[24] while the reduced Russian version was published only about 50 years later as part of Griboedov's 'oeuvre'.[25] It took another hundred years before the full text became available.[26] The much later Persian translation has been regarded as the most reliable testimony.[27] The main purpose of the 'Narrative' was to prove Willock's and MacNeill's non-involvement in the fatal event and to have their story circulated before any contradictory accounts, following the investigation undertaken by MacDonald's wife and his brothers, could be broadcast.[28] The barbaric acts of violence were committed solely by the enraged mob, while the shah and his entourage were innocent of any ill intentions.

On the Russian side, the folk narrative was even more imaginative; in one of the letters by a contemporary, Griboedov was described as 'swearing in the shah's presence, jumping up like a madman, wandering around, and spitting on the floor'.[29] Such an exaggerated image of a classical villain was recently recreated in the Iranian TV series, *Tabriz in the Fog*,[30] in which Griboedov is presented as a chubby young jerk ordering a whole village to be burnt down as a punishment for giving refuge to his wife, who ran away from his tyranny, despite attempts to restrain him by his wise and elderly secretary Maltsev.[31]

According to the *Blackwood* 'Narrative', one of Griboedov's main faults as the new ambassador was that he failed to produce the diplomatic gifts together with his credentials, while all the shah's presents to the Russian envoy and the members of his mission were listed in detail.[32] The royal gifts indeed travelled separately and, for some unknown reason, were redirected to Anzali. It was not uncommon for such precious objects to be sent separately, guarded by a military convoy. Griboedov, hurried by his superiors, despite his attempts to delay his arrival in Tehran nolens volens only had with him a very long list of the expected gifts. The only valuables he had with him to present to the shah were 55 rather exotic platinum coins.

The fashion of giving coins made of precious metals as diplomatic gifts was already established at the Persian court by his British counterparts and became quite popular, as Fath-'Ali Shah often questioned the value of their presents, insisting that they should cost more.[33] The coins helped to avoid such unpleasant arguments. It seems that Griboedov's coins scored quite a success, being a novelty for the shah, as they were the first platinum coins ever minted. They were struck just a few months earlier at the main state mint in the Peter and Paul Fortress from platinum brought from the Ural mines.

What is particularly remarkable is that the tsar's gifts, which Griboedov was supposed to present to the shah, arrived at the Russian mission at night only a few hours before the first attack of the bazaar mob. There were two attacks on the mission, after which no valuables survived. Among them there should have been the following precious objects:

1. The salary for all members of staff of the two Russian missions in Tehran and Tabriz for the whole year ahead (9,510 Dutch gold coins).[34]
2. The most precious possessions of the eunuch Mirza Ya'qub (Markaryants). It was he whom the mob used as a pretext for the attack, as he arrived at the Russian embassy the day before, seeking sanctuary as a Russian subject.
3. The tsar's gifts to the shah and his wives, including diamond decorations, a porcelain dinner service, crystal vases and wool textiles. The list also mentioned 400 swords and sables and 12 artillery guns.[35] However, it is questionable where and how the arms could have been stored in such quantities in the small, temporary accommodation offered to the mission during their short stay.
4. The shah's welcoming and farewell gifts to the tsar and his family, the ambassador and his entourage, which included diamond orders of the Lion and the Sun, Kashmir (Rezayi) shawls, pearl necklaces, Arab horses with bejewelled decorations and a sack with 1,000 Dutch guilders for the envoy.[36]
5. 1,700 gold *tuman*s, which Griboedov prepared for distributing as farewell gifts among the Persian members of staff.[37]
6. Personal money and valuables of the First Secretary of the mission, the millionaire Ivan Maltsev, who was intending to start his crystal and glass business in Persia.

7. Not less important and valuable was the mission's secret archive and particularly the envoy's personal papers – very likely the main target of the attack.

It is obvious that those who instigated the religious anger against Mirza Ya'qub, the shah's former eunuch who betrayed Islam and reconverted to Christianity, had a very easy task by arousing the mercantile interest in the bazaar mob. As the treasurer of the shah's harem, the eunuch could share with the Russians not only the secrets of the shah's private life but what was more important for them – given the indemnities owed – the real state of the reportedly empty royal treasury.

The reasons for the tragedy that befell the Russian mission in Tehran have been investigated ever since. Dozens of scholarly and many more journalist articles and monographs have been written, films, plays and novels produced,[38] but no trace of the above-mentioned treasures has ever been found. Some of them might have disappeared even before the start of the attack, possibly together with the mehmandar who secretly left the mission about an hour before the mob stormed the building, while the envoy and his staff were still asleep.[39]

As it happens, the fate of the gifts brought by the Persian mission, which was sent to St Petersburg to apologize for the incident, was rather similar.

The Persian Mission to the Russian Court

To avoid yet another seemingly inevitable military conflict with Russia, the Persian court was expected to send an apology instantly. However, it took the shah half a year to do so.[40] There were several reasons for this delay, apart from the purely financial, which comprised the special calculation needed to decide the amount of blood money (*khunbaha*, or *diya*) to be paid for the murdered envoy;[41] and the two korours (crores), or one million tumans, about four tons of gold at this period, of indemnities still to be paid under the terms of the Turkmanchay Treaty.

However, while aware of the dangers of such a delay, the shah was not in a hurry to prepare the mission and the presents: he was torn between two parties at court. The Tehran group under his son-in-law insisted on spending the money on the army and, instead of sending an apology, advocated joining the Ottomans against the Russians to regain the lost territories. The second party under his son and heir in Tabriz was desperately trying to convince his father that a third military disaster would put an end to the Qajar dynasty, as this time the Russians would indeed enter Tehran.

Eventually, it was not the shah but the crown prince who sent a 'temporary' mission. His intention, whatever his father would eventually decide, was to demonstrate to the Russians the good will of the Persians, as Russian intelligence was aware of the Perso-Turkish negotiations. It was 'Abbas

Mirza's seventh son, 16-year-old Prince Khosrow, who was eventually appointed head of the mission. There were two reasons for this: he was nowhere near to the throne in the long queue of potential successors and he was his father's favourite, considered by him to be the most suitable to inherit his own role in charge of the country's foreign affairs. It was the 'temporary' status of the envoy that was intended to explain to the Russians why such an insignificant and 'dispensable' figure was appointed to lead the mission. Supposedly, he was expected to be replaced later, most likely in Tiflis.

Khosrow Mirza was never replaced by either his father, who was very keen to go to St Petersburg when Griboedov was still alive, or by his elder brother Mohammad, who only five years later became the Shah of Persia. The main worry was that the envoy might be kept by the Russians as a hostage, or as a rival to the throne, as in the case of Mortaza-Qoli Khan, Fath-'Ali Shah's uncle, whom Catherine the Great welcomed at her court for a similar reason.[42] His portrait in full regalia commissioned by her favourite artist was a successful act of propaganda (see Plate VIa)*.

The insignificance of the envoy had to be offset by his entourage and the gifts. In fact, Khosrow Mirza's mission was an overwhelming success, in many cases ascribed to his own personality. The very handsome 16-year-old prince became a real fashion of the day at the Russian court, where it was a rare ball, masquerade or hunting party, ballet or theatre performance that took place without his presence (see Figure 5).

Fig. 5. Ball fan with Khosrow Mirza's autograph, № ЭПТ-6766 © State Hermitage Museum.

The 40-man entourage was indeed very strong: there were 17 VIPs, of whom the top four were Mirza Mas'ud Ansari Garmrudi, future foreign minister; Mirza Saleh,[43] professional diplomat, educated in England; Mirza Hajji Baba Afshar, also educated in England as a doctor and who became known as a protagonist of James Morier's novel and a British spy; and Mirza Taqi Khan Farahani, the famous Amir Kabir, later prime minister of Naser al-Din Shah, although at the time of the mission he was only 22.

It is remarkable that the *farman* (order) from the shah confirming Khosrow's credentials and his apology letter to the tsar arrived only in August, when the prince was already in Moscow waiting for the tsar to return from the Ottoman front. Exactly like Griboedov, the prince arrived for his first audience with the tsar almost empty handed, as the gifts sent from his grandfather's court only reached St Petersburg a month after the official ceremony in the Winter Palace. To avoid total embarrassment, Khosrow Mirza had to buy some token gifts for the tsar and his entourage in Moscow from the Persian merchants.

When the gifts eventually arrived, they consisted of quite an array of objects,[44] among which there were 100,000 gold tumans, 18 manuscripts and the yellowish, perfectly clear 88.7 carat 'Shah' diamond, offered specifically as blood money for the envoy. It has three names engraved on it by its previous owners, Borhan Nezam Shah of Ahmadnagar (1000/1591), Shah Jahan (1051/1641) and Fath-'Ali Shah (1242/1826). It is notable that for almost a hundred years this diamond was known under the name of Khosrow Mirza. The carved line around the upper tier of the stone could indicate that it was used as a decoration hanging above the Peacock Throne of Shah Jahan.[45] It is remarkable that there is no mention of the diamond in the records of the shah's treasury although other less precious items were well documented.[46]

The 18 manuscripts from Fath-'Ali Shah's personal library are now kept in the National Library of Russia in St Petersburg.[47] Thirteen of these represent Persian poetry, including the earliest (1466) surviving copy of 'Ali-Shir Nava'i's *Divan*. The rest are medieval chronicles and didactic works, some with important provenances. For example, Jami's *Kolliyat* of 1527 was produced in the royal atelier of Bahram Mirza, brother of Shah Tahmasp, and Sa'di's *Bustan* of 1578 bears the ex libris of the Mughal emperor Aurangzeb. Only six manuscripts have illustrations, but one of them, the *Shahnama* copy of 1651, commissioned for Shah 'Abbas II, has 192 miniture paintings. Of special importance in the context of the mission is the richly illuminated copy of Fath-'Ali Shah's own collection of poetry, *Divan-e Khaqan*, calligraphed in 1816 by Aqa Mohammad Ja'far Esfahani.

The rest of the Persian presents included two carpets, Arab horses, Rezayi shawls, a pearl necklace for the empress, a sword for the crown prince and other less precious items for the princesses. Looking at the list of the Persian gifts, two things seem obvious: first, that the objects were collected in haste and, second, that the shah did not have many resources, or that he wanted to show both the poor state of his treasury and that he had nothing to do with those valuables that had disappeared from the Russian embassy.

According to the reports of the Russian intelligence, the Persian treasury was valued at at least a hundred korours. By the time of the Turkmanchay Treaty, the Persian court was unable to produce fifteen, which were reduced to ten for the indemnity payments. However, when the eighth korour was paid with the intervention of the British envoy MacDonald, it was reported that the treasuries of both the shah and the crown prince were completely empty.[48]

Compared with the fiasco of the previous Persian mission to St Petersburg in 1815 under Mirza Abu'l-Hasan Khan Ilchi, who brought incomparably more luxurious gifts that were carried through St Petersburg on a caravan of elephants, Khosrow Mirza's lesser presents nevertheless achieved a striking success. To say the least, one of the remaining two korours of indemnities was waived and the payment of the other was postponed.[49]

The hospitality expenses spent on the maintenance of the Persian mission were much greater than those expended on any other mission before or after: all the way through Russia, Khosrow Mirza and his suite stayed in the best accommodation that the local administration could provide, and in St Petersburg the whole magnificent Taurida Palace, built for Prince Potemkin, and which later became the seat of the first Russian Parliament, was allocated for the embassy's use for two months. Overall, the significance attached to this mission was exceptional. Every single detail of the apology ceremony was specially designed and approved and became a template for receiving all other foreign embassies. Khosrow Mirza's entrée into St Petersburg was organized with unprecedented pomp: his arrival on the royal yacht from Peterhoff was greeted by a 21-gun salute from the Peter and Paul Fortress with crowds of thousands thronging along the embankments.[50]

On their departure, the prince and his entourage received very impressive farewell gifts. Among them there were orders and decorations, including diamond eagles with aigrettes, medals and bejewelled daggers, rings and snuff boxes for all the VIP members of the delegation. At the Imperial porcelain and crystal factories they received specially commissioned porcelain, crystal and glass dinner, tea and sherbet services, as well as vases, mirrors, lamps, textiles and guns. To carry all those gifts the mission was supplied with 193 horses, 16 carriages and 31 coaches. When the caravan was leaving Moscow, the loads almost tripled.[51] Out of all those loads of valuables which the members of the mission carried back to Persia, there is strong surviving evidence about only one precious object of exceptional value. It is a splendid diamond and emerald aigrette, which Khosrow Mirza received from the tsar in St Petersburg. According to Masoud Bonakdar, its total weight is 1728 grams and it contains 13 emeralds of tear-drop shape and 663 diamonds of various size arranged in the shape of a bouquet, tied at the base by a bow and a ribbon made of smaller diamonds. Most likely, the precious head decoration was confiscated from Khosrow Mirza's possessions by Mohammad when he became shah and it entered the royal treasury. It is now officially registered in the Museum of

Crown Jewels (National Bank), where it has been kept since 1960 as the former property of the Golestan Palace Museum, where it was deposited in 1875.[52] It was inherited together with Khosrow Mirza's diary by Naser al-Din Shah, who was depicted in great detail wearing it in an early portrait, which unfortunately perished during the turmoil of the Islamic revolution.[53]

As in the case of the tsar's gifts to the shah, few of the Persian artefacts brought by Khosrow Mirza survived in Russia, even excluding the live, mortal presents, like 'Arab horses'. The 'Shah' diamond is on permanent display in the Diamond Chamber of the Kremlin Museum in Moscow, the manuscripts are held in the National Library of Russia and some of the gold coins form part of the numismatic collection of the Hermitage Museum. Nevertheless, there is a series of objects that, although never mentioned as particularly important on the list of the gifts, are worthy of special attention. As part of the 'less precious items', Khosrow Mirza presented a set of teacups to the Empress Alexandra Fedorovna, the wife of Nicholas I (see Plate VIIa)*.

The Teacups and Holders presented by Khosrow Mirza

It is not known how many cups were originally presented to the tsarina. The current record of the Gold Room of the Treasure Gallery of the Hermitage mentions eight such cups.[54] A similar one is known to be part of the collections of the National Museum of Georgia.[55] It is possible that Khosrow Mirza presented it to Paskevich when enjoying his reluctant hospitality in Tbilisi on the way to St Petersburg.[56] In 2005, another two were sold at Bonhams, London.[57] However, only the empress' cups have the splendid gold holders executed in the traditional technique of Persian polychrome enamel on metal (*mina'i*).[58] They arrived together with the round gold mina'i tray, richly decorated with flowers with a female face in the compositional centre, symbolizing the 'Lady Sun' (*khanom-khorshid*). Cup holders became particularly popular in Middle Eastern and Mediterranean culture thanks to the fashion of tea and coffee houses and rapidly penetrated the Qajar court via the Ottomans. Such pieces were both produced locally and commissioned in Europe using various techniques involving precious metals and jewels. The Hermitage cross-cultural English cups with their Persian-style holders presented to the tsar seem to have carried a special message, as the English cups held inside the Persian holders could symbolize a strong alliance and a necessary support of Britain against Russia. In view of the notional assistance given by Britain to Iran, despite the treaty of Tehran in 1814, which promised help in the event of Russian aggression and was not respected when it came to the point (and was later revoked by a cash payment), this was a very optimistic message. Nevertheless, Britain's growing involvement in Persia and the potential for rivalry with Russia clearly created an opportunity for some leverage in Iran's relations with her northern neighbour.[59]

(a)

(b)

(c)

(d)

Plate I

(a)   (b)

(c)   (d)

Plate II

Plate III

Plate IV

(a)

(b)

Plate V

(a)

(b)

Plate VI

(a)

(b)

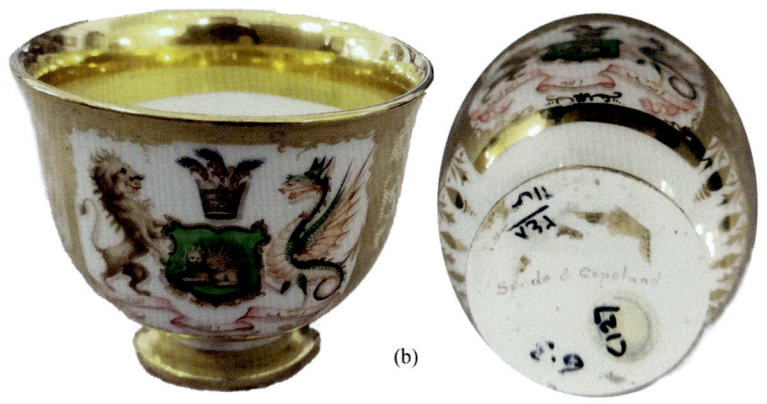

Plate VII

(a)

(b)

(c)

Plate VIII

(d)

It is not known whether the gold mina'i holders were produced specially to accompany the cups to St Petersburg as a gift targeting the Russian emperor through his wife, or had already been made when the shah received the cups from England. The holders were manufactured using a traditional Persian technique, which was also popular in both Persia and Russia since the earliest Romanovs. However, the holders do not bear the date of their production. The only inscription which might indicate the name of the master inside one of them is not legible;[60] it was not engraved but scratched. Among the suggested names for the master, who has not been identified so far, is Hafez Salim or Hafez 'Azim.[61] Either way, the choice of these holders to accompany the cups could be read as a deliberate allusion to an Anglo-Iranian collaboration.

The cups, according to their hallmark, were manufactured at Worcester, by Flight Barr and Barr.[62] It seems that there were several commissions of objects with the same portraits. The original one in the early 1820s consisted of a set of cabinet cups with the portraits of Fath-'Ali Shah and 'Abbas Mirza. Later the portraits were also transferred to medallions produced in 1825 in oval frames with a decor imitating a string of pearls.[63] The portraits of both Fath-'Ali Shah and 'Abbas Mirza (see Figure 6) had as their prototypes mirror reflections of the originals published in black and white by Sir Robert Ker Porter (1821–22).[64]

Fig. 6. Teacup with the portrait of Fath-'Ali Shah, 1825–30, Flight and Barr, soft-paste porcelain, hand-painted, № 1708 © Museum of Royal Worcester.*

As will be discussed below, Ker Porter made live portraits of both the shah and the crown prince during his audiences with each of them in Tehran and Tabriz and in several versions – as watercolours and as black and white drawings and etchings. Some of them were probably painted later, or even ascribed to the artist (see Figure 7).[65]

Fig. 7. Robert Ker Porter, Portrait of Fath-'Ali Shah Qajar, *Iran, ca. 1821–35, after a drawing made by the artist in 1819, Dreweatts, Chinese Ceramics and Works of Art (Part 2) and Japanese, Islamic and Indian Ceramics & Works of Art. London. 20 May 2021. lot 597.**

The version of the cups with a more restrained palette (in black, white and gold with a very light pink background) and without a hallmark is now in the collection of the Golestan Palace Museum in Tehran (Figure 8).[66] The Hermitage version is of the best quality of execution, most colourful, and decorated on both sides: portraits on the front and floral bouquets of elaborate design on the back.

Fig. 8. Teacup with the portrait of 'Abbas Mirza, porcelain, gold, Royal Worcester, Flight Barr and Barr, early 1820s, height 6.8 cm © Golestan Palace Museum.

The Tehran cups were produced as a cheaper, perhaps draft variant of the polychromic cups from the Hermitage and Bonhams. These tea services must have been made at about the same time as another teacup by Spode and Copeland, which is also kept in the Golestan Palace and represents the most spectacular attempt to combine two national symbols: Persian and English (see Plate VIIb)*.[67] The cup in question has the English Tudor-style coat of arms in the version going back to Henry VIII (1509–47), with the lion on the left and the dragon on the right. The Persian national symbol is represented by the Lion and the Sun inside the green shield in the compositional centre held by the English lion and the Welsh dragon. Above the shield, hanging in the air, is placed the Kayani crown of the King of Kings of the legendary dynasty from the *Shahnama* with three black heron feathers, adopted by Fath-'Ali Shah. The Welsh dragon and the English lion are standing on a floating pink ribbon bearing the Shi'i motto (*Asad-Allah al-Ghalib* – 'The Victorious Lion of God', the epithet of Emam 'Ali). Curiously, as far as the motto should be read from right to left, the Arabic word *asad* for the Shi'i lion happens to be not under the image of the lion but under the Welsh dragon. Obviously, the British designer had a very difficult task, trying to accommodate all the complications of such a multicultural amalgamation, and it was decided that the Welsh dragon labelled as the Arabic lion would be a better sacrifice than to produce the mirror image by swapping the English lion and the Welsh dragon, which would have distorted the British coat of arms.

It is possible that such an effort to merge the Persian and the British coats of arms was related originally to the cup commemorating of the 1801 Anglo-Persian Treaty against the French and the Russians,[68] which was later 'recycled' for Fath-'Ali Shah's farman dated Moharram 1224/March 1809 to honour Sir Harford Jones-Brydges as the British envoy to Iran in 1809–11 (Figure 9).[69]

Fig. 9. Royal order (farman) awarded by Fath-'Ali Shah to Sir Harford Jones-Brydges in Moharram 1224/March 1809, opaque watercolour, gold, ink, paper, 61.2 × 47.4 cm © Private collection.

This document, now in a private collection,[70] is a very curious testament to the rivalry between the London Foreign Office and the EIC, both of which happened to send their envoys to Persia simultaneously: Sir Harford Jones from London and Brigadier-General Sir John Malcolm from Calcutta. The extraordinary competition between the two envoys left quite an awkward impression on Fath-'Ali Shah, who had to choose between the two. The farman witnesses his decision to prefer Jones over Malcolm. Sadly for Malcolm, the situation was repeated when he arrived in Tehran again in 1810, but this time it was Sir Gore Ouseley who was sent from London and was again preferred by the shah. Malcolm had to return to India once more. A decade later, as noted above, Malcolm's brother-in-law John Kinneir MacDonald found himself in a very similar situation when he arrived from Calcutta to find Willock of the London Foreign Office as his rival. The Persian legend in the ribbon under the crest reads *az shafaqat khosravani* 'by royal favour', which for Jones was of such particular importance that he used it as part of his coat of arms.

Precedents and Cultural Sources for the Production of Fine Objects with Portraits

The adaptation of a European design to create the Persian national symbol is also seen in the decorative programme of the original Russian – although very Oriental – motifs used for the shah's dinner service produced in St Petersburg in 1838, where the central *Shir-o Khorshid* ('Lion and Sun') element (see Plate VIIIa)*,[71] replaces the double-headed eagle in the original Kremlin dinner service designed in 1837–38 by the antiques connoisseur F.G. Solntsev (see Plate VIIIb)*.[72] He was certainly inspired by the seventeenth-century objects of solid gold decorated with polychrome enamels, rubies and emeralds, like the plate that was presented to Tsarevich Alexey Petrovich by his grandmother Tsarina Natalya Kirillovna in 1694 (see Plate VIIIc)*.[73] However, it is quite possible that, in designing the dinner set for the shah, Solntsev also had in mind the gold tray which was brought by Khosrow Mirza to St Petersburg in 1829 (see Plate VIIId)*.[74] The main 'stately' feature of both services is the use of the national emblems of Russia and Persia positioned in the compositional centre of the plates, with the floral-arabesque ornament along the border that appealed to both the Russian and the Persian taste.[75]

The tradition of presenting objects made of porcelain or glass with portraits of the monarchs as diplomatic gifts had already been established between the Persian and European courts of France, Britain and Russia. Nile Green quotes the description of a very peculiar piece which was brought to London in 1819 by the Persian envoy Abu'l-Hasan Khan for George III: 'a gold enamelled looking-glass, opening with a portrait of his Persian Majesty, the object of which was to exhibit, at one view, the portraits of the two sovereigns – the one in painting the other by reflection, and around which were poetical allusions'.[76] Such a mirror object, where the two monarchs were gazing affectionately at each other with mutual admiration, was to express their close relationship, following the paradigm of the typical Persian lovers' gift. It is possible that objects like this could be a perfect fusion of the European fashion of depicting their monarchs on pieces of tableware[77] and the Classical literary tradition where the lovers' strong feelings are inspired by each other's portraits.[78] It is highly likely that a similar meaning of mirrors as a kind of portrait, with their ancient and deep symbolism, was applied to the mirror with a carved alabaster portrait of 'Abbas Mirza sent to the Tsar Alexander I in 1822 as an elegant and explicit statement about the important change of 'Abbas Mirza's status, to emphasize his appointment as crown prince, although he was not the most obvious candidate; one significant provision of the Treaty of Golestan in 1813 was Russia's support for the legitimate heir to the throne.[79]

The shah already had several objects in his palace that could have inspired him to commission the cups with his portrait. One such is a bowl depicting Alexander I,[80] which he received as a diplomatic gift brought back by the embassy of General Ermolov in 1816 to reciprocate Abu'l-Hasan Khan's mission of the previous year (Figure 10).

Fig. 10. Bowl with the portrait of Alexander I, porcelain, polychrome, gold, Imperial Porcelain Factory, St Petersburg 1815 (?) © Golestan Palace Museum.

The list of the gifts brought by Ermolov was exceptionally long and impressive, including various jewellery decorations made of gold, diamonds and other precious stones; crystal and gold qalyans; porcelain dinner and breakfast services; gold watches, including mechanical automata; mirrors, arms and armour covered with jewels; furs of different kinds, especially sables and ermines; and fabrics, especially silks and velvets.[81]

It is unlikely that the service bearing Alexander's portrait[82] had a similar admiring message to the shah as that of the magic mirror sent by Fath-'Ali Shah to George III in 1819, although the Russian emperor was aware of his own irresistible charms.[83]

Sir Robert Ker Porter and the Qajar Royal Portraits

The circumstances surrounding the portraits of the shah and the crown prince by Sir Robert Ker Porter (1777–1842) are of particular interest.[84] Ker Porter and Griboedov met in Tabriz in February 1819 at a special dinner given in honour of the Russian envoy Semen Mazarovich in the British Legation, run by chargé d'affaires Henry Willock and his brother and secretary Edward.[85] Ker Porter happened to be in Persia for several reasons. Officially, he was sent by Aleksey Olenin, president of the Russian Fine Arts Academy on an archaeological survey.[86]

Ker Porter had first come to St Petersburg in 1805 on the invitation of Alexander I, being recommended by the Russian anglophile ambassador in London, Count Semen Vorontsov (1744–1832).[87] He successfully married Princess Maria Scherbatova (1780–1827), who waited faithfully for five years for their wedding in 1812, by which time she was already 32. Ker Porter developed his skills in rather journalistic reporting on the current situation in his travel books[88] and on the Napoleonic campaign in Russia, which was published and translated several times.[89] It was thanks to his wife's connections[90] that he was introduced to the Russian court in both capitals, so that in 1813 the tsar and tsarina agreed to be the godparents of his newborn daughter Maria. This encouraged the English Prince Regent, the future George IV, to knight Ker Porter same year.

The couple did not spend much time together: in 1817 he left St Petersburg for Persia for a trip which lasted three years instead of the planned 12 months. Upon his return, he stayed at their family home in Ditton and came back to Russia only a year before his next posting in 1824 as British consul in Caracas. His wife stayed in St Petersburg looking after their daughter and died from typhoid in 1826.[91] Ker Porter spent 15 years in Venezuela and on his way back to England he visited in St Petersburg, where he met his daughter, other Russian relatives and friends, and celebrated his 65th anniversary. On the eve of his departure he had an audience with the tsar, after which, on the next day he suddenly died from a heart attack and was buried in Smolenskoe cemetery.[92]

Of particular importance to him was the support of his wife's cousin Alexey Olenin (1764–1843), a highly influential statesmen, who by that time was the director of the Imperial Public Library and the President of the Fine Arts Academy. Olenin engaged him on a research project to compare the existing records, both textual and visual, of the Persian antiquities and especially the ancient rock reliefs of the Achaemenid and Sasanian periods.[93] Ker Porter's meticulously precise drawings allowed scholars like Johann Christian Grotefend (1775–1853) to decipher the cuneiform inscriptions in Persepolis and elsewhere.[94] His resulting travelogue, published in 1817, immediately became exceptionally popular.[95]

Thanks to his official engagement from Olenin, Ker Porter could move easily around the territories in the north of Persia, which were controlled by Russia after the Golestan Treaty of 1813. Apart from producing drawings of the archaeological sites for the Russian academic authorities, he was also controversially collecting intelligence for the British about the political situation in the north. Elizaveta Renne published a top secret letter, discovered in the Bodleian Library, which reveals that the artist was sharing his incisive opinion about the importance of Georgia, Central Asia and especially the territories around the Caspian and Black Sea for British military and trading purposes, aiming not only to protect India but to change the confrontation with Russia in favour of England in Persia itself, even discussing the possibility of moving the capital back to Esfahan.[96]

Sir Robert and Lady Ker Porter established a warm friendship with the Persian ambassador, Abu'l-Hasan Khan Ilchi, during his mission in St Petersburg in 1815. The Ilchi reciprocated their hospitality with Abu'l-Hasan offering Ker Porter his full support in arranging personal audiences and drawing sessions with the shah in Tehran and crown prince 'Abbas Mirza in Tabriz. For his portraits, the shah awarded Ker Porter the Order of the Lion and the Sun. He later turned them into engravings to illustrate his travelogue. Both versions, in colour and in black and white, were transferred onto the porcelain cups and medallions, which as noted above are now kept in the Golestan Palace, the Hermitage, the National Museum of Georgia and the Museum of Royal Worcester.[97] It seems that Ker Porter's portrait of 'Abbas Mirza was used by Mohammad Ja'far, who was studying at the Academy of Fine Arts in St Petersburg, for his graduation piece (see Plate VIb)*.[98]

From the personal diaries and official reports of the Russian mehmandars of the Persian delegation it is known that during his stay in St Petersburg Khosrow Mirza commissioned several of his oil portraits, including the one painted by Gustav Hippius. Emulating his father and grandfather, the prince ordered it to be transferred to the dinner set commissioned at the Imperial Porcelain Factory. In the Taurida Palace, the portrait of his father 'Abbas Mirza 'in Persian style by Beggrov'[99] was borrowed by Suchtelen from Auguste de Montferrand (1786–1858) for one of the rooms. Khosrow returned the portrait when he left, adding his own lithographed portrait (Figure 11).[100] In October 1829, before his departure, Khosrow visited the Imperial porcelain and crystal factories, where he received as presents 200 various objects, including plates and vases with the portraits of the emperor, crown prince Alexander and Khosrow Mirza in polychrome with gold. Khosrow's portrait had a particular likeness, as he had been painted specially for this purpose by the factory's artist Golov, who was also using the oil painting of the prince that already existed.[101] Among the presents he received was a portrait of the tsar by Schulz.[102]

Fig. 11. Karl Gampeln, Portrait of Khosrow Mirza, *St Petersburg, 1829, ЭРГ-19106 © Hermitage Museum.*

So far it has been impossible to find any of those objects with Khosrow's portrait. The only image which I happened to come across was a black and white photograph of the oil painting (Figure 12).[103] In the portrait, Khosrow is wearing round his neck the diamond Order of the White Eagle, which he received as a farewell gift from the emperor. The reason for their disappearance could be explained by his attempt to seize the throne after the death of his father and grandfather. His half-brother Mohammad, when he became the shah with the support of both the Russian and British courts, ordered Khosrow and his other full brother Jahangir first to be imprisoned in the Ardabil fortress, blinded and then sent in exile to Hamadan for the rest of their life with their possessions confiscated. Khosrow's portraits were perceived as his pretension to the throne which he did not deserve. Perhaps by sending him to Russia as head of the mission, 'Abbas Mirza was hoping that Khosrow could jump the long queue to the throne, as had happened in his own case. If Khosrow could have become the shah with his experience, curiosity and the ability to observe European life he could have played the same role in developing his nation as Peter the Great did for Russia. After Peter's travels to Europe, he and his successors managed to turn his rather backward state into a superpower within just a couple of decades. Khosrow was the only Persian royalty to travel abroad before the grand tour of Naser al-Din Shah, who relied heavily on Khosrow's diary to prepare himself for his travels.[104]

Fig. 12. Portrait of Khosrow Mirza, *N 5682* © *National Library of Iran, Tehran.*

Khosrow's aspirations to become shah were probably encouraged by the role he was given to play during his embassy in Russia, where he was received by the tsar as a royal equal from an important state. At his tender age he was naturally emulating not only his counterpart Mirza Abu'l-Hasan Khan, who during his mission to London in 1809 had his portrait painted several times, including by such prominent English painters as Sir William Beechey and Sir Thomas Lawrence (Figures 13 and 14),[105] but also the shah and the emperor (Figure 15), even commissioning his own portraits as part of his elevated status.

Despite the very important role that both missions played in the political and cultural relations between the two countries, very little material evidence remains from them, including the exceptionally important and precious artifacts presented to the rulers of both countries, such as the specially commissioned porcelain bearing the prince's portraits. However, even one small teacup, like Darius and Alexander's ball, can say a lot about both giver and recipient, the circumstances of their lives and times and the ideas each had about themselves and the other.

Fig. 13. Sir Thomas Lawrence, Portrait of Mirza Abu'l-Hasan Khan Ilchi, *London, 1810, 1964.100* © *The Fogg Art Museum, Harvard University, Cambridge, Massachusetts.**

Fig. 14. Thomas Baxter, Cabinet cup with portrait of Mirza Abu'l-Hasan Khan, *Worcester, Flight Barr and Barr, ca. 1814–16* © *Bonham's, London, 29 September 2021.**

Fig. 15. Sir Godfrey Kneller, Portrait of Peter I the Great, Tsar of Russia, *1698, RCIN 405645* © *Royal Collection.**

Notes:

* For additional information; please see the List of Illustrations on page vii.
1. On his personality, perception and latest bibliography, see Firuza Melville, 'Paradox of Griboedov', pp. 299–314; idem, 'Alexander Sergeevich Griboedov', pp. 49–75 and Fig. 8. Also S.A. Fomichev, *Griboedov Entsiklopedia* and idem, *Aleksandr Griboedov, Biografiya*; N.A. Tarkhova, *Letopis' zhizni i tvorchestva Aleksandra Sergeevicha Griboedova (1790–1829)*.
2. Doris Behrens-Abouseif, *Practising Diplomacy in the Mamluk Sultanate*; on the elephants sent to the Russian court, see Daria Vasilyeva, 'Elephants as diplomatic gifts', pp. 281–310.
3. On the concepts of East–West royal gift-giving, see *Gifts of the Sultan*, edited by Linda Komaroff; *Dary Vostoka i Zapada imperatorskomu dvoru za 300 let*, edited by T.V. Rappe.
4. On symbolic dimensions of the diplomatic gifts, see Nile Green, *The Love of Strangers*, pp. 234–35.
5. See the catalogues by Layla S. Diba and Maryam Ekhtiar, *Royal Persian Paintings*. and Gwenaëlle Fellinger, *L'empire des roses*. On Russo-Persian royal and diplomatic gift exchange, see Adel Adamova, 'Rossiya i Iran: Diplomatiya i iskusstvo' and idem, 'Rossiya i Iran (XVI–XIX vv)', pp. 40–53 (Qajars) and esp. pp. 54–62. On the visit of Naser al-Din Shah in Michal Zichi's documentary watercolours, see A.S. Kantor-Gukovskaya and G.A. Printseva, *Pri dvore russkikh imperatorov*; and the current (July 2021) exhibitions: in Moscow, P.V. Korotchikova and M.V. Kullanda, *Splendour of the Sunset*; in London, John Curtis, Ina Sarikhani Sandmann and Tim Stanley, *Epic Iran*, and previously, in Washington, *The Prince and the Shah: Royal Portraits from Qajar Iran* (24 February–5 August 2018) in the National Museum of Asian Art, Smithsonian Institution, https://asia.si.edu/exhibition/the-prince-and-the-shah-royal-portraits-from-qajar-iran/ [accessed 6 December 2021].
6. Sara Nodjoumi, *Of Kings and Paintings*, with interviews by Abbas Amanat, Layla S. Diba, Maryam Ekhtiar, Mehran Haghighi and Sara Nodjoumi.
7. Similar to the Achaemenids appropriating the religious and political imagery of their conquered predecessors in Babylon, Assyria and other realms.
8. It would be enough to mention a recent review by Vanessa Martin, who refuses to admit the influence of Griboedov's British rivals on the shah and his role in the British Legation, calling the well-documented research a 'gross exaggeration' (V. Martin, 'Russians in Iran'). Such an attitude is a very symptomatic result of the British 'Narrative' produced immediately after the tragedy and promoted by the British writers ever since, cf. Laurence Kelly, *Diplomacy and Murder in Tehran*. As a result, the former British Foreign Minister, Jack Straw, in his book *The English Job*, mentions more than once the Turkmanchay Treaty and its consequences but not the person who was instrumental in its signing.
9. D.P. Costello, 'Murder of Griboedov', p. 85.
10. Interesting statistics are given by Maya Jasanoff, *Edge of Empire, Life, Culture and Conquest in the East*, p. 49, for the officers of the East India Company, of whom already in 1766 only 129 out of 231 were formally British.
11. Firuz Kazemzadeh, *Russia and Britain in Persia*, p. 6.
12. N.A. Tarkhova, 'O proekte russkoy zakavkazskoy kompanii', pp. 285–95.

13. Ryleev had 10 shares while, for example, the emperor had 20: E.A. Ivanyan, *Entsiklopediya rossiysko-amerikanskikh otnosheniy XVIII–XX veka*, p. 696; N.N. Bolkhovitinov, *Istoriya russkoy Ameriki*.
14. *Besedy v Obschestve lyubiteley Rossiyskoy slovesnosti*, p. 25; N.K. Piksanov, *Letopis zhizni i tvorchestva A.S. Griboedova*, pp. 89–90.
15. The trick was used by Sir Gore Ouseley who, accompanying the Persian ambassador Abu'l-Hasan Khan from London back home, travelled with his family via South America and Africa, taking 18 months to reach Persia, and eventually arriving in Tehran in November 1811. However, Fath-'Ali Shah did not appreciate his ambassadorial services, and Sir Gore had to leave Persia in April 1814, which he did via St Petersburg, Denis Wright, *The English Amongst the Persians*, pp. 13–16.
16. MacDonald managed to present his credentials only two years later, in 1826, see below. This was his second visit: earlier, he had accompanied Sir John Malcolm on the previous diplomatic mission on behalf of the EIC, in 1808–9, returning via Iraq, Turkey, Portugal, Spain, Sweden, Austria and Hungary; see John Kinneir MacDonald, *Narrative of Travels in Asia Minor, Armenia, and Kurdistan*.
17. John Malcolm, *Malcolm – Soldier, Diplomat, Ideologue of British India*, p. 327.
18. Griboedov's play in verse *Woe from Wit*, finished in 1824, was first published posthumously in 1833. His second, almost finished, play *Gruzinskaya noch* (Georgian night) perished with him.
19. Henry Manners Chichester, 'McNeill, Sir John'; Memoir of the Right Hon. Sir John McNeill; Maurice Chittenden, 'Passion for married doctor led Nightingale to humiliating error'.
20. Evelyn Harden, 'Griboedov and the Willock Affair'; idem, *Murder of Griboedov*.
21. E.I. Enikolopov, *A.S. Griboedov v Gruzii i Persii*, p. 144. N.K. Piksanov, ed., *A.S. Griboedov v vospominaniyakh sovremennikov*, pp. 198–200; V.E. Vatsuro, ed., *A.S. Griboedov v vospominaniyakh sovremennikov*.
22. 'Narrative of the Proceedings of the Russian Mission to Persia', pp. 496–512.
23. Russian Foreign Minister K. Nesselrode was the first to admit that it was Griboedov's 'own unnecessary excessive zeal that caused the massacre' (Nesselrode to Paskevich, 16 March 1829, Russian State Historical Archive (RGIA), St Petersburg).
24. 'Relation des événement que ont précédé et accompagné le massacre de la dernière ambassade russe', pp. 314–45.
25. Evgraf Serchevskii, ed., *A.S. Griboedov i ego sochineniya c prilozheniyami*.
26. Z. Davydov, ed., *A.S. Griboedov*, pp. 151–58.
27. Behnām Abu Torābiyān, *Gozar-e Ilchi: Qatlgah-e Griboedov dar Tehrān-e 'atiq*.
28. Emily MacDonald went with Captain Alexander to St Petersburg to meet the Russian Foreign Minister; however, her arrival coincided with the flamboyant visit of Khosrow Mirza, and nobody cared to hear about Griboedov as his 'affair was already closed' (Captain James Edward Alexander, *Travels to the Seat of War in the East*, p. 84).
29. I.S. Sidorov, ed. and annot., 'O gibeli A.S. Griboedova', esp. pp. 91–92 (letters by M.M. Bakunin).
30. *Tabriz in the Fog* (Iran TV, 2010), 28 episodes, directed by Mohammad-Reza Varzi.

31. Maltsev was 21 at that time.
32. 'Narrative', pp. 507–8.
33. To check and question the price and value of a gift was a general practice among Persian officials: when Abu'l-Hasan Khan, envoy at the court of George III, received a bejewelled dagger as a gift from the British monarch he complained when he discovered that the main jewel was made of glass, not a diamond. On the next day, the Prince Regent had to soothe his hurt feelings by presenting him with a ring with the real diamond (Green, *The Love of Strangers*, p. 235).
34. Natalya Myasoedova, *O Griboedove i Pushkine*, pp. 100–102.
35. Varvara Fomicheva, 'Perekhvachennye depeshi, p. 223. The inclusion of porcelain indicates Russia's desire to dominate this trade, while at this time it was British ceramics that were particularly popular; see Jaap Otte and Willem Floor, 'European ceramics in Iran', p. 120.
36. 'Narrative', pp. 507–8.
37. 'Narrative', p. 500.
38. Firuza Melville, 'Alexander Sergeevich Griboedov, pp. 50–56. Tynyanov's biographical novel about Griboedov, published in 1929, has recently been translated into English twice: Yury Tynyanov, *The Death of Vazir-Mukhtar*, trans. Susan Causey and trans. Anna Kurkina Rush and Christopher Rush.
39. 'Narrative', p. 510.
40. Firuza Melville, 'Khosrow Mirza's mission to St Petersburg in 1829', pp. 69–94; George Bournoutian, *From Tabriz to St. Petersburg*.
41. Vladimir Minorsky, 'Tsena krovi Griboedova. Neizdannyi document', pp. 333–45.
42. Adel Adamova and Galina Printseva, *Panorama*, pp. 8–9.
43. On Mirza Saleh, Mirza Mas'ud and Hajji Baba in England see Nile Green, 'The Madrasas of Oxford', pp. 807–29 and idem, *Love of Strangers*, especially on Mirza Saleh as a Persian Mr Darcy, pp. 2–5.
44. Melville, 'Khosrow Mirza's mission', p. 90.
45. A.E. Fersman, *Kristallografiya almaza*, pp. 459–547.
46. Masoud Bonakdar, 'Khosrow Mirza's aigrette'.
47. G.I. Kostygova, 'Sobranie persidskih rukopisey, postupivshee v Publichnuyu biblioteku v 1829 godu', pp. 336–45; O.V. Vasilyeva, *A String of Pearls*, p. 8.
48. Myasoedova, *O Griboedove i Pushkine*, p. 32.
49. A. Berzhe, 'Khosrow Mirza', p. 401; V. Potto, 'Khosrow Mirza', pp. 443–56.
50. M.G. Rozanov, 'Persidskoe posolstvo v Rossii 1829 goda', pp. 198–200.
51. Ibid., p. 217. Khosrow's delight at the porcelain factory and the numerous gifts he received are noted by Otte and Floor, 'European ceramics', p. 120.
52. Accession number 295-7174: 176 and the Museum of Crown Jewels inventory No. 33, box 7 (Bonakdar, 'Khosrow Mirza's aigrette', p. 8).
53. Sir Clements Robert Markham, *A General Sketch of the History of Persia*.
54. V3-732, 741, 743–750 (cups) and V3-751 (gold mina'i tray): A.A. Ivanov *et al.*, *Yuvelirnye izdeliya Vostoka*, pp. 120–23 and esp. p. 72. I thank Elena Malozemova and Daria Vasilyeva of the Hermitage Museum for their help in the museum archive regarding their provenance: notably, only two cups are mentioned there as being passed by the empress to the Keeper Labensky, although with no information about the gold enamelled holders (File 1, op. 2, 1830, no. 4); others arrived in 1934 from the collection of the Catherine Palace in Tsarskoe Selo. They

have been exhibited several times: e.g. Rappe, *Dary Vostoka i Zapada imperatorskomu dvoru za 300 let*, nos. 175, 176, p. 220. See also S. Varshavsky and B. Rest, *Podvig Ermitazha*, p. 336. Earlier exhibitions include: *Heaven on Earth*, p. 130; *Islam, konst och kultur*, pl. 2, p. 159.

55. I am grateful to Irina Koshoridze, keeper of Persian art at this museum, for this information.
56. It is also possible that the cups were sent to Tbilisi from Leningrad under a shared treasure policy during Soviet times.
57. Sold for £2,160: https://www.bonhams.com/auctions/13151/lot/203/ [accessed 11 August 2021].
58. B.W. Robinson, 'A royal Qājār enamel', pp. 25–30.
59. For general background, see Rose Greaves, 'Iranian relations with Great Britain', pp. 385–90; see also above n. 48. At this period, the rivalry was also expressed in terms of porcelain production, with Britain currently the source of the finest wares, as noted by Otte and Floor, 'European ceramics', pp.118–22.
60. I thank Daria Vasilyeva for the photograph of the inscription.
61. I thank Hamid-Reza Ghelichkhani for suggesting one of the readings of this name.
62. Five of them have the following inscription on the bottom: Flight & Barr. Royal Porcelain Works. Worchester. London House, 1 Coventry str. (Ivanov *et al.*, *Yuvelirnye izdeliya Vostoka*).
63. Museum of Royal Worcester (former Worcester Porcelain Museum and Dyson Perrins Museum), accession number 1707; see also nos. 1706, 1708. An undated bone-china unhandled cup with portraits of Fath-'Ali Shah and 'Abbas Mirza, made by Spode, is also noted by Jaap Otte and Willem Floor, 'English ceramics in Iran', p. 102; they also mention a dinner service by Wedgwood, made for Fath-'Ali Shah ca. 1810, ibid., p. 101 and Otte and Floor, 'European ceramics', p. 118.
64. Robert Ker Porter, *Travels in Georgia, Persia, Armenia, Ancient Babylonia*, flyleaf. I thank Moya Carey for pointing out these illustrations.
65. Cf. the portrait of Fath-'Ali Shah sold on 20 May 2021 at Dreweatts, London, 'Chinese Ceramics and Works of Art (Part 2) and Japanese, Islamic and Indian Ceramics & Works of Art', lot 597: https://auctions.dreweatts.com/auctions/7813/dreweal-10226/lot-details/271a29ee-65f4-4f95-8851-ad1100fcd329
[accessed 11 August 2021]. In 1833–35, there was another commission of 'the cabinet cups, medallions and spill vases' where the portraits, according to John Sandon, *Dictionary of Worcester Porcelain (1751–1851)*, p. 144, reproduced Thomas Dudley's prints. It seems that there were two versions of the second commission: in full colour and in sepia monochrome.
66. I am grateful to the management of the Golestan Palace Museum, and especially to Mansoureh Azadvari, Jabbar Ouj and Homayun Khodadad, for the opportunity to see the objects and obtain the photographs of them.
67. For the successful trade of Spode in Iran, see Otte and Floor, 'English ceramics', esp. pp. 102–3. As seen from Plate VII, there is no Persian inscription on the base. The authors do not refer to Flight Barr and Barr in either article. See note 66 for thanks once more to Golestan Palace officials for the image of the underside of the cup.

68. The cup has a hallmark which, according to Sandon (*Dictionary*, p. 376), could indicate that it was produced between 1813 and 1840. However, the Golestan cup, compared with the one described by Sandon, has a crown above the inscription.
69. Wright, *The English Amongst the Persians*, pp. 60–61.
70. Accession number AKM530. I am grateful to Bita Pourvash and Marika Sardar for their help in obtaining the image.
71. I am grateful to Anna Ivanova of the Hermitage Museum for pointing out this service to me. My special gratitude to Irina Bagdasarova for referring me to Tatyana Petrova's publications of this plate in the catalogues of the exhibitions of 2008 and 2016: *Podnesenie k Rozhdestvu*, pl. 28, p. 104 and *Iz serviznykh kladovykh*, pl. 43.3, p. 335.
72. V.V. Levshenkov, *Imperatorsky farfor*, p. 71.
73. Now in the Armoury Chamber, Museum of the Kremlin (MP-3365): https://collectiononline.kreml.ru/entity/OBJECT/42294?query=тарелка%201694&index=0 [accessed 11 August 2021].
74. Published in Ivanov *et al.*, *Yuvelirnye izdeliya Vostoka*, p. 118 (no. 72).
75. The plate is hallmarked with H and I for Nicholas I; however, without incorporating a crown.
76. Green, *Love of Strangers*, p. 234.
77. London Delft (Southwark), caudle-cup with the portrait of Charles II dedicated to his coronation in 1661, sold at Christie's, London, on 11 June 2010, lot 1007, for £49,250, https://www.christies.com/en/lot/lot-5323477.
78. For example, the iconic couples like Khosrow and Shirin or Yusof and Zoleykha.
79. Adamova and Printseva, *Panorama*, pp. 42–43; for the Russian commitment to support the heir to the throne, see for example F. Kazemzadeh, 'Iranian relations with Russia', p. 334.
80. Now in the collection of the Golestan Palace Museum. Cf. the cup in the collection of the Russian Museum, Goldovskiy, Grigoriy, Yuriy Epatko, *et al.*, *1812 god v proizvedeniyah iskusstva iz sobraniya Russkogo muzeya*, p. 111.
81. A. Berzhe, *Posolstvo A.P. Ermolova v Persiyu*, pp. 259–60.
82. Ibid., p. 83.
83. Cf. Napoleon's letter to his wife after he signed the 1807 Treaty of Tilsit with the very handsome Russian Emperor, whom he would have wanted to make his mistress if Alexander had been a woman.
84. T. Seccombe, 'Robert Ker Porter', pp. 190–92; W.M. Armstrong, 'The many-sided world of Robert Ker Porter', pp. 36–58; Walter Dupouy, ed., *Sir Robert Ker Porter's Caracas Diary*; R.D. Barnett, 'Sir Robert Ker Porter – Regency artist and traveller', pp. 19–24; Matthew Ancketill, 'The silver palette', pp. 70–72; Matthew Ancketill, *Strange Destiny*; Elizaveta Renne, 'Robert Ker Porter v Rossii', pp. 105–9; N.E. Vasilyeva, 'Albom R. Ker Portera s risunkami drevneyshikh pamyatnikov skulptury i arkhitektury', pp. 246–47; O.V. Vasilyeva, 'Chey albom', pp. 34–35; Elizaveta Renne, 'British artists in Russia', pp. 104–15; idem, 'Khudozhnik Sir Robert Ker Porter v Rossii'; Christopher Wright, 'Painting Persepolis'; Nodar Lakhuti, 'Chelovek mira', p. 9.
85. Tarkhova, *Letopis'*, p. 120.

86. Robert Ker Porter, having lost his father at the age of two in Edinburgh, was educated together with his four siblings by his mother Jane Porter, who correctly detected artistic talents in her children and helped them to flourish by hiring the best tutors. By the age of 16, Robert was awarded the Silver Palette prize from the Royal Society of Arts, and at 22 he was commissioned to decorate the chapel of St John's College, Cambridge. By this time, he and his family lived in what was formerly Joshua Reynolds' house on Leicester Square; his 13-year-old sister Anna Maria had by that time already published her first novel: Armstrong, 'The many-sided world of Robert Ker Porter', p. 38.
87. Count Semen Vorontsov preferred to stay in England when the term of his posting finished.
88. Robert Ker Porter, *Travelling Sketches in Russia and Sweden*; idem, *Letters from Portugal and Spain*.
89. Robert Ker Porter, *Narrative of the Campaign in Russia*.
90. Maria's parents belonged to high Russian nobility on both sides: her father was Prince Fedor Scherbatov and her mother was Princess Anna Mescherskaya, from whom she inherited several estates and a mansion in Moscow.
91. Barnett, 'Sir Robert Ker Porter', esp. p. 21.
92. Smolenskoe cemetery, burial place 3: https://spslc.ru/burial-places/porter-ker-robert.html [accessed 11 August 2021].
93. Barnett, 'Sir Robert Ker Porter', p. 20; Vesta Curtis, 'The British and archaeology in 19th century Persia', pp. 166–78; Elizabeth Errington and Vesta Sarkhosh Curtis, eds, *From Persepolis to the Punjab*, pp. 3–4.
94. Barnett, 'Sir Robert Ker Porter', p. 20; Curtis, 'The British and archaeology', pp. 169–73; J.P. 'The Qajar rock reliefs', pp. 31–49.
95. Ker Porter, *Travels in Georgia, Persia, Armenia, Ancient Babylonia*.
96. Notes by Sir Robert Ker Porter, mainly on military colonization in Russia and the situation in Persia in 1820, c.1820–1824, see *Notes on Russia and Persia*, pp. 32–34; Renne, 'British artists in Russia', esp. p. 107; idem, 'Khudozhnik Sir Robert Ker Porter v Rossii'.
97. See above, nn. 54, 61.
98. D. Safaralieva, 'Iranskiy uchenik Akademii, pp. 57–58; Adamova, 'Rossiya i Iran: Diplomatiya i iskusstvo', p. 194; idem, 'Rossiya i Iran (XVI–XIX vv.)', p. 56; *Aziatskiy vestnik*, p. 226.
99. Rozanov, 'Persidskoe posolstvo v Rossii 1829 goda', p. 216. Perhaps it was the lithograph from the portrait of 'Abbas Mirza painted in 1824 by Mohammad Ja'far, who was sent to St Petersburg by 'Abbas Mirza to study art at the Academy of Fine Arts (Museum of the Fine Arts Academy, P-588).
100. This lithographed portrait could have been the one which was produced by Karl Gampeln (1794–1880s).
101. Rozanov, 'Persidskoe posolstvo v Rossii 1829 goda', p. 230.
102. Ibid., p. 226. See also above, n. 51.
103. This photograph is now kept in the National Library in Tehran and Astan-e Qods in Mashhad. I thank Goodarz Rashtiani for drawing my attention to it.
104. Unfortunately, Khosrow Mirza's diary disappeared without a trace in Naser al-Din's Library.

105. Sir Thomas Lawrence, 'Portrait of Mirza Abu'l-Hasan Khan', 1810, 1964.100 © Fogg Art Museum, Harvard Art Museums; Sir William Beechey, 'Portrait of Mirza Abu'l-Hasan Khan Ilchi', 1809–10, F26 © British Library and CVCSC:0358.B © Compton Verney. It is interesting to note that, while in London, Abu'l-Hasan Khan joined the same Freemason lodge as that of his mehmandar Sir Gore Ouseley; see Hamid Algar, 'Freemasonry in the Qajar period'.

Bibliography:

Abu Torābiyān, Behnām, *Gozar-e Ilchi: Qatlgah-e Griboedov dar Tehrān-e 'atiq* (Tehran: Nashr-e Tarikh-e Iran, 1394/2015).

Adamova, Adel, 'Rossiya i Iran: Diplomatiya i iskusstvo', in *Iran v Ermitazhe* (St Petersburg: Slavia, 2004).

— 'Rossiya i Iran (XVI–XIX vv.): diplomatiya i iskusstvo', in *Persian Manuscripts, Paintings and Drawings of the 15th–early 20th Centuries. Catalogue of the Collections* (St Petersburg: The State Hermitage Publishers, 2010).

Adamova, Adel and Printseva, Galina, *Panorama Persii P.Ya. Pyasetskogo ot Enzeli do Tegerana* (St Petersburg: State Hermitage Museum, 2015).

Alexander, Captain James Edward, *Travels to the Seat of War in the East through Russia and The Crimea in 1829* (London: Henry Colburn and Richard Bentley, 1830).

Algar, Hamid, 'Freemasonry in the Qajar period, *Encyclopaedia Iranica*, online at https://iranicaonline.org/articles/freemasonry-ii-in-the-qajar-period [accessed 11 August 2021].

Ancketill, Matthew, *Strange Destiny: The Rediscovery of Sir Robert Ker Porter*, unpublished, Middle East Centre Archive, accession number GB 165 0009, St Antony's College, University of Oxford.

— 'The silver palette', in *Lantern* (July 1978), pp. 70–72.

Armstrong, W.M., 'The many-sided world of Robert Ker Porter', *The Historian* 25, no. 1 (1962), pp. 36–58.

Aziatskiy vestnik 3 (St Petersburg: Tipografiya departamenta ministerstva vnutrennikh del, 1825).

Barnett R.D., 'Sir Robert Ker Porter – Regency artist and traveller', *Iran* 10 (1972), pp. 19–24.

Behrens-Abouseif, Doris, *Practising Diplomacy in the Mamluk Sultanate: Gifts and Material Culture in the Medieval Islamic World* (London: I.B. Tauris, 2014).

Berzhe, A., 'Khosrow Mirza (1813–1875), chitano v Tiflise na Griboedovskon vechere 28–go yanvarya 1879 goda', in *Russkaya starina* 25 (St Petersburg: Pechatnya V.I. Golovina, 1879), pp. 333–52 and pp. 401–14.

— 'Posolstvo A.P. Ermolova v Persiyu. Istoricheskiy ocherk', *Russkaya starina* 6 (St Petersburg: Pechatnya V.I. Golovina, 1877).

Besedy v Obschestve lyubiteley Rossiyskoy slovesnosti, vol. II (Moscow: Tipografiya Gracheva & Co., 1868).

Bolkhovitinov, N.N., ed., *Istoriya russkoy Ameriki, 1732–1867*, vol. II, *Deyatelnost' rossiysko-amerikanskoy kompanii 1799–1825* (Moscow: Mezhdunarodnye otnosheniya, 1999).

Bonakdar, Masoud, 'Khosrow Mirza's aigrette and jewellery: Diplomatic gift exchange between Persian and Russian courts', *Qajar–Romanov Diplomatic Gift Exchange*, ed. Firuza Melville, forthcoming.

Bournoutian, George, *From Tabriz to St. Petersburg: Iran's Mission of Apology to Russia in 1829* (Costa Mesa: Mage, 2014).

Chichester, Henry Manners, 'McNeill, Sir John', in *Dictionary of National Biography, 1885–1900*, vol. 35: https://en.wikisource.org/wiki/Dictionary_of_National_Biography,_1885-1900/McNeill,_John_(1795–1883) [accessed 11 August 2021].

Chittenden, Maurice, 'Passion for married doctor led Nightingale to humiliating error. A new biography of the wartime nurse says she was driven to echo the severe criticism of the army made by her lover', *The Sunday Times* (22 August 2010): https://www.thetimes.co.uk/article/passion-for-married-doctor-led-nightingale-to-humiliating-error-5c5pqv3gs3p [accessed 11 August 2021].

Costello, D.P., 'Murder of Griboedov', *Oxford Slavonic Papers* 8 (1957), pp. 66–89.

Curtis, John, Ina Sarikhani Sandmann and Tim Stanley, *Epic Iran: 5000 Years of Culture* (London: Victoria and Albert Museum Publishing, 2021).

Curtis, Vesta, 'The British and archaeology in 19th century Persia', in *From Persepolis to the Punjab: Exploring the Past in Iran, Afghanistan and Pakistan*, ed. Elizabeth Errington and Vesta Sarkhosh Curtis, with contributions by Joe Cribb, Jean-Marie Lafont, St John Simpson, Helen Wang (London: British Museum Press, 2007), pp. 166–78.

Davydov, Z., ed., *A.S. Griboedov. Ego zhizn i gibel' v memuarakh sovremennikov* (Leningrad: Krasnaya gazeta, 1929), pp. 151–58.

Diba, Layla S. and Maryam Ekhtiar, ed., *Royal Persian Paintings: The Qajar Epoch 1785–1925* (London: I.B. Tauris and Brooklyn: Brooklyn Museum of Art, 1998).

Dupouy, Walter, ed., *Sir Robert Ker Porter's Caracas Diary (1825–1842): A British Diplomat in a Newborn Nation* (Caracas: Editorial Arte, 1966).

Enikolopov, E.I., *A.S. Griboedov v Gruzii i Persii* (Tiflis: Zakkniga, 1929).

Errington, Elizabeth and Vesta Sarkhosh Curtis, eds, *From Persepolis to the Punjab: Exploring the Past in Iran, Afghanistan and Pakistan* (London: British Museum Press, 2007).

Fellinger, Gwenaëlle, ed., *L'empire des roses: Chef d'ouvre de l'art Persan du 19e siècle présentée au Musée Louvre-Lens (28 mars – 22 juillet 2018)*, avec la collaboration de Carol Guillaume (Louvre-Lens: Snoeck, 2018).

Fersman, A.E., *Kristallografiya almaza* (Leningrad, Izdatelstvo Akademii nauk SSSR, 1955), pp. 459–547.

Fomichev, S.A., *Griboedov Entsiklopedia* (St Petersburg: Nestor-Istoriya, 2007).

— *Aleksandr Griboedov, Biografiya* (St Petersburg: Vita Nova, 2012).
Fomicheva, Varvara, 'Perekhvachennye depeshi', in *Khmelitsky sbornik. A.S. Griboedov: epokha, lichnost, tvorchestvo, sud'ba* 16 (Vyazma, 2014), pp. 219–25.
Goldovskiy, Grigoriy, Yuriy Epatko, *et al.*, *1812 god v proizvedeniyah iskusstva iz sobraniya Russkogo muzeya* (St Petersburg: Palace Editions 2012).
Greaves, Rose, 'Iranian relations with Great Britain and British India, 1798–1921', in *The Cambridge History of Iran, vol. 7, From Nadir Shah to the Islamic Republic*, ed. Peter Avery, Gavin Hambly and Charles Melville (Cambridge: Cambridge University Press, 1991), pp. 374–425.
Green, Nile, 'The Madrasas of Oxford: Iranian interactions with the English universities in the early nineteenth century', *Iranian Studies* 44 (2011), pp. 807–29.
— *The Love of Strangers: What Six Muslim Students Learned in Jane Austen's London* (Princeton: Princeton University Press, 2016).
Harden, Elizabeth, 'Griboedov and the Willock Affair', *Slavic Review* 30, no. 1 (March 1971), pp. 74–92.
— *Murder of Griboedov: New Materials* (Birmingham: Slavonic Monographs, 1979).
Heaven on Earth: Islamic Art from the State Hermitage and the Khalili Collection, exhibition catalogue (London: Prestel Publishing, 2004).
Islam, konst och kultur (Stockholm: Statens historiska museum, 1985).
Ivanov, A.A., V.G. Lukonin and L.S. Smesova, *Yuvelirnye izdeliya Vostoka, Kollekciya Osoboy kladovoy otdela Vostoka Gosudarstvennogo Ermitazha. Drevniy, srednevekovyi periody* (Moscow: Iskusstvo, 1984).
Ivanyan, E.A. *Entsiklopediya rossiysko-amerikanskikh otnosheniy XVIII—XX veka* (Moscow: Mezhdunarodnye otnosheniya, 2001).
Iz serviznykh kladovykh. Ubranstvo russkogo imperatorskogo stola XVIII-nachala XX veka (St Petersburg: Izdatelstvo Gosudarstvennogo Ermotazha, 2016).
Jasanoff, Maya, *Edge of Empire, Life, Culture and Conquest in the East (1750–1850)* (New York: Alfred A. Knoff, 2005).
Kantor-Gukovskaya, A.S. and G.A. Printseva, *Pri dvore russkikh imperatorov. Proizvedeniya Mikhaya Zichi v sobranii Ermitazha* (St Petersburg: State Hermitage Publishers, 2006).
Kazemzadeh, Firuz, *Russia and Britain in Persia: Imperial Ambitions in Qajar Iran* (New Haven: Yale University Press, 1968).
— 'Iranian relations with Russia and the Soviet Union, to 1921', in *The Cambridge History of Iran, vol. 7, From Nadir Shah to the Islamic Republic*, ed. Peter Avery, Gavin Hambly and Charles Melville (Cambridge: Cambridge University Press, 1991), pp. 314–49.

Kelly, Laurence, *Diplomacy and Murder in Tehran, Alexander Griboyedov and Imperial Russia's Mission to the Shah of Persia* (London: I.B. Tauris, 2002).

Komaroff, Linda, ed., *Gifts of the Sultan: The Arts of Giving at the Islamic Courts* (Los Angeles and New Haven: Los Angeles County Museum of Art and Yale University Press, 2011).

Korotchikova, P.V. and M.V. Kullanda, *Splendour of the Sunset: Iran of the Qajar Era (late 18th cent. – 1925)*. Catalogue of the Exhibition, Museum of Orient (Moscow: Muzey Vostoka, 2021).

Kostygova, G.I., 'Sobranie persidskih rukopisey, postupivshee v Publichnuyu biblioteku v 1829 godu', *Vostochnyi sbornik* 6 (St Petersburg: Rossiyskaya Natsionalnaya Biblioteka, 2003), pp. 336–45.

Lakhuti, Nodar, 'Chelovek mira', *Troitsky variant-Nauka*, no. 306 (16 July 2020), p. 9: https://trv-science.ru/2020/06/chelovek-mira/ [accessed 11 August 2021].

Levshenkov, V.V., *Imperatorsky farfor* (St Petersburg: Sankt-Peterburg orkestr, 2009).

Luft, J.P. 'The Qajar rock reliefs', *Iranian Studies* 34, nos. 1–4 (2001), pp. 31–49.

MacDonald, John Kinneir, *Narrative of Travels in Asia Minor, Armenia, and Kurdistan in 1813–14, with Remarks on the Marches of Alexander the Great and of the Ten Thousand Greeks* (London: John Murray, 1818).

Malcolm, John, *Malcolm – Soldier, Diplomat, Ideologue of British India: The Life of Sir John Malcolm (1769–1833)* (Edinburgh: John Donald Short Run Press, 2014).

Markham, Sir Clements Robert, *A General Sketch of the History of Persia* (London: Longmans, Green, 1874).

Martin, V., 'Russians in Iran: Diplomacy and Power in the Qajar Era and Beyond. Ed. Rudi Matthee and Elena Andreeva. London: I.B. Tauris, 2018', *Slavic Review* 78, no. 1 (Spring 2019), pp. 237–39.

Melville, Firuza, 'Khosrow Mirza's Mission to St Petersburg in 1829', *Iranian–Russian Encounters: Empires and Revolutions since 1800*, ed. S. Cronin (London and New York: Routledge, 2013), pp. 69–94.

— 'Paradox of Griboedov: At home among strangers, a stranger among his own', in *Na Pastbische mysli blagoy* (St Petersburg: Kontrast, 2015), pp. 299–314.

— 'Alexander Sergeevich Griboedov – Russian Imperial James Bond malgré lui', *The Russians in Iran*, ed. R. Matthee and E. Andreeva (London: I.B. Tauris, 2018), pp. 49–75.

Memoir of the Right Hon. Sir John McNeill, G.C.B. and of his second wife Elizabeth Wilson (London: John Murray, 1910).

Minorsky, Vladimir, 'Tsena krovi Griboedova. Neizdannyi document', *Russkaya mysl* III–V (Berlin–Prague, 1923), pp. 333–45.

Myasoedova, Natalya, *O Griboedove i Pushkine* (Kostroma-Nizhniy Novgorod: OOO Algol, 1997).
'Narrative of the Proceedings of the Russian Mission to Persia from its Departure from Tabreez for Tehran on 14th Jummade 2D [20 December 1828], until its Destruction on Wednesday the 6th of Sha'ban [11 February 1829]', *Blackwood's Edinburgh Magazine* (Edinburgh, September 1830), pp. 496–512.
Otte, Jaap and Willem Floor, 'European ceramics in Iran in the 19th and early 20th centuries', *American Ceramic Circle Journal* 20 (2019), pp. 117–43.
— 'English ceramics in Iran 1810–1910', *Northern Ceramic Society Journal* 36 (2020), pp. 91–125.
Piksanov, N.K., *Letopis zhizni i tvorchestva A.S. Griboedova, 1791–1829* (Moscow: Nasledie, 2000).
— ed., *A.S. Griboedov v vospominaniyakh sovremennikov* (Moscow: Federatsia, 1929), pp. 198–200.
Podnesenie k Rozhdestvu. Geraldika v russkom farfore, exhibition catalogue (St Petersburg: Izdatelstvo Gosudarstvennogo Ermitazha, 2008).
Porter, Robert Ker, *Letters from Portugal and Spain, Written during the March of the Troops under Sir John Moore* (London: Longman, Hurst, Rees and Orme, 1809; facsimile edition, Cambridge: Ken Trotman Ltd, 1985; second edition by Ulan Press, 2012).
— *Narrative of the Campaign in Russia during the Year 1812* (London: Longman, Hurst, Rees, Orme and Brown, 1813).
— *Travelling Sketches in Russia and Sweden During the Years 1805, 1806, 1807, 1808* (London: John Stockdale, 1813).
— *Travels in Georgia, Persia, Armenia, Ancient Babylonia, &c. during the Years 1817, 1818, 1819, and 1820* (London: Longman, Hurst, Rees, Orme and Brown, 1821).
— *Notes on Russia and Persia*, with some pages in the hand of Jane Porter. MS. Eng. hist. c. 409, Bodleian Library, pp. 32–34: https://archives.bodleian.ox.ac.uk/repositories/2/resources/4460 [accessed 11 August 2021].
Potto, V., 'Khosrow Mirza', *Kavkazskaya voyna*, vol. III (St Petersburg: Tipografiya Okruzhnogo Shtaba Kavkazskogo voennogo okruga, 1887), pp. 443–56.
Rappe, T.V., ed., *Dary Vostoka i Zapada imperatorskomu dvoru za 300 let, katalog vystavki* (St Petersburg: State Hermitage Publishers, 2014).
'Relation des événement que ont précédé et accompagné le massacre de la dernière ambassade russe en Perse', *Nouvelles Annales des Voyages des Sciences Géographique* (Paris, 1830), pp. 314–45.
Renne, Elizaveta, 'Robert Ker Porter v Rossii', in *Trudy Gosudarstvennogo Ermitazha*, t. 25 (Leningrad: Gosudarstvennyi Ermitazh, 1985), pp. 105–9.

— 'British artists in Russia in the first half of the nineteenth century', in *British Art Treasures from Russian Imperial Collections in the Hermitage*, ed. B. Allen and L. Dukelskaya (New Haven and London: Yale University Press, 1996), pp. 104–15.
— 'Khudozhnik Sir Robert Ker Porter v Rossii', *Nashe Nasledie*, no. 63–64 (Moscow, 2002): http://nasledie-rus.ru/podshivka/6412.php [accessed 22 August 2021].
Robinson, B.W., 'A royal Qājār enamel', *Iran* 10 (1972), pp. 25–30.
Rozanov, M.G., 'Persidskoe posolstvo v Rossii 1829 goda (po bumagam grafa P.P. Suchtelena)', *Russkiy arkhiv* 2 (Moscow: Universitetskaya tipografia (Katkov & Co.), 1889).
Safaralieva, D., 'Iranskiy uchenik Akademii', *Khudozhnik* 8 (Moscow, 1991), pp. 56–58.
Sandon, John, *Dictionary of Worcester Porcelain (1751–1851)*, vol. I (Woodbridge, Suffolk: ACC Art Book, 1993).
Seccombe, T., 'Robert Ker Porter', in *Dictionary of National Biography*, vol. XLVI (London, 1896), pp. 190–92.
Serchevskii, Evgraf, ed., *A.S. Griboedov i ego sochineniya c prilozheniyami* (St Petersburg: Glavnyi shtab Ego Impertarskogo Velichestva po uchebnym zavedeniyam, 1858).
Sidorov, I.S., ed. and annot., 'O gibeli A.S. Griboedova', in *Rossiyskiy arkhiv: Istoriya Otechestva v svidetelstvakh i dokumentakh 18–19 vv.* Almanakh, vv. 2–3 (Moscow: Studia Trite: Rossiyskiy arkhiv, 1992), pp. 91–97: http://az.lib.ru/g/griboedow_a_s/text_0170-1.shtml [accessed 11 August 2021].
Straw, Jack, *The English Job: Understanding Iran and Why it Distrusts Britain* (London: Biteback Publishing, 2019).
Tarkhova, N.A. 'O proekte russkoy zakavkazskoy kompanii (po materialam arkhiva I.F. Paskevicha v RGIA)', *Problemy tvorchestva A.S. Griboedova*, ed. S.A. Fomichev (Smolensk: TRUST-IMAKOM, 1994), pp. 285–95.
— *Letopis' zhizni i tvorchestva Aleksandra Sergeevicha Griboedova (1790–1829)* (Moscow: Minuvshee, 2017).
Tynyanov, Yury, *The Death of Vazir-Mukhtar*, trans. Susan Causey, ed. Vera Tsareva-Brauner (London: Look Multimedia, 2018); also trans. Anna Kurkina Rush and Christopher Rush (New York: Columbia University Press, 2021).
Varshavsky, S. and B. Rest, *Podvig Ermitazha* (Leningrad: Lenizdat, 1985).
Vasilyeva, Daria, 'Elephants as diplomatic gifts: Nādir Shāh's embassy of 1739–1742', *Doklady XXX-go Mezhdunarodnogo kongressa po istochnikovedeniyu i istoriografii stran Azii i Afriki*, t. 1 (St Petersburg: BP-Print, 2020), pp. 281–310.

Vasilyeva, N.E., 'Albom R. Ker Portera s risunkami drevneyshikh pamyatnikov skulptury i arkhitektury', in *Ermitazhnye chteniya (1986–1994), pamyati V.G. Lukonina* (St Petersburg: Gosudarstvennyi Ermitazh, 1995), pp. 246–47.

Vasilyeva, O.V., 'Chey albom', *Vostochnaya kollektsiys* (Summer 2004), pp. 28–41.

— *A String of Pearls: Iranian Fine Books from the 14th to the 17th Century in the National Library of Russia Collections* (St Petersburg: Rossiyskaya Natsionalnaya Biblioteka, 2008).

Vatsuro, V.E., ed., *A.S. Griboedov v vospominaniyakh sovremennikov* (Moscow, Khudozhestvennaya literatura, 1980).

Wright, Christopher, 'Painting Persepolis', in *British Library Picturing Places blog*: https://www.bl.uk/picturing-places/articles/painting-persepolis# [accessed 11 August 2021].

Wright, Denis, *The English Amongst the Persians during the Qajar Period (1787–1921)* (London: William Heinemann, 1977).

Films and TV series

Nodjoumi, Sara (producer), Mehran Haghighi (director), *Of Kings and Paintings* (Homa Films, 2019).

Varzi, Mohammad-Reza (director), *Tabriz in the Fog* (Iran TV, 2010), 28 episodes.

7

Proto-Nationalism in Early Modern Iran and Afghanistan

Sajjad Nejatie
(University of Toronto)

Introduction

The idea of 'Iran' has been subject to interpretation and reinterpretation throughout the ages, but perhaps never more so than in the decades following the Afghan invasion of Esfahan in 1722 and during the ensuing collapse of Safavid rule.[1] For it was during this transitional period that there emerged myriad polities (such as Ghelzay, Naderid, Abdali-Dorrani, Zand and Qajar) with opposing political agendas and also novel ideas concerning the fate of post-Safavid Iran. While the rule of most of these post-Safavid polities ultimately proved ephemeral, the Qajar and Dorrani dynasties established more enduring state structures in the second half of the eighteenth century. The process by which this dynastic stability was achieved forms the focus of this chapter. Specifically, this chapter explores the transformative impact that the emergent rivalry between the founders of each dynasty, Ahmad Shah Dorrani (r. 1747–72) and Agha Mohammad Khan Qajar (r. ca. 1779–97), had on the idea not only of 'Iran' but also of neighbouring 'Afghanistan' heading into the modern period.

The Qajar–Dorrani competition for supremacy over Iran and Khorasan has often been examined in the context of its entanglement in the so-called 'Great Game' between colonial Britain and Russia where, throughout the nineteenth century, this seemingly local/regional affair was played out on a global stage. But, as Benjamin D. Hopkins notes, the Great Game narrative, with its emphasis on the role of Britain and Russia's policies, has been challenged by those who instead emphasize the role of indigenous powers.[2] Yet, even among the studies that consider local perspectives, there is a tendency to gloss over or even overlook the interconnected histories of the Qajars and Dorranis. This is especially true of the Dorrani–Afghan vantage point, which occupies a rather narrow space in the historiography of eighteenth-century Iran. The present chapter thus revisits local sources on the early Qajar and Dorrani periods with an eye to expanding our knowledge of the nature of the conflict and its long-term consequences.

A number of studies have explored the emergence of Iran and Afghanistan as distinct territorial entities within the context of the Qajar–Dorrani rivalry in Khorasan.[3] Drawing insights from the work of Firoozeh Kashani-Sabet, in particular its emphasis on the centrality of land and territorial disputes in the development of nationalist discourses, this chapter focuses on the emergent Qajar–Dorrani conflict over Khorasan in the eighteenth century and its role in shaping the conceptual and physical boundaries that would come to define present-day Iran and Afghanistan.[4] Specifically, it considers the way in which the competing 'proto-nationalist' claims of the Qajars and Dorranis, as envisioned by each dynasty's founder, contributed to the construction of the boundaries that divide contemporary Iran and Afghanistan. At first glance, the use of the term 'proto-nationalist' in an eighteenth-century context may seem anachronistic, as it implies a connection to the distinctly modern concept of nationalism. But proto-nationalism is used here to describe a phenomenon that is not quite nationalist in the modern sense, with its fixation on delineating national borders. Rather, it is used in a broad sense to refer to pre-existing, indigenous conceptions of land, sovereignty and identity (ethnic and religious) that were later, through the influence of local and colonial actors in the nineteenth and twentieth centuries, reimagined and reshaped to fit the European mould of nation-states with clearly defined borders and distinctive ethno-religious identities.

Contesting the Safavid Legacy

The origins of the Qajar–Dorrani dispute may be traced back to the decline of Safavid authority in the first quarter of the eighteenth century. Like other post-Safavid aspirants, the founders of each dynasty had to contend with the legacy of over two centuries of Safavid rule but they adopted divergent approaches to this challenge.

The Qajars had been one of the Qezelbash (Turkish: Qızılbash) tribes who helped to form the Safavid Empire. Since the time of Shah 'Abbas I (r. 1587–1629), the ancestors of the Qajar dynasty migrated to the Caspian province of Astarabad (present-day Gorgan) and maintained a strong presence there. In the aftermath of the Ghelzay Afghan sack of Esfahan, the Qajar chief Fath-'Ali Khan (d. 1726) was among the local strongmen who came to the aid of the Safavid claimant Shah Tahmasp II (d. 1740) seeking to oust the Afghan invaders from the capital and restore Safavid authority. Fath-'Ali Khan remained loyal to the Safavid crown until superseded in influence by Nader-Qoli of the Afshar tribe, who is believed to have orchestrated the Qajar chief's downfall and execution. Fath-'Ali Khan's son Mohammad Hasan Khan (d. 1759) continued to show support for Safavid pretenders while engaging with his rivals, particularly Karim Khan Zand (r. 1751–79), for control over Iran. Though Mohammad Hasan's quest for power ended when he was killed by

Zand forces in 1759, his descendants Agha Mohammad Khan and Fath-'Ali Shah would continue the Qajar project of reconstituting the Safavid Empire.[5]

The forebears of Ahmad Shah were members of the Abdali Afghan tribe based in and around the Qandahar region throughout the seventeenth century, when the Mughals and Safavids competed for control of the province. The chiefs of the Abdali tribe emerged from historical obscurity in the decades following Shah 'Abbas II's (r. 1642–66) conquest of Qandahar in 1653, when they aided Safavid governors in guarding the local roads to ensure a steady flow of trade in the province. Contemporary sources point to the governorship of Gorgin Khan (r. ca. 1704–9) as a turning point, as his heavy-handed rule prompted an Afghan uprising that culminated in the Ghelzay Afghans seizing Qandahar and the Abdali Afghans invading Herat. The Abdali ruled Herat as an autonomous regime until the Naderid conquest in 1732, at which time Nader Shah (r. 1736–47) enlisted many of the Abdali defenders into his military.[6] When Nader was assassinated in 1747, the Abdali soldiers in his army, including Ahmad Shah, retreated to Qandahar, which would become the capital of the nascent Dorrani polity. Ahmad Shah and his fellow Abdali, whom he renamed 'Dorrani' after his epithet *Dorr-e Dorran*, or 'Pearl of Pearls', assumed control over the eastern lands of the Naderid empire.[7]

While the Qajar–Dorrani contest is usually traced to the reign of Agha Mohammad Khan, this feud had in fact emerged in the post-Naderid period. In his *Tarikh-e Ahmad Shahi*, the contemporary Dorrani chronicler Mahmud al-Hoseyni highlights the role of Mohammad Hasan Khan Qajar in the succession struggles between scions of the Afsharid dynasty in Khorasan. The author also lists the Qajar chief among the Qezelbash amirs who sought to defend Mashhad against the advance of Ahmad Shah's forces in 1750–51.[8] While the initial Dorrani foray to Mashhad proved unsuccessful, Ahmad Shah returned in the summer of 1754. It was during the course of this campaign that the Dorrani monarch issued a royal decree, or *farman*, which outlines his efforts to build an alliance with the chiefs of the Goklen (*Kukalan*) Turkmens against common Qezelbash adversaries in Khorasan. The following passage from this farman offers a unique insight into Ahmad Shah's attitude towards the Safavids, as well as his aspirations concerning Iran:[9]

> It is for this reason we have issued this confirmation. For during bygone eras in Rum, Turan and Hindustan when the Muslims engaged in jihad and guided [these] realms to the dignity of Islam, each one of the kings of these realms exerted themselves day and night in strengthening and illuminating the pristine religion of the Prophet (God's mercy be upon him!). As a result of their efforts, the Lord of the World, through His good graces [and] for the sake of the honour of Mohammad the Chosen (God's mercy be upon him!), strengthened each of the lands of the religion of Islam. Moreover, while the descendants of the foregone kings became preoccupied with seeking gratification and sensual pleasure,

during the reign of Shah Esma'il [I], the old custom (*dastur-e qadim*) was observed, but thereafter, some people, for the sake of personal benefit in putting in order the vital affairs (*mahamm*) of this territory [i.e. Mashhad], upended the foundation of their religion and took up the moniker 'Shi'a'. Their intent behind this act was that the people of Iran would not flee or travel to and from other lands. For under such circumstances, when an individual travelled [abroad], the Sunni community (*ahl-e Sonnat*) would not grant them passage and they would be compelled to return to this land [i.e. Mashhad] and submit to the [Safavid] sultan. Through this development, the fire of enmity was ignited and spread throughout the world such that the Qezelbash and their affiliates unjustifiably persecuted the Afghans. Those who possessed vigour (*gheyrat*) among the Afghans rose up and overran the entire realm of Iran to the point that they obtained kingship for themselves. However, at present it is only Mashhad the Holy that remains [to be subjugated].

Notwithstanding its rather superficial explanation for the conversion of Iran to Shi'ism or the intimation that the Afghans established their rule over all of Iran save Mashhad, the farman's claims would appear to reflect Ahmad Shah's desire to restore Iran to its perceived pre-Safavid, Sunni era of glory. It is likely that Ahmad Shah's campaigns in Khorasan were motivated by religious concerns, given his deeply spiritual worldview.[10] In light of Ahmad Shah's affiliation with the Mojaddedi branch of the Naqshbandi Sufi order, it is not surprising that the farman refers to the rulers of Central Asia, Anatolia and India which, like several of the core lands that fell under the sway of Dorrani authority, had long been prominent centres of Naqshbandi and Hanafi Sunni activity. It is also no coincidence that the farman is addressed to chiefs of the Goklen Turkmen – one of several local Sunni tribes that had long justified their inroads into the eastern peripheries of the Safavid Empire on religious grounds and who may thus have been inclined to ally with Ahmad Shah on similar pretexts.

However, while Ahmad Shah's claims against his Qezelbash rivals represent just one example of a centuries-old *topos* of religious strife between Shi'i rulers based in Iran and Sunni adversaries on its peripheries, the sectarian nature of the conflict should not be exaggerated. For all the farman's emphasis on the heavy-handedness of the Qezelbash, it will be recalled that Shi'is from Iran contributed significantly to the establishment of Dorrani rule. This includes the small but influential cadre of Iranian secretaries employed by Ahmad Shah who managed the administrative affairs of state as well as the Qezelbash soldiers who played an integral part in the extension of Dorrani rule into Khorasan and Hindustan.[11] It would thus appear that the farman's criticism was directed specifically towards hostile Qezelbash factions, especially those opposed to Ahmad Shah's ambitions, while its appeal to Sunni solidarity was designed primarily to galvanize the support of Turkmen tribesmen with whom the Dorranis shared a common religious basis on which to build an alliance. But whatever its underlying motivations, the farman clearly emphasizes the Sunni identity of the Dorrani state – one of the features that distinguished the Afghan polity from its Qajar counterpart in Iran, which followed the Safavid precedent in embracing a Shi'i identity.

The religious elements of the farman were certainly entwined with Ahmad Shah's broader political objectives. As in Ahmad Shah's correspondence with the Ottoman sultan Mostafa III, Dorrani designs on Iran are depicted as pre-emptive measures intended to quell the rise of tyrannical Qezelbash forces in Iran which might threaten Dorrani dominion.[12] The farman was issued when Iran was in a state of flux; Karim Khan Zand was still in the process of consolidating his rule in western Iran while competing with the military adventurer Azad Khan 'Afghan'. The Qajars under Mohammad Hasan Khan were important power brokers, but it was not until the rise of Agha Mohammad Khan that they became sufficiently powerful to assert dominance. At this juncture, there would have been a sense that Iran was ripe for the taking and Dorrani sources make it clear this was one of Ahmad Shah's aims. For instance, in his description of the early Dorrani invasions of Mashhad, Feyz Mohammad Kateb Hazara, a prominent historian of the Afghan polity, echoes the farman's sentiments, writing: 'At this time Ahmad Shah had so much power that he could contemplate the extension of his authority over all of Iran'.[13]

The Mashhad campaign took place at the height of Ahmad Shah's power and it is plausible that the Dorranis not only planned on, but could well have succeeded in, bringing much of western Iran under their authority. After successfully annexing north India with its lucrative tax base, Ahmad Shah set his sights on capturing Mashhad from forces loyal to Nader Shah's grandson Shahrokh (d. 1796). Before setting out for the Mashhad campaign, Ahmad Shah appointed Mirza Mohammad Taqi Khan Shirazi (d. 1756) as his 'overseer of the affairs of the province of Iran' (*saheb-ekhteyari-ye velayat-e Iran*).[14] There is an indication that Ahmad Shah intended to extend his authority westward. During the Mashhad campaign, Ahmad Shah dispatched his amir Shah-Pasand Khan to capture the Qajar strongholds of Astarabad and Mazandaran; but, near Sabzavar, the Dorrani contingent was repelled by the forces of Mohammad Hasan Khan Qajar in what was a prelude to future Qajar–Dorrani altercations.[15] Just prior to the winter of 1755, Ahmad Shah retreated to Herat with the intention of resuming operations in Khorasan. However, the prospect of an immediate follow-up campaign never materialized due to more pressing affairs in India, and perhaps also because of Taqi Khan's fall from grace and death in Kabul in 1756. As it turned out, Ahmad Shah focused his energies in the ensuing years on consolidating Dorrani authority in India and did not return to Mashhad until 1770, when he confirmed Shahrokh's vassalage in Khorasan. In the roughly 15-year period between Ahmad Shah's two

Mashhad campaigns, the lands of Khorasan east of Mashhad fell within the Dorrani sphere of influence and Karim Khan Zand succeeded in consolidating his rule over much of western Iran. While no explicit evidence of a Dorrani–Zand agreement has surfaced to date, it seems plausible that an informal understanding was reached whereby Mashhad, along with the Lut and Kavir deserts to its south, would serve as a buffer between the Dorrani and Zand states and that such a *modus vivendi* remained intact until the end of Zand rule.

There is evidence that Ahmad Shah saw in Karim Khan Zand a potential partner in his bid for power in Iran. As John Perry has observed, periodic contacts were made between the Dorranis and Zands, aimed at forging alliances against common foes.[16] During the aforesaid Dorrani campaign against Mashhad in 1754–55, Ahmad Shah sought Karim Khan's support against Azad Khan while also seeking to ally with the Zand ruler in his Iranian campaigns.[17] There is also an indication that cordial relations continued after the death of Karim Khan, motivated in part by the threat that Agha Mohammad Khan posed to Zand authority. One chronicler of the late Zand period notes that, in 1793, the last of the Zand dynasts, Lotf-'Ali Khan (r. 1789–94), reached out to Ahmad Shah's son and successor, Timur Shah (r. 1772–93), seeking aid against the growing Qajar danger. However, this partnership was never consummated due to Timur Shah's death in 1793.[18] Lacking any strong ally against the increasingly powerful Qajars, Lotf-'Ali Khan was soon defeated and killed by the forces of Agha Mohammad Khan in 1794, thus bringing an end to Zand rule.[19] One can only speculate on the outcome of a Dorrani–Zand alliance against the Qajars. But what is certain is that the spectre of a Dorrani invasion of a war-ravaged western Iran remained a possibility throughout the latter half of the eighteenth century – a prospect of which Agha Mohammad Khan and his successors were wary.[20]

Contesting the Naderid Legacy

While Qajar and Dorrani attitudes towards the Safavids differed markedly – with the Qajars seeking to resuscitate old norms of Safavid sovereignty and the Dorranis aspiring to restore Iran's pre-Safavid, Sunni identity under their own leadership – both dynasties shared, at least initially, a critical view of Nader Shah and the Afsharids.

In the case of the Qajars, their disdain for Nader Shah can be traced back to the Afghan sack of Esfahan in 1722, around which time the Qajar chief Fath-'Ali Khan emerged as one of the local strongmen of Khorasan who aided Shah Tahmasp II in the latter's quest to re-establish Safavid rule. However, in the ensuing competition for Tahmasp II's patronage, Fath-'Ali Khan was executed, allegedly in a plot orchestrated by Nader-Qoli of the Afshar tribe, a rival strongman who was thus able to secure his own position as Tahmasp II's deputy.[21] Fuelled by a bitter enmity towards Nader, Fath-'Ali Khan's son Mohammad Hasan Khan spent much of the Naderid and post-Naderid era circulating between the Qepchaq Steppe and his ancestral homeland of Astarabad. Throughout this period, he would return to Astarabad when opportunities arose, then retreat back to the steppe when his ambitions were checked.[22] Upon Nader's death, Mohammad Hasan Khan served as a powerful actor in the political affairs of Khorasan, with Nader's chronicler Mahdi Khan Astarabadi portraying him as strong candidate to assume power after Nader's assassination.[23] Apprehensive of the potential threat posed by this Qajar khan, Nader's nephew and successor 'Adel Shah (r. 1747–48) led a campaign against Mohammad Hasan Khan in Astarabad, where he captured the latter's eldest son, Mohammad Khan, and had the boy castrated, hence his epithet *agha* or 'eunuch'.[24]

The execution of his grandfather by Nader Shah and his own castration by order of 'Adel Shah only intensified Agha Mohammad Khan's animus towards the Afsharids. While he spent most of his early years in power campaigning in the west in an effort to extend Qajar control over former Zand territories, towards the end of his career Agha Mohammad Khan set his sights on eradicating the last vestiges of Afsharid rule in Khorasan to the east. This motivation unmistakably undergirded Agha Mohammad Khan's capture of Mashhad, which was at the time governed by Shahrokh Afshar with the backing of the Dorranis – an alliance strengthened by the marriage of Shahrokh's daughter Gowharshad to Timur Shah during the third Dorrani campaign of Mashhad in 1770–71.[25] Although Agha Mohammad Khan initially avoided direct confrontation with the Dorranis in Khorasan, the situation changed after the death of Timur Shah in 1793, when the Dorrani polity was weakened by internecine conflict. In 1796, Agha Mohammad Khan made preparations to visit Mashhad, ostensibly to make the pilgrimage to the shrine of 'Ali al-Reza (d. 818), but, in fact, to depose Shahrokh. Upon assuming control of the city, Agha Mohammad Khan had Shahrokh tortured and eventually killed. He is also said to have ordered the bones of Nader to be exhumed and transported from Mashhad to his capital in Tehran.[26] With the removal of the Afsharids from Mashhad, the Qajars turned their attention to the Dorrani lands of Khorasan. Agha Mohammad Khan would certainly have continued this eastward march himself if not for his assassination in 1797. However, his mandate in Khorasan would be carried out by his nephew and successor Fath-'Ali Shah (r. 1797–1834).

Sources commissioned under Ahmad Shah mirror the anti-Naderid rhetoric found in Qajar sources. This critical outlook may be attributed to a number of factors. For one, the Abdali tribesmen who assumed control over Herat in post-Safavid times represented perhaps the most significant challenge to Nader Shah's eastward expansion and thus bore the brunt of his campaigns in Khorasan. At the tail end of his second invasion of Abdali Herat (1731–32), Nader recognized that victory could not be achieved by sheer force and instead assumed control of the province through a process of mediation with its Abdali defenders.[27] Following the conquest, many of the Abdalis were admitted into the ranks of Nader's army and were largely responsible for Nader's military successes. However, Mahmud al-Hoseyni notes that Nader Shah was cautious not to elevate members of the old Abdali nobility, such as Ahmad Shah – whose father Mohammad Zaman Khan and brother Zu'l-Faqar Khan served as rulers of Herat prior to the Naderid conquest in 1732 – to senior military ranks lest their pride and ambition compel them to rebel.[28] Instead, Nader elevated those on the lower rungs of a tribe's social organization to positions of leadership so that they would recognize that their newfound status derived solely from him. Moreover, for reasons similar to those behind Agha Mohammad Khan's period of captivity at the Zand capital, Nader had Ahmad Khan, a member of the Abdali tribe's chieftain class, serve as a retainer at the Naderid court in order to ensure the good behaviour of his kin.

Nader Shah's tumultuous relations with the Abdali help to explain why sources on the reign of Ahmad Shah refer to Nader in unambiguously disparaging terms, as an unjust tyrant whose bloody reign was destined to fail.[29] However, this anti-Naderid sentiment represents a clear contrast to later sources on the Dorranis, which depict Nader Shah in more favourable terms, even going so far as to portray Ahmad Shah as one of his favourites. Perhaps the most influential example is a history of the Dorrani dynasty written by Emam al-Din Hoseyni, called *Hoseyn Shahi*, which contains a peculiar anecdote of Nader Shah's premonition that Ahmad Shah would succeed him as king. The passage in question reads as follows:

> One day, Nader Shah sat upon his golden throne enjoying the weather as Ahmad Khan – that is, the renowned Ahmad Shah – stood before him observing all manners of respect. Suddenly Nader Shah said, 'O Ahmad Khan Abdali, come near'. When the latter did so, [Nader] again said, 'Come nearer still'. As he approached nearer observing all manners of respect and deference, [Nader] said, 'O Ahmad Khan! Remember that after me sovereignty (*saltanat*) will pass on to you. You must treat my descendants with kindness'. Ahmad Shah responded, 'May I be your sacrifice! If his highness the king of kings should order for my execution, I am at his service. There is no need to utter such speech'. [Nader] reiterated, 'I am certain that you will be king after me. Tread the path [of kindness] with my descendants' ... Ahmad Shah thus acted in accordance with those words of Nader Shah by striving to treat the descendants of Nader with courtesy and esteem ... To the present, it being the year 1213 AH [1798], that conduct towards Nader's progeny is observed by the heirs of Ahmad Shah.[30]

There is no evidence to support Emam al-Din's assertion that Nader Shah regarded Ahmad as his successor, but the anecdote has nevertheless often been repeated in the historiography of the Dorranis.[31] Beyond its fictive and anachronistic elements, what is often overlooked is the subtext of Emam al-Din's account of Nader Shah's premonition, in particular how the shifting attitude of the Dorranis towards Nader was occasioned by Qajar expansionism in Khorasan.

It should be noted that the *Hoseyn Shahi* was completed in circa 1798, shortly after Agha Mohammad Khan captured Mashhad and removed Shahrokh from power there. On the eve of this Qajar invasion, Shahrokh sent his eldest son, Nader Mirza (d. 1803), to the provincial Dorrani court at Herat. From there, Nader Mirza made his way to the capital of Kabul, where he was received by Zaman Shah b. Timur Shah Dorrani (r. 1793–1801), who assigned him a residence and a pension in Peshawar. Upon learning of Agha Mohammad Khan's death, Zaman Shah had a Dorrani force escort Nader Mirza back to Mashhad, where Afsharid power was restored.[32] But this restoration proved short-lived, as Fath-'Ali Shah's forces recaptured Mashhad in 1803 and had Nader Mirza killed soon thereafter, thus bringing an end to the Afsharid dynasty.[33]

The author of the *Hoseyn Shahi*, Emam al-Din, was in the retinue of Zaman Shah at the time of Agha Mohammad Khan's capture of Mashhad and would have been keenly aware of the Qajar ruler's ambitions to invade the western territories of the Dorrani polity. Emam al-Din's account of Nader repeatedly imploring the future Ahmad Shah to treat his descendants with kindness reflected the contemporary state of affairs, with Zaman Shah giving refuge to Nader's great-grandson, Nader Mirza. It would appear that the rehabilitation of Nader Shah in the *Hoseyn Shahi* was a product of Zaman Shah's efforts to reinstall an Afsharid satellite in Mashhad as a way to rebuff Qajar expansionism in Khorasan.

This analysis shows how the Naderid legacy, much like its Safavid counterpart, became a focal point in the emergent Qajar–Dorrani competition for the right to exercise sovereignty over Khorasan. In their efforts to establish a new Qajar ruling dispensation, Agha Mohammad Khan and Fath-'Ali Shah disparaged the Naderid era since its ascent had come at the expense of their forefathers. From the Qajar perspective, the removal of Shahrokh and his successors from power in Mashhad righted an old wrong and restored a semblance of the previous Safavid imperial order in Khorasan that had been sullied during the Afsharid interregnum. While Ahmad Shah Dorrani was likewise critical of Nader Shah due to his oppressive reign, he nevertheless presented himself as the inheritor of the Naderid imperial mandate, due in part to the central role of the Abdali-*cum*-Dorrani Afghans in Nader's military triumphs. Yet, decades later, when faced with the challenge of looming Qajar expansionism in Khorasan, Ahmad Shah's grandson Zaman Shah endorsed the invented tradition that Nader Shah had prophesied the rise of the Dorranis – a gesture designed to present the Dorranis as legitimate successors to the Naderid empire and to thereby reinforce the Afghan polity's claims to rule in Khorasan.

The Qajar–Dorrani Duel for Khorasan

Although rooted in the late-Safavid and Afsharid eras, the Qajar–Dorrani rivalry did not develop into a direct diplomatic and military stand-off until the final decade of the eighteenth century. During the reigns of Ahmad Shah and Timur Shah (1747–93), the Dorrani polity was at the height of its power, whereas the nascent Qajar state was not yet in a position to challenge Afghan supremacy in Khorasan. However, by the 1790s, the tides of power had shifted in favour of the Qajars, leading to a new, more contentious chapter in Qajar–Dorrani relations that had lasting repercussions. This reversal of fortunes was in large part a reflection of each dynasty's relative ability to solve the dilemma of succession. Whereas the immediate successors of Agha Mohammad Khan established comparatively stable reigns, after the death of Timur Shah, in 1793, the Dorrani polity faced a debilitating crisis of succession that went largely unresolved until the second half of the nineteenth century. Within this period of protracted Dorrani crisis, the peripheral territories in Khorasan and Hindustan fell beyond the state's control. Meanwhile, the core provinces of Kabul, Qandahar and Herat likewise fragmented into appanages controlled by scions of the Dorrani royal family. As a result of this internecine conflict, Ahmad Shah's descendants, collectively known as the Sadozay dynasty, would eventually be replaced by the amirs of a collateral Dorrani line, the Barakzay, who formed a neo-Dorrani dynasty.[34]

Under Agha Mohammad Khan and his successors, the Qajars exploited the internal turmoil faced by the Dorrani rulers. Shortly after the death of Timur Shah, Agha Mohammad Khan saw an opportunity to sow divisions between Timur Shah's son and successor Zaman Shah, based in Kabul, and the latter's brother, Shahzada Mahmud, the *wali*, or governor, of Herat who was treated as a Qajar protégé. Acting as nominal heir to the Safavid Empire, Agha Mohammad Khan sent an envoy to the court of Zaman Shah outlining his desire to reassert what he regarded as 'Iranian' authority over the Dorrani territories in Khorasan, with the former Safavid province of Herat being among the territories particularly coveted. The Qajar chronicler Reza-Qoli Khan Hedayat recounts Agha Mohammad Khan's overtures towards Zaman Shah as follows:

> For this reason, at the present time the world-conquering king of kings, his highness Agha Mohammad Khan, dispatched Mohammad Hoseyn Khan Qaraguzlu-ye Hamdani along with a cordial letter to Shah Zaman Afghan at Kabul. The object of his mission was to discuss the surrender of Balkh, which had always been part of the realms of Iran (*zamima-ye belad-e Iran*). When the emissary of the world-protecting monarch, Soltan Mohammad Shah, reached Kabul and Qandahar, Shah Zaman agreed to the surrender of Balkh. He dispatched a certain Gadu Khan on a mission to his royal highness alongside Mohammad Hoseyn Khan

Qaraguzlu. [Gadu Khan] was deferential in the capitulation of Balkh and carried a letter of supplication that was penned and sent [by Shah Zaman] professing fealty. Moreover, Shahzada Mahmud, the governor of Herat, demonstrated his devotion and said, 'For many years during Safavid times Herat, too, was a part of Iran. If it is accepted, I, too, will be one of the governors and appointees of the king of Iran. Since I exercise control over this province, I have girded the waist of servitude and lie in wait of the commands of his highness [i.e. Agha Mohammad Khan]'.[35]

Not surprisingly, Dorrani recountings of this episode differ substantially. Feyz Mohammad, for instance, roundly rejects Hedayat's account of events as a product of Iranian bias and provides an alternative narrative of events. According to Feyz Mohammad's account, following the arrival of Mohammad Hoseyn Khan Qaraguzlu, Zaman Shah in turn sent an envoy of his own to the Qajar court rejecting Agha Mohammad Khan's overtures. Upon returning, the Afghan envoy Gadu Khan recommended Zaman Shah to invade 'Iran' and annex it to 'Afghanistan', but the plan was interrupted by the news of Agha Mohammad Khan's death in 1797. This turn of events instead provided an opportunity for Zaman Shah, as described above, to restore Afsharid rule in Mashhad under the leadership of Nader Mirza, a protégé of the Dorrani shah.[36]

While Hedayat and Feyz Mohammad wrote their accounts of this episode retrospectively, after Iran and Afghanistan had congealed into distinct territorial entities, both authors agree that Agha Mohammad Khan sought to incorporate Dorrani-controlled lands of Khorasan into what the Qajars regarded as a part of Iranian territory. Following in his predecessor's footsteps, Fath-'Ali Shah pitted Shahzada Mahmud against Zaman Shah, but after a failed attempt to defeat his brother in battle, Shahzada Mahmud fled to the court of Fath-'Ali Shah at Tehran in 1798. With this Dorrani vassal-prince in tow, Fath-'Ali Shah sent an emissary to the court of Zaman Shah reiterating Agha Mohammad Khan's demand for the withdrawal of Dorrani forces from the lands of Khorasan extending to Balkh, which constituted 'part of the territories of Iran' (*jozv-e mamalek-e Iran*).[37] In the subsequent correspondence between Fath-'Ali Shah and Zaman Shah in 1799–1800, the Dorrani ruler balked at the Qajar demands on the basis that the lands of Khorasan were legitimately conquered by his ancestors and thus represented his birthright.[38]

What began as a diplomatic clash would quickly escalate into a complex sequence of armed confrontations between Qajar and Dorrani-aligned forces in and around Herat in the opening decades of the nineteenth century. The entanglement of competing colonial powers, particularly Russia and Britain, in the conflict further complicated matters. In 1800, the British Government of India dispatched Sir John Malcolm as an envoy to the Qajar court to form an alliance designed to prevent Dorrani-led encroachments into India. However, French and later Russian support for Qajar ambitions in Khorasan compelled the British to enter into a pact with the Dorrani shahs. A British mission led by Mountstuart Elphinstone reached Peshawar in 1809 and concluded a treaty whereby the British agreed to support the Dorranis against any Qajar attempt to invade Afghan territories.[39] This agreement set a precedent for British support of the Dorranis in future clashes with the Qajars. Fath-'Ali Shah and his heirs succeeded in extending Qajar influence over the province throughout the first half of the nineteenth century, but the last campaign against Herat, in 1856–57, ended in defeat and the signing of the 1857 Treaty of Paris, the terms of which required the Qajars to withdraw all claims to sovereignty over Herat.[40] In retrospect, this final Qajar defeat cemented Herat's status as part of the Afghan polity.

While the British involvement in the Qajar–Dorrani dispute is seen as the primary catalyst for Herat being separated from Iran and incorporated into the Afghan polity, this view tends to rely too heavily on Safavid and Qajar epistemologies. The Qajar claim over Herat on the basis of its Safavid heritage is controversial, given that the province had long been a site of political contest even during the Safavid epoch. Prior to the Safavid takeover of Herat in 1510, the province was under Ozbek rule from 1507 to 1510. The Ozbeks had taken Herat from the Timurids, who had ruled the province during the preceding century. Herat was a thriving cultural and political centre under Shahrokh b. Timur (r. 1405–47) and Soltan-Hoseyn Bayqara (r. 1469–1506).[41] Throughout the sixteenth century, the Safavids and Ozbeks duelled for control of Herat, with the Safavids ultimately wresting control of the province from the Ozbeks.[42] But, although Herat remained in Safavid control for much of the seventeenth century, throughout the eighteenth century it was administered by multiple regimes, the most enduring of which were those of the Abdali-*cum*-Dorrani Afghans. Indeed, Ahmad Shah and his successors derived legitimacy from their status as descendants of the Abdali chiefs who established rule over Herat in the 1710s. For instance, in response to the challenges issued by the amirs of Iran to Ahmad Shah's authority, Mahmud al-Hoseyni asserts that Herat represented the hereditary domain of the Dorranis since it had previously served as the seat of governance for the shah's elder brother and father in the post-Safavid era.[43] While it is true that Herat was later conquered by Nader Shah, soon after the latter's death in 1747, Dorrani forces recaptured the province and it remained under Afghan control thereafter. In this way, from the Dorrani perspective, Herat constituted an inheritance (*miras*) of the royal family – a view echoed by Zaman Shah in his aforesaid correspondence with Fath-'Ali Shah.

We know from this same Qajar–Dorrani correspondence that the early Qajars viewed sovereignty over Khorasan not only as their duty as heirs of the Safavid legacy, but also as their birthright on account of the province being the resting place of their forefathers.[44] Probably in response to such claims, the *Hoseyn Shahi* of Emam al-Din establishes a historical association between the

Abdali forebears of the Dorrani dynasts and the tenth-century Sufi master Abu Ahmad Abdal (d. 966), the patron saint of the shrine town of Chesht just east of Herat. According to this narrative, the name 'Abdal' was bestowed upon the tribe by Abu Ahmad Abdal, the spiritual master of the tribe's progenitor. Not unlike Emam al-Din's anecdote of Nader Shah predicting that Ahmad Shah Dorrani would succeed him as king, the lack of any corroborating evidence to support this Abdali–Cheshti relationship has not prevented it from being uncritically reproduced in the historiography. But when considered in the light of the emergent Dorrani–Qajar dispute over Herat, it is apparent that this tradition was invented in order to assert the presence of the Abdali-*cum*-Dorrani Afghans in the province dating back to the tenth century and to thereby trump any comparable claims to authority over Herat advanced by the Qajars and their supporters.[45]

Understood in their historical context, then, the claims and counter-claims forwarded by the Qajars and Dorranis represented a more recent manifestation of a lengthy history of political competition over the sovereignty of Herat. What differentiated the Qajar–Dorrani duel from its antecedents, however, was that it coincided with the intervention of colonial powers in the nineteenth century and the introduction of new forms of political organization, especially the notion of the nation-state, which resulted in the delineation of the boundaries along the Iran–Afghanistan frontier. Indeed, recent studies have aptly demonstrated how the physical and conceptual mapping of Afghanistan as a distinct nation took place during the era of colonial intervention.[46] But, as Hopkins has noted, it should be recalled that the construction of Western-style nation-states in the region was not merely a product of colonial policies but a process endorsed and effected by local actors, including later rulers of the Qajar and Dorrani polities as well as their representatives.[47]

Conclusion

The establishment of the Qajar and Dorrani dynasties in the eighteenth century coincided with the formulation and expression of new political strategies that may be aptly described as 'proto-nationalist' in so far as they contained the conceptual precursors to some of the salient features of the modern nationalist discourses in Iran and Afghanistan. An example drawn from the early Dorrani context is Ahmad Shah's emphasis on the Afghan identity of the Dorrani polity, a fact that is alluded to in various primary sources, including the farman cited earlier in this chapter.[48] It should be noted here that any notion of a territorially bounded nation would have been alien to Ahmad Shah, who followed the example of his predecessors, especially Nader Shah, in seeking to create a Timurid-style 'world-empire'. Moreover, the borders of this 'Dorrani empire' were not fixed but instead expanded into Iran, Hindustan and Central Asia and this trans-regional character attests to the reality that Ahmad Shah's worldview was more globalist than nationalist in orientation. Further, at the societal level, the Dorrani monarch nurtured a form of Islamic cosmopolitanism not uncommon in pre-modern Muslim societies across Asia. Nonetheless, it should also be stressed that the Afghan character of the polity established by Ahmad Shah contributed to the Dorrani territories of Khorasan eventually becoming refashioned by nationalist ideologues and colonial authors alike as 'Afghanistan' or 'the land of the Afghans'. For a pertinent example, we may refer to the works of the Turkophile Afghan statesmen Mahmud Tarzi (d. 1933), one of the founding ideologues of nationalism in Afghanistan. In the writings of Tarzi, who, incidentally, belonged to the Dorrani tribe like Ahmad Shah, Afghan (read: Pashtun) identity is tactfully utilized as one of the core features that distinguished Afghanistan from Iran.[49] In this respect, ideas of Afghan identity continually disseminated by the ruling elite of the Dorrani state since the reign of Ahmad Shah played a decisive role, arguably even more so than the activities of colonial Britain, in the creation of a distinctly Afghan polity. Another example covered in this chapter is Ahmad Shah's utilization of Sunni Islam to mobilize support against Shi'i adversaries in post-Safavid Iran, which represents an early expression of Sunnism as the creed sponsored by the Dorrani dynasty and one of the key attributes that would differentiate the Afghan polity from the decidedly Shi'i orientation of its Qajar counterpart.

With respect to the proto-nationalist sentiments cultivated by the Qajars, the dynasty's efforts to reconstitute the Safavid Empire mirrored the development of the now prevalent notion of 'Greater Iran' – a broad territorial expanse that encompassed various traditionally 'Iranian' territories, including most if not all the lands of present-day Afghanistan, which were separated by various historical forces. In the specific case of Herat, the role of British intervention in the failure of the Qajars to maintain control over the province fed into the perception that Herat was separated from Iran primarily due to the machinations of colonial powers. However, beyond carrying disputed irredentist undertones, this view tends to overlook the decades of Afghan rule of post-Safavid Herat. Interestingly, the initial efforts of the Qajars to recapture Herat as heirs of the Safavids elicited various subtle responses from the rulers of the Afghan polity, including the invented tradition of Herat as the ancestral homeland of the Dorrani dynasty's ruling class. Its ahistoricity aside, this tradition was aimed at buttressing Dorrani claims to authority over Herat and thereby solidifying the province's status as part of the Afghan polity. These examples suggest that the conceptual origins of the distinct Iranian and Afghan political domains were already in place well before the intervention of colonial powers in the Herat conflict. As such, while there is no denying the influence of colonial powers in Qajar and Dorrani affairs, the seeds of nationalism, or what we have loosely termed 'proto-nationalism', sown by the Qajars and Dorranis in their duel for the fate of Khorasan throughout the eighteenth century, arguably exerted an equal if not greater impact on the construction of the boundaries between Iran and Afghanistan in modern times.

Notes:

1. Throughout this chapter the term 'Afghan' is used in its pre-modern sense denoting 'Pashtun'.
2. Benjamin D. Hopkins, 'The bounds of identity', pp. 239–42; Firoozeh Kashani-Sabet, *Frontier Fictions*, pp. 3–10.
3. David Charles Champagne, 'The Afghan–Iranian Conflict over Herat Province and European Intervention 1796–1863'; Benjamin D. Hopkins, *The Making of Modern Afghanistan*; Christine Noelle-Karimi, *The Pearl in its Midst*.
4. Kashani-Sabet, *Frontier Fictions*, pp. 6–9.
5. A concise review of the careers of Fath-'Ali Khan and Mohammad Hasan Khan is given in Gavin R.G. Hambly, 'Āghā Muḥammad Khān and the establishment of the Qājār dynasty', pp. 104–14. On the continued Qajar support of Safavid pretenders, see John R. Perry, 'The last Safavids', pp. 59–69. For the depiction of the Qajars as inheritors of the Safavid throne, see Mohammad Taqi Sepehr Lesān al-Molk, *Nāsekh al-tavārikh*, p. 81; Rezā-Qoli Khān Hedāyat, *Tārikh-e Rowzat al-safā-ye Nāseri*, vol. IX/1, pp. 7396–398; Gavin R.G. Hambly, 'Aqa Mohammad Khan and the establishment of the Qajar dynasty', pp. 126–36, 144–46; Kashani-Sabet, *Frontier Fictions*, pp. 19–20; Noelle-Karimi, *The Pearl in its Midst*, pp. 196–97.
6. Sajjad Nejatie, 'The Pearl of Pearls', pp. 183–98, 212–83.
7. Nejatie, 'The Pearl of Pearls', pp. 294–412.
8. Mahmud al-Hoseyni, *Tārikh-e Ahmad Shāhi*, vol. I, pp. 78b–79a and 94a.
9. Sayyed Hoseyn Shahshahāni, 'Farmān-e tārikhi-ye Ahmad Shāh Dorrāni', pp. 159–63.
10. Nejatie, 'The Pearl of Pearls', pp. 341–46.
11. Sajjad Nejatie, 'Iranian migrations in the Durrani Empire, 1747–93', pp. 494–509.
12. Ahmad Shah's plans for further campaigning in Iran are described in Gholām Jeylāni Jalāli, *Nāma-ye Ahmad Shāh Bābā be-nām-e Soltān Mostafā sālesi-ye 'Osmāni*, pp. 14–23, 76–78; also see Ernest S. Tucker, *Nadir Shah's Quest for Legitimacy in Post-Safavid Iran*, p. 108.
13. Feyz Mohammad Kāteb Hazāra, *The History of Afghanistan*, vol. I, p. 23.
14. Mahmud al-Hoseyni, *Tārikh-e Ahmad Shāhi*, vol. I, pp. 214b–15a.
15. Mohammad Fath-Allāh Sāru'i, *Tārikh-e Mohammadi*, pp. 36–37; Mahmud al-Hoseyni, *Tārikh-e Ahmad Shāhi*, vol. I, pp. 252b–57b; Abu'l-Hasan Golestāna, *Mojmal al-tavārikh*, pp. 75–78.
16. John R. Perry, *Karim Khan Zand*, p. 206; 'Abd al-Karim 'Bokhāri', *Histoire de l'Asie Centrale*, vol. II, p. 9.
17. Mann suggested that the text reads *'ahd-e mosāfāt bast*, but it is unclear exactly where his reading derives from, as this statement is not mentioned in either the manuscript of 'Abd al-Karim's work (folio 7a) that is housed in the Bibliothèque Nationale de France, or Schefer's edition, which is based on the same. Rather, the text contains a single passing reference to Karim Khan in which the author asserts that Ahmad Shah had 'established peace' (*solh namud*) with the Zand ruler; see Oskar Mann, 'Quellenstudien zur Geschichte des Ahmed Šāh Durrânî', p. 356; 'Abd al-Karim 'Bokhāri', *Histoire de l'Asie Centrale*, vol. II, p. 9.

18. This information is derived from the supplement (*zeyl*) to the *Tārikh-e giti-goshā* by Āqā Mohammad Rezā Shirāzi; see Mohammad Sādeq Musavi Nāmi, *Tārikh-e giti-goshā dar tārikh-e Zandiya*, pp. 380–81; Perry, *Karim Khan Zand*, p. 300; Hambly, 'Āghā Muḥammad Khān', p. 125.
19. Perry, *Karim Khan Zand*, pp. 299–301.
20. Perry, *Karim Khan Zand*, p. 206; Hambly, 'Aqa Mohammad Khan', p. 167.
21. Laurence Lockhart, *Nadir Shah*, pp. 14–16, 24–27.
22. Mohammad Hasan Khan's regular circulation between the Caspian region and the Qepchaq Steppe closely resembles the *qazaqliq* phenomenon which, as Joo-Yup Lee describes, was a common feature in the political culture of post-Mongol Central Asia; see Joo-Yup Lee, *Qazaqlïq, or Ambitious Brigandage, and the Formation of the Qazaqs*.
23. As noted by Tucker, *Nadir Shah's Quest for Legitimacy*, p. 107, referring to Sir William Jones's 1770 French translation of Astarābādi's *Jahāngoshā-ye Nāderi*, not found in the Persian edition of the text.
24. Peter Avery, 'Nādir Shāh and the Afsharid legacy', p. 59; Perry, *Karim Khan Zand*, pp. 5, 36.
25. Mahmud al-Hoseyni, *Tārikh-e Ahmad Shāhi*, vol. II, pp. 618b–19a; Abu'l-Hasan Golestāna, *Mojmal al-tavārikh*, p. 119.
26. Sir John Malcolm, *The History of Persia from the Most Early Period to the Present Time*, vol. II, p. 274; Lockhart, *Nadir Shah*, p. 264 n2; Hambly, 'Āghā Muḥammad Khān', pp. 130–31. According to the well-known tradition, recorded by Lockhart, Agha Mohammad Khan had the remains of Nader Shah, as well as those of Karim Khan, interred under the threshold of his palace so that whenever he left he could trample on them.
27. Nejatie, 'The Pearl of Pearls', pp. 261–73.
28. Mahmud al-Hoseyni, *Tārikh-e Ahmad Shāhi*, vol. I, pp. 11b–13a.
29. Jalāli, *Nāma-ye Ahmad Shāh Bābā*, pp. 8–10.
30. Emām al-Din Hoseyni, *Hoseyn Shāhi*, pp. 11a–12a. My translation differs from that in Ganda Singh, *Ahmad Shah Durrani*, pp. 19–20.
31. Singh, *Ahmad Shah Durrani*, pp. 18–20. Concerning the wide impact that *Hoseyn Shāhi* has exerted on the scholarship pertaining to Ahmad Shah and the Dorranis, see Nejatie, 'The Pearl of Pearls', pp. 89–94.
32. 'Abd al-Karim 'Bokhāri', *Histoire de l'Asie Centrale*, vol. II, pp. 64–66; Feyz Mohammad Kāteb Hazāra, *The History of Afghanistan*, vol. I, pp. 87–88.
33. Noelle-Karimi, *The Pearl in its Midst*, pp. 216–17.
34. Nejatie, 'The Pearl of Pearls', pp. 427–35.
35. Hedāyat, *Tārikh-e Rowzat al-safā-ye Nāseri*, vol. IX/1, pp. 7399–400. A similar sequence of events is recounted by Lesān al-Molk, *Nāsekh al-tavārikh*, vol. I, pp. 81–83. Also see Champagne, 'The Afghan–Iranian Conflict', pp. 48–54; Noelle-Karimi, *The Pearl in its Midst*, pp. 196–97.
36. Hazāra, *The History of Afghanistan*, vol. I, pp. 73–83, 87–88.
37. Lesān al-Molk, *Nāsekh al-tavārikh*, vol. I, p. 81. Further details on Fath-'Ali Shah's activities in Khorasan at this juncture are provided in Hedāyat, *Tārikh-e Rowzat al-safā-ye Nāseri*, vol. IX/1, pp. 7447–448; Hazāra, *The History of Afghanistan*, vol. I, pp. 92–94, 97–100; 'Abd al-Karim 'Bokhāri', *Histoire de l'Asie Centrale*, vol. II, pp. 16–18.

38. On the correspondence between Fath-'Ali Shah and Zaman Shah, see especially 'Aziz al-Din Wakili Pupalza'i, *Dorrat al-zamān fi tārikh-e Shāh Zamān*, pp. 137–44; Noelle-Karimi, *The Pearl in its Midst*, pp. 197–99.
39. Hazāra, *The History of Afghanistan*, vol. I, pp. 124–27.
40. Abbas Amanat, 'Herat vi. The Herat question', pp. 219–24; Noelle-Karimi, *The Pearl in its Midst*, pp. 200–34.
41. Maria E. Subtelny, *Timurids in Transition*.
42. Martin B. Dickson, 'Sháh Tahmásb and the Uzbeks'.
43. Mahmud al-Hoseyni, *Tārikh-e Ahmad Shāhi*, vol. I, p. 110a; Jalāli, *Nāma-ye Ahmad Shāh Bābā*, pp. 26–27; Nejatie, 'The Pearl of Pearls', pp. 355–56.
44. Wakili Pupalza'i, *Dorrat al-zamān*, pp. 142–43; Noelle-Karimi, *The Pearl in its Midst*, pp. 198–99.
45. Sajjad Nejatie, 'Reflections on the prehistory of the Abdāli Afghans', pp. 552–54.
46. Noelle-Karimi, *The Pearl in its Midst*; Hopkins, *The Making of Modern Afghanistan*.
47. Hopkins, 'The bounds of identity', p. 239.
48. On the Afghan identity of the Dorrani polity under Ahmad Shah, see Nejatie, 'The Pearl of Pearls', pp. 419–28.
49. For a recent assessment of Tarzi and his role in constructing the discursive framework of Afghan nationalism, see Jonathan L. Lee, *Afghanistan*, pp. 436–42.

Bibliography:

'Abd al-Karim 'Bokhāri', *Histoire de l'Asie Centrale (Afghanistan, Boukhara, Khiva, Khoqand) depuis les dernières années du règne de Nadir Chah (1153), jusqu'en 1233 de l'Hégire (1740–1818)*, ed. and trans. Charles Schefer, 2 vols (Paris: E. Leroux, 1876); cf. [*History of Central Asia*], MS, Bibliothèque nationale de France, Supplément Persan 1391.

Amanat, Abbas, 'Herat vi. The Herat question', *Encyclopaedia Iranica*, vol. XII, fasc. 4 (2003), pp. 219–24, online at https://iranicaonline.org/articles/herat-vi [accessed 5 July 2021].

Avery, Peter, 'Nādir Shāh and the Afsharid legacy', in *The Cambridge History of Iran, vol. 7, From Nadir Shah to the Islamic Republic*, ed. Peter Avery, Gavin Hambly and Charles Melville (Cambridge: Cambridge University Press, 1991), pp. 3–62.

Champagne, David Charles, 'The Afghan–Iranian Conflict over Herat Province and European Intervention 1796–1863: A Reinterpretation', doctoral dissertation (Austin: University of Texas Press, 1981).

Dickson, Martin B., 'Sháh Tahmásb and the Uzbeks: The Duel for Khurásán with 'Ubayd Khán, 930–946/1524–1540', doctoral dissertation (Princeton University, 1958).

Golestāna, Abu'l-Hasan, *Mojmal al-tavārikh*, ed. Mohammad Taqi Modarres-Razavi (Tehran: Ebn-e Sinā, 1320/1941; 2nd edn, 1344/1965).

Hambly, Gavin R.G., 'Āghā Muḥammad Khān and the establishment of the Qājār dynasty', in *The Cambridge History of Iran, vol. 7, From Nadir Shah to the Islamic Republic*, ed. Pater Avery, Gavin Hambly and Charles Melville (Cambridge: Cambridge University Press, 1991), pp. 104–43.

— 'Aqa Mohammad Khan and the establishment of the Qajar dynasty', *Journal of the Royal Central Asian Society* 50, no. 2 (1963), pp. 161–74.

Hazāra, Feyz Mohammad Kāteb, *The History of Afghanistan: Fayz Muhammad Kātib Hazārah's Sirāj al-tawārikh*, trans. R.D. McChesney and M.M. Khorrami, 6 vols (Leiden: Brill, 2013).

Hedāyat, Rezā-Qoli Khān, *Tārikh-e Rowzat al-safā-ye Nāseri*, ed. Jamshid Kiyānfar, 10 vols (Tehran: Asātir, 1380/2001).

Hopkins, Benjamin D., 'The bounds of identity: The Goldsmid Mission and the delineation of the Perso-Afghan border in the nineteenth century', *Journal of Global History* 2, no. 2 (2007), pp. 233–54.

— *The Making of Modern Afghanistan* (New York: Palgrave Macmillan, 2008).

Hoseyni, Emām al-Din, *Hoseyn Shāhi*, British Library, Ms. Or. 1663.

Jalāli, Gholām Jeylāni, ed., *Nāma-ye Ahmad Shāh Bābā be-nām-e Soltān Mostafā sālesi-ye 'Osmāni ke az ru-ye noskha-e vāhed-e khatti-e ārshif-e saltanati-ye Istanbul tartib shoda ast* (Kabul: Anjoman-e Tārikh-e Afghānestān, 1346/1967).

Kashani-Sabet, Firoozeh, *Frontier Fictions: Shaping the Iranian Nation, 1804–1946* (Princeton: Princeton University Press, 2000).
Lee, Jonathan L. *Afghanistan: A History from 1260 to the Present* (London: Reaktion Books, 2018).
Lee, Joo-Yup, *Qazaqlïq, or Ambitious Brigandage, and the Formation of the Qazaqs: State and Identity in Post-Mongol Central Eurasia* (Leiden: Brill, 2016).
Lesān al-Molk, Mohammad Taqi Sepehr, *Nāsekh al-tavārikh: Tārikh-e Qājāriya*, ed. Jamshid Kiyānfar, 3 vols (Tehran: Entesharāt-e asātir, 1377/1998).
Lockhart, Laurence, *Nadir Shah: A Critical Study based mainly upon Contemporary Sources* (London: Luzac, 1938).
Mahmud al-Hoseyni, *Tārikh-e Ahmad Shāhi*, facs. ed. Dustmorād Sayyed Morāduf, 2 vols (Moscow: Nauka, 1974).
Malcolm, Sir John, *The History of Persia from the Most Early Period to the Present Time*, 2 vols (London: John Murray, 1815).
Mann, Oskar, 'Quellenstudien zur Geschichte des Ahmed Šāh Durrânî (1747–1773)', *Zeitschrift der Deutschen Morgenländischen Gesellschaft* 52 (1898), pp. 97–118, 161–72, 323–58.
Nāmi, Mohammad Sādeq Musavi, *Tārikh-e giti-goshā dar tārikh-e Zandiya*, ed. Sa'id Nafisi ([Tehran:] Eqbāl, 1363/1984–85).
Nejatie, Sajjad, 'Iranian migrations in the Durrani Empire, 1747–93', *Comparative Studies of South Asia, Africa and the Middle East* 37, no. 3 (2017), pp. 494–509.
— 'The Pearl of Pearls: The Abdāli-Durrāni Confederacy and its Transformation under Ahmad Shāh, Durr-i Durrān', doctoral dissertation (University of Toronto, 2017).
— 'Reflections on the prehistory of the Abdāli Afghans', *Central Asian Survey* 38, no. 4 (2019), pp. 548–69.
Noelle-Karimi, Christine, *The Pearl in its Midst: Herat and the Mapping of Khurasan (15th–19th Centuries)* (Vienna: Austrian Academy of Sciences, 2014).
Perry, John R., 'The last Safavids, 1722–1773', *Iran* 9 (1971), pp. 59–69.
— *Karim Khan Zand: A History of Iran, 1747–1779* (Chicago: University of Chicago Press, 1979).
Sāru'i, Mohammad Fath-Allāh, *Tārikh-e Mohammadi: Ahsan al-tavārikh*, ed. Gholāmrezā Tabātabā'i-Majd (Tehran: Amir Kabir, 1371/1992).
Shahshahāni, Sayyed Hoseyn, 'Farmān-e tārikhi-ye Ahmad Shāh Dorrāni', *Farhang-e Irān Zamin* 6 (1337/1958), pp. 159–63; online at http://www.asnad.org/en/document/195/ [accessed 6 July 2021].
Singh, Ganda, *Ahmad Shah Durrani: Father of Modern Afghanistan* (London: Asia Publishing House, 1959).

Subtelny, Maria E. *Timurids in Transition: Turko-Persian Politics and Acculturation in Medieval Iran* (Leiden: Brill, 2007).

Tucker, Ernest S., *Nadir Shah's Quest for Legitimacy in Post-Safavid Iran* (Gainesville: University Press of Florida, 2006).

Wakili Pupalza'i [Fufalzā'i], 'Aziz al-Din, *Dorrat al-zamān fi tārikh-e Shāh Zamān* (Kabul: Matba'a-e dowlati, 1337/1958).

8

Fraying at the Edges: Iran and the Khanates of Central Asia

Fatema Soudavar Farmanfarmaian
(Independent scholar)

It may have been an inevitability that Turkic tribes should eventually take over much of Central Asia in the wake of Chinggis Khan and Timur, yet the surviving prestige of Persianate culture was such that those very same tribes were motivated more by the leadership of a bi-cultural Turko-Persian imperial entity than by separatist inclinations. The Idea of Iran lived on for a while longer under 'foreign' dynasties that, as in the past, claimed to be its staunch upholders. That was certainly the case with the largest Turkic tribe, the Afshars, who were empowered when Nader Shah assumed the throne after the fall of the Safavids. That was also the case with the first Qajar ruler, Agha Mohammad Khan, whose ancestral base of Marv was considered by his clan as integral to Iran, and who was equally committed to preserving Transcaucasia, where the Qajar branch of the Qezelbash had been invested by the Safavids with the governorships of Ganja and Qarabagh. Their intentions were sincere, their methods brutal and their opponents determined to carve their own fiefdoms out of the ruins of empire by appropriating patches of distorted history. Sic transit gloria mundi.

I would like to begin with a homage to the memory of the late Michael Axworthy. Several years ago, following his brilliant talk at the Iran Society on Nader Shah's army, I asked him about Panah 'Ali Khan (d. 1763) of the Caucasian Javanshir tribe and whether it was true, as I had been informed according to a family tradition, that he was the herald and standard-bearer of Nader Shah's army as they entered Delhi. Panah 'Ali Khan was deported with his tribe to Khorasan to prevent them from stirring up mischief in the Caucasus against Nader in favour of the Safavids; but, once there, they were recruited for the Indian campaign. After the assassination of Nader Shah (1698–1747), Panah 'Ali Khan appropriated the Khanate of Qarabagh, which remained under the suzerainty of his clan for three generations, the last two of which juggled between Russian expansionism and Iranian irredentism. His son and successor, Ebrahim Khalil Khan (d. 1806), was besieged in his fortress at Shusha (Shushi) by Agha Mohammad Khan Qajar (1742–97) – a siege often remembered for the poetic exchange incorporating a pun on the words *shisha* and *panah*.[1] Here were the proud chiefs of two Turkic clans negotiating war with improvised Persian poetry, which was integral to their upbringing, but would soon cease to be so, with distortive results on literary history. Ebrahim Khalil, having pledged loyalty to Qajar kingship in return for uncontested rule over Qarabagh, reneged on the agreement and sought Russian protection when Catherine the Great's army crossed into Transcaucasia in 1796. His betrayal provoked a second siege just five days before Agha Mohammad's assassination and, although the shah was buried honourably, the khan's loyalty would thereafter vacillate between Russia and Iran as he gauged his chances for survival. He opted for a precarity that ultimately led to his murder by the same saviours whose protection he had sought.[2]

Thus the period preceding the Russian aggressions of the early eighteenth century was a grey zone of dual fealty that would end up to Russia's advantage. It was the Russian rise to power that tilted Erekle II of Georgia (1720–98) to their side and it was the Russian encroachment on former Iranian provinces that aroused the most vicious instincts of Agha Mohammad Khan during his ruthless sack of Tiflis, which in turn precipitated the final loss of Georgia. And it was the Russian advance in Central Asia that pushed the British to separate Herat from Iran. This new balance of world power had a clear effect on local elites.

Axworthy confirmed a propensity among Nader Shah's military chiefs to found independent states after the shah's assassination. He specifically referred to Erekle and Ahmad Khan Abdali (1722–72) who, in 1747, was nominated by a Pashtun tribal council as the first king of Afghanistan, with the epithet *Durr-e Durran* (pearl of pearls), but he chose not to infringe on the legitimate rule of Nader Shah's grandson, Shahrokh (1734–96).[3]

Missing from this list of the multinational components of Nader Shah's front line were the Ozbek amirs of Transoxiana, although large numbers of their tribesmen were recruited as mercenaries.[4] The Shibanids and Ozbeks had pushed across the Jaxartes and wrested control of Transoxiana and Khvarazm in the dying days of the Timurids, so these regions had, in effect, been drifting away from Iran since 1500. There was no inclination among their elites to join the campaigns of the self-proclaimed inheritor of the Safavid mantle.

The Shibanid era in Transoxiana was the culmination of mass migrations, the seeds of which were sown as early as the third or fourth century AD. In the tenth century, the Ghaznavid slave guards of the Samanids were the first Turkic clan to harbour ambitions of hegemonic rule. Close on their heels came the unstoppable 24 tribes of the Oghuz (22 without the Khalaj), whose first incursions in the periphery of Transoxiana date to the late eighth century, shortly after the initial appearance of Arab armies and Muslim proselytizers in the region.[5] The oases of northern Khorasan provided a fertile arena for these pastoralist groups. Some were assimilated into settled communities, others were recruited to fight for one patron or another, and many more pursued their habitual way of life that combined plunder with pastoralism.[6] The repercussions of these mass migrations determined the historical course of Western Asia and Eastern Europe for centuries to come.

The Oghuz have been described by Roemer as carrying 'the lightest of cultural burdens', so that Persian culture 'exercised upon them a peculiar attraction to which they readily responded'.[7] Their leaders converted to Islam and adopted Persian culture and institutions, but their illiterate rank and file, little affected by the sophistication of their leaders and clinging to their unruly ways, were a menace to chiefs who aspired to a vast sultanate covering the ancient civilizations of Western Asia. Upon the advice of their Persian vizier Nezam al-Molk (1018–92), the sultans dispatched large contingents of their troublesome tribesmen to the frontiers of Rum – Azerbaijan, Transcaucasia, eastern Anatolia – as militant missionaries, though 'pasture and plunder' may have held greater attraction for those undisciplined hordes.[8] Their marauding continued well into the Seljuq period, when one of their leaders claimed Marv as his personal *eqta'* (land grant), or when a band of Oghuz looted and slaughtered the inhabitants of Nishapur and torched its famous library. Nor did they spare their own, as evidenced by their capture and caging of Sultan Sanjar and the massacre of his amirs and religious scholars.[9] This was despite the fact that those 'in the neighbourhood of Marv and on the borders of the empire apparently regarded themselves as the special subjects of the sultan'.[10]

The significant presence of Turkic tribes launched a gradual Turkification of the vernacular on both sides of the Caspian Sea, mainly in rural areas, but the pace of linguistic change was quicker in Transoxiana where the local population became bilingual earlier at the expense of Iranian languages, principally Old Khvarazmian and Sogdian, which died out gradually except as isolated dialects in the Pamirs.[11] The Turkification of the spoken language did not, however, dethrone the primacy of New Persian from its high pedestal. Bokhara was, after all, a major centre of its gestation after the Arab conquest. From a Turkic perspective, Mahmud Kashghari (1008–1102), author of the *Divan loghat al-Tork*, was critical of the 'slurred' speech of urban bilinguals and favoured the pure elegant Turkic idiom of his kindred Qarakhanids who ruled contemporaneously with the Persianized Ghaznavids and Seljuqs, using a Middle Turkic language and the Uighur script. Yet his choice of an epic ancestor to bestow legitimacy on his patrons fell upon a character from the *Shahnama*, the Turanian Afraseyab.[12]

The conditions were less amenable to the Persianization of the Chinggisids, Ozbeks and other Turko-Mongolian groups of the northern steppes than had been the case for the Ghaznavids and Seljuqs when they moved into Persian-speaking lands. The Mongols themselves were few in number, but their leaders retained an unabated prestige at the head of the Turkic tribal formations and polities that held sway at one time or another over central, western and southern Asia.

In the dying days of the Timurids, Ozbeks under Abu'l-Kheyr Khan (d. 1468) crossed the Syr Darya and raided Khvarazm and Transoxiana. When, after the demise of Abu Sa'id, the empire of Timur disintegrated precipitously, the stars were auspiciously aligned for the grandson of Abu'l-Kheyr, Mohammad Shibani (d. 1510), also known as Sheybak or Shahbakht, to conquer Samarqand in 1500 with the backing of Ozbek amirs, barely a year before the establishment of a Shi'i state in Iran by the adolescent Esma'il Safavi (1487–1524). Having taken control of the whole of Transoxiana, Shibani Khan went on to conquer Khvarazm, Timurid Herat and much of the rest of Khorasan, but he met his end in 1510, fighting Shah Esma'il I during their confrontation at Marv. His death opened up an opportunity for another branch of the same lineage, the 'Arabshahis (or Yadegarids), to establish a separate khanate in Khvarazm in 1511.[13] Even though the Abu'l-Kheyrids and the 'Arabshahis traced their lineage to Chinggis Khan's eldest son, Jochi (d. 1227), through the latter's son, Shiban, a family feud had poisoned relations between them. The 'Arabshahis did not join forces with Mohammad Shibani on his Khorasan campaign.[14] They are believed to have dispatched an informant to alert Shah Esma'il of Shibani Khan's hostile intentions with respect to Khorasan, and their khan, Ilbars I (d. 1518), even joined the Safavids at Marv in a bid to secure his rule over Khvarazm. The khan's association with the Shi'i elements of his domains was strongly resented by the Sunni ulema and their devotees, as a result of which he had to change policy with regard to Iran's Trojan horse, the Shi'is of Khvarazm.[15] Thereafter relations alternated between periods of hostility, manifested through plundering raids and abductions, and interludes of goodwill bordering on vassalage and sustained by the regular exchange of envoys and the consignment of hostages to the court of Esfahan. This lasted up to the time of Shah Soleyman (r. 1666–94).[16]

Shibani Khan had studiously prepared his conversion to orthodox Islam under the guidance of Naqshbandi sheykhs, and became a stalwart defender of Sunni orthodoxy.[17] Folk Shi'ism and eccentric heterodoxies, which had been rampant throughout Iranian lands before the Safavids, were congenial to nomads bred on shamanism, but the dogmatization of Shi'ism through the agency of Lebanese religious scholars, deepened the gulf between Shi'i Iran and its mainly Sunni periphery.[18] With the Safavid declaration of Shi'ism as the state religion, the Persian language came to be conflated with Shi'i heresy.[19]

Another development that threatened the supremacy of Persian was the refinement of the Chaghatay language into an elegant literary tongue, modelled on Jami, through the efforts of Mir 'Ali-Shir Nava'i (1441–1501), the erudite vizir of Soltan-Hoseyn Bayqara (1438–1506), who undertook the task at the latter's behest.[20] Adherence to Sunnism and the claim to the Chinggisid legacy, complemented by the Chaghatay language, were therefore the cultural tenets that alienated the khanates from Safavid Iran and enabled them to emphasize their pride in Mongol ancestry and the legitimacy thereby bestowed on their rule.

As the Khvarazmians had long been engaged in trade with the northern steppes, they were the first to Turkicize, even before the Mongols burst onto the scene.[21] Their adoption of Chaghatay for literary production and administration had a limited effect, given that the retention of nomadic lifestyles and of steppe traditions were inimical to the cultural sophistication that builds up over generations. Khvarazm, which, from the tenth to the twelfth centuries, had given birth to luminaries such as Biruni, Zamakhshari (author of the Arabic dictionary, *Moqaddamat al-adab*) and Jorjani (author of the first pharmacological compendium in Persian, *Zakhira-ye Khvarazmshahi*), became culturally sterile. The only writing with any literary pretension consisted of chronicles penned by Abu'l-Ghazi Khan (1603–66) in the seventeenth century, after ten years of exile in Esfahan spent browsing through Persian historical works.[22]

The Shibanids were better placed within an uninterrupted tradition of artistic and literary excellence that maintained the creative flow, primarily in Persian, and continued to attract talents from Iran, especially from Timurid Herat.[23] The majority of Shibani Khan's successors were also well-versed in Persian, sponsoring classical Persian poetry right up to the seventeenth century. Historiography had pride of place, paradoxically using the Persian language to immortalize their exploits and triumphs in perpetuation of Chinggisid precedents that, in their worldview, bypassed Timur (1336–1405) and linked them in a direct line to the Mongol legacy.[24] Shibani Khan commissioned (or partially wrote) the *Tavarikh-e gozida-ye nosratnama* to celebrate his conquest of Samarqand.[25] Two other early chronicles on the same theme were likewise composed in Persian: the versified *Fathnama* by the poet 'Shadi' produced for Shibani Khan's brother, Mahmud Soltan, who ruled in Samarqand; and the *Shibaninama* by Kamal al-Din Bana'i Haravi (1453–1512), who left Herat for Bokhara after falling out with Bayqara over his denial of the literary merits of Chaghatay.[26] With all their insistence on their Turko-Mongolian lineage, no more than three of the early Shibanid histories were composed in Chaghatay, while the majority of the dozens commissioned under later bibliophile khans throughout the rest of the sixteenth century and thereafter employed Persian (except in Khvarazm), due largely to an influx of talent from Khorasan. Some of the later chronicles, including many of those dedicated to 'Abdollah Khan, followed the format of the *Shahnama* and repurposed its material with the same aim of exalting the dynasty and its Chinggisid ancestry.[27]

A degree of bilingualism therefore persisted in Transoxiana and, to a lesser extent, in Khvarazm, where it was mainly limited to the Iranian urban population known as Sarts.[28] Chaghatay or any other developed Turkic idiom would have compromised the survival of Persian only if decontextualized from the cultural baggage that initiated the steppe tribes into the ways of sedentary societies and their handling of commerce, statecraft and high culture. Even in societies with a preponderance of nomadic elements, cultural links were not fully severed, as Turkic idioms and literary Chaghatay were infused with Persian terminology (and that goes for Ottoman Turkish too).[29]

Cities with a long history of Persian literacy, especially Bokhara, steadfastly clung to their Persianate culture and language within a Sunni mould. Although Bokhara was ruled by clans who were alienated from Safavid Iran, to this day the city remains Persian-speaking. Even Stalinist efforts to throw a wrench into their Tajik identity were ineffective. Time and again on my trips, I have been surprised by the tenacity of ancient links despite official discouragement. In 2003, a Bokharan woman, whose father hailed from Azerbaijan, proposed to circumambulate my person solely because of my Iranian origin; a few bemused Ozbek women in her party, with embroidered velvet caps and multiple braids, followed suit blindly.[30]

In brief, since the separation of Herat from Bokhara under the later Timurids, Transoxiana had, to all intents and purposes, broken away from Iran, while remaining partially beholden to its cultural legacy. The khans and amirs still had eyes on Khorasan. Failing to conquer the province, they raided and ravaged it multiple times in between periods of peaceful relations, mostly when trouble brewing at home impeded adventurism abroad. Whenever they penetrated deeper into Iranian territory, down to Astarabad (Gorgan), it never lasted long. They were happy to reap the spoils from repeated sackings of the Emam Reza shrine in Mashhad, which offered rich pickings, and at least on one occasion in the seventeenth century was accompanied by a vicious slaughter of local inhabitants. In the last years of the long-lived and powerful 'Abdollah Khan, all of Khorasan, including Herat, was conquered by Ozbek amirs who raided as far as Yazd and Kashan. This time they stayed on, for about a decade (1588–98). Attempts to drive them out remained inconclusive until the death of 'Abdollah Khan in 1598, when Shah 'Abbas (1571–1629) retrieved Khorasan. However, he failed to recapture Balkh, which had been added to the Ozbek appanages of Samarqand, Bokhara and Tashkent by the nephew of Shibani Khan after he ousted Babor from his ancestral fiefdoms. Relations remained relatively peaceful for the remainder of the reign of Shah 'Abbas, but hostilities resumed after his death. Despite the rift, a certain interdependence persisted; a renegade khan from Bokhara or Khiva, when threatened on the home front, had little choice but to seek asylum at the court of Esfahan, where he was welcomed and granted assistance.[31]

These campaigns were unsustainable over a longer period and there seems to have been little compulsion to hold on to Khorasan permanently. The khanates were happy to plunder, while the Safavids were primarily bent on protecting the frontiers of Khorasan and repelling marauders.[32] Sectarian hostility took its toll, sometimes viciously, but there were more pressing reasons for hostilities.[33] The most contentious issue was the abduction of thousands of Persians to sell in the slave markets of Bokhara and Khiva, justified on the grounds that infidels were fair game.[34] The intermediaries were often unaffiliated Turkmen tribes who moved between Khvarazm and northern Khorasan, selectively backing one khan or another according to expediency.[35]

Khiva, which had replaced the former capital of Urganj after the latter's water source (a tributary of the Oxus) dried up in the late sixteenth century, briefly acquired the upper hand in the mid-seventeenth century before confronting Nader Shah's wrath a century later.[36]

The seventeenth century was beset with other crises: while the khans of Khiva were raiding Bokhara, large numbers of nomadic Kazakhs crossed the Syr Darya to the Zarafshan valley and joined Ozbek rebels to wreak such havoc that famine and cannibalism ensued.[37] By the early eighteenth century the khanates were in disarray and the Safavid and Mughal Empires had also become moribund. The moment was ripe for Nader Shah to perform.

The northern borderlands of Khorasan, Nader's home territory, were afflicted by Turkmen depredations; Marv, in particular, had its water supply cut off while the population was stricken by the plague. We know from Mohammad Kazem 'Vazir-e Marv', a native of Marv and one of two important historians of Nader Shah, that the early stages of the Nader's career were devoted to Marv and the Atrak region in order to secure the road from Tus to Transoxiana. Another aim was to restore Marv and its famous dam, to which end he dispatched funds and engineers, whose incompetence did not deliver the expected results.[38] While Nader was ascending the rungs of power, he was too engaged elsewhere to react to slave raids. Making peace with the Ottomans, pacifying the Caucasian and Afghan provinces and the ambitious Indian campaign were prioritized. His son, Reza-Qoli (1719–47), was entrusted with the khanates pending his return from India. By the time a triumphant Nader Shah was free to venture into Transoxiana, only Balkh had been recaptured, though it would be retaken eventually by Ahmad Shah Dorrani and integrated into the new state of Afghanistan.[39]

Nader Shah's campaigns to Bokhara and Khiva do not seem to have targeted the elimination of the khanates; rather he sought to subjugate them by backing supportive clans in exchange for tribute in the form of supplies (grain, fodder, horsemen).[40] The khanates, with all their infighting, were firmly ensconced; even with Nader Shah's formidable battle-hardened army, the reintegration of breakaway provinces into a reconstituted Iranian empire could scarcely be envisaged. Nader Shah may have entertained hopes that his proposition for the creation of a fifth Ja'fari *mazhab* might eventually result in a loose reunification, though that would come at the price of major concessions, similar to those on which the peace treaty with the Ottomans was predicated.[41] The khan of Bokhara and his amirs, awed by Nader Shah's military exploits, visited his camp to offer their submission, so there was no need to enter the city. Khiva, however, was besieged, all the slaves were liberated and the incumbent ruler, Ilbars II (r. 1728–40), was executed with 20 of his amirs in retaliation for their gratuitous murder of the Juybari sheykhs who had delivered the shah's ultimatum.[42]

By then the power behind the khan of Bokhara was the *ataliq* (a tutor similar to the *atabeg* in post-Seljuq Iran), who belonged to the Ozbek Mangit tribe. Mohammad Rahim, the son of the first ataliq, enjoyed the patronage of Nader Shah and was the first Ozbek to lead a contingent of his tribesmen in the shah's army.[43] After Nader Shah's assassination, the Mangits assumed the leadership of Bokhara and its dependencies, initially in the name of a Janid puppet.[44] After eliminating the latter, they were the first non-Chinggisids in over two centuries to hold the reins in Bokhara and Khvarazm; their rule was cut short in Khvarazm unlike in Bokhara, where they held fast.[45] With their newfound hegemony they would betray the trust of Nader Shah by attacking Marv, which had been intermittently raided but never annexed to a khanate or to an appanage.

After the devastating onslaught of the Mongols on Marv, the whole oasis had become a no-man's land, though still nominally part of Khorasan and Iran. Despite the ravage and depopulation from which it never recovered, the ancient history of Marv awarded it a special place and an indelible prestige in Iranian memory. It was one of the 16 perfect lands named in the Avesta; it was where the Silk Road was launched officially when a delegation from the Han emperors of China was met ceremoniously by Parthian cavalrymen; it was where the last Sasanian emperor, Yazdegerd III (d. 653), was murdered on his flight from the Arab armies; it was a hub of religious interaction between Zoroastrians, Buddhists, Manichaeans and Christians (with a large bishopric); and it was from there that Abu Moslem Khorasani (d. 755) launched the 'Abbasid Revolution; it then became the capital of the Eastern Caliphate of Ma'mun (d. 833).[46] Throughout much of its history Marv was a seat of learning with libraries that attracted some of the greatest early Islamic polymaths and held a treasure trove of tales for the *Shahnama*. It had its last great days under the Seljuqs, when it became the capital of Khorasan for most of the duration of the sultanate, as is still evident in the mausoleum (or palace) of Sultan Sanjar (d. 1157), which has been disfigured by misguided restoration entrusted to Turkish experts who adorned it with Arabo-Andalusian windows beneath the drum of the dome – a flagrant example of how a sham identity can go wrong.[47] After the destruction inflicted by the Mongols on the Marv oasis and its famous Soltanband dam on the Morghab river, the ruined landscape, still enveloped in an aura of myth, became a roaming ground for Turkmen tribes and their flocks.

The tricky designation 'Turkmen', which has as many applications as there are Turkmen clans, calls for more elucidation. Several definitions have been proposed, the most widely accepted of which is given by early Islamic sources such as Biruni, namely that the Oghuz tribes who converted to Islam were thereafter designated as 'Turkmen'.[48] Over the centuries the composition of the

Turkmen tribes was inevitably reconfigured as a result of widespread movements, contacts with other tribes and fluctuating political and economic ties. Having absorbed Persians, Kurds and Arabs, as well as various Turko-Mongolian tribes, not all the Turkmen were Oghuz, nor even Turks. The Turkmen were particularly numerous in Khvarazm and, augmented by infiltrations by various other groups, they added up to a quarter of the population of the khanate on the eve of the nineteenth century. With no fixed allegiance, they were intermittently subordinate to Khiva, Bokhara or Iran, as dictated by the pursuit of pasture and of captives to enslave. As the main intermediaries of the slave trade, they came under frequent attack from the Iranian side while serving the khans as an unofficial and unreliable military arm.[49] The clash of Yomut Turkmen with the Ozbek elites of Khvarazm in 1770 resulted in anarchy after their capture of Khiva from the ruling Qongrats, following which the Yomuts were banished en masse. They then joined the Turkmen who had migrated to northern Khorasan after the fall of the Safavids, further disrupting the life of rural communities.[50]

Meanwhile the Turkmen who had become sedentary or joined confederations lost the designation 'Turkmen' and came to be known by the name of their tribal or political affiliation.[51] The expulsion of the Qezelbash by the Ottomans, whose aspirations to the caliphate were jeopardized by the presence of militants devoted to Shi'i heterodoxy, resulted in a reverse flow of Turkmen Qezelbash to Safavid service. The Qajars, as followers of Sheykh Heydar (d. 1488), the ancestor of the Safavids, were among the earliest tribes to join the Qezelbash confederacy. Thereafter they would be known by the name of their tribe and its subdivisions rather than as Turkmen. Regarding the origins of the Qajars, one version alleges that they reached the borders of Khorasan with the first Oghuz migrations, when the tribes had to coexist with Arabs and Iranians who had preceded them there. Another version traces their origin to the Turkic tribes who followed Hülegü Khan (d. 1265) to Iran. Their own tradition ascribes their ancestry to a Qajar Noyan, the son of a general in the Mongol army. As the Qajars do not figure in Rashid al-Din's list of Oghuz tribes, Hambly conjectures that they may have been a sub-group of a larger tribe, such as the Bayat.[52]

With their promotion to administrative posts in the Safavid period, the Qajars were granted the governorships of Ganja, Erivan and Qarabagh. When Shah 'Abbas moved Kurdish and Turkmen tribes to defend the north-eastern marches, Qajar contingents are reported to have been resettled at Astarabad and Marv as a shield against Turkmen and Ozbek raids.[53] The mobility of Turkmen groups makes it difficult to pinpoint their precise locations at any given time. The Qajar presence in Marv and Astarabad may even predate the Safavids, given that Iranian historians of the nineteenth century refer to Marv as the original homeland of the Qajars.[54] The presence of the Qoyunlu clan is already attested at the fort of Mobarakabad (Aq Qal'a) near Astarabad at the time of

Shah Tahmasp. That was where Agha Mohammad Khan was born, while his father was a fugitive in the Karakum desert.[55] The Yomut Turkmen, who migrated unimpeded between the Karakum desert and Khvarazm, had given refuge in the forbidding vastness of the desert to the fugitive Mohammad Hasan Khan Qajar, whose ambitions of kingship and multiple campaigns had incurred the enmity of the Afsharids and the Zands, and of rival Qajars.[56] The earliest recorded name of a Qajar governor (*beglarbegi*) to Marv is Mehrab Khan Qarabaghi who was appointed in 1017/1608 by Shah 'Abbas and who held the post until 1032/1623.[57] This concurs with another passage in Eskandar Beg about Mehrab Khan's Qezelbash and *tofangchi* fighting off the troops of Emam-Qoli Khan as they approached Marv after raiding Nishapur and Mashhad.[58] The son of Mehrab Khan, Morteza-Qoli Khan, was appointed to the same post in 1042/1633, but was later replaced by a royal *gholam*, 'Ali-Qoli Khan.[59] So the governorship of Marv was assigned preferentially, though not exclusively, to a Qajar.

The only major monument erected after the Mongol ravages at Marv was the citadel of Bahram 'Ali Khan (Turkicized to Bairam 'Ali Khan) from the 'Ezzedinlu (or 'Azodanlu) Qajar clan, who was the respected chief of the tribal Qajars of Marv in the mid-eighteenth century.[60] It is not clear for how long the 'Ezzedinlu had been based there; they seem to have dominated the oasis from at least the early Safavid period until 1785, entertaining variable relations with local Turkmen tribes and weathering the influx of Yomuts from Khiva.

Among the Turkmen tribes, the Tekke and the Saruq were the most actively engaged in the slave trade, while the Salur lived a more settled life between Sarakhs and the oasis of Marv.[61] The Salur were considered the noblest of them all, descended as they were from Chinggis through his fourth son, Tolui (d. 1232), and as such enjoyed 'a certain paramountcy' among the original Oghuz.[62] They had the dignity not to get involved in the slave traffic, and traded instead in horses and skins.[63] Their daughters were sought as brides by Qajar chiefs. Bahram 'Ali Khan's mother was a Salur, as was the mother of Fath-'Ali Shah (born 1772 of an 'Ezzedinlu–Qajar union).[64] An 'Ezzedinlu (Hoseyn-Qoli Khan) was entrusted with the transfer of Agha Mohammad Khan's remains from Shusha to the shrine of 'Abd al-'Azim in Rayy before reburial in Najaf.[65] All this speaks for their revered status as tribal elders among their kinsmen.[66]

Having lost Khiva, the third Mangit, the fanatical Shah Morad (r. 1784–1801) proceeded in 1785 to attack Marv relentlessly until 1789–90. He killed Bahram 'Ali Khan and destroyed his citadel, while the Iranian Shi'i inhabitants of Marv, including the family of Bahram 'Ali Khan, were deported in waves to Bokhara and Samarqand, where they resettled separately from the local Persian-speakers. Like their predecessors, the Mangits had hoped to reach Mashhad and strip the shrine, but found the city too well defended.[67] Instead, their troops engaged in plunder and slaughter in the surrounding villages.[68] The

Mangit hold on Marv was contested and fought over more than once by Khiva in the nineteenth century.[69] Khivan expansionism, the strong presence of Turkmen tribes, internecine rivalry and Iranian claims prevented the Mangits from maintaining an uninterrupted hold on the Marv oasis.

The Qajar connection with Marv may have been physically severed, but they were not about to forget and forgive. The long narrow strip of land between the Karakum desert and the Kopet Dagh mountains was still considered integral to Khorasan and Iran; with the consolidation of the new dynasty on the throne of Iran, several attempts were made to liberate the captives and to reassert time-honoured links with Marv and beyond. After his coronation, Agha Mohammad was determined to retrieve the lost regions of eastern Iran: Herat, Balkh, Marv and eventually Bokhara. He wrote to Zaman Shah (1770–1844) of Kabul to reclaim Balkh (a polite refusal arrived posthumously).[70] In another letter addressed to the khan of Bokhara, he affirmed that Balkh-e Bami, Marv-e Shahijan, Zamindavar, Sistan, Qandahar and Kabul were inseparable from the territory of Iran's *padeshah*s. 'What has seized you to occupy Balkh-e Bami and Marv-e Shahijan?' The letter vows not to transgress the ancient limits of Iran nor to cross the Jeyhun (Oxus) if Iran's rightful claims are respected. He goes on to complain about the killing of his kinsman Bairam 'Ali (Bahram 'Ali) Khan 'Ezzedinlu.[71] On his barefoot and tearful pilgrimage to the shrine of Emam Reza, where he stopped to grieve at the latter's grave, Agha Mohammad reported hearing the voice of 'Aqa Bahram Qoli' imploring him to avenge his blood, and to take punitive action, now that the kingship was theirs, for the cruel fate inflicted on the inhabitants of Marv.[72] Had he lived, Agha Mohammad Khan would have doubtless reacted as violently to the occupation of Marv and Balkh as he did to that of Tiflis.

Meanwhile Shah Morad had sent his son, the Amirzada Naser al-Din Ture, to govern Marv, but upon the accession of his brother, Amir Heydar, the Amirzada was summoned to Bokhara. Suspicious of his brother's intentions, he disobeyed and stayed on in rebellion until his funds dried up. He was thinking of applying for sanctuary in Afghanistan, but the new Qajar governor of Khorasan, Prince Mohammad Vali Mirza (1789–1864), fearing an Ozbek–Afghan alliance and intending to restore the frontiers of Khorasan, invited him to stay on in Mashhad as his personal guest. The next governor, Prince Hasan 'Ali Mirza Shoja' al-Saltana (1789–1853), unwisely cut off his allowance, so the Amirzada was mulling an appeal to Russia or England when he met James Baillie Fraser in Mashhad. Through Fraser's conversations with the Amirzada we learn that the son of Bahram 'Ali Khan, Mohammad Hoseyn Khan, who resided as an honourable captive at the court of Bokhara, had been plotting revenge. He contacted the Amirzada to help him recover Bokhara from Amir Heydar. When news of a conspiracy reached the khan, the Amirzada and Mohammad Hoseyn Khan Marvi had to escape to Mashhad. The latter proceeded to the encampment of Agha Mohammad Khan, who bade him deliver a message to Shah Morad demanding capitulation.[73] He could ill afford to take such a risk and ended up instead at the court of Fath-'Ali Shah as a respected dignitary who amassed substantial wealth, much of which was spent on building a mosque and *madrasa* complex that is still known as Marvi, though it is presently at risk of falling victim to greedy developers.[74] A despondent Amirzada proceeded to Istanbul and, unable to obtain support, ended his days in Russia.[75] Any attempt by Khiva to fill the void was short-lived in the face of the looming Russian threat.

The issue of Marv continued to plague relations with Bokhara and Khiva throughout the first half of the nineteenth century. The Qajar government made multiple attempts by diplomatic means or by the force of arms to free the Iranian slaves held in Bokhara and Khiva and to reclaim Marv. In 1831, when the heir apparent, 'Abbas Mirza, was appointed governor of Khorasan, he undertook two successive campaigns, respectively in 1831 and 1832, and attacked the Turkmen in the area of Sarakhs, razed their forts and obtained the release of 20,000 captive slaves after pacifying the Salur.[76] Following 'Abbas Mirza's untimely death in 1833, it was left to his son, Mohammad Mirza (1808–48), to pursue the same task in 1836, on his way to attempt to recover Herat from the British-backed Afghans.[77] After ascending the throne as Mohammad Shah he dispatched two diplomatic missions: in 1842 to Khiva, and in 1844 to Bokhara, both of which were recorded in the memoirs of the respective envoys. Heading the first one was Mohammad 'Ali Khan Ghafur, who arrived concurrently with embassies from Russia and England. His main mission was to obtain the liberation of the lieutenant and nephew of Mashhad's Qajar governor who were captured by Turkmen raiders while they were out hunting. He took the opportunity to demand that the slave trade be terminated and that all Iranian slaves be freed. The new shah had been contemplating war to enforce those demands but was dissuaded by the Russian and English envoys in Tehran. The memoirs of Ghafur, *Ruznama-ye safar-e Khvarazm*, offer glimpses into the arguments advanced by each side. Ghafur complains that the khan had not kept his promise to stop the Turkmen of his domains from capturing Iranians, and the khan, for his part, refers to transgressions by Iranian governors and the shah's refusal to reciprocate when his envoy took some slaves to Tehran as a gesture of goodwill; he offers to ransom some slaves, just as he had to buy back Khvarazmian captives held by the Qajars, but that would only involve a small number, as most of the captives had been bought and were in private possession. In the end, only the nephew of the governor was released.[78]

The second mission of 1844 was unveiled recently when the anonymous *Safarnama-ye Bokhara* was published in Tehran in 1995 and reviewed in English by James Gustafson in 2013.[79] These memoirs have since been identified as the travelogue of 'Abbas-Qoli Khan, who was tasked with the mission upon the request of the British chargé d'affaires, Justin Sheil. In the wake of the murder of two British agents, Colonel Stoddart and Captain Connolly in Bokhara, Sheil was concerned that the same fate might befall Joseph Wolff, a convert to Christianity and Anglican missionary who travelled there to inquire about their fate.[80] 'Abbas-Qoli Khan, having spent four days in Marv en route, reminded the khan that Marv was the homeland of the Qajars. He further invoked the historical and cultural unity of Iran and Greater Khorasan with Transoxiana, and, by implication, Iran's hereditary right to Marv, which he dated to the reign of the first epic king, Manuchehr, grandson of Fereydun in the *Shahnama*. With Manuchehr begins the conflict with Turan, represented by Afraseyab, which was resolved by the arrow of the archer Arash landing on the Oxus at Balkh to demarcate the frontier between Iran and Turan. Reference to epic heroes presents, to quote Gustafson, 'a conceptual geography of Central Asia' that supports 'their difference as well as unity in a Persianate cultural sphere'.[81] Despite the amir's dread of the Qajar empire 'as a particularly significant threat', the envoy was able to return with Wolff and 1,000 released captives.[82] What the amir felt to be a 'significant threat' was the epic attachment of Iran to those regions rather than military aggression or occupation.

It was this emotionally charged devotion to a historical or mythological memory that also turned Nader Shah or Agha Mohammad Khan into fierce upholders of a broader identity that was alien to the amir's blinkered view of Bokhara's place in the longue durée. Finally, under Naser al-Din Shah (1831–96), his prime minister, Amir Kabir, sent the author and chronicler Reza-Qoli Khan Hedayat to Khiva, where he hosted slaves at his residence and flaunted his support by walking in public with them. Nevertheless, he left empty-handed. The incumbent khan, Mohammad Amin, made no concessions for fear of emboldening the Qezelbash to make further demands.[83] A more pragmatic view was expressed by Soltan Morad Mirza Hesam al-Saltana (1818–83), who led the final unsuccessful campaign during the Herat war of 1856–57. His lengthy argument is reproduced in a book by British chargé d'affaires Edward Eastwick: the gist of it is that the frontiers of Persia 'being coterminous with the country of the Turkomans', are too long to prevent inroads and kidnappings, except through the possession of the stronghold of Marv; that was what made the reoccupation of Marv so vital, in addition to its being the 'homeland of a large part of the Qajar tribe' and 'as rightfully belonging to Persia as any of the Shah's dominions'.[84] Empty words at a time when Russian and British colonial intrigues determined frontiers, though that did not discourage the Qajars from feeble attempts at asserting their rights.

Between 1852 and 1860, two armed campaigns were undertaken. The first one was led in 1851 by Fereydun Mirza, the governor of Khorasan, jointly with the Turkmen. By 1855, they had routed the army of Mohammad Amin Khan, who lost his life in the battle. An Iranian governor was once again established at Marv, but he did not last long due to feuding between the Saruqs and the

Tekke. That led to one last disastrous Qajar intervention in 1860–61.[85] The army, led by Prince Hamza Mirza Heshmat al-Dowla in 1860, was soundly defeated by Tekke Turkomans. The corruption and ineptitude of the troops were wittily satirized by Joseph Arthur, comte de Gobineau in *Les nouvelles asiatiques*.[86]

Conclusion

Less than a quarter of a century later the Russians were in Marv. The Great Game was in full swing and the traditional frontiers of Khorasan were breached. The prospects were not favourable for Persian literacy, which had been eroding but would thereafter face a more serious threat from artificial borders wreaking havoc with historical identity. History would be rewritten more than once according to shifts in ideology. While the Shibanids considered Timur a usurper of the Chinggisid legacy, in the post-Soviet period, Timur is adulated and the Shibanids are ignored or subsumed under the Timurids, who are now hailed as the progenitors of the Uzbek nation. Regional history has been fragmented with a giant Sovietized statue of Timur in Uzbekistan, of Oghuz Khan in Turkmenistan and of Esma'il Samani in Tajikistan, with no apparent connection between any of them. This selective approach serves short-term politics but seen from a world-historical perspective, it diminishes and obfuscates the panoramic sweep of cultural awareness in all its splendid diversity.

Notes:

1. Shushi is the older Armenian pronunciation, hence the play on words with *shisha*, meaning glass. Relations with the Armenian *melik*s varied from outright alliance and intermarriage to clannish hostility. See George A. Bournoutian's translation of Mīrzā Jamāl Javānšīr Qarābāġī's *A History of Qarabagh*.
2. George A. Bournoutian, 'Ebrahīm Khalīl Khan Javānšīr', pp. 71–73.
3. Peter Avery, 'Nādir Shāh and the Afsharid legacy', pp. 59–62. The Abdalis had twice besieged Mashhad in the early eighteenth century. Nader's priority was to neutralize them before taking on the Ghilzais; he engaged them in battle several times before they entered his service as some of his 'most dependable and hard-fighting troops', according to Michael Axworthy, *The Sword of Persia*, pp. 76, 81–83.
4. Avery, 'Nādir Shāh', p. 51.
5. Peter B. Golden, *An Introduction to the History of the Turkic People*, pp. 206–7.
6. C.E. Bosworth, 'The Iranian world', pp. 82–86, 195–96.
7. H.R. Roemer, 'The Turkmen dynasties', p. 149.
8. Golden, *An Introduction to the History*, p. 221. According to Bosworth, 'The Iranian world', pp. 61–62, 'a crusade against the Christians does not appear to have been one of the mainsprings of the sultan's policy', and the Turkmen were driven by their quest for 'pasture and plunder'. Other *ghazi* elements – Arabs, Kurds, Deylamites – had preceded them in Anatolia to convert Christians.
9. Bosworth, 'The Iranian world', pp. 151–57.
10. A.K.S. Lambton, 'The internal structure of the Saljuq Empire', pp. 246–47.
11. Golden, *An Introduction to the History*, pp. 224–25. The Sogdian traders, who travelled back and forth to China through the Tarim basin, left the mark of their language and writing on Uighur, which adopted Aramaic-based Sogdian scripts vehicled through trade and religion: Buddhism, Manichaeism and Nestorian Christianity (ibid., p. 151).
12. Ibid., pp. 5, 172, 197, 228–29. For the history of the appropriation of Afraseyab and Turan by Turkic dynasties in Central Asia, see Richard Payne, 'The making of Turan'.
13. See Yuri Bregel, "Arabšāhī', pp. 243–45.
14. Mohsen Rahmati, 'Ravābet va monāsebāt-e khānedān-e 'arabshāhi', p. 93. Bregel, "Arabšāhī', p. 243.
15. Rahmati, 'Ravābet va monāsebāt', pp. 92–93. Citing from *'Ālam-ārā-ye Shāh Esmā'il*, the author affirms that to conciliate Shah Esma'il and secure his support, the 'Arabshahi khan agreed to profess Shi'ism. Some of the information in the latter book may be propagandistic, as the author admits; conversion of the khan to Shi'ism would top the list of suspect information. Bregel, "Arabšāhī', p. 243, mentions a massacre of the Qezelbash garrison in the town of Vazir after the townspeople offered the protection of the town to the grandsons of Yadegar Khan ('Arabshahi), who, together with Ozbek tribes from the steppe, went on to conquer Khvarazm and subjugate Turkmen tribes down to the Kopet Dag range. This would imply that Shi'ism had made inroads into Khvarazm with the support of Shah Esma'il.
16. See sequel in Rahmati, "Ravābet va monāsebāt', pp. 93–104.
17. Yuri Bregel, 'Bukhara iii. After the Mongol invasion', p. 516.

18. H.R. Roemer, 'The successors of Timur', p. 136. See Rula Jurdi Abisaab, *Converting Persia*.
19. Bertold Spuler, 'Central Asia v. In the Mongol and Timurid periods', pp. 172–76.
20. Spuler, 'Central Asia v'; Roemer, 'The successors of Timur', p. 139. More than half of the vocabulary of Chaghatay in Nava'i's poetry was derived from Persian. See Gerhard Doerfer, 'Chaghatay language and literature', p. 340.
21. Golden, *An Introduction to the History*, p. 228.
22. Bregel, "Arabšāhī', p. 244. Abu'l-Ghazi's two works on the origins of the Turkmen and the Turks, *Shajara-ye Tarākama* and *Shajara-ye Tork* ('Genealogy of the Turkmen' and 'Genealogy of the Turks'), use the local Turkic dialect that contains less Persian than classical Chaghatay. See http://feb-web.ru/feb/litenc/encyclop/le1/le1-0152.htm [accessed 12 January 2020].
23. Jaimee Comstock-Skipp, 'Heroes of Legend, Heroes of History', p. 18. The short-lived patronage of Behzad by Shibani Khan is mentioned only by Babor, see Priscilla Soucek, 'Behzād, Kamāl-al-dīn', p. 114. If this is correct, the portrait of Shibani Khan attributed to his hand may be a faithful likeness.
24. Barbara Brend, 'A sixteenth-century manuscript from Transoxiana', p. 103. See also Comstock-Skipp, 'Heroes of Legend', pp. 15–17.
25. Brend, 'A sixteenth-century manuscript', p. 105. A single copy of the later illustrated version of the *Nosratnāma* is in the British Library. Copies of the *Jāme' al-tavārikh* may have reached Samarqand as booty from Herat, but Brend speculates that Timur may have taken a copy from Tabriz to Samarqand after his conquest of the former city in 1386.
26. Yuri Bregel, 'Historiography xii. Central Asia', pp. 395–96. See also Z. Safa, 'Banā'i Heravi'. For Banā'i's disagreement with Bayqara, see Chad Lingwood, *Politics, Poetry, and Sufism in Medieval Iran*, p. 114. Bregel provides a well-rounded account of the little-known chronicles of the Ozbek khanates. He also refers to an eye-witness account of the campaign against the Kazakhs written by the Iranian Sunni émigré author, Fazlollāh b. Ruzbehān Khonji, under the title, *Mehmān-nāma-ye Bokhārā*, dedicated to his host. See also Shahzad Bashir, 'Arbiters of Iran' and Ali Anooshahr, *Turkestan and the Rise of Eurasian Empires*, pp. 84–113.
27. According to Karin Ruehrdanz, 'The Samarqand *Shahnama*s in the context of dynastic change', pp. 213–14, 'the only extant complete illustrated *Shahnama* of Shaibanid provenance' was made for 'Abdollah Khan. A copy from Khiva is dated to the 1550s, but the illustrations are described as 'provincial'. See Comstock-Skipp, 'Heroes of Legend', p. 5, n. 15, and p. 12.
28. Bregel, "Arabšāhī'; Golden, *An Introduction to the History*, p. 408.
29. Golden, *An Introduction to the History*, pp. 33, 302.
30. Reciprocity of affinities is expressed in the choice of the title *Bokhara* for the foremost Persian literary journal.
31. Yuri Bregel, "Bukhara iv. Khanate of Bukhara and Khorasan', pp. 521–24. Bregel refers, in particular, to Wali Mohammad Khan who, under threat from his nephews, took refuge with Shah 'Abbas and received assistance to regain control. For several cases from Khvarazm, see Rahmati, '*Ravabet va monasebat*'.
32. Bregel, 'Bukhara iv'.

33. Ibid. Bregel refers to gruesome atrocities, such as the total annihilation of the Sunni population of Qarshi in 1512 (Bana'i Haravi was among the casualties), and the slaughter of Qezelbash by 'Abdollah Khan's troops in Herat. Tales of Sunni persecution inside Iran were reported by Iranian refugees in Transoxiana.
34. Ibid.
35. Ibid. The slave raids are said to have begun under 'Abdollah Khan and continued into the early twentieth century. However, the English merchant Anthony Jenkinson saw Indian and Iranian merchants buying slaves in Bokhara as early as 1558. See Jeff Eden, *Slavery and Empire in Central Asia*, p. 48.
36. Golden, *An Introduction to the History*, p. 38.
37. Bregel, 'Bukhara iii', p. 516.
38. Avery, 'Nādir Shāh', pp. 22–24, 54–55.
39. Yuri Bregel, 'Central Asia vii. In the 18th and 19th centuries', pp. 193–94. See also V. Fourniau, 'Balkh iii. From the Mongols to modern times', p. 591, regarding the Abdali recapture of Balkh.
40. Bregel, 'Central Asia vii', pp. 193–194.
41. Avery, 'Nādir Shāh', pp. 25–26, 45–46, 49.
42. Bregel, 'Central Asia vii', pp. 193–94.
43. Bregel, 'Bukhara iii', p. 517. Anke von Kügelen, 'Manghits', alleges that Nader Shah 'sent him at the head of a thousand men to pacify Bukhara', probably in response to rebellions by Ozbek amirs.
44. Bregel, 'Bukhara iii', pp. 518–19.
45. Ibid. Mohammad Rahim 'legitimized' his rule on the basis of his marriage to the daughter of the last khan, Abu'l-Feyz, whom he killed after Nader Shah's death.
46. Recently, the Islamic Republic of Iran identified a ruined structure in Marv as the house of Emam Reza. To my knowledge, there is no archaeological justification for this attribution other than that the Eighth Imam resided in Marv when he was summoned there by Ma'mun as his heir.
47. The misguided restoration of the Sanjar mausoleum and other monuments was discussed by Robert Hillenbrand in his keynote lecture at the Iran Heritage Foundation conference, *From Persepolis to Isfahan: Safeguarding Cultural Heritage*. The lecture, entitled 'The restoration of medieval monuments in the Iranian world, especially Central Asia', is available as a podcast on the Iran Heritage Foundation website.
48. Golden, *An Introduction to the History*, pp. 212–13.
49. Bregel, 'Central Asia vii', p. 196.
50. Ibid., p. 193.
51. Ibid, pp. 193–97.
52. 'Qājār', *Dāneshnāma-ye jahān-e eslām*, 1/7243. Gavin Hambly, 'Āghā Muḥammad Khān and the establishment of the Qājār dynasty', p. 104. The latter source mentions Qajar Noyan as a putative ancestor of Timur.
53. 'Qājār', *Dāneshnāma-ye jahān-e eslām*.
54. Ibid. See also James M. Gustafson, 'Qajar ambitions in the Great Game', p. 544.
55. Ibid. and 'Āghā Mohammad Khān Qājār', *Dāneshnāma*, 1/298.
56. Avery, 'Nādir Shāh', p. 48. John R. Perry, 'The Zand dynasty' pp. 74–77.
57. 'Qājār', *Dāneshnāma-ye jahān-e eslām*, 1/7243.
58. Eskandar Beg Monshi, *Tārikh-e 'ālam-ārā-ye 'Abbāsi*, vol. II, p. 684.

59. Vahid Qazvini, '*Abbāsnāma*, p. 62. Morteza-Qoli Khan was promoted to *sepahsalar* by Shah 'Abbas II, and eventually beheaded, ibid., p. 331.
60. Bahram 'Ali Khan must be the correct name, if Agha Mohammad Khan addressed him thus. After the destruction of his citadel and the mass immigration of Turkmen to Marv, the name was Turkicized to Bairam 'Ali, the name cited in all later Iranian, Russian and English sources, with the sole exception of Gavin Hambly who uses Bahram 'Ali in a footnote on the marriage between Qajars and Turkmen without mentioning his source. It is possible that he was known by both names. As for the tribal name, Persian sources give 'Ezzedinlu, with 'Azodanlu in brackets. In *Tārikh-e Zu'l-Qarneyn*, Mirzā Fazlollāh Shirāzi – cited by Abbas Amanat and Arash Khazeni, 'The steppe roads of Central Asia', p. 123 – calls him Bairam 'Ali Khan 'Azodanlu.
61. See Amanat and Khazeni, 'The steppe roads', p. 118, regarding the distribution of various Turkmen tribes. See also Golden, *An Introduction to the History*, p. 400. According to questionable information given by a tribal elder to O'Donovan, most of the Turkmen tribes (Tekke, Saruq, Salur) in the Marv oasis had moved there around the middle of the eighteenth century; Edmund O'Donovan, *The Merv Oasis*, vol. II, pp. 168–70.
62. Golden, *An Introduction to the History*, p. 208. Amanat and Khazeni, 'The steppe roads', p. 123, cite Mirzā Fazlollāh Shirāzi, according to whom 'in the time of Bayram 'Ali Khan 'Azodanlu Qajar's rule in Merv, Salur Khan invaded that region several times, turning the place upside down and creating havoc', then adds that the Salurs 'who considered themselves lords and princes' and never killed or took slaves from Iran, petitioned the royal court to move their encampment to Sarakhs where they 'were allowed to stay in peace'.
63. The same passage cited by Amanat and Khazeni in 'The steppe roads', p. 123, confirms that the Salur were 'merchants of horses and Bukhara skins in Khurasan and Khvarazm'.
64. Hambly, 'Āghā Muḥammad Khān', p. 113.
65. 'Āghā Mohammad Khān Qājār', *Dāneshnāma*, 1/298.
66. Their respected status among other Qajars was confirmed to me orally by older members of the family.
67. Bregel, 'Bukhara iv', p. 522. Bregel, 'Bukhara iii', p. 518.
68. Feyzollāh Bushāsp Gusha, 'Marv dar nakhostin daha-hā-ye hokumat-e Qājār', pp. 27–28. Citing from Mirzā Shams Bokhārā'i's *Tārikh-e Bokhārā*, the author writes that Shah Morad, to save face, pretended that Emam Reza appeared in his dream to dissuade him.
69. Bregel, 'Central Asia vii', pp. 197–98.
70. Mahmud Mahmud, *Tārikh-e ravābet-e siyāsi-ye Irān va Ingilis*, vol. I, p. 174.
71. Bushāsp Gusha, 'Marv', p. 28. The extract is taken from the original letter as reproduced in E'temād al-Saltana, *Tārikh-e montazam-e Nāseri*, vol. III, pp. 1432–33.
72. Fatema Soudavar Farmanfarmaian, 'An Iranian perspective of J. B. Fraser's trip', p. 229, n. 54. The same episode is also quoted in the Persian translation of Amineh Pakravan, 'Agha Mohammad Khan', translated from French into Persian by Jahāngir Afkāri, p. 270. Pakravan believes that it was a ploy on the part of Agha Mohammad to report hearing a voice from beyond the grave.

73. See Soudavar Farmanfarmaian, 'An Iranian perspective', pp. 229, 231–32 (cited from James Baillie Fraser's *Diaries*, pp. 172–73. See also n. 66 in the same article). According to Fraser, Mohammad Hoseyn Khan had been in touch with the clergy of Mashhad and had communicated to them a plan regarding Shi'ism. The *Diaries* give a confused account of his flight, after he was threatened with execution. On another page Fraser has him escaping, being caught, pardoned and given a village to live in until his death. This is obviously wrong, but Bushāsp Gusha, 'Marv', p. 27, also mentions an itinerary via Shahr-e Sabz.
74. Reported in Jām-e Jam Online, 27 Tir, 1389. According to the same article, the Khan-e Marvi endowed the adjacent garden and his numerous properties (farms, houses, shops) for the maintenance of the mosque and madrasa.
75. Bushāsp Gusha, 'Marv', p. 33.
76. Amanat and Khazeni, 'The steppe roads', p. 117. Here the authors contradict Mirzā Fazlollāh Shirāzi about the Salurs not dealing in slaves. See footnote 62.
77. Ibid. Eden, *Slavery and Empire*, p. 38, blames the failure of the Herat campaign in part on the interruption of Iranian supply lines by Khvarazmian forces before their eviction by Saruq Turkmen, who rejected any submission to Khvarazm.
78. Eden, *Slavery and Empire*, pp. 40–45.
79. Gustafson, 'Qajar ambitions', p. 537.
80. Ibid., p. 540. See also Eden, *Slavery and Empire*, pp. 7–8, about Wolff writing to all the monarchs of Europe to plead for the plight of 200,000 Iranian slaves, 'many of them people of high talent', and receiving no reaction.
81. Gustafson, 'Qajar ambitions', pp. 542–52, makes a comparison with 'European authors' own conceptual geographies presented through constant reference to Alexander and Marco Polo as enlightened travellers and adventurers in a foreign, unfamiliar land'.
82. Ibid., p. 539. Gustafson gives the impression that 'Abbas-Qoli Khan was only able to save Wolff, but Bushāsp Gusha, 'Marv', pp. 40–41, refers to his return with 1,000 freed slaves. They were all intercepted on their way to Mashhad by Turkmen who wanted to ransom or swap them for their own captives in Mashhad, but they were allowed to leave on the order of Amir Nasrollah.
83. Eden, *Slavery and Empire*, p. 40.
84. Edward B. Eastwick, *Journal of a Diplomate's Three Years' Residence*, vol. I, pp. 251–54.
85. Bregel, 'Central Asia vii', p. 198.
86. Joseph Arthur, comte de Gobineau, 'L'histoire de Gamber Aly', in *Les nouvelles asiatiques*, III.

Bibliography:

Abisaab, Rula Jurdi, *Converting Persia* (London: I.B. Tauris, 2004).

Amanat, Abbas, and Arash Khazeni, 'The steppe roads of Central Asia and the Persian captivity narrative of Mirza Mahmud Taqi Ashtiyani', in *Writing Travel in Central Asian History*, ed. Nile Green (Bloomington: Indiana University Press, 2014), pp. 113–34.

Anooshahr, Ali, *Turkestan and the Rise of Eurasian Empires: A Study of Politics and Invented Traditions* (Oxford: Oxford University Press, 2018).

Avery, Peter, 'Nādir Shāh and the Afsharid legacy', in *The Cambridge History of Iran, vol. 7, From Nadir Shah to the Islamic Republic*, ed. Peter Avery, Gavin Hambly and Charles Melville (Cambridge: Cambridge University Press, 1991), pp. 3–62.

Axworthy, Michael, *The Sword of Persia, Nader Shah, from Tribal Warrior to Conquering Tyrant* (London: I.B. Tauris, 2006), pp. 75–98.

Bashir, Shahzad, 'Arbiters of Iran: Chroniclers and patrons in an age of literary bounty', in *The Timurid Century: The Idea of Iran*, vol. 9, ed. Charles Melville (London: I.B. Tauris, 2020), pp. 7–24.

Bosworth, C.E., 'The political and dynastic history of the Iranian world (A.D. 1000–1217)', in *The Cambridge History of Iran, vol. 5, The Saljuq and Mongol Periods*, ed. J.A. Boyle (Cambridge: Cambridge University Press, 1968), pp. 1–202.

Bournoutian, George A., *A History of Qarabagh: An Annotated Translation of Mirza Jamal Javanshir Qarabaghi's Tarikh-e Qarabagh*, English translation (Costa Mesa, CA: Mazda Publishers, 1994).

— 'Ebrāhīm Khalīl Khan Javānšīr', *Encyclopaedia Iranica*, vol. VIII, fasc. 1 (1997), pp. 71–73.

Bregel, Yuri, ''Arabšāhī', *Encyclopaedia Iranica*, vol. II, fasc. 3 (1986), pp. 243–45.

— 'Bukhara iii. After the Mongol invasion', *Encyclopaedia Iranica*, vol. IV, fasc. 5 (2000), pp. 515–21, online at https://iranicaonline.org/articles/bukhara-iii [accessed 27 April 2021].

— 'Bukhara iv. Khanate of Bukhara and Khorasan', *Encyclopaedia Iranica*, vol. IV, fasc. 5 (2000), pp. 521–24, online at https://iranicaonline.org/articles/bukhara-iv [accessed 27 April 2021].

— 'Central Asia vii. In the 18th–19th centuries', *Encyclopaedia Iranica*, vol. V, fasc. 2 (2000) pp. 193–205, online at http://www.iranicaonline.org/articles/central-asia-vii [accessed 27 April 2021].

— 'Historiography xii. Central Asia', *Encyclopaedia Iranica*, vol. XII, fasc. 4 (2004), pp. 395–403, online at https://iranicaonline.org/articles/historiography-xii [accessed 27 April 2021].

Brend, Barbara, 'A sixteenth-century manuscript from Transoxiana: Evidence for a continuing tradition in illustration', *Muqarnas* 11 (1994), pp. 103–16.

Bushāsp Gusha, Feyzollāh, 'Marv dar nakhostin daha-hā-ye hokumat-e Qājār', *Pajuheshnāma-ye Tārikh* 9 (1386/2007), pp. 21–50.
Comstock-Skipp, Jaimee, 'Heroes of Legend, Heroes of History: Militant Manuscripts of the Shaybanid Uzbeks in Transoxiana', master's dissertation (The Courtauld Institute of Art, London, 2015).
Doerfer, Gerhard, 'Chaghatay language and literature', *Encyclopaedia Iranica*, vol. V, fasc. 4 (1991), pp. 339–43, online at https://iranicaonline.org/articles/chaghatay-language-and-literature [accessed 27 April 2021].
Eastwick, Edward B., *Journal of a Diplomate's Three Years' Residence in Persia*, vol. I (London: Smith, Elder & Co., 1864).
Eden, Jeff, *Slavery and Empire in Central Asia* (Cambridge: Cambridge University Press, 2018).
Eskandar Beg Monshi Torkamān, *Tārikh-e 'ālam-ārā-ye 'Abbāsi*, vol. II, ed. Shahrudi (Tehran: Nashr-e tolu' va sirus, 1364/1985).
E'temād al-Saltana, Mohammad Hasan Khān, *Tārikh-e Montazam-e Nāseri*, vol. III, ed. Mohammad Esmā'il Rezvāni (Tehran: Donyā-ye ketāb, 1367/1988).
Fourniau, V., 'Balkh iii. From the Mongols to modern times', *Encyclopaedia Iranica*, vol. III, fasc. 6 (1988), online at https://iranicaonline.org/articles/balk-town-and-province#pt3 [accessed 27 April 2021].
Fraser, James Baillie, *Diaries*, manuscript formerly at Reelig House, now in the National Records of Scotland.
Gobineau, Joseph Arthur, comte de, 'L'histoire de Gamber Aly', in *Les nouvelles asiatiques* (Paris: René Aussourd, 1876); 1922 edition by Perrin & Cie, online at http://www.gutenberg.org/files/48279/48279-h/48279-h.htm [accessed 27 April 2021].
Golden, Peter B., *An Introduction to the History of the Turkic People: Ethnogenesis and State Formation in Medieval and Early Modern Eurasia and the Middle East*, Turcologica Bd. 9 (Wiesbaden: Harrassowitz, 1992).
Gustafson, James M., 'Qajar ambitions in the Great Game: Notes on the embassy of 'Abbas Qoli Khan to the Amir of Bokhara, 1844', *Iranian Studies* 46, no. 4 (2013), pp. 535–52.
Hambly, Gavin, 'Āghā Muḥammad Khān and the establishment of the Qājār dynasty', in *The Cambridge History of Iran, vol. 7, From Nadir Shah to the Islamic Republic*, ed. Peter Avery, Gavin Hambly and Charles Melville (Cambridge: Cambridge University Press, 1991), pp. 104–43.
Javānšīr Qarābāġī, Mīrzā Jamāl, trans. G.A. Bournoutian as *A History of Qarabagh* (Costa Mesa, CA: Mazda Publishers, 1994).
von Kügelen, Anke, 'Manghits', *Encyclopaedia Iranica*, online edition (2004), at https://iranicaonline.org/articles/manghits [accessed 27 April 2021].
Lambton, A.K.S., 'The internal structure of the Saljuq Empire', in *The Cambridge History of Iran, vol. 5, The Saljuq and Mongol Periods*, ed. J.A. Boyle (Cambridge: Cambridge University Press, 1968), pp. 203–82.

Lingwood, Chad, *Politics, Poetry, and Sufism in Medieval Iran: New Perspectives on Jāmī's Salāmān va Absāl* (Leiden: Brill, 2014).

Mahmud, Mahmud, *Tārikh-e ravābet-e siyāsi-ye Irān va Ingilis dar qarn-e nuzdahom*, 8 vols (Tehran: Nashr-e eqbāl, 1328/1949).

O'Donovan, Edmund, *The Merv Oasis: Travels and Adventures East of the Caspian During the Years 1879–1880–1881, Including Five Months' Residence Among the Tekkes of Merv*, vol. II (London: Smith, Elder & Co., 1882).

Pakravan, Amineh, 'Agha Mohammad Khan', trans. from French into Persian by Jahāngir Afkāri (Tehran: Jāmi, 1377/1998).

Payne, Richard, 'The making of Turan: The fall and transformation of the Iranian east in late antiquity', *Journal of Late Antiquity* 9 (2016), pp. 4–41.

Perry, John R., 'The Zand dynasty', in *The Cambridge History of Iran, vol. 7, From Nadir Shah to the Islamic Republic*, ed. Peter Avery, Gavin Hambly and Charles Melville (Cambridge: Cambridge University Press, 1991), pp. 63–103.

Rahmati, Mohsen, 'Ravābet va monāsebāt-e khānedān-e 'arabshāhi-ye khvārazm bā safaviyān', *Pajuhesh-hā-ye tārikhi* (Dāneshkada-ye adabiyāt va 'olum-e ensāni, Dāneshgāh-e Esfahān), Dowra-ye jadid 3, no. 2 (1390/2011), pp. 89–112.

Roemer, H.R., 'The successors of Timur', in *The Cambridge History of Iran, vol. 6, The Timurid and Safavid Periods*, ed. Peter Jackson and Laurence Lockhart (Cambridge: Cambridge University Press, 1986), pp. 98–146.

— 'The Turkmen dynasties', in *The Cambridge History of Iran, vol. 6, The Timurid and Safavid Periods*, ed. Peter Jackson and Laurence Lockhart (Cambridge University Press, Cambridge 1986), pp. 147–88.

Ruehrdanz, Karin, 'The Samarqand *Shahnama*s in the context of dynastic change', in *Shahnama Studies II: The Reception of Firdausi's Shahnama*, ed. Charles Melville and Gabrielle van den Berg (Leiden: Brill, 2012), pp. 213–33.

Safa, Z., 'Banā'ī Heravī', *Encyclopaedia Iranica* (1988), online edition (2011), at http://www.iranicaonline.org/articles/banai-heravi [accessed 27 April 2021].

Soucek, Priscilla, 'Behzād, Kamāl-al-dīn', *Encyclopaedia Iranica*, vol. IV, fasc. 2 (1989), pp. 114–16, online at https://www.iranicaonline.org/articles/behzad-kamal-al-din [accessed 27 April 2021].

Soudavar Farmanfarmaian, Fatema, 'An Iranian perspective of J. B. Fraser's Trip to Khorasan in the 1820s', *Iranian Studies* 44, no. 2 (2011), pp. 217–42.

Spuler, Bertold, 'Central Asia v. In the Mongol and Timurid periods', *Encyclopaedia Iranica*, vol. V, fasc. 2 (1990), pp. 172–76, online at http://www.iranicaonline.org/articles/central-asia-v [accessed 27 April 2021].

Vahid Qazvini, Mohammad Tāher, *'Abbāsnāma, sharh-e zendegāni-ye 22 sāla-ye Shāh 'Abbās Thāni (1052–1073/1642–1663)*, ed. Ebrāhim Dehgān (Arak: Ketābforushi-ye Dāvudi, 1329/1950).

Online resources:

'Āghā Mohammad Khān Qājār', *Dāneshnāma-ye jahān-e eslām*, 1/298, http://lib.eshia.ir/23022/1/298 [accessed November 2020].

Jām-e Jam Online, https://jamejamonline.ir/fa/news/340493, 27 Tir 1389/22 June 2010 [accessed January 2021].

'Qājār', *Dāneshnāma-ye jahān-e eslām*, vol. 1/7243, online at http://lib.eshia.ir/23019/1/7243, 10 Bahman 1391/29 January 2013 [accessed December 2020].

9

Sir William Jones and the Migration of the Idea of Iran to India

John R. Perry
(The University of Chicago, Emeritus)

India had long been familiar to the West, from early Sasanian times, as the land of fabulous wealth, wonders and wisdom. The Sanskrit collection of animal fables known as the *Panchatantra* was translated into Middle Persian, then in eighth-century Baghdad by Ebn al-Moqaffa' into Arabic as *Kalila wa Demna*, and rapidly acquired versions in Greek, Latin, old Spanish, Hebrew, English and indeed most medieval European languages, to become an early self-motivational bestseller, a rival to Aesop's fables or the *Disciplina Clericalis*.[1] This was later reinforced by translations of trickster tales with the parrot as theme (known in India as the *Tutinama*), which filtered into Persian literature of Iran (most famously two parables in the *Masnavi* of Jalal al-Din Rumi) and via Turkey to Europe and America as fabliaux, ballads and oral humour.[2]

The actual Persianization of north Indian literary and administrative culture began with Sultan Mahmud of Ghazna's conquest of Lahore and Panjab province in the early eleventh century. His destructive incursions, targeting the fabled wealth of Hindu temples, did have a positive side – the philosopher and pioneering Indologist Abu Reyhan al-Biruni, embedded with the army, learned Sanskrit and consulted with Hindu pandits, publishing two volumes in Arabic of his impressions of Indian science and theology. Subsequent dynasties of Turkish military mamlukes consolidated the Muslim mastery of the Panjab, and poets such as Mas'ud-e Sa'd-e Salman (d. 1121) and Amir Khosrow Dehlavi (d. 1325), who gloried in being of mixed Turco-Persian and Indian birth, secured Persian's position as the language and literary currency of Indian courts.[3]

In 1525–26, Babor the late Timurid prince of Ferghana, descended from Chinggis Khan on his mother's side and Tamerlane on his father's, a former client of Esma'il Safavi and an accomplished poet and memoirist in Chaghatay Turkish and Persian, conquered Delhi and Agra, founding the Mughal Empire. This venerable institution was to remain the principal patron of Indo-Persian literature for more than three centuries – even when politically subordinate to more powerful regional conquerors, such as Nader Shah, in 1739, and the English East India Company (EIC) from 1765, when General Robert Clive 'persuaded' Shah 'Alam to cede the *divani*, i.e. the monopoly of revenue collection in Bengal, and thus the de facto government of India.

Hot on the heels of poets, as ever, came lexicographers, initially more native to India than immigrant. From the early fourteenth to the late nineteenth century, dozens more Persian dictionaries were produced in India than in Iran, by both Indians and Iranian visitors and immigrants. Examples are the *Borhan-e qate'* ('Decisive Proof', 1651) of Mohammad-Hosayn Borhan from Tabriz and the popular *Farhang-e Jahangiri* of Hoseyn Enju from Shiraz, completed in 1602 at Akbar's court: the extent of its circulation is seen in its citation by Thomas Hyde, Laudian Professor of Arabic at Oxford, in his Latin monograph on the religions of the ancient Persians in 1700.[4] The contributions of Indian lexicographers and later literary-linguistic critics, such as Tek Chand Bahar and Seraj al-Din Khan Arzu, informed the work both of Iranian scholars in late Qajar and Pahlavi times, notably Malek al-sho'ara Bahar (*Sabkshenasi*, 'Stylistics', 1952) and 'Ali-Akbar Dehkhoda (*Loghatnama*, 'Lexicon', first published posthumously in 1980) and of Western scholars, such as Richardson, Johnson and Steingass (*Comprehensive Persian Dictionary*, 1892) and Douglas C. Phillott (*Higher Persian Grammar*, 1919).

Then, in 1722, came the Afghan invasion of a dying Safavid Empire. Among the first and most directly affected by the fall of Esfahan, and who has left us the most complete picture of the catastrophe and its aftermath in his memoirs (completed in 1742), was the Shi'i poet and scholar Sheykh Hazin Lahiji from Gilan. As a boy, he grew up with his father at the Safavid court as a precocious polymath and poet. In 1721, as the Afghan army closed in to blockade the starving capital, he tried in vain to persuade Shah Soltan-Hoseyn, and his own family, to flee before it was too late; then, leaving behind his precious library, he slipped away disguised as a peasant. After two years spent teaching among the Lur at Khorramabad, organizing a militia to defend the town against the advancing Ottoman army, and a dispiriting visit in 1734 to his homeland, Russian-occupied Gilan, horrified by the continued oppression under Nader Shah, he left Iran and settled in the Mughal court of Delhi. Here, five years later, he went into hiding to avoid a massacre when Nader Shah invaded and plundered the city. He moved on, to Agra and then Benares (Varanasi), where he died and was buried in 1766.

In his exile, despite his avowed dislike of India, Hazin was treated as a celebrity; open-minded, he sought out fellow scholars of all faiths. According to Sir Gore Ouseley (British Orientalist of the next generation, a colleague of Jones), Hazin was 'equally admired and esteemed by the Muselman, Hindoo, and English inhabitants of India'.[5]

In the half-century between the final calamitous years of, respectively, the Safavid and the Zand dynasties (ca. 1730s to 1780s), some hundreds of literate and variously prominent Iranians, not solely Safavi survivors, fled to India, often with their families.[6] Several, like Abu'l-Hasan Golestana, became rueful chroniclers of this period. His three uncles served Nader, but two fell into disfavour and fled to India; Abu'l-Hasan was a hostage in Karim Khan's retinue during the contest for power in western Iran, but in 1756 slipped away to the Shi'i shrine city of Najaf and joined his family in India. Here, at Morshedabad in 1782, he wrote his *Mojmel al-tavarikh*, a detailed history of the early Zand period.

It is instructive to note how many of these exiles were Shi'i scholars or administrators, the cream of the loyal products of the Muslim sect recently established as the state religion of the Iranian empire, now bereft of political and military support. There remained the *'Atabat*, the holy shrine cities of Najaf and Karbala in Iraq, neutral territory for pilgrims even under Sunni Ottoman Turkish rule; from here such refugees could reach Basra or the Gulf port of Bushire and take a local ship or, with luck and connections, an East India Company merchant vessel (as did another memoirist, the Safavid Mirza Khalil Mar'ashi), heading east to India. Morshedabad in Bengal, at that period the headquarters of the EIC, already had an established Shi'i community.

Of those who stayed in Iran, the poet and literary biographer Azar Bigdeli famously lamented in the preface to his *tazkera*, the *Atashkada*, that the situation 'had reached a point where no one has the heart to read poetry, let alone write it'.[7] In India, meanwhile, composition and recital of Persian verse, especially the *ghazal*, were all the rage, and not only at the rulers' courts, or by Iranian refugees and Indian natives. By this time, French, Armenian and British traders and commercial agents were settled in several cities. In the course of the eighteenth and nineteenth centuries, more than 60 of these resident *farangi*s or their mixed offspring, including eight women, had sufficient command of Persian and, later, Urdu, to dabble in the mild intoxicant of ghazal or *roba'i*, basking in the applause of indulgent Indians to compose poems at the convivial *mosha'era* verse readings; some even accumulated considerable *divans*.[8]

Into this fluid social and cultural environment in September 1783 stepped Sir William Jones, newly knighted, and married to Anna Maria Shipley, the daughter of the radical Bishop of Grafton, as a judge on the Bengal bench.[9] Born in London in 1746, Jones' father was a distinguished Welsh mathematician, a Fellow of the Royal Society and friend of Sir Isaac Newton, with a cousin in Anglesey, Lewis Morris, who helped to pioneer the Celtic Revival. He died before William turned three, but the boy's gifted mother, Mary Nix, made sure that her son's mind was stimulated from an early age. The boy entered Harrow Public School on a scholarship as a child prodigy at the age of seven, and graduated from Oxford in 1768, having sailed through the Greek and Roman classics, to Hebrew and Arabic. In the same year, Jones accepted a prestigious commission from King Christian VII of Denmark, the brother-in-law of George III, to translate from the Persian (into French) Astarabadi's *Jahangosha-ye Naderi*, a life of the late Nader Shah. This secured a useful emolument and his election as a Fellow of the Royal Society of

Copenhagen. Jones actually despised the tyrant Nader, and gratuitously appended a treatise on Persian and Arabic poetry, with 24 pages of odes by Hafez, rendered into elegant French.

So already we see where he stands. Jones was something of a quiet rebel, not alone among his peers in an England that still somewhat distrusted its Celtic, non-conformist or cosmopolitan fringes. 'Let us study the ancient Indians as we do the Greeks and the Romans', Jones urged his literate contemporaries; but some rated him too 'pompous and imaginative', and British liberals such as William Wilberforce and John Stuart Mill were also evangelical Christians, with a knee-jerk bias against Indian paganism. Despite his Romantic bravado, Jones was not averse to using his intellectual energy to climb the thorny slopes of English and Continental high society. He had earlier taken a post tutoring the seven-year-old Lord Althorp, which gave him access to influential Whig aristocrats and politicians, and was now planning a history of Turkey, where Persian literature was appreciated and steady diplomatic relations with the French provided fitful news of the sad state of his ultimate goal, Iran. Perhaps fortunately for Indo-Persian studies, he failed to land the post of ambassador at Constantinople. However, he was elected a Fellow of the Royal Society in 1772, and the next year, even more advantageously, voted into Dr Johnson's prestigious Turk's Head Club, to enjoy coffee and conversation with such as Burke, Gibbon and Goldsmith; and a more promising consolation prize was soon to come his way.

He had meanwhile been studying law and was called to the Temple Bar in London in 1770. He did not neglect Persian, publishing a series of verse translations and juxtaposing prose versions of odes by Hafez and Horace; and in 1771 he wrote the first modern grammar of the language, primarily for employees of the East India Company, but leavened with quotations from Persian literature, such as the opening ghazal of Hafez's divan, the 'Maid of Shiraz' ode. He also translated into English the *Mo'allaqat*, the seven celebrated odes of pre-Islamic Arabia. In 1778, he applied for the post of a judge in the Bengal Supreme Court, which would bring him into direct daily contact with Persian language and literature. The response to this was delayed for five years, probably as various officials weighed proven achievements against his political reputation in some quarters as a radical Whig and a supporter of the American revolutionaries. Meanwhile, he practised on the Carmarthen circuit from 1775 to 1783, where he 'proudly rediscovered the colonized land of his fathers, and was angered at the erosion of ancient Celtic liberties by a rack-renting Anglicized squirearchy'.[10]

Jones readily admitted that his catalogue of languages did not include Welsh, joking later with Louis XVI that he knew almost every language but his own.[11] For light relief during vacations he initiated a Druid circle and, as chief bard, entertained the company on the banks of the river by Cilgerran Castle (in Cardigan, North Wales) with occasional verses anticipating Wordsworth, and an extempore piece 'Kneel to the Goddess whom all Men Adore', i.e., Diana, Mary, Astarte, or Ganga. On one level this was just another academic prank, yet it uncannily foreshadows not only his own later discourse to the Asiatic Society 'On the Gods of Greece, Italy, and India' (1784) but a theory not seriously discussed by archaeologists and comparative folklorists until the 1960s. Using evidence from the latest excavations throughout Eurasia that unearthed paintings and figurines of female deities from the late Paleolithic into the Neolithic age, and characterizations of goddesses in Babylonian–Sumerian times, scholars such as Merlin Stone[12] and Marija Gimbutas[13] (citing James Frazer, Margaret Mead and Joseph Campbell) have argued that the earliest Goddess was not just a member of a primarily male pantheon but, as the actual creator of life through childbearing, was the Supreme Deity. Until, that is, the Hebrews and the Romans respectively introduced a male 'King of the Gods' and finally a single male deity. There were tentative reassertions in later Christianity (the Virgin Mary) and Islam (Fatima), but their enhanced status was short of the divine, and not permitted to improve that of women in general. At any rate, Jones was well prepared to meet Lakshmi and Saraswati in his new career.

In Calcutta, Jones hit the ground running. He was not an employee of the East India Company; his immediate superior was Warren Hastings, appointed in 1773 as the first Governor General of India, Governor of the Presidency of Fort William and Head of the Council of Bengal, after Lord North's parliament enacted the Regulating Act for India in an attempt to establish some oversight of the Company's irresponsible excesses. More of a scholar than a sabre-rattling conqueror, Hastings introduced his new colleague to members of the Bengal intelligentsia and actively supported his academic pursuits, in particular the founding of the 'Asiatick Society' of Bengal within a few months of his arrival. This institution, starting with some 30 members, was designed for research and publication on all aspects of Asian, in particular Indian, culture. Here, in a famous lecture in 1786, Jones would propose his theory of the relationship between Greek, Latin, Persian and Sanskrit, which inaugurated the sciences of comparative Indo-European philology and historical linguistics.

To prepare for this enterprise, Jones decamped shortly to Krishnagar, 60 miles up the Ganges from Calcutta, where he donned Indian dress, rented a bungalow and engaged Brahmins to help him learn Sanskrit. His letters to friends at this time reflect his enormous enthusiasm and respect for Hindu religion and philosophy,[14] an excitement such as he had earlier felt in engaging with ancient Greek and Celtic lore at Harrow, Oxford and by the river at Cilgerran Castle.

A recent book by William Dalrymple projects a novel view of the EIC during the eighteenth century:[15] that of a predatory multinational corporation with its own private army, authorized by its founding charter a hundred years earlier to 'wage war' and by 1765, after Robert Clive had defeated the young

Mughal emperor Shah 'Alam and extorted the right to collect the revenue of Bengal, Bihar and Orissa, '250 company clerks, backed by the military force of 20,000 locally recruited Indian soldiers, had become the rulers of the richest Mughal provinces'.[16] Thereafter, Clive and other successful generals of the EIC's army were able to retire and return home with millions of pounds worth of Indian *loot* (a Hindustani word borrowed during this period).

Unlike the Safavid state in Iran, the Mughal Empire did not collapse after this signal defeat; the Emperor, whoever he was, remained a revered, or at least useful figurehead, even as rival powers – the Sultans of the Deccan in Mysore in the south, the Marathas in the centre and the Rajputs in the north-west – at different times and in various alliances challenged the Company's hegemony, and intermittently won control of the unfortunate Emperor or deposed him for a compliant relative. But the Company bounced back time and again, by bribery, intimidation and occasionally by sheer superiority of arms and generalship. The carnage, the treachery, the cruelty and suffering of this process was inflicted and borne by all sides; and yet, despite the economic and human toll, India's fertile fields, busy factories and tolerant communities were able to sustain a functioning civilization. And even in the famine years of 1769–70, as Indian families starved by dry wells and parched fields, the Company's 'nabobs' kept their tax rates high and their collectors busy, even as their stocks in London plunged.

In 1773, Lord North's parliament responded to a growing suspicion in Britain that the Company was too reckless and overbearing for its own good and that of the motherland. This was prompted by the sudden demand for a huge bailout of a corporation 'too big to fail' (since many of its shareholders were Members of Parliament). In return for this mercy, the Directors of the EIC were required to submit to a Regulating Act for India. Clive, by now afflicted with gout and prone to depression, was one of those investigated for bribery and extortion; he responded with outrage and was cleared in a vote, but later committed suicide. Three Crown Councillors sailed to Calcutta to oversee Hastings' implementation of the Regulation Act and were unceremoniously received. One, Sir Philip Francis, conceived a particular animus against Hastings and schemed to replace him. After six years of his obstruction, by 1780 Hastings had had enough and publicly denounced him. Francis challenged him to a duel, and lost, narrowly escaping a fatal wound.

In the same year, a surprise military defeat further degraded the Company's prestige in India. Heydar Ali of Mysore and his son Tipu Sultan, in a triple alliance with the Marathas and the Nezam of Hyderabad, and with a shipment of arms from France, inflicted a devastating defeat on a smaller and unprepared Company force from Madras. The 7,000 survivors captured by Tipu were forcibly converted to Islam, variously humiliated and tortured, and held for up to ten years in his fortress at Seringapatam. The ship bearing the news of this

'Battle of Pollilur' reached Fort William on 20 September, adding to Hastings' troubles.[17]

Despite the horrors of this defeat, it did not spell the end of the Company's presence in the Deccan. The triple alliance dissolved without capitalizing on its victory, and Hastings' quick dispatch of reinforcements from Calcutta and conclusion of a separate treaty with Scindia, the Maratha leader, preserved this vital southern foothold. A related EIC manoeuvre did, however, emphasize that this was well and truly the age of globalization: it was the Company's attempt to offload its surplus East Asian tea on the American colonial market, with additional taxes, that provoked the 'Boston Tea Party' in that same month, when the Patriots made their point of 'No taxation without representation' by dumping the tea into the harbour, thereby igniting the American Revolutionary War.[18]

Francis submitted his case against Hastings as the fount and locus of all Company corruption, derelict in his appointed mission, and for seven years Westminster Hall was packed with the capital's elite: royalty, ministers, and the artistic and literary celebrities of the day savouring the theatrical hyperbole of Edmund Burke, Charles James Fox and Brinsley Sheridan. And finally, in 1795, when no personal malfeasance was actually proven against Hastings, he was acquitted – dazed, ruined and disillusioned.[19]

Hastings had been replaced during his recall to London by Charles, Marquis Cornwallis, eager to redeem his reputation after the surrender to Washington at Yorktown in 1781, seen by some as a noble diplomatic gesture, but by others as an inglorious defeat. Arriving in Calcutta in August of 1786, he enforced the self-disciplinary goals mandated by the Regulating Act, such as a ban on private trading by administrators, and increased their salaries; he also regulated the land and revenue system of Bengal. It was during his nine-year tenure that the government and civil service of India as a whole began to resemble that of British Imperial India after 1857, and indeed of its independent successor. The threat from Napoleon, whose invasion of Egypt was seen as a stepping-stone to India, galvanized Cornwallis to end the continuing menace of Tipu, who was killed in the siege of Seringapatam in 1799.[20]

Jones and his academic colleagues seem to have steered clear of these disruptive episodes. Calcutta, to which Hastings had transferred the headquarters of the Presidency from Morshedabad soon after his appointment, had grown into a flourishing commercial and cultural hub with excellent communications, spared the stresses of an imperial capital or major military base. Members of the Asiatic Society responded with a spate of serious Indo-Persian studies, such as Francis Gladwin's translations of the *A'in-e Akbari* ('Institutes of Akbar') on Mughal statecraft, and the classic work of Persian *adab*, Sa'di's *Golestan*. In 1823, the Royal Asiatic Society would be formed in London, modelled on that in Calcutta, with a series of research projects and publications continuing the work of Jones and his colleagues.[21]

In Indology, Jones followed the lead of Dara Shokoh, Shah Jahan's scholarly son, who with a team of pandits from Benares had commenced a translation of the Sanskrit *Upanishads* into Persian in 1657. Jones' continuation of this project was the first direct translation from Sanskrit into a Western language. He also launched a veritable craze among the German Romantics with his 1789 translation of Kalidasa's erotic drama *Śakuntala* (even though bowdlerized). Curiously, although many more university chairs of Sanskrit were established in Germany than in Britain, none of the professors, or their graduates, appear to have visited India.[22]

Not that he neglected his judicial duties: the long-established Persian-Islamic Indian administrative and judicial systems, with roots in the practice of the *mobad*s, the Zoroastrian priesthood and provincial administrators of the Sasanian Empire, put him in the position of the chief *qadi*, with a Persian secretariat and abundant scribes, most of them non-Muslims, to prepare copies of petitions, depositions, deeds, certificates – a range of documents generically called *mazhar-nama*.[23] When not presiding on the bench, he pursued a project to record an exhaustive digest of Hindu and Muslim law to legitimize British rule through the integration of native traditions, a first step towards the goal of a comprehensive Anglo-Indian Law that was intermittently pursued by others in later years. He also found time to pen helpful notes in favour of stipends for indigent Persian poets. He read and translated contemporary Persian Sufi poets, including exiles such as Hazin. And, behind it all, he ached for a chance to visit Iran, where he had established friendly contact with Mirza Hoseyn Farahani, the erudite Zand vizier with a famous library.

In the spring of 1791 he wrote to his envoy in Shiraz, Harford Jones–Brydges (no relation), acknowledging receipt of a letter from the young Lotf-'Ali Khan Zand, the last ruler of the dynasty, to be forwarded to Timur Shah Dorrani in Kabul (evidently a plea for help against an imminent attack by Agha Mohammad Khan Qajar);[24] he thanks Jones–Brydges for sending him also a copy of Mirza Sadeq Nami's definitive history of the Zand dynasty, and looks forward to visiting Shiraz within the next two years. But this was not to be: the Dorrani ruler died a year later, Shiraz fell to the Qajars, Lotf-'Ali was killed by Agha Mohammad in 1794; and Jones died in Calcutta on 27 April of that same year, of a severe liver infection.

He was buried in Calcutta, in the Park Street Cemetery under an obelisk gravestone, mourned, like Hazin, by British, Indian and Iranian alike. He openly cherished the Idea of Iran, as he eloquently expressed it, and may be compared in some measure with the Persian exiles from the post-Safavid wasteland, or even with Rumi's reed, which in the opening lines of the *Masnavi* is 'sundered from its root' to make a pipe and 'makes hope of homecoming its sole pursuit'.

A new era for Indo-Persian language and literature had already been foretold by a little-known contemporary of Jones in Calcutta (though they may never have met). Army officers and Company clerks needed to be taught the local contact language, assumed by the top brass to be Persian, the language of bureaucracy and high culture. John Borthwick Gilchrist, a Scottish surgeon with the Company's Bengal Army, became interested in the languages actually *spoken* in northern India, particularly the vernacular of both Hindus and Muslims, later to be called Hindi and Urdu, which Gilchrist termed 'Hindustanee'. A tour of the region during 1785, in particular Feyzabad near Lucknow, where Gilchrist sought out local poets, convinced him that this vernacular was a sophisticated medium, with a literary register called *rekhta*, *Hindavi* or *Hindi*. He reported that the pidgin variety called 'Moors', which English soldiers and clerks were generally content to use, was inadequate for the purpose, and that Hindustani was more suitable than Persian, the usual medium taught – often in Britain, perfunctorily – to most EIC employees. Gilchrist was accepted to tutor them in Persian and Hindustani, and from 1787 compiled a Hindustani grammar and a dictionary. In 1801, he was appointed the first professor of Hindustani at the newly established College of Fort William. Hiring *monshi*s (native scribes), Gilchrist set them to translating stories from Persian into a simple but elegant style of Hindustani, to be printed in a modified Perso-Arabic script. Some of these even became popular among Indian readers. The momentous transitioning to Hindi-Urdu as the medium of oral communication and popular literature had been recognized.[25]

So I hail this otherwise obscure Edinburgh medic as a pioneer field sociolinguist *avant la lettre*, with a notable policy impact: the EIC did finally announce (in 1824), and slowly implement, its reluctant switch to Urdu as the official language of administration. It soon become clear to all that Persian's *dowlat*, its hallowed authority as a living language beyond its home in Iran, Afghanistan and Tajikistan, was yielding to the age of national vernaculars and that, with the rise of a stable Qajar dynasty in Iran, the 'outsourcing' of Persian to India was effectively discontinued.

Nevertheless, the idea of Iran as it had filtered via language and literature into the ethos of India remains there until this day. In the course of the next 150 years, *rekhta* was used and refined by poets and scholars who also wrote in Persian, such as Mirza Asadullah Ghalib (1797–1869) and *'Allama* Iqbal (1877–1938). After Independence, Hindu-majority India established Hindi in Nagari script as the official national language, with emphasis on Sanskrit as a lexical and stylistic source in preference to Persian. Hyderabad, capital of Andra Pradesh under the Nezam, kept its autonomy and Persian secretariat for a short time after Independence before switching to the regional vernacular, Telugu; and at Bombay in Gujarat (where Iranian Zoroastrian émigrés first made landfall following the Muslim Arab invasion) the Parsee community continues to treasure the language as a link with their ancient homeland and its culture (scholars publish in Persian and English, while using Gujarati for everyday communication). Muslim-majority Pakistan promoted Urdu in a modified Persian script, and favoured Persian lexis, appointing a National Language Authority. Urdu of Pakistan today is the only Persianate language that retains access to Arabic as an occasional source for technical neologisms, and frozen Persian syntagms in Urdu texts are a boon to Persianists with little knowledge of Hindi. Educated Indians, Pakistanis and Bangladeshis at home and abroad generally have some degree of Persian, and Bollywood and Lollywood lyrics feature Persian-style ghazals. The Turkish Republic, where *ta'liq* calligraphy is still a popular art 90 years after the Latinization of the writing system, holds an annual prize competition.

British, European and American scholars of Persian language and culture followed the trend, turning increasingly in the early twentieth century from India to sources in Iranian libraries and editions by Iranian publishers, and to colleagues at Iranian universities established under the Pahlavis for instruction and support. But we will always remember the indefatigable Jones and his colleagues, British and Indian, who took up the challenge of a temporarily disabled Iran and helped her through the crisis.

Notes:

1. S.v. 'Kalila wa Demna', *Encyclopaedia Iranica*, online edition (2012), at https://iranicaonline.org/articles/kalila-demna-index [accessed 8 April 2021].
2. John R. Perry, 'Monty Python and the *Mathnavi*', pp. 63–73.
3. Alyssa Gabbay, 'Establishment of centers of Persian court poetry', pp. 34–47.
4. John R. Perry, 'The Persian language sciences in India', pp. 76–93.
5. Francis C. Belfour, trans., *The Life of Sheikh Mohammed Ali Hazin*; see also John R. Perry, 'Hazin Lāhiji'.
6. For an account of the members of the Safavi family after the fall of Esfahan, see John R. Perry, 'The last Safavids', pp. 59–69.
7. Cited in E.G. Browne, *A Literary History of Persia*, vol. IV, p. 282.
8. Ram Babu Saksena, *The European and Indo-European Poets of Urdu and Persian*.
9. A detailed account of Jones' life and career is given by Michael J. Franklin in *Encyclopaedia Iranica*, vol. XV (2009) and Wikipedia (last edited 11 March 2021); see also Sam Miller, *A Strange Kind of Paradise*, pp. 210–48. There is some discrepancy in the dating of Jones' arrival at Calcutta: William Dalrymple, in *White Mughals*, p. 32, has 15 January 1784. Since the Asiatic Society was founded in 1784, the earlier date of arrival appears more likely.
10. Franklin, 'Jones', p. 7.
11. Miller, *A Strange Kind of Paradise*, p. 241 n. 10.
12. Merlin Stone, *When God was a Woman*.
13. Marija Gimbutas, *The Language of the Goddess*.
14. Dalrymple, *White Mughals*, pp. 32–34.
15. William Dalrymple, *The Anarchy: The East India Company*.
16. Ibid., p. xxv.
17. Ibid., pp. 250–57.
18. Ibid., pp. 257–58.
19. Ibid.; Percival Spear, *A History of India*, vol. II, pp. 91–103.
20. Spear, *A History of India*, vol. II, pp. 308–14.
21. See Charles Melville, 'Great Britain, x', pp. 262–63, and *Encyclopaedia Iranica* online edition, for other contributions of Jones, his contemporaries and successors in Persian studies.
22. Miller, *A Strange Kind of Paradise*, pp. 243–45.
23. Nandini Chatterjee, '*Mahzar-nama*s in the Mughal and British Empires', pp. 397–406.
24. See John R. Perry, *Karim Khan Zand*, pp. 115–16. I am indebted to Professor Franklin for the copy of this correspondence.
25. John R. Perry, 'Gilchrist, John Borthwick'.

Bibliography:

Belfour, Francis C., trans., *The Life of Sheikh Mohammed Ali Hazin, Written by Himself* (London, 1830).

Browne, E.G., *A Literary History of Persia, vol. IV, A History of Persian Literature in Modern Times, A.D. 1500–1924* (Cambridge: Cambridge University Press, 1924).

Chatterjee, Nandini, '*Mahzar-nama*s in the Mughal and British Empires: The uses of an Indo-Islamic legal form', *Comparative Studies in Society and History* 58, no. 2 (2016), pp. 397–406.

Dalrymple, William, *White Mughals: Love and Betrayal in Eighteenth-Century India* (London: Penguin Books, 2002).

— *The Anarchy: The East India Company, Corporate Violence, and the Pillage of an Empire* (New York: Bloomsbury, 2009).

Franklin, Michael J., 'Jones, Sir William', *Encyclopaedia Iranica*, vol. XV (2009), online at https://iranicaonline.org/articles/jones-sir-william [accessed 8 April 2021].

Gabbay, Alyssa, 'Establishment of centers of Persian court poetry', in *A History of Persian Literature*, vol. IX, *Persian Literature from Outside Iran*, ed. John R. Perry (London: I.B. Tauris, 2018), pp. 34–47.

Gimbutas, Marija, *The Language of the Goddess* (New York: Harper & Row, 1989).

Melville, Charles, 'Great Britain, x. Iranian studies in Britain: Islamic period', *Encyclopaedia Iranica*, vol. XI (2002), pp. 260-67, online at https://iranicaonline.org/articles/great-britain-x [accessed 8 April 2021].

Miller, Sam, *A Strange Kind of Paradise* (London: Jonathan Cape, 2014).

Perry, John R., 'The last Safavids, 1722–1773', *Iran* 11 (1971), pp. 59–69.

— 'Monty Python and the *Mathnavi*: The parrot in Persian, Indian and English humor', *Iranian Studies* 36, no. 1 (2003), pp. 63–73.

— 'Hazin Lāhiji', *Encyclopaedia Iranica*, vol. XII (2003), pp. 97–98, online at https://iranicaonline.org/articles/hazin-lahiji [accessed 8 April 2021].

— *Karim Khan Zand* (Oxford: Oneworld Publications, 2006).

— 'Gilchrist, John Borthwick', *Encyclopaedia Iranica*, online edition (2015), at https://iranicaonline.org/articles/gilchrist-john [accessed 8 April 2021].

— 'The Persian language sciences in India', in *A History of Persian Literature, vol. IX, Persian Literature from Outside Iran*, ed. John R. Perry (London: I.B. Tauris, 2018), pp. 76–93.

Saksena, Ram Babu, *The European and Indo-European Poets of Urdu and Persian* (Allahabad, 1943).

Spear, Percival, *A History of India*, vol. II (Harmondsworth: Penguin, 1965).

Stone, Merlin, *When God was a Woman* (New York: Dorset Press, 1966).

Wikipedia.org, 'William Jones (philologist)' (last edited 11 March 2021).

Index:

A

'Abbas I, Safavid Shah .. 2, 35, 46, 47, 48, 59, 60, 66, 69, 71, 83, 86-88, 90-91, 93, 104, 172, 173, 196, 200
'Abbas II, Safavid Shah ... 11, 33, 35, 36, 46, 47, 48, 66, 142, 208
'Abbas III, Safavid Shah 11, 66
'Abbas Mirza, Qajar prince ...5, 84, 94, 115, 118, 132, 133, 136, 141, 145, 147, 150, 152, 154, 160, 162, 202
'Abbasid 47, 198
'Abbas-Qoli Khan 202, 209
'Abd al-'Azim, shrine 200
'Abd al-Beg 42
'Abd al-Razzaq, *see* Donboli
Abdali, Afghan tribe 171, 173, 177, 179, 182, 183, 207
'Abdollah Khan, court painter 108, 109, 111, 112, 113, 115-118, 121, 122, 123
'Abdollah Khan, Ozbek 195, 196, 206, 207
Abu Ahmad Abdal 183
Abu'l-Hasan Khan, Ilchi 143, 149, 150, 152, 154, 155
Abu'l-Hasan Mostowfi, *see* Ghaffari
Abu'l-Feyz Khan 11, 15
Abu Moslem Khorasani 198
Afghanistan, Afghans 3, 7, 165, 171, 172, 181, 183-189, 192, 197, 201, 223
Afraseyab 193, 203, 205
Afshar, Afsharid, tribe, dynasty ...8,16, 18, 28, 30, 37, 59, 62, 68, 69, 70, 83, 84, 87, 88, 91, 92, 93, 94, 103, 172, 173, 176, 177, 179, 180, 181, 191, 200
Agha Mohammad Khan Qajar 3, 4, 37, 57, 58, 59, 60, 64, 67, 68, 71, 72, 81, 82, 83, 85, 87, 88, 91, 92, 94, 95, 107, 108, 113, 171, 173, 175, 176, 177, 178, 179, 180, 181, 186, 191, 192, 200, 201, 203, 208, 212, 222
Ahmad Khan Abdali 178, 192

Ahsan al-tavarikh 83
A'in-e Akbari 221
Alexander I, tsar 150-151
Alexander the Great ...29, 129-130, 154
Alexander, Capt. James Edward ...158
Alexandra Fedorovna, Empress 144
Alexey Petrovich, Tsarevich 149
'Ali Morad Khan Zand 59
'Ali-Qoli Jebadar 34, 36, 42
al-Soweydi, 'Abdollah 19, 22, 25
Amburger, Andrey 136
Amir Heydar 201
Amir Khosrow Dehlavi, poet 215
Amirzada Naser al-Din Ture 201
Anatolia 13, 174, 193, 205
Anglican 203
Anzali (Enzeli) 7, 59, 164
appanage 198
Aq Qal'a 199
Aq Qoyunlu 86
Aqa Bahram Qoli 201
Aqa Mohammad Ja'far, artist 142, 152, 162
Arab 34, 47, 139, 142, 144, 192, 193, 198, 223
Arabo-Andalusian 198
'Arabshahi 205
Aras, river 65, 109
Arash 203, 208, 210
Ardabil 66, 71, 154
Ardashir 92, 98
Armenians 17, 18, 23, 63, 65, 105, 137, 138, 205, 217
Arthashastra 16
Asiatic Society, Bengal 219, 221
Ashraf 2, 59, 60, 69, 70, 71, 72
Astarabad 57-61, 64, 67-70, 72, 76, 108, 172, 175, 177, 196, 199
Astarabadi, Mirza Mahdi Khan, historian 15, 34, 42, 84, 95, 97, 177, 217
Astrakhan 1, 57, 58, 59, 63, 64, 135
atabeg 198
ataliq 198
Atashkada, tazkera 217
Atrak 197
Avesta 198
Axworthy, Michael 1, 6, 191

Azad Khan 'Afghan' 68, 70,175
Azerbaijan 12, 68, 70, 74, 90, 109, 112, 193, 196
Azodanlu 200, 208

B

Bahar, Malek al-sho'ara 216
Bahram, artist 38
Bahram (Bairam) 'Ali Khan 200, 201, 208
Bahram Mirza..................................142
Bakikhanov, 'Abbas-Qoli 65
Baku 59, 63, 64, 65, 66, 76, 77, 78
Balkh 3, 180, 181, 196, 197, 201, 203, 207, 211
Barakzay..180
Barforushi, Mohammad Nadim, historian..92
Bay of Astarabad........................58, 59
Bayat 199
Beechey, Sir William, artist 154
Bengal 33, 216, 217, 219, 220, 222, 223
Bigdeli, Azar, see *Atashkada*
al-Biruni, Abu Reyhan....195, 198, 215
Blackwood, magazine 138
Bokhara (Bukhara) 69, 70, 193, 195-203, 205-208, 210-211
Bonakdar, Masoud..........................143
Borhan Nezam Shah 142
Borhan-e qate' 216, see also langauge
Boston 'Tea Party' 221
Britain 184, 220; idea of Iran in 5; and Persian studies 5, 222, 224; and India 33; and Russia 129, 132, 133, 144, 149, 171, 181, 203, 222, 223
British ....5, 33, 147, 148, 218; and Central Asia 151, 152, 181, 182, 184, 192, 202, 203; in India 5, 28, 33, 216, 217, 221, 222, 224; in Iran 132, 133, 134, 136, 137, 138, 139, 142, 143, 148, 152, see also East India Company
Bulgarin, Faddey 134
Bustan of Sa'di 142

C

Calcutta 132, 144, 149, 219, 220, 221, 222
campaigns, military
   Astarabad 176
   Herat 182, 203, 209
   India 15, 19, 191, 197
   Khorasan 194
   Mashhad 173, 175, 176, 177
   Napoleonic 151
   Ottoman 18
   Qarshi 69
Caspian Sea 4, 57-72 *passim*, 152, 172, 193
Catherine II, the Great 4, 58, 59, 64, 141, 192
Catherine Palace, Tsarskoe Selo ...159
Caucasus 2, 3, 6, 9, 18, 28, 32, 64-69, 71, 93, 129, 132, 133, 135, 136, 137, 191, 192, 193
Central Asia 3, 13, 14, 15, 16, 19, 20, 29, 32, 57, 69, 71, 86, 133, 152, 174, 183, 191, 192, 203
Chavchavadze, Alexander......134, 137
Chavchavadze, Princess Nina 136, 137
Chehel Sotun Palace... 34, 35, 103, 104
Chengiz Khan..................................13
Chesht, Cheshti 183
Chinggis Khan......... 191, 194, 200, 215
Chinggisid 193, 194, 195, 204
Christian VII, King of Denmark 217
Christians 138, see also Armenians
chroniclers 18, 69
   Naderid 9, 11, 12, 15, 16, 17, 42, 68, 84, 177
   Zand 65, 216
   Qajar ......67, 68, 81, 83-95 *passim*, 180; *see also* historiography
Cilgerran Castle 218, 219
Clive, General Sir Robert 33, 215, 219, 220
coins 32
   platinum 4, 139
confederacy 86, 199
Connolly, Captain Arthur..............203
Cornwallis, Marquis Charles ..220, 221
coronations 2, 12, 14, 17, 19, 32, 34, 37, 82, 87, 108, 161, 201

crystal 4, 137, 139, 143, 150, 152

D

Daghestan 61, 64, 65, 74
Dalrymple, William 219
Dara Shokoh 222
Dehkhoda, 'Ali-Akbar 216
Delhi ...5, 9, 15, 28, 29, 31, 33, 37, 42, 191, 215, 216
diamonds 4, 37, 138, 139, 143, 150, 153
    Darya-ye nur 37
    Kuh-e nur 37
    Shah 142, 144
    Taj-e mah 37
diplomatic gifts 33, 112, 113, 122, 129-130, 135, 138, 139, 149, 150
Divan (court, chancery) 6, 36, 94, 114, 116, 216
Divan (collected poems) 217
    of 'Ali-Shir Nava'i 142
    of Hafez 218
Divan loghat al-Tork 193
Divan-e Khaqan 41, 142
Donboli, 'Abd al-Razzaq 'Maftun'..84, 94, 98, 99
Dorrani ....3, 70, 171-184 passim, 197, 222
Durr-e Durran 192

E

East India Company (EIC) 33, 132, 133, 135, 136, 148, 215, 217, 219-221, 223
Eastwick, Edward 203
Ebrahim Khalil Khan.............. 191, 192
Elphinstone, Mountstuart............... 182
Emam al-Din Hoseyni 178
Emam Reza ...2, 17, 68, 87, 114, 177, 196, 201, 207, 208
Emam Reza shrine.......................... 196
Emam-Qoli Khan............................ 200
'Emarat-e Divani 103, 114
ensan-e kamel (Perfect Man) 29, 30
Enzeli, *see* Anzali

Erekle II..................................... 67, 192
Erivan 134, 137, 199
Ermolov, General Alexey......114, 135, 150
Esfahan ....5, 9, 18, 30, 33, 34, 35, 58, 103, 104-106, 113, 152, 194, 195, 196; fall of 14, 60, 61, 69, 81, 85, 87, 171, 172, 176, 216, 225; school of 11
Eskandar Beg Monshi 90, 91, 200
Esma'il Samani 204

F

famine 81, 197, 220
Farhang-e Jahangiri 216, *see also* language
farman 18, 142, 148, 149, 173, 174, 175, 183
farr 9, 15, 29, 31, 37
Fath-'Ali Khan of Quba 64-67, 76
Fath-'Ali Khan Qajar . 67, 69, 85, 172, 176
Fath-'Ali Shah Qajar.....3, 5, 8, 31, 58, 71, 83, 84, 88, 89, 90, 91, 92, 93, 94, 102-116 *passim*, 118, 121, 122, 123, 130, 132, 139, 142, 145, 147, 148, 149, 151, 158, 173, 177, 179, 181, 182, 200, 202, *see also* royal portraits
Fathnama 195
Fereydun............................ 34, 48, 203
Feyz Mohammad Kateb Hazara 175
Feyzabad 223
films 140
    Of Kings and Paintings 130
    Tabriz in the Fog 138
Flight Barr and Barr, Worcester ...145, 147, 155
Fort William, Calcutta ... 219, 221, 223
Francis, Sir Philip 220
Fraser, James Baillie.............. 201, 209
Freemasonry 163
    Flaming Star 134
    Free Society of Lovers of Russian Literature 134

G

Gadu Khan.............................. 180, 181
Gampeln, Karl, artist 153
Ganja 86, 112, 191, 199
   Treaty of, *see* Treaties
Garmrudi, Mirza Mas'ud Ansari 141
genealogy 86, 90, 206
Georgia ...3, 67, 72, 82, 121, 126, 133, 134, 137, 144, 152, 160, 162, 168, 192
Ghaffari, Abu'l-Hasan Mostowfi, artist and historian .28, 37, 39, 42, 47, 49, 65
Ghalib, Mirza Asadullah 223
Ghaznavid... 192
Ghelzay........... 9, 11, 61, 171, 172, 173
gholam.......................... 35, 37, 49, 200
gifts, gift exchange ...4, 17, 31, 62, 66, 82, 87, 89, 129, 140-144, 154, *see also* diplomatic gifts
Gilan 58, 59, 61, 63, 64, 66, 67, 73, 74, 75, 76, 77, 216
Gilchrist, John Borthwick 223
Goklen Turkmen (Kukalan).... 173, 174
Golestan of Sa'di 221
Golestan, Treaty of (1813), *see* Treaties
Golestan Palace, Tehran .94, 105, 109, 112, 115, 130, 144, 147, 150, 152
Golestana, Abu'l-Hasan, historian ..75, 216
Golov, artist 153
Gorgan.............................. 87, 172, 196
Gorgin Khan 173
governorships ...86, 92, 114, 173, 191, 199, 200
grammars .... 5, 216, 218, 223, *see also* language
Great Game ...129, 132, 171, 204, 207, 211
Griboedov, Alexander 4, 129, 130-142 *passim*, ... 151
Grotefend, Johann Christian 152
Gustafson, James 202

H

Hambly, Gavin 199
Hamza Mirza Heshmat al-Dowla ...204
Hanafi.. 174
Hanway, Jonas........................... 24, 53
Hasan 'Ali Mirza Shoja' al-Saltana 201
Hastings, Warren 219, 220, 221
Hazin Lahiji, Sheykh 216, 222
Hedayatollah Khan............... 63, 75, 76
Herat 1, 3, 37, 118, 173, 175, 177-184, 192, 194, 195, 196, 201, 202, 203
heresy 194
Hermitage State Museum, St. Petersburg 116, 130, 131, 141, 144, 147, 152, 153
heterodoxy...................................... 199
Hettier, Pierre-Theodor 135
Heydar, Sheykh 199
Heydar 'Ali .... 220, *see also* Mysore
Hindustan 3, 24, 173, 174, 180, 183
Hippius, Gustav, artist 152
historiography 2, 44, 54, 82, 84, 95, 96, 97, 99, 102, 171, 178, 183
Homa films................................ 170
Hoseyn Shah Afghan....................... 11
Hoseyn-Qoli Khan.......................... 200
Hülegü Khan 199
Hyde, Thomas 216

I

Ilbars I 194, 198
il-e jalil-e Torkman........................... 13
India 5, 16, 17, 27, 28, 29, 30, 31, 32, 33, 42, 57, 61, 62, 63, 106, 174, 215-224 *passim*; British interests in 5, 132, 133, 136, 149, 152, 181, 219, 221; Dorranis in 175; Nader Shah in 2, 6, 14-16, 20, 28, 32, 37, 106, 191, 197; Persian literature in 5, 216, 217, 222, 223, *see also* East India Company, Mughals
invented tradition 9, 38, 179, 182, 183, 184
Iqbal, 'Allama, poet 223
Iran, Iranian *passim*, and

Idea of Iran 1, 2, 3, 5, 6, 27, 29, 34, 171, 191, 215, 222, 223; under Nader Shah 9-21 *passim*
and Afghanistan ....28, 171-184 *passim*
and Britain 4, 5, 144, 145, 148,
and Central Asia .... 3, 191-204 *passim*
and Europe 1, 2
and Russia ...4, 57-70 *passim*, 129-156 *passim*, 192
religion, *see* Shi'ism, Sunnism, Islam, Zoroastrianism
scholarship ..5, 216, 217, 222, 224
territory, borders .... 4, 91, 93, 132, 180, 181, 192, 196, 201, 203, *see also* language................................
Iran-zamin 34, 48
Iraq 1, 7, 9, 10, 19, 20, 158, 217
Islam 2, 9, 10, 11, 12, 13, 19, 20, 30, 31, 32, 70, 103, 140, 173, 184, 219; conversion to 193, 194, 198, 220, *see also* Muslim, Sunnism, Shi'ism
Islamic revolution 144

J

Ja'fari mazhab ...10, 12, 13, 19, 20, 23, 32, 71, 197
Jahangir Mirza Qajar 154
Jahangosha-ye Naderi, *see* Astarabadi
javanmardi 29, 30, 37, 45, 47, 55
Javanshir...191
Jones, Sir William 5, 215, 217, 218, 220, 222, 224
Jones-Brydges, Sir Harford ...148, 149, 222
Jaxartes...192
Jorjani...195

K

Ka'ba...13, 23
Kabul.............. 175, 179, 180, 201, 222
Kalat-e Dar al-Sebat 17
Kalat-e Naderi 16, 17, 18, 30, 106
Kalila wa Demna 215

Kamal al-Din Bana'i Haravi...........195
Karabagh, *see* Qarabagh
Karakum..................................200, 201
Karim Khan Zand ..7, 8, 38, 57, 63, 65, 66, 68, 70, 71, 81, 82, 87, 96, 106, 107, 172, 175, 176, 185, 186, 189, 225, 226, see also royal portraits
Karminagi, Mohammad Qazi Vafa, historian 69
Karnal, battle of 9, 15, 37, 106
Kartli-Kakheti.............................59, 65
Kashan...196
Kashgari, Mahmud 193
Kayanid crown 82, 87, 95, 122
Kayanids..11
Ker Porter, Sir Robert 145, 146, 151, 152, 162
Anna Maria 162
khadim al-harameyn al-sharifeyn.....13
khanates 65, 72, 74,194, 196, 197, 198, 199, 206
Khiva........... 7, 196, 197, 199-203, 206
Khonji, Fazlollah, historian.......18, 206
Khorasan ....3, 4, 6, 11, 16, 18, 28, 45, 60, 69, 70, 82, 87, 93, 106, 171-182 *passim*, 184, 191, 192, 194-199, *passim*, 201, 202, 203, 204
Khosrow Mirza, son of 'Abbas Mirza 4, 129, 133, 141, 142, 143, 144, 149, 152, 153, 154
Khvarazm......192, 194, 195, 197, 198, 199, 200, 205, 208, 209
kingship.............. 49, 52, 101, 121, 125
Kneller, Sir Godfrey 156
Koca Mehmet Rağıp Pasha 13, 22
kolah-e Naderi 12
Kordan, *see* Treaties
Kura, river 61, 65

L

language, linguistics
 bilingualism..............................195
 Chaghatay . 194, 195, 196, 206, 215
 Iranian Turkish............................13
 Middle Turkic 193
 New Persian 193
 Old Khvarazmian 193
 Ottoman Turkish 96

Pashtun 184, 185, 192
Persian 194, 195, 218, 222, 224, 225, 226
languages, Indian
   Gujarati 223
   Hindustani (Hindi) 223, 224
   Nagari 223
   Sanskrit 215, 219, 222, 223
   Telegu 223
   Urdu 223, 224
Lankaran (Lenkoran) 65
Lazarev, Admiral Mikhail 134
Lawrence, Sir Thomas, artist .154, 155
Lebanon, Lebanese 10, 194
Levashov, General Vasiliĭ 61, 63
Lion and Sun (*Shir-o Khorshid*) 139, 147, 149, 152
Lotf-'Ali Khan Zand 82, 176, 222
Lord North, British Prime Minister 219, 220

M

MacDonald, John Kinneir 136, 137, 138, 143, 149
Ma'aser-e soltaniyya 84
Malcolm, Sir John 75, 98, 136, 148, 158, 167, 181, 186
Maftun, *see* Donboli
Mahmud I, Ottoman sultan 13
Mahmud al-Hoseyni, chronicler 173, 178, 182
Mahmud Mirza, chronicler ... 84, 87, 88
Mahmud Soltan 195
Mahmud Tarzi 184
Majma' al-tavarikh 85
Malek Mahmud Sistani 11
Malek Mohammad Khan 63, 66
Maltsev, Ivan .. 130, 136, 137, 138, 139
Mangit 198, 200
Manuchehr 203
Mar'ashi, Mir Sayyed Mohammad .. 68, 75
Mar'ashi, Mirza Khalil, historian ... 217
Marv 3, 34, 69, 191, 193, 194, 197, 198, 199, 200, 201, 202, 203, 204, 207, 208, 209
Marv-e Shahijan 201
Marvazi, 'Homa' 84, 86, 87, 88

Mashhad ... 3, 7, 16, 17, 18, 23, 24, 30, 68, 70, 87, 94, 162, 173-177, 179, 181, 196, 200, 201, 202, 205, 209
Mas'ud-e Sa'd-e Salman, poet 215
mausoleum 44, 198, 207
Mazandaran .57, 58, 59, 60, 71, 73, 76, 82, 175
Mazarovich, Count Semen, ambassador 151
mazhab 10, 12
mazhab-e Ja'fari 12
mazhar-nama, legal document 222
Mecca 10, 12, 13, 18
Medina 10, 12, 13, 18
Mehrab Khan Qarabaghi 200
Merk, Consul Grigoriĭ 63
Mir 'Ali-Shir Nava'i 194
Mir Sayyed Mohammad 68, 75
Mirza Baba, artist 40, 41, 42, 109, 110, 111, 112, 115, 121, 122
Mirza Fazlollah 84
Mirza Hajji Baba Afshar 142
Mirza Hoseyn Farahani, Zand vizier 222
Mirza 'Isa, Qa'em-Maqam 94
Mirza Jani 34, 38
Mirza Mahdi Khan, *see* Astarabadi
Mirza Mohammad Reza Tabrizi 84
Mirza Mohammad Sadeq 84
Mirza Sadeq Nami, Zand historian 222
Mirza Saleh 142
Mirza Taqi Farahani (Amir Kabir) 142
Mirza Ya'qub (Markaryants) 137, 139
Mobarakabad 69, 199
Mofarreh al-qolub 83, 92, 96, 98, 99
Moghan 12, 13, 17, 19, 37
Moghisa 70
Mohammad, the Prophet 90, 173
Mohammad 'Ali Khan Ghafur 202
Mohammad 'Ali Tusi 3, 29, 34
Mohammad Amin Khan 203
Mohammad Baqer, artist 39, 40, 42
Mohammad Fathollah b. Mohammad Taqi 67
Mohammad Hasan Khan Qajar 57, 58, 64, 67, 68, 69, 70, 85, 86, 172, 173, 175, 176, 177, 200
Mohammad Hoseyn Khan Marvi ... 201
Mohammad Hoseyn Khan Qaraguzlu-ye Hamdani 180

INDEX

Mohammad Kazem 'Vazir-e Marv' 11, 68, 197
Mohammad Mirza 202
Mohammad Qasem, artist 35
Mohammad Rahim 198, 207
Mohammad Reza Hendi, artist ..30, 31, 41, 42
Mohammad Sadeq, artist.....37, 40, 42,
Mohammad Shah, Naser al-Din, Mughal 15, 23, 31, 44
Mohammad Shah Qajar ...4, 114, 141, 143, 154, 180, 202
Mohammad Shibani........................194
Mohammad Taqi Khan Shirazi.......175
Mohammad Vali Mirza 201
Mohammad Zaman Khan 178
Mojaddedi sufis 174
Mongol ...2, 12, 81, 97, 101, 193, 195, 198, 199, 200
Moqaddamat al-adab 195
Morghab, river...............................198
Morris, Lewis 217
Morshedabad (Murshidabad) 217
Mortaza-Qoli Khan Qajar...58, 59, 141
Morteza-Qoli Khan.................200, 208
Moscow ...64, 135, 137, 142, 143, 144, 162
Mughal, Mughals 5, 9, 12, 13, 14, 15, 16, 18, 28, 29, 31, 32, 37, 106, 133, 142, 173, 197, 215, 216, 220, 221, *see also* India
Musa al-Kazem, Imam 10
Musa Bek..65
Muslim ..9, 13, 14, 15, 19, 21, 32, 115, 173, 184, 192, 215, 217, 222, 223
Mysore 220

N

Nader Mirza, son of Shahrokh...... 179, 181
Nader Shah Afshar (Nader-Qoli Khan) 1-5, 9-21 *passim*, 27-43 *passim*, 66, 67, 92, 93, 106, 108, 173, 176-179, 182-183, 191-192, 215, 216, 217; conquest of Bokhara .... 197-198; conquest of India .2, 15, 16, 28, 30; and the Ottomans .2, 10, 13, 14, 20, 28; and Turko-Mongol legitimacy 2, 9, 12, 13, 71; and Shi'ism 12, 18, *see also*, Ja'fari mazhab, Kalat-e Naderi, Moghan, royal portraits
Naderi(d) ...6, 8, 45, 46, 48, 50, 51, 84, 110, 120, 121, 171, 173, 176, 177, 178, 179, 217
Najaf............... 14, 18, 19, 20, 200, 217
Naqshbandi.............................174, 194
Naser al-Din Shah Qajar ...37, 97, 106, 112, 114, 121, 122, 142, 144, 154, 157, 203
Nasrollah Mirza................................15
Natalya Kirillovna, Tsarina 149
National Library of Russia . 37, 142, 144
Nesselrode, Count Karl 136, 137
New Jolfa 18
New Nakhjavan 18, 23
Nezam al-Molk..............................193
Nishapur 193, 200
Nizovoĭ Korpus................................62
nomadic lifestyle 9, 13, 18, 195, 196, 197

O

Oghuz 86, 192, 193, 198, 199, 200, 204
Oghuz Khan 86, 204
Olenin, Aleksey 151
Order of the White Eagle 153
Orumia 70
Ottomans 4, 10, 11, 12, 13, 14, 18, 19, 20, 28, 31, 32, 66, 71, 93, 144, 197, 199, 216, 217; and the Afghans 175; conflict in the Caucasus 69, 74, 129, 140; war with Russia 57, 61, 142
Ouseley, Sir Gore 112, 113, 149, 216
Oxus 197, 201, 203
Ozbek, Ozbeks ....9, 12, 13, 15, 18, 93 182, 192, 193, 194, 196-199, 201, *see also* Shibanids

P

Pahlavi.............. 27, 109, 112, 125, 216

Palace of the Sun 16
Pamirs 193
Panah 'Ali Khan 191
Panchatantra 215
Park Street Cemetery, Calcutta 222
Parthian 110, 121, 198
Paskevich, General Ivan 133, 135, 136, 144
Peacock throne 142
Pearl of Pearls 173, 185, 186, 187, 189
Persian culture 130, 193
Persianate 2, 3, 9, 10, 69, 70, 191, 196, 203, 224
Persianization 193, 215
Peshawar 179, 182
Peter the Great, Tsar 34, 154
Peter and Paul Fortress, St Petersburg 134, 139, 143
porcelain 4, 5, 139, 143, 145, 147, 149, 150, 152, 154
portraits 5, 35, 36, 41, 43, 89, 104, 105, 107, 113, 122, 130, 145, 146, 147, 149, 150, 151, 152, 154, 206; equestrian 33, 34, 38, 42, 48, 112, *see also* royal portraiture, wall painting
portraits, Qajar 42, 108, 115, 120, 121, 141, 144, 152, 155, 160
portraits, Zand 37, 42
Potemkin, Prince Grigoriĭ ...57, 58, 59, 60, 71, 143

Q

Qajar, Qajars *passim*, *see also* chroniclers, diplomatic gifts, portraits, royal portraiture, Tehran
Qandahar 3, 11, 173, 180, 201
Qarabagh (Karabagh) 65, 191, 199, 205, 210, 211
Qarshi 69, 207
Qasr-e Khorshid 16, 30, 106
Qepchaq Steppe 177, 186
Qezelbash (Qızılbash) ...2, 3, 13, 36, 37, 69, 70, 71, 86, 172, 173, 174, 175, 191, 199, 200, 203, 205, 207
Qom ... 6, 94, 103, 113, 114, 115, 116, 118, 123, 124, 125, 126
Qoyunlu clan 199

quriltay 2, 12, 13, 22

R

Rashid al-Din, historian 199
Rasht ...7, 58, 59, 61, 62, 63, 64, 66, 72, 76
religious scholars, *see also* ulema.. 193, 194
reunification 2, 197
Reza 'Abbasi, artist 48
Reza Khan 27, 37, 44, 58
Reza Shah 55
Reza-Qoli, son of Nader Shah ...28, 38, 197
Reza-Qoli Khan Hedayat 180, 203
Reza-Qoli Khan Qajar 58
Reza-Qoli Mirza Afshar 69
Roemer, Hans 7, 22, 25, 193, 205, 206, 212
Rostam al-tavarikh 84
Royal Asiatic Society 221
royal portraiture 5, 28, 30, 35, 42, 43, 112, 130
   'Abbas Mirza 5, 145, 147, 150, 152, 162
   Alexander I, tsar 150, 151
   Fath-'Ali Shah 5, 6, 41, 42, 110-113, 116, 117, 121, 122, 130, 131, 145, 146, 160
   Karim Khan Zand.... 38, 39, 40, 107
   Khosrow Mirza 153, 154
   Nader Shah 5, 28-43 *passim*, 106
   Napoleon 131
   Peter the Great 156
   Shah 'Abbas .... I 35
Rum (Anatolia) 29, 173, 193
Rumi, Jalal al-Din, poet 215
Russia, Russian 3, 4, 17, 31, 45, 48, 49, 93, 108, 109, 118, 129, 130, 134, 171, 181, 191, 192, 201, 202; and the Caspian 4, 57-72 *passim*, 132, 192; in Central Asia 204, 216; in Iran 4, 6, 118, 133, 134, 135, 136, 137, 138, 139, 140-154 *passim*, 203, 216; and the Ottomans 4, 31, 129, 140, 142, *see also* Britain
Russian-America Company ... 134, 135

S

Russian Trans-Caucasian Company 133, 134
Ruznama-ye Mirza Mohammad Kalantar-e Fars 84
Ruznama-ye safar-e Khvarazm 202
Ryleev, Kondraty 134, 135, 158

Saba, Fath-'Ali Khan, poet 3
sabb (ritual cursing) 12
Sabzavar 70, 175
Sadozay 180
Safarnama-ye Bokhara 202
Safavid, Safavids 1, 2, 3, 4, 5, 9, 10, 12, 13, 14, 18, 20, 28, 37, 65, 104, 105, 173, 174, 176, 191, 194, 196, 199, 216, 220; fall 11, 61; image 5, 29, 30, 31, 32, 34, 35, 36, 37, 42, 103, 104, 105, 107, 108; legitimacy 11, 12, 58, 59, 60, 64, 67, 69-72 *passim*, 173, 175, 179, 182, 184; nostalgia 81-95 *passim*, 109
Safavid pretenders ...11, 14, 64, 66, 70, 81, 172; restoration 11, 28, 58, 66, 67, 68, 70, 71, 72, 85
Safavid revivalism 60, 71, 108, 172, 173, 174, 176
Saffarids 11
saff-e salam (court audiences) 112, 113, 117, 119, *see also* wall painting
Safinat al-Mahmud 85
Salur Turkmen 200, 202, 208
Salyan 64, 65, 66, 76
Samarqand 194, 195, 196, 200, 206, 212
Sarakhs 200, 202, 208
Saru'i, Mohammad Fathollah, historian 67, 68, 69, 70, 84, 86, 87, 97
Saruq Turkmen 200, 208, 209
Sasanian 27, 32, 34, 47, 55, 92, 94, 110, 111, 152, 198, 215, 222
Scherbatova, Princess Maria 151
Schulz, artist 153
sedentary lifestyle 13, 195, 199
Sefidrud 61
Seljuq 104, 111, 193, 198

Semën Arapov 62
Seringapatam .... 220, 221, *see also* Mysore
Servitor of the Two Holy Places 13
Shadi 195
Shah 'Abbas I, *see* 'Abbas I
Shah 'Abbas II, *see* 'Abbas II
Shah 'Alam, Mughal emperor 216, 220
Shah Esma'il I 10, 194
Shah Jahan, Mughal emperor . 142, 222
Shah Morad, Mangit 200, 201, 202
Shah Soleyman 34, 35, 68, 194
Shah Soltan-Hoseyn ...3, 61, 69, 85, 97, 216
Shah Tahmasp II 11, 172, 176
shahanshah 9, 15, 32, 47, 109
shah-e din 32
Shahnama ..3, 8, 10, 16, 22, 24, 30, 34, 43, 47, 48, 92, 122, 142, 147, 193, 195, 198, 203, 206, 212
Shahnama-ye Naderi 3, 34, 43
Shah-Pasand Khan 175
Shahrokh Shah Afshar, grandson of Nader Shah 3, 8, 68, 175, 177, 179, 192
Shahrokh b. Timur 177, 182
Shahzada Mahmud, governor of Herat 180, 181
Shamakhi 62, 65
shamanism 194
shari'a 12
shawls 139, 142
Sheykh 'Abbasi, artist 35
Sheykh Heydar 199
Shi'ism ...36, 3, 69, 70, 109, 110, 114, 147, 174, 175, 184, 194, 199, 200, 205, 209, 217
under Nader Shah 2, 9, 10, 12, 14, 19, 20, 22, 32, 71
Shiban 192, 194, 195, 196, 204, 206
Shibani Khan, Mohammad .... 18, 194, 195, 196, *see also* Ozbeks
Shipley, Anna Maria 217
Shiraz ...27, 57, 59, 65, 66, 70, 82, 94, 104, 106, 107, 109, 216, 222
Shirvan 64, 65, 69, 74
Shusha 191, 200
simultaneous rulership 13, 22
Sistan 104, 201
slave trade 199, 200, 202

Sogdian 193, 205
Soltan Morad Mirza, Hesam al-Saltana
   203
Soltan-Ahmad Mirza, 'Azod al-Dowla
   89
Soltanband 198
Soltan-Hoseyn Bayqara 182, 194
South Caucasus .64, 65, 66, 67, 69, 71, 74
Spode and Copeland, Stoke-on-Trent 147, 160
St Petersburg 4, 28, 58, 59, 62, 64, 66, 129, 131, 135, 136, 137, 140-145, 149-153
   Album 36, 42
Stalinist 196
Stoddart, Colonel Charles 203
succession 1, 3, 35, 59, 64, 67, 68, 88, 173, 180
Sufi 174, 183, 222
Sulak, river 61
Sunnism 3, 10, 11, 12, 19, 20, 31, 32, 70, 71, 217
   under the Dorranis 174, 175, 176, 184
   under the Shibanids 194, 196, 207
Sunni orthodoxy 194
Suvarov, General A.V. 57
Syr Darya (Jaxartes) 194, 197

T

Tabriz ...70, 84, 97, 99, 136, 138, 139, 140, 146, 151, 152, 158, 159, 165, 170, 206, 216
Tahkik ve Tevfik 13, 22, 25
Tajik 70, 196
Tajikistan 104, 204, 223
taqiya (prudent dissimulation) 19
Tarikh-e 'alam-ara-ye 'Abbasi ... 90, 92
Tarikh-e 'alam-ara-ye Naderi 11
Tarikh-e 'Azodi 89
Tarikh-e jahan-ara ... 83, 84, 86, 88, 89
Tarikh-e Mohammadi 83, 84, 86, 87
Tarikh-e Saheb-Qerani ... 83, 84, 86, 87
Tashkent 196
Taurida Palace, St Petersburg 152
Tavarikh-e gozida-ye nosratnama .. 195
tazkera 85, 98, 99

Tazkera-ye Al-e Davud 85
Tazkera-ye Anjoman-e Khaqan 85
Tazkera-ye Khavari 85
Tazkera-ye Negarestan-e Dara 85
Tbilisi ...67, 70, 71, 87, 132, 134, 137, 141, 144, 160, 165, 192, 201
teacups 4, 144, 145, 147, 154
teacup holders 4, 144, 145, 159
Tehran 4, 20, 28, 94, 99, 103, 105, 107, 108, 109, 110, 112, 113, 114, 115, 123, 129, 130, 132, 133, 139, 140, 144, 146, 147, 149, 152, 158, 177, 181, 202
Tekke Turkmen 200, 204, 208
textiles 4, 139, 143
Tiflis, *see* Tbilisi
Tilsit, *see* Treaties
Timur 1, 2, 12, 15, 16, 17, 19, 176, 177, 179, 180, 191, 204, 206, 222
Timur Shah Dorrani 176, 177, 180, 222
Timurid ..2, 7, 9, 15, 71, 104, 182, 183, 192, 194, 195, 196, 204, 215
Tipu Sultan of Mysore 220, 221
tofangchi (rifleman) 200
trade 18, 60, 62, 63, 64, 66, 67, 72, 74, 76, 134, 137, 173, 195, 217
   Caspian 57, 59, 60, 61, 63
   ceramics 160
   horses 200
   pilgrimage 12
   silk 61
   skins 200
   slave trade 199, 200, 202
Transcaucasia, *see* Caucasus
Transoxiana 192, 193, 194, 195, 196, 197, 203, 206, 207, 210, 211
Treaty, treaties 15, 67, 137, 161, 197, 221
   Anglo-Persian Treaty (1801) ... 148
   Ganja (1735) 61, 62, 63, 66, 72
   Georgievsk (1783) 67
   Golestan (1813) 118, 150, 152
   Kordan (1746) 10, 14, 20, 21
   Paris (1857) 182
   Rasht (1732) 58, 61, 62, 63
   Tehran (1814) 144
   Tilsit (1807) 161
   Turkmanchay (1828) 4, 132, 133, 135, 136, 140, 143

Zohab (1639) 14, 20
Tumanovskiĭ, Ivan, consul..........59, 63
Turan 11, 13, 15, 48, 173, 203, 205, 212
Turkification...............................3, 193
Turkmanchay, *see* Treaties
Turkmen 9, 10, 13, 15, 16, 19, 20, 57, 68, 69, 71, 173-175, 197-203, 208-209
Turkmen Steppe 60, 68, 70
Turkmenistan..................................204
Turko-Mongol tradition ...2, 9, 10, 12, 13, 15, 82, 193, 195, 199; *see also* Timurid
Turk's Head Club 218
Tutinama (Tales of a parrot) 215

U

Uighur script....................................193
ulema............ 18, 19, 87, 108, 114, 194
umma........................9, 12, 13, 15, 21
Uzbekistan.......................................204

V

Voĭnovich, Count Marko ...57, 58, 59, 60, 71, 72, 76, 79
Volga...57, 61
Volynskiĭ, Artemiĭ 61
Vorontsov, Count Semen 151
Vsevolozhsky, Alexander 135

W

wall paintings 37, 45, 94, 103-106, 107
  Agha Mohammad Khan 107-108
  Fath-'Ali Shah ... 108-110, 112-119 *passim*
  Zand era 107, 110
Western Asia 193
Willock, Henry 132, 136, 137, 138, 149, 151
Woolf, Joseph 203

Y

Yazd...196
Yomut Turkmen ... 57, 68, 75, 199, 200

Z

Zakhira-ye Khvarazmshahi 195
Zamakhshari...................................195
Zaman Shah ...179, 180, 181, 182, 187, 201
Zamindavar 201
Zands ....37, 42, 83, 87, 91, 92, 94, 98, 103; art .104, 106, 107, 110, 171, 216, 217; forces . 173; and Dorranis, 176, 177; and Russians . 62, 63, 65-67, 72
Zarafshan, river 197
Zavalishin, Dmitry 134, 135
Zaveleysky, Petre 134
Zohab, *see* Treaties
Zoroastrian 27, 222, 223